Financing Africa

Through the Crisis and Beyond

Financing Africa
Through the Crisis and Beyond

Thorsten Beck

Samuel Munzele Maimbo

Issa Faye

Thouraya Triki

BMZ ⊕ | Federal Ministry
for Economic Cooperation
and Development

THE WORLD BANK

ISBN: 978-0-8213-8797-9
eISBN: 978-0-8213-8798-6
DOI: 10.1596/978-0-8213-8797-9

Library of Congress Cataloging-in-Publication Data

Beck, Thorsten.
    Financing Africa : through the crisis and beyond / Thorsten Beck . . . [et al.].
        p. cm.
    Includes bibliographical references and index.
    ISBN 978-0-8213-8797-9—ISBN 978-0-8213-8798-6 (electronic)
    1. Financial institutions—Africa. 2. Finance—Africa. 3. Monetary policy—Africa. I. Title.
    HG187.5.A2B43 2011
    332.096—dc23

                                                                                          2011034178

Cover design by Debra Naylor of Naylor Design.

Contents

Figures

Maps

Tables

Foreword

For too long, firms and households in Africa have faced severe constraints to affordable finance—costly fees and commissions, insufficient and inefficient financial infrastructure, and short tenor, to name a few. But things are changing, albeit slowly. This book, a joint effort of the African Development Bank, the German Federal Ministry of Economic Cooperation and Development, and the World Bank, demonstrates that Africa is making progress in relaxing these constraints. New players and products, enabled by new technologies and business models, have helped broaden access to financial services, especially savings and payment products. Critically, African finance has been stable for quite a while now; after a peak of banking crises in the 1980s, there have been few systemic banking crises since then. Despite the recent global financial crisis, banks in Africa are, on average, well capitalized and liquid.

At the same time, Africa faces persistent but not insurmountable challenges, namely its small scale, informality, volatility, and poor governance. Many firms and most households are still excluded from access to financial services, especially long-term finance. Infrastructure financing needs remain largely unmet. Agricultural finance has been ignored by commercial financiers for being too high-cost and high-risk, aggravated by the same challenges enumerated above.

Financing Africa: Through the Crisis and Beyond is a call to arms for a new approach to Africa's financial sector development. First, policy makers should focus on increasing competition within and outside the banking sector to foster innovation. This implies a more open regulatory mindset, possibly reversing the usual timeline of legislation-regulation-innovation for new players and products. It also implies expanding traditional infrastructure, such as credit registries and payment systems beyond banks. Second, the focus should be on services rather than existing institutions and markets. Expanding provision of payment, savings and other financial services to the unbanked might mean looking beyond existing institutions, products, and delivery channels, such as banks, traditional checking accounts, and brick-and-mortar branches. Third, we should focus on the demand constraints as well as the supply ones; expand financial literacy programs for households and enterprises; and address nonfinancial constraints, especially for small enterprises and in rural areas.

All financial sector policy is local. To reap the benefits of globalization, regional integration, and technology, policy makers have to recognize the politics of financial deepening and build constituencies for financial sector reform. While the challenges of expanding access, lengthening contracts, and safeguarding the financial system are similar, the ways of addressing them will depend on the circumstances and context of each country.

With its cautiously optimistic tone, this book creates an opportunity for Africa's policy makers, private sector, civil society, and development partners to harness the progress of the past as a way to address the challenges of the future and enable the financial sector to play its rightful role in Africa's transformation.

Shantayanan Devarajan
Chief Economist, Africa Region
World Bank

Mthuli Ncube
Chief Economist
African Development Bank

Thomas Albert
Director Africa
German Federal Ministry for Economic Cooperation and Development

Acknowledgments

The principal authors of this report are Thorsten Beck, Samuel Munzele Maimbo, Issa Faye, and Thouraya Triki. The report also draws on draft material specially provided by Mike Coates, Robert Cull, Florence Dafe, Michael Fuchs, Robin Hofmeister, Thomas Losse-Müller, Margaret J. Miller, Thilasoni Benjamin Musuku, David Porteous, Lemma Senbet, Mircea Trandafir, Simon Christopher Walley, Makayo Witte, and Alice Zanza. Excellent research assistance has been provided by Mohammad Hosseini, Thierry Kangoye, Ines Mahjoub, Pranav Ramkrishnan, Tania Saranga, David Symington, Radomir Todorov, and, in particular, Alexandra Jarotschkin, who also contributed with textual revisions on the completion of the consultation process. We are grateful to Stephen McGroarty and Susan Graham and the World Bank Office of the Publisher for coordinating the book design, editing, and production process. The data collection effort on financial structure and regulations in Africa was carried out by the African Development Bank's Department of Statistics led by Charles L. Lufumpa (Director) and, especially, the team of Beejaye Kokil (Division Manager), Letsera Nirina (Statistician), and Tarak Hasni and Slaheddin Saidi (Statisticians-Consultants).

External peer reviewers for the study were Patrick Honohan, (Governor, Central Bank of Ireland), Perks Ligoya (Governor, Reserve Bank of Malawi), Louis Kasekende (Deputy Governor, Bank of Uganda), Laurence Harris (Professor of Economics, School of Oriental and African Studies, University of London), Allen Franklin (Professor of Finance and Economics, The Wharton School), Mohammed Omran (Vice Chairman, Insurance Holding Company, Arab Republic of Egypt), Ghada Waly (Assistant Resident Representative, UN Development Programme, Egypt), Ismail Douiri (Co-Chief Executive Officer, Attijariwafa Bank, Morocco), Ziad Oueslati (Founding Partner Tuninvest-Finance Group), Bouakez Hafedh (Professor of Economics, HEC Montreal), and Lemma Senbet (Professor of Finance, University of Maryland).

The African Development Bank and World Bank reviewers were Simon C. Bell, Mohamed Damak, Asli Demirgüç-Kunt, James Emery, Michael Fuchs, Devinder Goyal, Leonce Ndikumana, Gabriel Victorien Mougani, Charles Muthuti, Sebastian O. Okeke, Tilahun Temesguen, and Désiré Vencatachellum.

We are grateful for the insights of officials and market participants visited for the study in Egypt, Kenya, Libya, Mauritius, Morocco, Senegal, South Africa, Tunisia, and Uganda. We have benefited from comments during consultation events in Dakar, Frankfurt, Johannesburg, Nairobi, Tunis, and Washington, DC. At these events, we appreciate the institutional support we received from the Kenya School of Monetary Studies in Nairobi, the Bankers Association of South Africa, and FinMark Trust in South Africa. We are also grateful for the comments and assistance provided by Ed Al-Hussainy, Abayomi A. Alawode, Henry K. Bagazonzya, Gunhild Berg, Johannes Braun, Irma I. Grundling, Juliet Kairuki, Zachary A. Kaplan, Maya Makanjee, Hannah Messerli, Stephen N. Ndegwa, Ismail Radwan, Oliver Reichert, David Scott, Riham Shendy, and Smita Wagh.

The study was carried out under the overall guidance of Shantayanan Deverajan (Chief Economist, Africa Region, World Bank) and Ncube Mthuli (Chief Economist and Vice-President, African Development Bank). It also benefited from the support and guidance from management: Gabriela Braun and Karen Losse (both Deutsche Gesellschaft für Internationale Zusammenarbeit), Leonce Ndikumana (Director at the Operations Policy Department, African Development Bank), Marilou Uy (Director, Africa Finance and Private Sector, World Bank), and Désiré Vencatachellum (Director of the Research Department, African Development Bank). Coordination and management support was ably provided by the Secretariat of the Making Finance Work for Africa Partnership, led by Stefan Nalletamby (Coordinator) and his team: Habib Attia, Alessandro Girola, Hugues Kamewe, Sarah Mersch, and Carlotta Saporito.

On behalf of the African Development Bank and the World Bank and on their own behalf, the authors are especially grateful to the German Federal Ministry for Economic Cooperation and Development (BMZ) for providing financial support for the preparation of the study.

Abbreviations

AIDS	acquired immune deficiency syndrome
AML	anti–money laundering
ATI	African Trade Insurance
ATM	automated teller machine
BCP	Basel Core Principle for Effective Banking Supervision
BH	Banque de l'Habitat (Tunisia)
BRIC	Brazil, Russian Federation, India, and China
CDG	Caisse de Dépôt et de Gestion (Morocco)
CEMAC	Economic and Monetary Community of Central Africa
CFT	Combating the Financing of Terrorism
CGAP	Consultative Group to Assist the Poor
DBSA	Development Bank of South Africa
DFI	development finance institution
FDI	foreign direct investment
G-7	Group of Seven
G-20	Group of Twenty
GDP	gross domestic product
ICT	information and communication technology
LBC	licensed buying company (Ghana)
LIA	Libyan Investment Authority
m-banking	mobile banking
MFI	microfinance institution
MIX	Microfinance Information Exchange

MOU	memorandum of understanding
MRFC	Malawi Rural Finance Corporation
NAFIN	Nacional Financiera (Mexico)
NGO	nongovernmental organization
NMB	National Microfinance Bank (Tanzania)
OPCR	*organisme de placement en capital risque* (venture capital investment fund)
PPP	public-private partnership
PPT	Pesewa Power Trust (Ghana)
RBM	Reserve Bank of Malawi
SACCO	savings and credit cooperative
SIM	subscriber identification module
SME	small and medium enterprise
SWF	sovereign wealth fund
TPS	Tenant Purchase Scheme
UEMOA	West African Economic and Monetary Union

Note: All dollar amounts are U.S. dollars (US$) unless otherwise indicated.

Country Abbreviations

Code	Country name	Code	Country name	Code	Country name
ABW	Aruba	BHS	Bahamas, The	COL	Colombia
ADO	Andorra	BIH	Bosnia and	COM	Comoros
AFG	Afghanistan		Herzegovina	CPV	Cape Verde
AGO	Angola	BLR	Belarus	CRI	Costa Rica
ALB	Albania	BLZ	Belize	CUB	Cuba
ANT	Netherlands Antilles	BMU	Bermuda	CYM	Cayman Islands
ARE	United Arab	BOL	Bolivia	CYP	Cyprus
	Emirates	BRA	Brazil	CZE	Czech Republic
ARG	Argentina	BRB	Barbados	DEU	Germany
ARM	Armenia	BRN	Brunei	DJI	Djibouti
ASM	American Samoa	BTN	Bhutan	DMA	Dominica
ATG	Antigua and Barbuda	BWA	Botswana	DNK	Denmark
AUS	Australia	CAF	Central African	DOM	Dominican Republic
AUT	Austria		Republic	DZA	Algeria
AZE	Azerbaijan	CAN	Canada	ECU	Ecuador
BDI	Burundi	CHE	Switzerland	EGY	Egypt, Arab Rep.
BEL	Belgium	CHI	Channel Islands	ERI	Eritrea
BEN	Benin	CHL	Chile	ESP	Spain
BFA	Burkina Faso	CHN	China	EST	Estonia
BGD	Bangladesh	CIV	Côte d'Ivoire	ETH	Ethiopia
BGR	Bulgaria	CMR	Cameroon	FIN	Finland
BHR	Bahrain	COG	Congo, Rep.	FJI	Fiji

Code	Country name	Code	Country name	Code	Country name
FRA	France	LTU	Lithuania	SAU	Saudi Arabia
FRO	Faeroe Islands	LUX	Luxembourg	SDN	Sudan
FSM	Micronesia, Fed. Sts.	LVA	Latvia	SEN	Senegal
GAB	Gabon	MAC	Macao, China	SGP	Singapore
GBR	United Kingdom	MAR	Morocco	SLB	Solomon Islands
GEO	Georgia	MCO	Monaco	SLE	Sierra Leone
GHA	Ghana	MDA	Moldova	SLV	El Salvador
GIN	Guinea	MDG	Madagascar	SMR	San Marino
GMB	Gambia, The	MDV	Maldives	SOM	Somalia
GNB	Guinea-Bissau	MEX	Mexico	STP	São Tomé and
GNQ	Equatorial Guinea	MHL	Marshall Islands		Principe
GRC	Greece	MKD	Macedonia, FYR	SUR	Suriname
GRD	Grenada	MLI	Mali	SVK	Slovak Republic
GRL	Greenland	MLT	Malta	SVN	Slovenia
GTM	Guatemala	MMR	Myanmar	SWE	Sweden
GUM	Guam	MNG	Mongolia	SWZ	Swaziland
GUY	Guyana	MNP	Northern Mariana	SYC	Seychelles
HKG	Hong Kong, China		Islands	SYR	Syrian Arab Republic
HND	Honduras	MOZ	Mozambique	TCD	Chad
HRV	Croatia	MRT	Mauritania	TGO	Togo
HTI	Haiti	MUS	Mauritius	THA	Thailand
HUN	Hungary	MWI	Malawi	TJK	Tajikistan
IDN	Indonesia	MYS	Malaysia	TKM	Turkmenistan
IMY	Isle of Man	MYT	Mayotte	TMP	Timor-Leste
IND	India	NAM	Namibia	TON	Tonga
IRL	Ireland	NCL	New Caledonia	TTO	Trinidad and Tobago
IRN	Iran, Islamic Rep.	NER	Niger	TUN	Tunisia
IRQ	Iraq	NGA	Nigeria	TUR	Turkey
ISL	Iceland	NIC	Nicaragua	TWN	Taiwan, China
ISR	Israel	NLD	Netherlands	TZA	Tanzania
ITA	Italy	NOR	Norway	UGA	Uganda
JAM	Jamaica	NPL	Nepal	UKR	Ukraine
JOR	Jordan	NZL	New Zealand	URY	Uruguay
JPN	Japan	OMN	Oman	USA	United States
KAZ	Kazakhstan	PAK	Pakistan	UZB	Uzbekistan
KEN	Kenya	PAN	Panama	VCT	St. Vincent and the
KGZ	Kyrgyz Republic	PER	Peru		Grenadines
KHM	Cambodia	PHL	Philippines	VEN	Venezuela, RB
KIR	Kiribati	PLW	Palau	VIR	Virgin Islands (U.S.)
KNA	St. Kitts and Nevis	PNG	Papua New Guinea	VNM	Vietnam
KOR	Korea, Rep.	POL	Poland	VUT	Vanuatu
KWT	Kuwait	PRI	Puerto Rico	WBG	West Bank and Gaza
LAO	Lao PDR	PRK	Korea, Dem. Rep.	WSM	Samoa
LBN	Lebanon	PRT	Portugal	YEM	Yemen, Rep.
LBR	Liberia	PRY	Paraguay	YUG	Serbia and
LBY	Libya	PYF	French Polynesia		Montenegro
LCA	St. Lucia	QAT	Qatar	ZAF	South Africa
LIE	Liechtenstein	ROM	Romania	ZAR	Congo, Dem. Rep.
LKA	Sri Lanka	RUS	Russian Federation	ZMB	Zambia
LSO	Lesotho	RWA	Rwanda	ZWE	Zimbabwe

Chapter 1

Financing Africa: Setting the Stage

Introduction

Cautious hope is in the air for finance in Africa. While the global crisis may have dented some of the progress made since the beginning of the 21st century, one feels the optimism and sees the positive trends. A deepening of financial systems can be observed in many African countries, with more financial services, especially credit, provided to more enterprises and households. New players and new products, often enabled by new technologies, have helped broaden access to financial services, especially savings and payment products. Innovative approaches to reaching out to previously unbanked parts of the population go beyond cell phone–based M-Pesa in Kenya and basic transaction accounts, such as Mzansi accounts in South Africa. Competition and innovation dominate African financial systems, and, for every failure, there is now at least one success. However, many challenges remain, and the journey toward deeper, more-efficient, and more-inclusive financial systems will be long and fraught with many difficult choices in many countries in Africa.

Africa's financial systems have progressed over the past 20 years. Yes, the promise of the efforts at liberalization, privatization, and stabilization in the 1980s has only been partly fulfilled, though African finance has been stable for quite a while now. Since the peak of the banking crises in the 1980s, there have been few systemic banking crises, though pockets of fragility persist, often related to political crisis or deficiencies in governance. On average, banks in Africa are well capitalized and liquid. Still, the benefits of deeper, broader, and cheaper finance have not yet been reaped. Finance in Africa still faces problems of scale and volatility. And the same liquidity that helps reduce volatility and fragility in the financial system is also a sign of the limited intermediation capacity on the continent. Nonetheless, as we discuss below, globalization, technology, and increasing regional integration may provide new opportunities for finance in Africa.

1

As a consequence of recent positive trends, African financial sectors entered the crisis with a cushion of high levels of capitalization and liquidity. Financial institutions on the continent largely evaded the direct impact of the global financial crisis. Low levels of integration with international financial markets limited the exposure to toxic assets and to the volatility of international markets. With a number of important exceptions, nonperforming loans remained stable despite the slowdown in economic growth. Notwithstanding the limited impact of the global financial crisis and the improvements in overall stability, several countries have been suffering from homegrown financial fragility related to governance challenges and sociopolitical unrest.

Africa's economies have been hit by the ensuing Great Recession through reduced trade flows and reduced portfolio flows and remittances. The fall in demand and, consequently, in the prices of commodities has hit commodity-based economies significantly. The rapid decline in global trade that started in late 2008 (by up to 45 percent in real terms year on year) affected all African economies and, to a large extent, explains the lower growth the region experienced in 2009. The increasing spreads and reduced maturities resulting from the shortage of liquidity in the global financial system have made investment and trade more difficult as well. Africa has also experienced a rapid reduction in capital flows, which has depressed stock exchange indexes throughout the continent and forced governments and companies to cancel bond and stock issues. Nonetheless, the overall impact of the Global Recession seems to have been milder on Africa than on other regions of the world, and the continent is already expected to match precrisis growth rates of 5 percent in 2011 (IMF 2011).

More importantly, Africa will be affected by long-term trends that started before the crisis and have been reinforced by the crisis, especially the shifts in the distribution of global economic power. The shift of weight away from the North (the G-7) toward the East (especially China and India) and the South (to the G-20) has been another consequence of the crisis not only for Africa, but also for the global financial and economic system. In the context of globalization, the BRIC countries, especially China and India, but, more recently, also Brazil, are playing a growing role in Africa.[1] This is reflected in capital flows and also the structure of banking systems. While Indian banks have long had a presence in East African countries, the purchase of a 20 percent stake by a Chinese bank in Standard Bank in South Africa represents a new trend for China. The foreign direct investment of Brazil, China, and India has been increasing across the continent. It began mostly in natural resource extraction and agriculture, but has now extended to other sectors. Additional funds have been forthcoming from the Gulf region, often in the form of sovereign funds. This shift in capital flows and international governance offers opportunities and challenges for Africa: opportunities in terms of urgently needed resources and challenges in terms of managing the resources properly.

This chapter opens with a description of the book's objectives and contributions, including the main policy messages. It then develops the basic analytical framework through which we view financial sector development in Africa, distinguishing among beneficiary concepts and groups so as to focus our policy messages. We highlight the importance of financial sector development for economic growth and poverty alleviation and conclude with a summary of the persistent problems in Africa—limited scale, informality, volatility, and governance issues— that require new solutions. Opportunities for solutions are possible within the new trends of globalization, regional integration, and technology.

Financing Africa, the Book

This book targets the stakeholders in Africa's financial systems. Stakeholders are understood widely: policy makers, regulators, practitioners, development partners, academics, and others. The book includes a stocktaking and forward-looking exercise that indicates viable paths to financial sector deepening and broadening. It represents an effort to document new and existing trends in Africa's financial sectors, taking into account Africa's many different experiences. It focuses on general trends and, thus, does not encompass an exhaustive, detailed discussion of the development and structure of each of the 53 African financial systems (for example, see Allen, Otchere, and Senbet 2010).

The book intends to contribute to the efforts of African policy makers to capture opportunities and overcome challenges. It outlines broad policy messages for financial systems in Africa on the premise that one size does not fit all. It does not outline strategies for the financial sector in every country across the continent, but, rather, offers general policy messages. It also discusses specific segments of the financial sector, such as rural and housing finance; it does not, however, offer an exhaustive and conclusive coverage of these segments. We leave that to more specialized publications in these areas.

The book builds on and extends substantially the World Bank publication *Making Finance Work for Africa*, which drew attention to the opportunities and challenges of financial system development across Africa (see Honohan and Beck 2007). First, it relies on a much broader array of data than the previous publication. Second, it includes North African countries in the analysis, which, along many dimensions, have followed a different path of financial sector development. Finally, it expands on the analysis of the previous publication, including a thorough discussion of the regulatory challenges of finance in Africa. Critically, the world is different in 2011 from the world in 2007. Box 1.1 summarizes the main differences between the two publications.

An Analytical Framework

In theory, financial institutions and markets exist to help overcome market frictions that make direct exchanges between economic agents difficult. Academics typically distinguish between specific functions of financial service providers, such

Box 1.1   What's New?

Financing Africa is a follow-up to *Making Finance Work for Africa*. What has changed since early 2007, and what distinguishes this publication from the previous one?

The environment has changed

The environment in which African financial systems operate has changed dramatically over the past four years. The number of African countries experiencing a systemic banking crisis has fallen from a peak of 15 in the mid-1990s to a sporadic outlier in the 2000s. Credit to the private sector (as a ratio of gross domestic product [GDP]) has risen by more than 20 percentage points since 1990. There has been a growing trend toward regional integration within the continent in recent years, though this trend started well before 2007. Kenyan, Moroccan, Nigerian, and South African banks are rapidly expanding operations in the region. Over the past four years, the transformational impact of the deepening and broadening of financial system technology has become clear as well. With over 13 million clients in Kenya, M-Pesa is the world's most widely used telecommunications-led mobile money service.

Globally, too, the environment is different. We might be at the tail end of the first global financial crisis of the 21st century and the Great Recession, but the global financial system has changed dramatically. The center of economic and financial power has shifted to the South and East, which is also reflected in the replacement of the G7 by the G20 as the major international policy coordination body.

The set of information and experiences is larger

Relative to four years ago, we have a much richer and more detailed set of data available. Specifically, we can draw on a systemic data collection effort by the African Development Bank and the Deutsche Gesellschaft für Internationale Zusammenarbeit of indicators on the development and structure of financial systems across Africa, as well as the regulatory framework. Furthermore, the international community has made enormous progress in collecting data on the outreach of financial systems and the barriers to access among enterprises and households; we draw on this experience.

A critical difference with respect to the previous publication is the inclusion of the North African subregion. The inclusion of these countries—different in income level and economic and financial structure—and the comparison with other parts of Africa enrich the discussion in the book and provide additional insights into the process of financial sector deepening and broadening. The recent turmoil in this part of Africa, however, makes many conclusions on the related financial systems appear tentative.

While Africa can learn from the rest of world, the world can learn from Africa, as we lay out in this publication. The experience with mobile phone banking, for example, shows the power of technology and the potential that payment-led inclusion strategies possess relative to credit- or savings-led inclusion strategies. We therefore refer to experiences in other regions, but also experiences in different African countries and how these experiences may be used across the continent.

The focus has expanded

The altered global environment also calls for a somewhat different emphasis. In light of the recent regulatory reform debate in Europe and the United States and in the context of the

Box 1.1 What's New? *(continued)*

G20 process, we focus more prominently on the regulatory framework. We argue that the reform suggestions developed in response to the recent crisis have to be adapted with caution to the African context and, even within the African region, to the level of development of different financial systems.

Including North Africa also reemphasizes the benefits of focusing on differences across Africa. Thus, needs and policy options vary between small and large and between low- and middle-income countries, while landlocked, resource-rich, and fragile states face yet another set of challenges.

Honohan and Beck (2007) present two main policy recommendations: (1) strengthen credit and property registries and streamline court procedures and (2) establish independent supervisors. This publication follows a different path by presenting three main general messages, which are then fine-tuned in each of the thematic chapters and also detailed for different country groups.

Some themes and contrasts are maintained from the previous book. The contrast between the modernist and the activist approach is also used in this publication to highlight the advantages of a careful assessment of the role of government, a role that should help create and develop markets rather than replace them. We also build and expand on the distinction between Finance for All and Finance for Growth by highlighting the importance of finance for basic market transactions beyond fostering long-term investment activities.

as (1) facilitating the exchange of goods and services by providing a medium of exchange; (2) pooling society's savings for investment in large investment projects beyond the savings capacity of small individual savers; (3) screening potential investment projects, thus putting society's savings to the best use; (4) monitoring enterprises and thus making sure money is used for the best purpose; and (5) investing in risk management services, such as diversifying across different projects or smoothing volatility over time.[2] These functions overlay with the practitioner's distinction among (1) payment and transaction services, (2) deposit and savings services, (3) credit services, and (4) insurance and risk management services. These services are often provided by different institutions or in different markets. Yet another, partly overlaying distinction is based on different beneficiary groups and time horizons. Expanding on a distinction made by Honohan and Beck (2007), this book distinguishes between three concepts: Finance for Markets, Finance for Growth, and Finance for All. This distinction helps us frame our discussion throughout the book.

- *Finance for Markets* relates to financial services that underlie short-term commercial market transactions, such as trade finance, remittance payments, and various types of short-term credit facilities. This concept relates primarily to the financial system function of enabling market-based transactions within the economy and across borders. By facilitating commerce, financial systems allow the market-based exchange of goods and services beyond the immediate family and community. Finance for Markets refers to financial services for enterprises and households, thus cutting across all possible beneficiary groups. The concept covers transaction and payment services, including remittances from emigrant workers to their families back home. It covers deposit services for households and enterprises, as well as short-term credit facilities for enterprises of all sizes, including trade credit. These basic services are provided by almost every financial system in the world, even the most rudimentary ones, although at different degrees of efficiency. They are mostly provided by banks, but may also be provided by nonbank financial service providers, including telecommunications companies. The recent crisis and the reduction in the supply of trade finance underline the importance of Finance for Markets.

- *Finance for Growth* relates to the finance for enterprises, households, and governments that supports medium- and long-term activities (longer than 12 months). Finance for Growth is finance mainly for investment purposes, and it is here that financial institutions and markets fulfill their key function of the maturity transformation of short-term liquid claims—be they deposits or marketable securities—into long-term investment finance. Finance for Growth thus involves a key function of financial systems: pooling society's savings and putting them to their best use. This comprises risk management techniques and the screening and monitoring of entrepreneurs and projects. It relates to large-scale finance, including for infrastructure and agriculture, and finance for small and medium enterprises and to debt and equity instruments, as well as hybrid instruments, such as mezzanine debt and guarantees. These services are provided by an array of institutions, including banks, insurance companies, pension funds, mutual funds, and private equity funds, and relate to activities on different financial markets, including stock and bond markets. Moving from Finance for Markets to Finance for Growth constitutes a major challenge for many low-income countries, including in Africa.

- *Finance for All* relates to the process of expanding financial services both for markets and for growth to the largest possible segment of the population, including households, small enterprises, and large firms. Finance for All overlaps the concepts of Finance for Markets and Finance for Growth, but refers to the process by which short- and long-term financial services, including payment, savings, credit, and insurance services, are pushed out to previously unserved segments of the population. It overlaps with Finance for Markets to the extent that access to basic transaction services is being extended to all segments of the population. It overlaps with Finance for Growth to the extent that more segments of the population gain access to contractual savings services, while microenterprises gain access to investment finance. In discussing Finance for All, we refer to all types of formal financial institutions, but also semiformal financial institutions such as cooperatives or savings and credit cooperatives. Finance for All has been a challenge throughout the world not only for low-income countries, but also for many middle-income countries that have made substantial progress in the dimensions of Finance for Markets and Finance for Growth.

The three concepts overlap, including in policy prescriptions, but it is important to keep in mind the different focus of each. Countries at different levels of economic and financial development might focus on different concepts. Postconflict or low-income economies might focus mainly on the basic services implied by Finance for Markets, and middle-income and socioeconomically more stable countries might focus on Finance for Growth strategies.[3] Finance for All has remained a challenge for low- and middle-income countries and even for some high-income countries, such as the United Kingdom or the United States.

It is important to note that these three concepts do not involve a trade-off, least of all the Finance for All approach. It is more about sequencing than trading off. For instance, the existence of efficient financial services for market exchange is the basis for longer-term financial contracts.

The Main Messages and a Caveat

In Africa, distinguishing among these three concepts is critically important for policy design. While African economies and financial systems share many features, there are critical differences along notable dimensions. Financial systems face different challenges in low- and middle-income countries across the continent. Basic financial services for commercial transactions and short-term credit (Finance for Markets) characterize the financial systems of many low-income countries, where formal financial services are often limited to a small share of enterprises and households. Middle-income countries are characterized by a much larger outreach of banking systems to households and enterprises, a larger variety of financial services and products, and a diversification of financial institutions and markets. Size matters: even among low-income countries, larger economies are able to sustain larger and more diversified financial systems.

There are also important geographical differences. North African financial systems are dominated by government-owned financial institutions to a much larger extent than systems in Sub-Saharan Africa, where many systems are weighted toward foreign-owned banks. Even there, though, governments are preponderant in other segments of the financial system, such as the pension sector and the bond market. However, there are also important differences in the challenges that financial systems in densely populated economies, such as Rwanda and Uganda, face from systems in countries with more dispersed populations, such as Ethiopia or Tanzania. There is an important distinction between common law and civil code countries. Common law countries typically have a more flexible legal and regulatory framework that offers more room for innovation, while civil code countries rely more steadily on written codes and often take longer to adjust the legislative and regulatory framework to new developments. Finally, postconflict countries and economies with abundant natural resources face their own unique set of challenges in achieving financial deepening and broadening.

We refer to these distinctions throughout the book and provide policy recommendations for the various subgroups in chapter 6.

Taking into account these large differences across the continent, we use the framework above to develop the three main messages resulting from our analysis, as follows:

- *Competition is the most important driver of financial innovation that will help African financial systems deepen and broaden.* Competition, in this context, is broadly defined and encompasses an array of policies and actions. On the broadest level, it implies a financial system that is open to new types of financial service providers, even if they are nonfinancial corporations. It allows the adoption of new products and technologies. The example of cell phone–based payment systems across the continent is one of the most powerful illustrations in this category. Within the banking system, competition implies low entry barriers for new entrants, but also the necessary infrastructure to foster competition, such as credit registries that allow new entrants to draw on existing information. To achieve more competition in smaller financial systems, more emphasis has to be placed on regional integration. However, this might also mean more active government involvement by, for example, forcing banks to join a shared payment platform or contributing negative and positive information to credit registries. While it is important to stress that the focus on innovation and competition should not lead to the neglect of financial stability, there has been a tendency in many African countries to err too much on the side of stability.

- A second and related message is that *there should be an increasing focus on financial services rather than on specific institutions.* Across all three dimensions discussed above (Finance for Markets, Finance for Growth, and Finance for All), we care primarily about the necessary financial services and, only in a second instance, about the institutions or markets that provide the services. Banks are an important component of every financial system, but if nonbanks are better at providing certain financial services, they should be allowed to do so. If the small economies of Africa cannot sustain organized exchanges, the emphasis should be placed instead on alternative sources of equity finance, such as private equity funds. If the local economy is not sufficiently large to sustain certain segments of a financial system, then the import of such services should be considered. One size does not fit all: smaller and low-income countries are less able than larger and middle-income countries to sustain a large and diversified financial system and might have to rely more heavily on international integration.

- Finally, *there is a need for increased attention on the users of financial services.* Turning unbanked enterprises and households into a bankable population and ultimately banked customers involves more than pushing financial institutions down-market. Achieving such a change requires financial literacy, that is, knowledge about products and the capability to make good financial decisions among households and enterprises. It also means that nonfinancial constraints must be addressed, such as, most prominently, in agriculture. It includes a stronger emphasis on equity financing for often overleveraged enterprises. It also includes a consumer protection framework, though what suits South Africa, for example, may be too costly in resources and skills for Malawi.

Financial Sector Development: Why Do We Care?

The provision of financial services for specific beneficiary groups is important, but the ultimate goal is economic development. What is the role of finance in the development process in Africa? How important is financial sector development relative to development in other policy areas? Where should the emphasis lie: in banks or markets? Broad cross-country comparisons, but also experiences in the region, have provided insightful evidence in this respect.

Ultimately, financial deepening and broadening can contribute to Africa's move out of poverty and low-income status toward middle-income and emerging market status. The vision is of a financial system that fulfills the three concepts discussed above by providing a sound and effective platform for the market-based exchange of goods and services, attracting and intermediating the necessary resources for long-term private and public investment, and expanding financial services to larger segments of the population so as to offer, at least, access to transaction services.

Two decades ago, financial system development was an afterthought in the mind of a development economist designing a policy agenda. Today, financial sector policies have become a centerpiece in the debate on how to foster growth in low-income countries, reduce stark poverty levels, and, ultimately contribute to the achievement of the Millennium Development Goals. Over this period, ample evidence based on various levels of aggregation and distinct methodologies has been accumulated on the growth-enhancing effect of financial sector development. Even accounting for reverse causation, research has established the robust positive impact of financial sector deepening on economic development. Figure 1.1 illustrates the conclusion of a well-established body of empirical evidence: countries with higher levels of credit to the private sector relative to GDP experienced higher average annual real GDP per capita growth rates over the period 1980–2007. The relationship holds not only for a broad cross-section of countries, but also within Africa. The conclusion is confirmed by cross-country, panel, and time-series estimation techniques.[4]

The effect of finance on growth is not only statistically, but also economically significant. To illustrate the effect of financial deepening, compare Ethiopia with Thailand. Over the period 1980–2007, the ratio of private credit to GDP averaged 18 percent in Ethiopia, but 87 percent in Thailand. The cross-country comparisons illustrated in figure 1.1 suggest that Ethiopia's real GDP per capita would have

Figure 1.1   Finance and Growth across Countries, 1980–2007

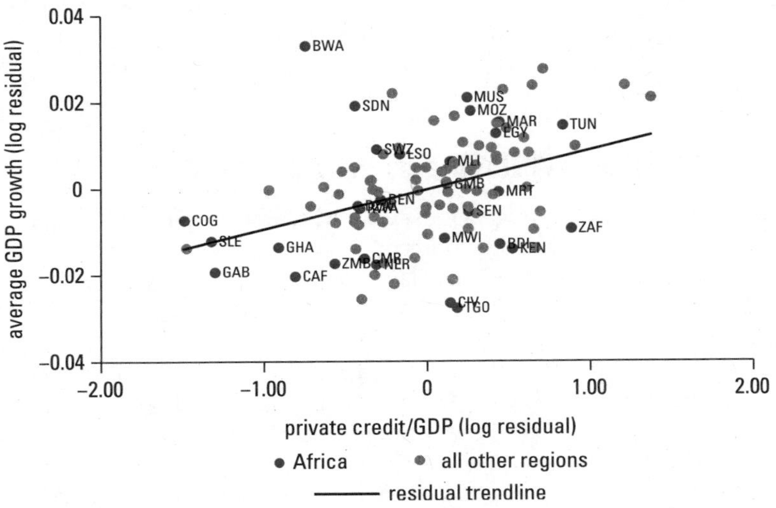

Source: Author calculations.
Note: Sample size: 99 countries. The figure shows a partial scatter plot of private credit to GDP and GDP per capita growth averaged over 1980–2007 and controlling for initial GDP per capita, government consumption, inflation, trade openness, and education. For a complete listing of 3-letter country codes and the respective country names, see pages xvi–xvii.

grown by 1.3 percentage points more had the country been at the same level of financial development as Thailand, or 1.4 percent instead of the actual 0.1 percent. Under this scenario, GDP per capita would have been over 40 percent greater in 2007.[5] We can also compare the financial development and corresponding growth performance in Africa with that in low- and middle-income countries in East Asia. While financial development measured according to the ratio of private credit to GDP stood, on average, at 21 percent across Africa over the period 1980–2007, it was 32 percent in East Asia. During the same period, the East Asian economies grew 2.3 percent per year on average, while the African economies grew 0.7 percent on average. The estimates illustrated in figure 1.1 suggest that 0.4 of a percentage point of this difference in average annual growth—a quarter of the difference— was caused by the lower level of financial development. Thus, the estimates suggest that, today, Africa could have a GDP per capita greater by 13 percent than the actual GDP per capita. This is, indeed, a significant loss.

The positive impact of financial development on growth does not mean that growth has no influence on financial deepening and broadening. On the contrary, by helping to increase incomes, financial deepening can create additional demand for financial services, thus generating a positive feedback loop. Policies that help foster financial sector development ultimately also help establish a virtuous growth cycle. Moreover, many of the policies that foster financial sector deepening and broadening, including an effective contractual and information framework and macroeconomic stability, also have a direct positive impact on economic development and poverty alleviation.

What are the channels through which financial development helps increase economic growth? While financial systems assist in pooling savings, transforming maturity, and converting savings into capital accumulation, it is ultimately through improvements in resource allocation and productivity growth that finance helps economies grow more quickly (Beck, Levine, and Loayza 2000; Love 2003; Wurgler 2000). The functions of attracting deposits and investment and transforming short-term claims into long-term assets, thereby financing investment, should obviously not be ignored; they are the basis for the ultimate function of finance, which is to put the savings of society to the best use, that is, put savings where they can reap the highest (expected) returns, thus translating into growth. Financial deepening especially helps industries that rely heavily on external finance, but it also helps reduce the financing constraints on enterprises, particularly smaller firms (Rajan and Zingales 1998; Beck, Demirgüç-Kunt, and Maksimovic 2005). Financial deepening thus has a transformative effect on economies by shaping industrial structure, distribution by firm size, and even organizational structures (Demirgüç-Kunt, Love, and Maksimovic 2006). It is the facilitating role of financial systems that helps foster economic growth. Finance provides opportunities for new entrepreneurs and fosters innovation and competition as well.

Providing external finance to enterprises in the form of equity, debt, or some hybrid thus seems critical to the positive impact of finance on growth. Recent cross-country comparisons have indeed found that it is enterprise credit, rather than household credit, that explains the positive impact of finance on growth (Beck et al. 2009). This does not mean that credit services for households are not important; the growth effect of financial development, however, seems to come mainly from enterprise finance. One therefore has to look beyond credit services to other financial services in discussing the welfare impact of financial service provision on households. This casts doubt on the credit-led inclusion strategy often propagated by microcredit institutions and puts a premium on enhancing access to savings and transaction services. We return to this topic in chapter 3.

Financial sector development is important not only for fostering the economic growth process, but also for dampening the volatility of the growth process. As shown by Aghion et al. (2010), financial systems can alleviate the liquidity constraints on firms and facilitate long-term investment, which ultimately reduces the volatility of investment and growth. Similarly, well-developed financial markets and institutions can help dampen the negative impact that exchange rate volatility has on firm liquidity and thus investment capacity (Aghion et al. 2009). This is especially important in economies that depend heavily on natural resources and are thus subject to high terms of trade and real exchange rate volatility.

What has the recent crisis taught us about the importance, but also the risks of financial deepening?[6] First and foremost, it has shown us the enormous risks that financial system fragility can create in the overall economy and for people's livelihoods. The global crisis and the ensuing Great Recession have put in doubt the paradigm that financial deepening is good for growth under any circumstance. Consumer credit booms in several European countries and the United States, fueled by the combination of regulatory neglect, the feeling that "this time is different," and the liquidity glut linked to global macroeconomic imbalances, ended in the global financial crisis. International links through global financial markets helped propagate the shock, first, through financial markets, while trade links ultimately resulted in the propagation of the real sector slump. For students of financial systems, the bright (growth-enhancing) and dark (instability) sides of financial development go hand in hand. The same mechanism through which finance helps growth also makes finance susceptible to shocks and, ultimately, fragility. Specifically, the maturity transformation from short-term savings and deposit facilities into long-term investments is at the core of the positive impact of a financial system on the real economy, but also renders the system susceptible to shocks. The role that finance has as a lubricant for the real economy likewise exacerbates the effect of financial fragility on the real economy. However, the externalities that the failure of financial institutions and markets impose on the real economy and the heavy government support for incumbent financial institutions that financial fragility therefore typically triggers are taken into account by the stakeholders in financial systems and give these stakeholders an incentive to be aggressive in the face of risks. It is thus critical to harness financial market forces for the benefit of the real economy and the population at large, rather than focus on finance for its own sake.

Instead of throwing out the baby with the bathwater, it is therefore important to construct a regulatory and governance framework that minimizes the risk of fragility and provides policy makers with better possibilities for managing bank failures in a way that is incentive-compatible. If there is a lesson to be learned in Africa from the crisis, it seems to be that the growth benefits of a well-developed financial system can only be reaped in a stable macroeconomic environment protected by an appropriate regulatory and supervisory framework and strong internal bank governance. This means there should be more transparency and accountability in bank management, less direct government intervention in the regulatory and supervisory process, and a focus on building up mechanisms of market discipline. However, the situation also highlights the demand-side constraints in terms of financial literacy and consumer protection, a topic we take up in several parts of the publication.

Ultimately, the financial systems of Africa are significantly less sophisticated than systems elsewhere, and most are far from becoming overheated as several financial systems in Europe and North America did before the crisis. This does not mean that there is no fragility (see chapter 5). Nonetheless, most of the fragility in recent years has not arisen because of too much finance, but because of misallocated finance generated by governance challenges. In a nutshell, Africa's financial

Figure 1.2 Finance and Poverty Alleviation across Countries

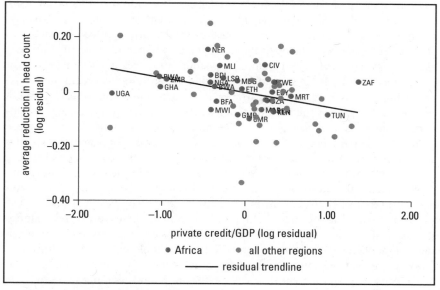

Source: Beck, Demirgüç-Kunt, and Levine (2007).
Note: Sample size: 68 countries. The figure shows a partial scatter plot between the ratio of private credit to GDP and growth in the headcount—the share of the population living on less than a dollar a day—averaged over the period 1980 to 2003 and controlling for the initial headcount. For a complete listing of 3-letter country codes and the respective country names, see pages xvi–xvii.

systems stand to gain significantly from deepening and broadening. If there is a decreasing marginal benefit from financial deepening or even a threshold where more financial deepening may have a negative effect, Africa's financial systems are far from reaching it.[7]

Who benefits the most from financial deepening? While theory provides conflicting analyses about whether it is the rich or the poor who benefit most from financial sector development, cross-country comparisons indicate that financial deepening has a pro-poor effect (Beck, Demirgüç-Kunt, and Levine 2007). Figure 1.2 illustrates the pro-poor effect of finance: countries with deeper financial systems see poverty levels drop more rapidly. As in the case of economic growth, the economic effect of financial deepening on poverty reduction is strong. Again, a comparison between Ethiopia and Thailand illustrates. Specifically, the cross-country comparisons shown in figure 1.2 suggest that, instead of a reduction in the poverty headcount from 33 to 23 percent over the period 1981 to 2000, a level of financial development similar to that of Thailand would have allowed a reduction of the headcount to 9 percent in Ethiopia.[8]

Financial deepening can have broader effects on socioeconomic development than those captured by GDP per capita and the poverty headcount. While eradicating extreme poverty by 2015 is one of eight Millennium Development Goals adopted in 2000, financial development may also be linked to the other seven goals, which refer to education, gender equality, health, the environment, and global partnerships.[9] In the case of education and health, one important outcome of access to financial services occurs through the income effect: better access to financial services improves incomes and therefore the possibility of accessing health and education services, while, at the same time, reducing the need to rely on children as laborers in the household. Allowing women direct access to financial services might improve the possibility they could become entrepreneurs, thus increasing their individual incomes and their chance to be more independent. This is reflected in greater female participation in family and community decision making. There is also an important insurance effect: better access to credit, savings, or insurance services reduces the need to use child labor as a buffer in the case of seasonal income fluctuations and transitory income shocks and allows consumption smoothing in the case of transitory income reductions caused by health shocks. It also allows more rapid attention to health problems. Finally, there is an aggregate infrastructure effect: more efficient financial institutions and markets allow more private and public investment in the construction of schools and health facilities.

What are the mechanisms of this poverty-reducing impact of financial deepening? Theory suggests different channels. On the one hand, providing access to credit among the poor might help the poor overcome financing constraints and allow them to invest in microenterprises and human capital accumulation (Galor and Zeira 1993; Galor and Moav 2004). On the other hand, there might be indirect effects through enterprise credit. By expanding credit to new and existing enterprises and allocating society's savings more efficiently, financial systems can expand the formal economy and pull larger segments of the population into the formal labor market. The first explorations of the channels through which finance affects income inequality and poverty levels point to an important role for such indirect effects. Specifically, evidence from Thailand and the United States suggests that an important effect of financial sector deepening on income inequality and poverty is an indirect one. By changing the structure of the economy and allowing more entry into the labor market by previously unemployed or underemployed segments of the population, finance helps reduce income inequality and poverty, but not by giving access to credit to everyone (Beck, Levine, and Levkov 2010; Giné and Townsend 2004). It is important to stress that this is preliminary evidence to be confirmed or refuted by future research, but it has centered the debate on an important question: should policy makers focus on deepening or on broadening financial sectors? It has also helped widen the debate on financial services for the poor beyond microcredit to other financial services, such as savings services, payment services (especially in the context of remittances from family members who have emigrated to other parts of the country or outside the country), and insurance services.[10]

A long-running discussion has centered on whether policy makers should focus more on banks or on capital markets. While both provide important financial services, the related technologies are different. Banks create proprietary information about their clients, especially borrowers, while capital markets collect and process information from different sources and reflect this information in prices. Banks offer better intertemporal risk diversification tools, while markets are better in diversifying risk cross-sectionally. Markets are better at offering standardized products, while banks are better at offering tailored solutions. However, banks and markets can also be complementary through the application of instruments such as securitization, by allowing exit strategies for venture capitalists, and by providing competition with each other. However, cross-country comparisons have shown that it is not really the structure of the financial system that matters, but rather the provision of financial services, whether these are supplied by banks or markets (Levine 2002; Beck and Levine 2002; Demirgüç-Kunt and Maksimovic 2002). The attempts of policy makers to push artificially for the development of a specific segment of the financial system over another are typically not fruitful. Yet, comparing financial systems across countries, one can discern clear patterns. Such a comparison suggests that there is an ordering in the development of different segments of the financial system. Systems in low-income countries are typically based much more on banks, while capital markets and contractual savings institutions, such as insurance companies, develop at a later stage.[11] Beck et al. (2008) estimate an income elasticity for different components of the financial system, which illustrates the different speeds at which different segments develop as GDP per capita rises (see table 1.1). Given the level of GDP per capita on the continent, it is not surprising that all African financial systems are based heavily on banks and exhibit underdeveloped markets. Not only is the capital market segment of these financial systems underdeveloped, but also the contractual savings component (insurance, pensions, and mutual funds) is small in most African countries. Finally, there is a

Table 1.1 Income Elasticities across Different Segments of the Financial System

Variable	Rank	Income elasticity
Public bonds to GDP	1	0.20
Bank deposits to GDP	2	0.35
Bank assets to GDP	3	0.44
Pension funds to GDP	4	0.45
Bank credit to GDP	5	0.49
Stock market capitalization to GDP	6	0.56
Insurance assets to GDP	7	0.66
Institutional investor assets to GDP	8	0.77
Mutual funds to GDP	9	0.88
Private bond capitalization to GDP	10	1.20
Value traded to GDP	11	1.30

Source: Beck et al. (2008).

scale element to the development of capital markets, and small economies therefore have difficulty—even in the developed world—in sustaining liquid markets.

The above discussion does not imply that policy makers in Africa should be content with the underdeveloped nonbank segments of the financial system. There is a need to diversify the financial center away from a heavily bank-dominated system, but it is also important to recognize that artificially creating certain components of the financial system without the necessary demand and infrastructure will have limited economic benefit.

Time for New Solutions to Old Problems

Financial institutions and markets exist to help overcome market frictions related to transaction costs and risk. However, the efficiency with which financial institutions and markets can overcome these market frictions is critically influenced by country characteristics. Fixed transaction costs in financial service provision result in decreasing unit costs as the number or size of transactions increases. These fixed costs exist at the level of the transaction, client, institution, and even financial system. Processing an individual payment or savings transaction entails costs that are, at least in part, independent of the value of the transaction. Maintaining an account for an individual client also implies costs that are largely independent of the number and size of the transactions the client makes. At the level of a financial institution, fixed costs span a wide range—from the brick-and-mortar branch network to computer systems, legal and accounting services, and security arrangements—and are independent of the number of clients served. Fixed costs also arise at the level of the financial system, including regulatory costs and the costs of payment, clearing, and settlement infrastructure, which are, up to a point, independent of the number of institutions regulated or participating in the payment system. The resulting economies of scale at all levels make it unprofitable to stay in the business of financial service provision unless the associated scale economies are captured in some form.[12]

In addition to costs, the outreach in the supply of financial services, especially credit and insurance services, is constrained by risks, particularly the risk of default. The risks can be either contract specific or systemic. Systemic risk can be defined as risk that is nondiversifiable within a given economy and that, as a consequence, affects all financial contracts. Systemic risk typically stems from high macroeconomic uncertainty (reflected in high inflation and exchange rate volatility), weaknesses in the contractual and informational environment, or geographical limitations. Regardless of its origin, systemic risk hinders the supply of financial services because it raises the default probability or the loss, given default, for all contingent contracts written in a given jurisdiction. This leads to a higher cost for funds and, hence, a higher floor for the interest rate required to grant a loan, shorter maturities as risk increases with the loan horizon, or higher premiums to write insurance policies. As systemic risk increases, it enlarges the set of borrowers and projects that find the cost of credit unaffordable and are thus priced out of the credit market. Similarly, this makes insurance policies unaffordable for larger segments of the population.

Idiosyncratic credit risks are specific to individual borrowers or projects and therefore are not correlated with systemic risk. As a result, the cost of finance and the availability of credit or insurance services differ across debtors and projects depending on the related differences in idiosyncratic riskiness. Importantly, however, the ability of the lender to manage idiosyncratic risk is influenced by the systemic risk environment. Two factors are particularly important in explaining the differences in interest spreads across debtors (for a given type of loan) that are induced by idiosyncratic risk: agency problems and limits to the diversification of risks that are not related to agency problems. The first can be linked to the lack of information, but also to volatility, while the second can be linked to diseconomies of scale. Agency problems arise from information asymmetries between debtors and creditors, whereby a debtor is privy to relevant information about herself and her project that the creditor may not be able to secure or only at a prohibitively high cost; this can lead to two conceptually distinct sources of credit risk: adverse selection and moral hazard.[13] The former refers to higher interest rates that attract riskier borrowers and projects, while the latter refers to the borrower's incentive to use the proceeds of the loan in endeavors that are riskier than those specified in the credit contract, while concealing this behavior from the creditor.

A lack of scale and a lack of tools to deal with idiosyncratic and systemic risk can limit the capacity of financial systems to effectively serve the host economy, foster growth, and reduce poverty. However, the characteristics of the host economy provide the backdrop before which financial institutions and markets have to operate. African economies are characterized by several adverse circumstances—pointed out by Honohan and Beck (2007)—that make it more difficult to overcome the two market frictions of size and risk, as follows:

- The *small scale* of many economies does not allow financial service providers to reap the benefits of scale economies. The small size of African economies, as shown in figure 1.3, is driven by the low income level across the continent, but also by the small size of countries. The limited demand for savings, insurance, credit, or even simply payment transactions means that large parts of the population of African economies are not commercially viable customers. The dispersed populations in many African countries means that financial service provision outside urban centers is not cost-effective. Despite the increasing trend toward urbanization, large parts of populations in Africa still live in rural areas. The small size of financial systems does not allow financial institutions to recover the fixed costs of basic systems and might undermine competition if the system does not sustain more than a small number of institutions.

- As documented in figure 1.4, large parts of the economy and a large share of all economic agents operate in the *informal sector* and do not have the necessary formal documentation, such as enterprise registration, land titles, or even formal

Figure 1.3   GDP across Countries, 2009

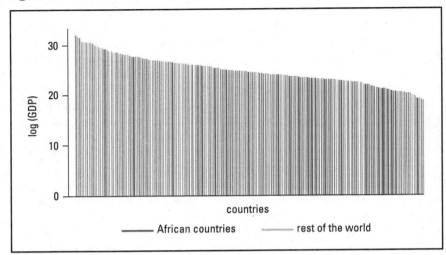

Source: World Bank (2010a).
Note: Sample size: 188 countries. GDP is measured in current U.S. dollars.

Figure 1.4   The Informal Economy across Countries, 2007

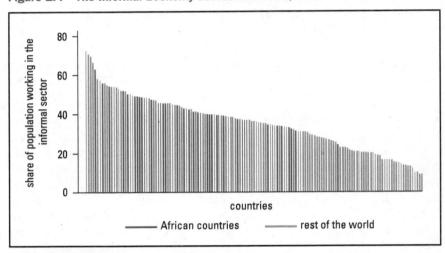

Source: Schneider, Buehn, and Montenegro (2010).
Note: Sample size: 145 countries.

addresses. This increases the costs and risks for financial institutions and excludes large segments of the population from formal financial services.

• *Volatility* on the individual and aggregate levels increases costs and undermines risk management. At the individual level, volatility is related to informality and

Map 1.1   Reliance on Natural Capital across the World

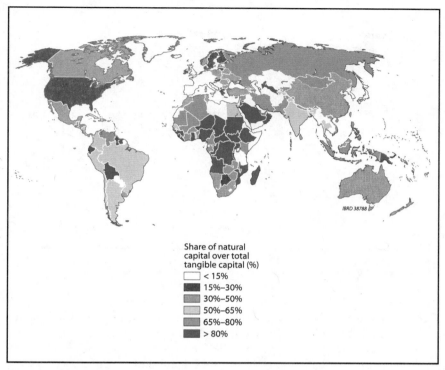

Share of natural
capital over total
tangible capital (%)
- < 15%
- 15%–30%
- 30%–50%
- 50%–65%
- 65%–80%
- > 80%

Source: Gylfason (2010).

the consequent fluctuations in the income streams of many microenterprises and households. This means these agents are less attractive for financial institutions. At the aggregate level, volatility refers to the dependence of many African economies on commodity exports, which makes economies vulnerable to the large price swings characteristic of commodities (see map 1.1). Volatility at the aggregate level also refers to political and social unrest, from which Africa has suffered over the past 50 years of independence. Volatility increases the costs, but especially the risks faced by financial institutions and markets.

- *Governance* problems continue to plague many private and government institutions throughout the continent and undermine not only the market-based provision of financial services, but also reform attempts and government interventions aimed at fixing market failures. These governance challenges are widespread and affect many financial institutions, ranging from banks, microfinance institutions, and cooperatives to government institutions, including development finance institutions. Governance problems have been at the root of many financial crises on the continent. They also affect directly the ability of financial institu-

Figure 1.5   Governance across Countries, 2008

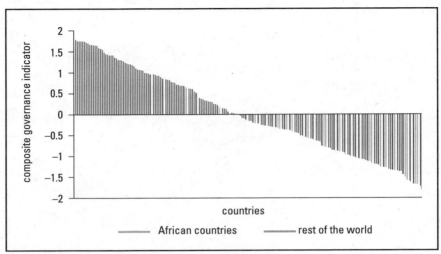

Source: Kaufman, Kraay, and Mastruzzi (2009).
Note: Sample size: 197 countries.

tions and markets to manage idiosyncratic and systemic risks. The governance challenge and the related agenda contain a large number of dimensions, ranging from political stability and accountability in the control of graft to the rule of law. Along all these dimensions, Africa ranks significantly below other countries, although there are positive examples of reforms (figure 1.5).

Not all countries show these four characteristics. Africa has large economies, such as Kenya and Nigeria. Middle-income countries such as Mauritius and South Africa are able to benefit from their higher income levels in terms of scale economies. The prevalence of the informal economy is significantly lower in the middle-income countries of North Africa than in Sub-Saharan Africa. Noncommodity exporters are subject to much less volatility than commodity exporters, and countries such as Botswana and Mauritius have shown significant and increasing levels of governance. However, many countries across the continent are affected by at least one of these characteristics, which make them less receptive to hosting a thriving financial system.

In analyzing the long-standing challenges described above, the book draws attention to three recent trends and phenomena—globalization, regional integration, and technology—that offer new solutions, but also represent new challenges.

- *Globalization:* Integration in international financial markets has been an important, but controversial aspect of financial sector policy throughout the world in past decades and even more so since the recent crisis. While most African countries have opened up their financial systems to the entry of foreign banks, capital account restrictions are still in place in many countries, although often more de jure than de facto. Capital account liberalization has long been considered an important component of the modernist agenda of the Washington Consensus (Rodrik 1998). Yet, the crisis experience in East Asia and other emerging markets in the 1990s has led to a more cautious approach. The underlying economic model has also faced severe criticism: cross-country comparisons do not yield consistent results on the benefits of capital account liberalization. In addition, there may be a threshold value in economic, institutional, and financial development below which countries do not benefit from capital account liberalization because capital inflows critically depend on financial markets and institutions.[14] Foreign investors need capital markets to invest in equity or debt, unless they create subsidiaries or joint ventures. Even portfolio investors need institutions or markets in which to invest. Governance is therefore important so that countries may reap the benefits of international capital flows, as shown by the example of resource-based economies in which the corresponding capital inflows are not always properly accounted for or used in the public interest. Overall, a cautious approach is called for that focuses more on long-term capital inflows (foreign direct investment) rather than short-term portfolio flows and that imposes additional safety lines on macroeconomic management. This debate has gained fresh significance in light of the current attempt of emerging markets to use capital flow restrictions to counter the negative repercussions of the capital inflows from developed markets that are a consequence of the application of quantitative easing policies.

- *Regional integration*: Regional integration has been on the agenda of African policy makers since many countries achieved political independence. The successful example of Europe in creating a large regional market with a joint currency, joint institutions, and coordinated policy making has been inspiring, although the recent euro crisis may have dampened the enthusiasm somewhat. Prima facie, there is an enormous potential for Africa in overcoming scale diseconomies by coming together. Not surprisingly, there have been numerous attempts at such cooperation. However, the results have been limited. Apart from three currency unions, two joint bank regulation and supervision authorities, a joint insurance regulatory authority, and two regional stock exchanges, most efforts have occurred at the level of coordination and the exchange of experiences. One reason for the limited success at integration has been political; another is overambition, as is obvious from the failure to establish a pan-African currency union; yet another is weak implementation. It is important to note that—as in the European Union—regional integration cannot and will not move at the same speed in all areas and all segments of the financial sector. For this reason, focusing on smaller and economically and institutionally more homogeneous subregions, such as East Africa, might be more promising than trying to integrate larger regions with countries at different levels of financial development and relying on different institutional and legal structures. By harmonizing the bank regulatory framework, authorities can reduce the regulatory costs for banks active across several countries of the respective subregion (World Bank 2007a). Integrating payment systems can significantly reduce the cost of crossborder transactions, including remittances, and help increase intraregional trade. Creating regional stock exchanges and allowing cross-listing can assist in creating the necessary scale for liquid capital markets in the region.

- *Technology.* Technology can help mitigate scale- and risk-related frictions. Technology can help reduce transaction costs, especially the fixed cost component. It can help reduce operational risk, while it minimizes the opportunities for theft and fraud. Financial services via mobile phones offer African financial systems the chance for a transformational banking model that leapfrogs conventional banking models by substantially reducing transaction costs. Moving away from the brick-and-mortar model of banking with high fixed costs toward mobile phone technology, where most of the costs are variable, can help overcome diseconomies of scale. Similarly, weather insurance built on exogenous indicators can help resolve information asymmetries between the insured and insurance companies at low cost.

Globalization, regional integration, and technology offer new opportunities, but also represent challenges, which we discuss throughout the book. All three trends will also have an impact on the relative role of the private and public sectors. There will be more space for private service providers to deepen and broaden financial systems, while the public sector has to redefine its role and face new challenges in regulation and supervision. Globalization, regional integration, and technology will raise new challenges to financial sector regulators. Globalization and regional integration will require home and host country regulators to cooperate more closely in regard to crossborder banks, and these home and host countries will increasingly be outside the developed world. Technology, especially in mobile financial services, will require closer cooperation among regulators across sectors, but also a more agile regulatory approach.

The changes in globalization and the new opportunities that technology provides also raise new challenges for governments. The crisis has reinforced the need for an open debate on the role of government. Honohan and Beck (2007) address this debate by distinguishing two approaches to financial sector policy: *modernism* and *activism.* While modernism focuses on creating the necessary conditions for the emergence of modern financial markets, including the necessary legal and regulatory reforms, activism aims at replacing nonexistent markets through government intervention, including government-owned financial institutions.

Many elements of this debate are reflected in this book as well. The recent crisis might trigger an increasingly activist role for governments throughout the continent, partly driven by the examples set in industrialized countries, but also by the different role of government in Brazil, China, and India, three emerging countries with growing influence and weight in Africa. This trend toward an activist role of government can also be seen in the desire of African governments to establish new development banks. Still, the memories of activist failures are too fresh to expect a full-fledged return to government-dominated financial systems. However, the limitations of the modernist approach are also evident.

As Honohan and Beck (2007) emphasize, we, too, stress a nuanced view that recognizes the limitations of modernism while pointing to the pitfalls of activism. Government has to play an important role in (1) expanding outreach, (2) lengthening financial contracts, and (3) safeguarding financial systems. This role goes beyond setting the rules of the game and building institutions. Government might have to play an important part in fostering competition, but also cooperation. The important message is that one size does not fit all; while learning from other countries in the region and other regions is important, the contextual framework has to be stressed. We are also far from possessing a rigorous metric that can be used to categorize and judge government interventions; there will be a lot of trial and error. It is thus important to put in place better assessment tools for government interventions.

The Outline of the Book

The remainder of the book is organized into five chapters. In the next chapter, we landscape financial systems in Africa. We use an array of (new) data on the country, firm, and household levels to quantify the development and structure of financial systems across the continent. We show that Africa's financial systems continue to be small in absolute and relative terms. They are based heavily on banks; few stock markets have sufficient liquidity; and the contractual savings industry is small and weak in most countries. The small size of financial systems also explains the high costs of intermediation and financial service provision, as well as the limited competition. The chapter also documents the progress Africa's financial systems made before the crisis and recent trends since the crisis. Africa's banking systems are well integrated in global financial systems, as shown by the dominance of many banking systems by foreign-owned banks. However, the face of globalization has changed in Africa: the multinational banks of the former colonial powers have been slowly replaced in importance by regional banks based in southern and western Africa, while capital flows from emerging markets such as Brazil, China, and India have slowly overtaken the capital flows of the industrialized world. Access to financial services by households and enterprises is still limited across Africa, though recent trends are promising.

Chapter 3 focuses on the challenge of expanding financial systems in Africa. We build on the issues of scale and risk introduced in this chapter to derive the concept of an access possibilities frontier. This provides a framework for benchmarking access to formal financial services and discussing policies that help turn the unbankable into the bankable population and the bankable into the banked population. We then focus on four specific dimensions of the access agenda. First, we discuss the role of different financial service providers, and, in line with our main messages mentioned elsewhere above, we focus on the importance of competition in alleviating supply-side constraints. Second, we discuss the need to concentrate on users of financial services as much as on suppliers through financial literacy programs. Third, we discuss the possibilities and challenges that technology represents in the need to promote an expansion in access. In this context, we discuss the possibility that a new transaction-led approach toward financial inclusion might be more promising in Africa than a credit- or savings-oriented approach. We discuss the role of government in pushing the frontier outward through institution building, as well as in pushing toward the frontier by fostering competition. We also focus on specific sectors, such as the ongoing challenges of agricultural and rural credit and the challenges of finance for small and medium enterprises.

Chapter 4 focuses on the issue of lengthening financial contracts. Financial services for households and enterprises are characterized by short maturities. At the same time, Africa faces enormous gaps in infrastructure, housing, and long-term firm finance. We discuss the current landscape among providers of long-term resources, including banks and capital markets, as well as institutions with unused potential to contribute to long-term finance, such as contractual savings institutions. We explore the possibilities that globalization offers in the form of sovereign wealth funds and private equity funds. We offer policy options for expanding long-term finance by adopting a similar approach as in the previous chapter and distinguishing between policies that help Africa optimize the current possibilities to expand long-term finance—partial risk guarantee schemes, public-private partnership structures, and the use of development finance institutions, among others—and policies that push the frontier outward, such as policies aimed at macroeconomic stability and institution building.

Chapter 5 focuses on safeguarding finance. Africa has made enormous progress over the past 20 years in improving the regulation of banking, with the result that financial systems are much more stable. However, progress in banking regulation has not always been accompanied by progress in the quality of supervision. Furthermore, the recent crisis has reinforced the lesson that safeguarding a financial system requires constant updating and adaptation to new circumstances. The relevance for Africa of the regulatory reform in the North, including Basel III capital requirements, are discussed. One specific issue we focus on is bank resolution and crisis preparedness, an area where there is a significant need for reform, especially in view of the increase in regional integration in banking. Expanding the regulatory and supervisory perimeter beyond banking has to be undertaken carefully, distinguishing between segments in which the savings of the poor may be at risk and in which there is a call for regulatory oversight and segments with sophisticated investors in which a caveat emptor approach might be more appropriate. Governance challenges are as important as regulation, especially in the contractual savings segment of the financial system. User protection, however, is as important as the supervision of suppliers, and we therefore discuss issues of consumer protection.

Chapter 6 is the "who does what" chapter, highlighting the role of different stakeholders. It focuses on the facilitating role of governments and the changing role of state-owned financial institutions. It also highlights the potential for regional integration in Africa and how to go about achieving it. It discusses the politics of financial sector reform and the challenge of the creation of a constituency for financial sector reform. Finally, we revisit a theme developed throughout the book—one size does not fit all—by discussing challenges and priorities among certain subgroups of countries.

Notes

1. The BRIC countries are Brazil, the Russian Federation, India, and China.
2. See Levine (2005) for an in-depth discussion.
3. This does not imply that postconflict countries do not have enormous funding needs; however, their financial systems may not be the best conduit for the funding of reconstruction efforts.
4. See Levine (2005) for a literature review. It is important to note that, while figure 1.1 illustrates a partial correlation, numerous studies using different aggregation levels have shown that this relationship is robust to controls for reverse causation and biases arising from the omission of other potential factors influencing growth.
5. Such comparisons are only illustrative because the coefficient estimates measure marginal changes rather than large discrete changes.
6. Among many others, see the following on the recent financial crisis: Acharya and Richardson (2009), Brunnermeier (2009), Levine (2010), Rajan (2010), and Stiglitz (2010).
7. A recent paper by Arcand, Berkes, and Panizza (2011) shows that, above a threshold of private credit to GDP of 150 percent, the effect of finance on growth is significantly negative.
8. As in the case of figure 1.1, the significant relationship between finance and poverty reduction illustrated in figure 1.2 is only a partial correlation, but is confirmed if one controls for reverse causation and the omitted variable bias.
9. See Claessens and Feijen (2006) and Littlefield, Morduch, and Hashemi (2003) for a closer discussion.
10. For an in-depth discussion of these issues and the relevant literature, see World Bank (2008a).
11. This is also consistent with theory; see, for example, Boyd and Smith (1998).
12. See Beck and de la Torre (2007) for a more detailed discussion.
13. For the classic article on the effects of information asymmetry on credit supply, see Stiglitz and Weiss (1981).
14. See Kose et al. (2009), and, for a discussion on Uganda, see Kasekende (2001).

Chapter 2

Landscaping
African Finance

Introduction

The global economy and the global financial system are at the tail end of the Great Recession, the worst crisis since the Great Depression, and a first assessment of the impact on African financial systems can be made. This is not to say that risks of additional shocks and heightened volatility do not exist, but, according to all indications, the worst of the crisis is over, notwithstanding the ongoing crisis in several European countries and recent political turmoil in North African countries. However, it is also clear that there will be no return to the easy, cheap money of the early years of the 21st century, a theme we pick up below. Moreover, continuing global imbalances will make the global financial system susceptible to further shocks and fragility.

In this chapter, we (1) assess the impact of the crisis on Africa's financial systems and (2) present a broad quantitative analysis of these systems. In doing so, we benefit from a much broader set of data sources than did Honohan and Beck (2007). Specifically, we draw on a data collection exercise that was undertaken for this book and that focuses on the structure and various segments of financial systems in Africa, including the market, portfolio, and maturity structure of financial institutions and instruments. We also draw on significant advances in measuring access to financial services achieved at the Consultative Group to Assist the Poor and the World Bank. Finally, we benefit from the growing interest of academics and analysts in African financial systems and the consequent data collection efforts.

The Effect of the Crisis

As the recent global financial crisis starts to fade into the distance, the debate on the impact of the crisis on Africa and the related long-term implications is alive with varying degrees of relief and caution.[1] Many are relieved that the direct impact has not been as severe as it might have been. Others remain concerned that the impact on the financial sector, through the secondary effects on the real economy, may actually be more significant and long-lasting than was first assumed. This chapter argues that, more important than either position, is the fact that the crisis not only stalled the gains in financial inclusion achieved in Africa in the run-up to the crisis, but also exposed the structural weaknesses in the sector that had remained unresolved even as the continent was making progress on key access indicators.

The conventional wisdom at the height of the crisis was that, with the exception of large and globally more connected economies such as Kenya, Nigeria, and South Africa, the crisis would have little impact on Africa because the transmission mechanisms between the financial systems in Africa and the systems in the rest of the world were weak. African financial institutions, it was argued, were not exposed to the risks emanating from the complex instruments in international financial markets because most of the banks in Africa rely on deposits to fund their loan portfolios (that they keep on the books to maturity), most of the interbank markets are small, and the markets for securitized or derivative instruments are small or nonexistent. African financial institutions reportedly experienced increases in their international lending costs and shorter maturities as a consequence of the crisis, but the effect remained small given the modest level of external lending.

In time, however, this conventional view started to give way to concerns about the second-round effects through the real sector. In addition, the impact was significant through reduced capital flows, especially lower portfolio flows, but also lower foreign direct investment (FDI) and aid flows. International capital flows to African dried up. Africa also suffered from a drop in remittances from Europe, though with a lag after the onset of the Great Recession and though part of this effect was caused by devaluations in local currencies (see figure 2.1).[2] Finally, there was a wealth effect in countries with stock markets: stock indexes dropped substantially, though they recovered in most cases. The initial expectations during the crisis, the current view, and the anticipated policy implications of these trends are discussed below.

Stock market performance

Initial hopes that investors, weary of the markets in developed countries, would seek opportunities in African and other developing economies were misplaced. The most immediate effect of the crisis was felt on stock markets throughout the region. The small size and illiquidity of Africa's stock markets were amplified rather than overlooked because local and international investors had become more cautious in their investment strategies. Thus, while the price-earnings ratios on many African stock markets were above comparators in mature markets in 2007, the fallout from the subprime mortgage crisis in the United States dampened investment plans significantly (figure 2.2). In 2008, the market turnover on the Uganda Bourse dropped 60 percent during the third quarter, the Nairobi Stock Exchange 20 share index in Kenya fell 31 percent, and the Johannesburg Stock

Figure 2.1 Remittance Flows through the Crisis and Beyond, 2004–10

Source: World Bank (2011a).

Figure 2.2 Stock Market Performance through the Crisis, 2008–10

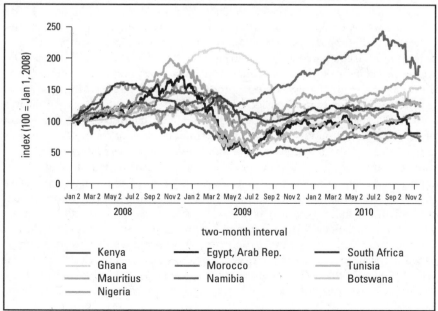

Source: Bloomberg.

Exchange all-share index lost 22.6 percent in October, following a 14 percent decline in September, all in all a 42 percent decline since May the same year. African stock exchanges also experienced limited issues during the crisis, which further delayed market recovery. Box 2.1 summarizes the experience on some stock exchanges during the crisis.

This was disappointing. Until the recent crisis, African stock markets had been experiencing a resurgence and displaying an energy that had not been felt for years. Prior to 1989, there were only five stock markets in Sub-Saharan Africa, and only three in North Africa. By 2010, there were more than 20 stock exchanges, ranging from start-ups in Mozambique and Uganda to the well-established Lagos and Johannesburg stock exchanges. With the exception of South Africa, most African stock markets had doubled their market capitalization between 1992 and 2002, while total market capitalization for African markets had increased from US$113.4 billion to US$244.7 billion during those years. Ghana had five new equity listings in 2004; the initial public offering of Kenya Electricity Generating Company in 2006—the country's first in five years—attracted strong demand and enormous public interest. The 2008 initial public offering for the cell phone companies Safaricom and Celtel in Kenya and Zambia, respectively, had both been oversubscribed. This emerging confidence in African stock markets was negatively affected by the crisis.

Real sector performance

As the financial crisis surged into all parts of the real economy in developed countries, African countries experienced a substantial decline in exports when the rapid pace of trade expansion in the early 2000s decelerated sharply (figure 2.3). The sectoral and geographical concentration of exports in most African countries exacerbated the impact. Growth among Sub-Saharan African countries fell to 5 percent in 2010 compared with 6.6 percent over 2004–08 (IMF 2011). In countries where the fall in investments was coupled with a decline in export earnings, a slowdown in the growth of gross domestic product (GDP), and a sharp drop in domestic asset prices (for example, a local housing market correction), the result was weakened bank balance sheets and, in some cases, bank failures. Overall, the impact of the Great Recession varied with the economic structure of countries. Mauritius and South Africa, both middle-income countries and financial centers, suffered because of reductions in crossborder bank flows and because of their dependence on export markets in Europe. Meanwhile, Morocco was affected through a reduction in revenues that was observed mainly in the secondary and tertiary sectors, as well as through the luxury segment of the real estate market. Commodity exporters such as Gabon, Guinea-Bissau, and Zambia suffered because of the rapid decline in commodity prices. Finally, several countries—most prominently Nigeria—experienced domestic crises that were triggered by the exogenous shocks of the global crisis. In Nigeria, the crisis was initiated by a vicious cycle of capital outflows and commodity price drops that affected local investor sentiment and the appetite for

Box 2.1   Performance on Selected Stock Markets during 2008–09

In *Nigeria,* the stock market witnessed a sharp decline beginning in March 2008, and the Nigeria all-share index lost more than 60 percent of its value. The correction (from high price-earnings ratios) was triggered, among other causes, by foreign investor withdrawal and led to margin calls and increases in the required collateral, precipitating additional declines. The decline in the Nigerian stock market was of particular concern to banks in Nigeria. Not only did it generate increases in the nonperforming loans of the banks, which had provided loans for stock purchases, but it also raised the cost of issuing new capital. (Banking shares accounted for over 60 percent of the total market capitalization.)

In *Kenya* between July 2008 and April 2009, the Nairobi Stock Exchange 20 share index fell 48 percent. To some extent, this reflected domestic factors, such as rising domestic political uncertainty following the postelection political turbulence in early 2008 and the third in a series of broker fraud scandals that reflected the underlying weaknesses in governance in the Kenyan capital market. Kenya's macroeconomic prospects were also heavily impacted by food and fuel price inflation in early 2008, which resulted in growing pressure on consumer prices. Some part of the fall in the Nairobi Stock Exchange index may also be ascribed to the Safaricom initial public offering in June 2008, which, although heavily oversubscribed at the time, drowned the market with a massive increase in equity supply at the moment sentiment was turning. As a result, the many small investors who had been attracted by the issue suffered sizable losses. Subsequently, the initial public offering by Cooperative Bank in November 2008 was 30 percent undersubscribed against a target of K Sh 6.7 billion.

In *Ghana,* the Ghana Stock Exchange all-share index, which had experienced an impressive 64 percent increase between January and October 2008, while stock markets around the world were collapsing, lost almost 46.6 percent during 2009, making it the world's most poorly performing stock market over this period. The effect of the financial crisis was exacerbated by the migration to a new automated trading system to which investors needed time to adjust and the rise in domestic interest rates, which made money market instruments more attractive. Domestic mutual funds were under pressure as investor redemptions could not be offset by sales in the illiquid equity markets; indeed, at least one fund had to borrow for redemptions.

In *Tunisia,* despite a 14 percent correction during the last quarter of 2008, the Bourse de Tunis Tunindex closed the year with a moderate 10.7 percent increase. Similarly, the Bourse de Tunis led African markets in 2009, closing the year with a 48 percent return on the Tunindex. Countercyclical measures taken by the government during the crisis helped sustain the performance of listed companies, which experienced a 10 percent rise in profits during the first semester of 2009. The confidence of investors was also strengthened by the implementation of a guarantee fund *(Fonds de Garantie de la Clientèle du Marché des Valeurs Mobilières et des Produits Financiers),* which covered noncommercial risks arising from the failure of financial intermediaries, as well as the enactment of a new code governing the provision of financial services to nonresident investors.

Sources: Data of the World Bank; data of the Ghana Stock Exchange; Bourse de Tunis (2010).

Figure 2.3   African Exports through the Crisis and Beyond, 2006–10

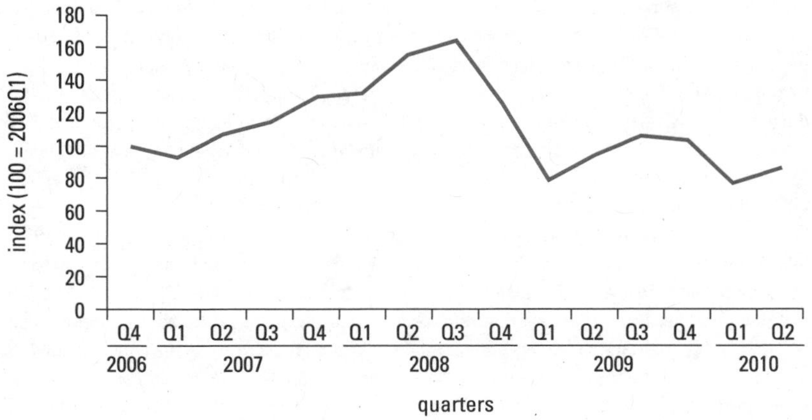

Source: Analytical Trade Tables (database), International Merchandise Trade Statistics Section, UN Statistics Division, New York, http://unstats.un.org/unsd/trade/imts/analyticaltradetables.htm.

Box 2.2   The Real Economy Impact of the Financial Crisis in Zambia

The Zambian economy was significantly impacted by the global crisis as a result of the sharp decline in copper prices, which, during the third and fourth quarters of 2008, fell by more than 60 percent relative to the peak in mid-2008. The mining sector, a mainstay of the Zambian economy, was hit hard by this decline. Mining accounts for some 70 percent of Zambia's foreign exchange earnings, and Zambia's revenue earnings from copper sales tumbled from US$3.6 billion in 2008 to US$2.9 billion in 2009, an 18 percent drop (figure a). Banks responded by cutting loans and advances to the private sector. Economic activity in communities dependent on mining stuttered; loan impairment increased; and bank liquidity and profitability declined. The slump in copper prices led to mine closures, which rendered thousands of people jobless.

The International Monetary Fund approved US$256.4 million in financial support to Zambia during the second quarter of 2009. Despite a recovery in copper prices, economic growth was still slow in the aftermath of the crisis: the government revised the GDP growth estimate downward to 4.5 percent compared with the 5.0 percent projected at the beginning of 2009. During the first six months of 2009, the government received US$339 million less in tax receipts and aid. The shortfall was offset largely by cuts in government expenditures to keep the fiscal deficit within the target of 3.1 percent of GDP for 2009.

At the peak of the recession, many western investors scaled back their presence in Zambia's copper belt. Their departure at the height of the recession saw the FDI of Chinese investors taking up the abandoned positions. At the height of the price slump, Chinese firms

Box 2.2 The Real Economy Impact of the Financial Crisis in Zambia *(continued)*

Figure a. Zambian Exports

Figure b. The Performance of Three Large Banks

leveraged the low prices to stockpile copper and purchase mines. China invested over US$400 million in FDI in the Zambian mining industry in 2009 and pledged more than 60 percent of the expected FDI in the following years. Zambia's mining industry is now benefiting from the global recovery. Closed mines have reopened, and growth in the copper belt region is forecast at 5.0–6.5 percent between 2010 and 2012.

While the Zambian banking system is currently stable and well capitalized, the slowdown in economic activity and the steep decline in copper prices resulted in an increase in nonperforming loans from 8.8 percent of total assets at the end of March 2009 to 10.4 percent at the end of June 2009 (figure b). In addition, banking system lending to the private sector decelerated as a result of sluggish economic activity, and there was an increase in average bank lending rates owing to a rise in yields on government short-term treasury bills. As the pressure on the exchange rate eased, short-term yields on government securities began stabilizing.

Sources: Losse-Müller (2010); data of Bankscope; Direction of Trade Statistics (database), International Monetary Fund, Washington, DC, http://elibrary-data.imf.org/FindDataReports.aspx?d=33061&e=170921 (accessed in 2010).

bank risk. Box 2.2 reports the experience of one country during the crisis, Zambia, a typical natural resource–based economy. The case illustrates the feedback processes from real to financial sectors and policy reactions.

In this environment, large projects in Africa that required external financing to complement shorter-term bank financing faced difficulties in sourcing these finances, and, where they did find the resources, they faced higher interest rates and short maturities because of the flight to safety and the greater risk aversion of lenders. At the same time, portfolio outflows exerted pressure for currency devaluations. Reductions in official development assistance, remittances, and tourism receipts also had an initial negative impact on the economy. As investments fell, some projects could not be completed, causing them to be unproductive and saddling bank balance sheets with nonperforming loans. Lower commodity prices, combined with a credit crunch and increased risk aversion, made the financing and development of capital investments more difficult.

Private sector lending and loan portfolio performance

An immediate concern at the time of the crisis was that banks would become excessively conservative in their policies and curtail the growth of private sector lending on the continent, especially long-term finance. To analyze the effect of the crisis at the microlevel, we consider bank balance sheets (figure 2.4). While the majority of banks on which we have data still expanded their loan books in 2009, one-fifth reduced their loan books, and some quite aggressively. Asset quality and profitability also do not seem to have been affected by the crisis, as shown by only a small uptick in nonperforming loans to 8 percent, high in international comparison, but low by historic comparison in Africa. A closer look at the group of banks that reported an increase in nonperforming loans reveals that most of them are located in Ghana

Figure 2.4   Bank Stability in Africa, 2005–10

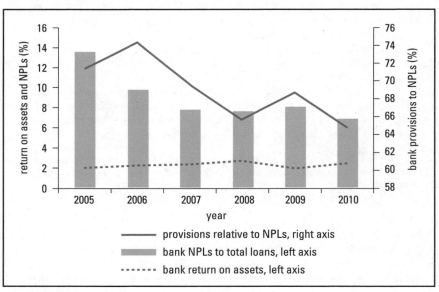

Source: IMF (various).
Note: NPLs = nonperforming loans.

and Nigeria, two countries that suffered from domestic crises triggered by the global economic recession. The banking systems in Côte d'Ivoire, Democratic Republic of Congo, and Togo also suffered from systemic distress for longer periods; this was related to political turmoil and governance deficiencies in these countries. In most other countries, large increases were confined to individual banks, while the performance of other banks was better. (Here, we measure large increases as year-on-year increases in nonperforming loans by 150 basis points or more relative to gross loans.)

In the aftermath of the crisis, early indications, according to a World Bank study, are that fears of large increases in nonperforming loans were premature (see Losse-Müller 2010). More than half of the 152 African banks reviewed for the study data on credit quality reported stable or declining nonperforming loans.

So far, the performance is encouraging, especially because loans in Africa have relatively short maturities, and banks therefore register poor loan performance relatively rapidly. Also, the risk of portfolio deterioration was larger when GDP growth tapered off in 2009, and, provided growth holds up, the risk might not be that great anymore. However, this benign picture should not be misunderstood: the rapid pace of growth in the past might still entail a buildup of credit risks in the region's banking systems. In general, country experiences around the world highlight that rapid credit growth often challenges the ability of banks to manage risk and the supervisory capacity of regulators.

Where credit is still available, banks have increased the cost and shortened the tenor of finance. This is disappointing after recent years, when funds had started to enter African markets looking for equity and portfolio investments. Real private sector credit, in particular, has been growing at an accelerating rate, and its median value has doubled over the past decade. Even as a share of GDP, it has turned the corner; the median share approached 18 percent in 2007, about a third higher than at the anemic trough in 1996. Much of this increase was on the back of innovative noncollateralized lending practices. Salary and other cash flow–based lending have been emerging, with positive outcomes for customers in the form of consumer loans.

To their credit, banking systems across Africa entered the crisis equipped with low leverage, high levels of capitalization, and ample liquidity, putting them in good shape in the face of a potential worsening in credit performance as a result of the domestic and global economic downturns. Early indications are that credit growth picked up again throughout 2010 and that credit provision might be about to return to the previous high-growth path. Nonetheless, in African countries, as in other developing countries, policy makers must face a new reality: the times of cheap, easy money are over. This is true of private funds, but also of official funds. In the wake of severe budget cuts in most industrialized countries, foreign aid budgets are likely to be cut. This will put a higher premium on private funding, including commercial and private donor money. It will also put a premium on domestic financial intermediation and regional integration.

Africa's Financial Systems in International Comparison

With the benefit of hindsight, one should not be surprised by the performance of Africa's financial sector through the crisis given the size of the sector, its lack of international and domestic integration, and the nature of the structural deficiencies that remained in financial systems even as they were achieving progress prior to the crisis. The recent global crisis mainly served to remind policy makers how vulnerable Africa is to shocks. While the absence of financial sophistication helped Africa reduce the contagion effects through financial market channels, it also prevented the financial sector from mitigating the impact of the shocks on the real economy. Policy design and development should therefore focus beyond the crisis and address these structural deficiencies.

A first step in the analysis of Africa's financial systems is an assessment and exploration of key statistics on the depth, breadth, efficiency, stability, and components of the systems. Such an analysis has to compare Africa with other regions, but also within a historical African perspective over the past, while focusing as much on similarities across the continent as on differences among countries within the continent. Critically, such an analysis has to benchmark Africa's financial systems by considering the low income level of most African economies and other country characteristics. Such an analysis is a first, though important step in better understanding Africa's financial systems. The remainder of this chapter thus sets the stage for the subsequent chapters, in which we look more closely at the challenges of the outreach, maturity structure, and stability of these financial systems.

In the following, we use an array of indicators at the country, firm, and household levels to document the development of finance in Africa. We point to the overall low level of development, but also positive trends over the past 10 years. We highlight strengths, such as strong and stable banks, and weaknesses, such as limited nonbank financial service providers, and discuss the trend away from North-South toward South-South capital flows. Africa's financial systems are based heavily on banks, and banks are therefore a large emphasis in the following. However, we also discuss other segments of these financial systems, including capital markets and contractual savings institutions, such as insurance companies and pension funds.

Relative to Honohan and Beck (2007), we have a much richer set of data sources we can use to assess quantitatively the development, efficiency, and outreach of financial systems in Africa. In addition to broad cross-country databases on the development and structure of financial systems (Beck, Demirgüç-Kunt, and Levine 2010), this publication uses much better cross-country data on the access to financial services by households and firms (CGAP and World Bank 2010), financial infrastructure (World Bank 2008b; World Bank and IFC, various; and so on), and remittance prices across corridors. In addition, we have available a detailed Africa-specific database on financial structure and the regulatory framework that contains data on 46 of the 53 countries on the continent.

The size of African banking systems

Standard indicators of banking system development show that Africa's banking systems are small in absolute and relative size. Many African banking systems would be mid-sized banks in high-income countries. Using a sample of banks included in Bankscope, which typically covers 90 percent of a country's banking system, we find that the average African bank has total assets of US$220 million, while the total balance sheet size of a non-African bank is, on average, almost US$1 billion. Behind this average, however, is a large variation. Standard Bank of South Africa has total assets of over US$100 billion, while the average bank in Madagascar has assets below US$200 million. Figure 2.5 shows the log of liquid liabilities—currency, plus demand and the interest-bearing liabilities of banks and nonbank financial intermediaries—in U.S. dollars. Most African banking systems are toward the right of the scale, with the notable exception of banking systems in Algeria, the Arab Republic of Egypt, Morocco, and South Africa, which are relatively large. If measured in relative size based on the claims on the private domestic nonfinancial sector relative to GDP (private credit), for example, we find that most African financial systems have relatively small banking sectors (figure 2.6). While the median for African countries was 19 percent in 2009, it was 49 percent for non-African developing countries. Behind this median, however, is significant variation across Africa. While private credit to GDP is less than 3 percent in Chad, it is over 70 percent in Mauritius, Morocco, and South Africa. The North African subregion shows the

Figure 2.5   Absolute Size of African Banking Systems, 2009

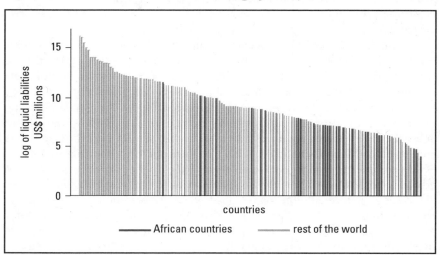

Source: Beck, Demirgüç-Kunt, and Levine (2010).
Note: Sample size: 154 countries. The highest African values are for Algeria, the Arab Republic of Egypt, Morocco, and South Africa.

Figure 2.6   Relative Size of African Banking Systems, 2009

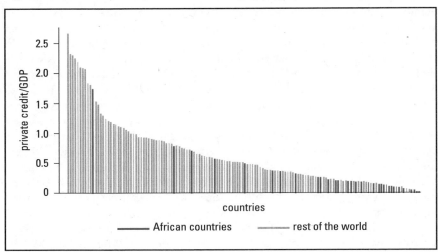

Source: Beck, Demirgüç-Kunt, and Levine (2010).
Note: Sample size: 140 countries. The highest African values are for Mauritius, Morocco, South Africa, and Tunisia.

highest levels of financial development, a median of 48 percent, which is at the same level as non-African developing countries, while Central Africa and West Africa show the lowest level, with a median of 16 percent.

African banking systems are not only small, but also characterized by low intermediation. One simple method of gauging intermediation efficiency is the loan-deposit ratio. Banks have funding sources other than deposits and other purposes besides lending to the private sector, but the loan-deposit ratio gives a good, though crude indication of intermediation efficiency. The loan-deposit ratio ultimately captures one of the core tasks of financial intermediaries, that is, putting society's savings to its best use: private sector development. We see that African banking systems intermediate, on average, only 74 percent of their deposits, while banks in non-African developing countries intermediate 109 percent of their deposits. As pointed out by Honohan and Beck (2007), countries in Africa showing lower levels of deposits intermediate an even lower share of these scarce deposit resources into private sector loans. While in the Republic of Congo the ratio of liquid liabilities to GDP is 33 percent and the loan-deposit ratio is 17 percent, the corresponding ratios in Tunisia are 62 and 107 percent, respectively (figure 2.7). It seems that, for most banking systems in Africa, especially in Sub-Saharan Africa, the resource constraint is not currently binding; yet, these systems suffer from an intermediation constraint.

The low intermediation ratios point to a critical problem in African banking: while the lack of resources might be a longer-term impediment to the economic

Figure 2.7   Intermediation Efficiency Versus Financial Depth, 2009

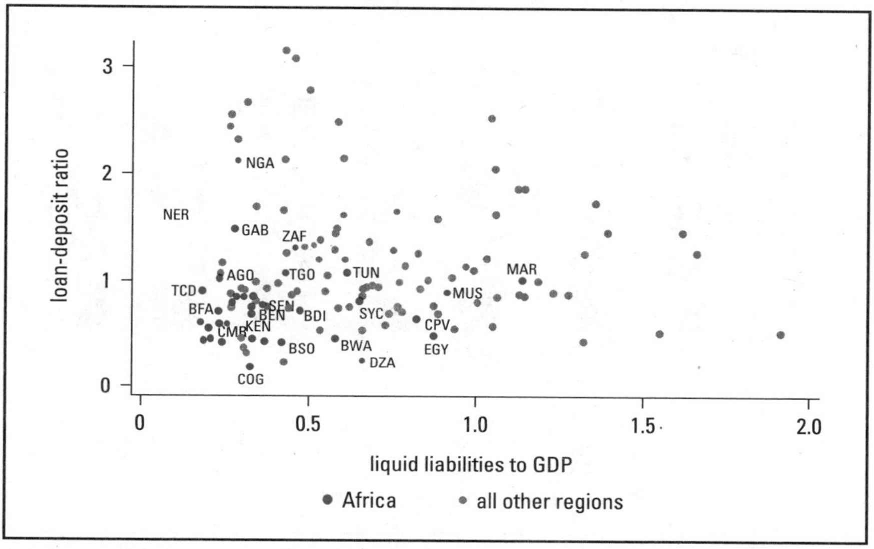

Source: Beck, Demirgüç-Kunt, and Levine (2010).
Note: Sample size: 133 countries. For a complete listing of 3-letter country codes and the respective country names, see pages xvi–xvii.

growth of the continent, a more immediate problem is the fact that existing re-sources are not intermediated efficiently into the private sector, where they are needed most. This is consistent with the observation across the African region that banks prefer to invest in government securities rather than private sector loans and that the credit channel of monetary policy only functions weakly. Banks react little to the changes in interest rates set by monetary authorities by lending more or less to the private sector, but, rather, they shift assets among government bonds and foreign asset holdings.

The relatively limited intermediation efficiency is confirmed if one digs deeper into the asset side of bank balance sheets to explore where banks invest their re-sources. Figure 2.8 shows the asset composition of banks across different regions. Unlike banks in other regions of the world and banks in high-income countries, African banks hold a much smaller share of their assets in private sector loans and a much larger share in government securities, foreign assets, and liquid assets.

There were significant improvements across African financial systems in the years leading to the global crisis. There was a persistent increase in the ratios of liquid liabilities to GDP, bank deposits to GDP, and private credit to GDP that were not driven by individual countries, but that occurred throughout the region (figure 2.9). In the years leading up to the global crisis, 75 percent of all countries experi-enced financial deepening. Africa's banking systems now also intermediate a larger

Figure 2.8   Asset Composition of Banks across Regions, 2009

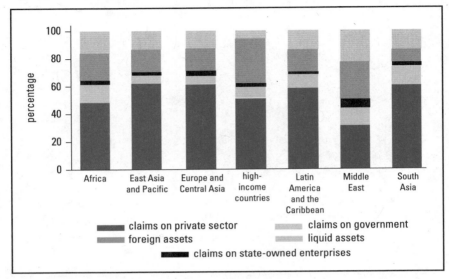

Source: International Financial Statistics (database), International Monetary Fund, Washington, DC, http://elibrary-data.imf.org/FindDataReports.aspx?d=33061&e=169393 (accessed in 2010).

Figure 2.9   Financial Deepening across Africa, 1990–2009

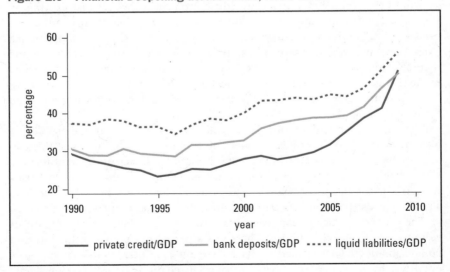

Source: Beck, Demirgüç-Kunt, and Levine (2010).
Note: Sample size: 25 countries. The number of countries indicated represents the situation following the balancing of the data set.

Figure 2.10 Private Credit across Africa, 1990–2009

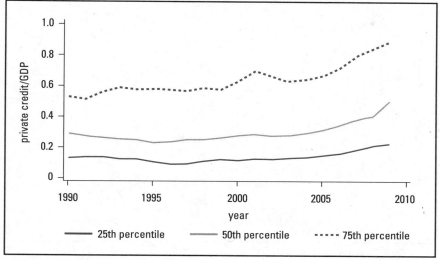

Source: Beck, Demirgüç-Kunt, and Levine (2010).

share of deposits into loans. This has led to a broad increase in the ratio of private credit to GDP across the continent (figure 2.10).

Banking outreach and maturity structure

African banking systems lack not only depth, but also breadth. In the absence of reliable indicators of the share of households that use bank accounts across a large number of countries, we have used proxy indicators to gauge the outreach of banking systems. The number of branches per capita shows the limited outreach of African banking systems compared with systems in other regions (figure 2.11). While Benin has less than one branch per 100,000 people, Bolivia has almost seven. While Egypt has four branches per 100,000 adults, Malaysia has 11. Data on the penetration of automated teller machines and point-of-sale systems shows a similar picture. While Morocco has nine automated teller machines per 100,000 adults, Malaysia has 47.5.

African banking is mostly short term, as evidenced by the maturity structure on the asset and liability sides of bank balance sheets. More than 80 percent of deposits are sight deposits or are deposits with a maturity of less than one year; less than 2 percent of deposits have a maturity of more than 10 years (figure 2.12, chart a). The maturity distribution is not as extreme on the loan side, though it is biased toward the short end. Almost 60 percent of loans are for less than one year, and less than 2 percent of loans are for more than 10 years (figure 2.12, chart b). This maturity structure of African banks is consistent with the low level of financial develop-

Figure 2.11   Branch Penetration across Countries, 2009

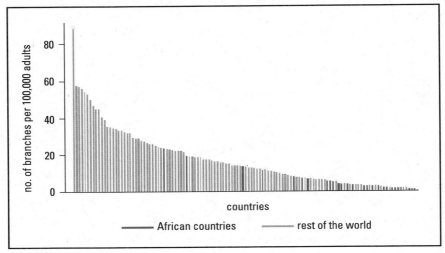

Source: CGAP and World Bank (2010).
Note: Sample size: 123 countries.

Figure 2.12   The Maturity Structure of Deposits and Loans across Africa, 2005–09

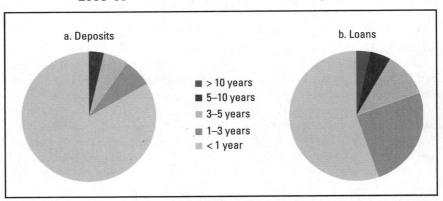

Source: Making Finance Work for Africa (database), Partnership Secretariat, African Development Bank, Tunis, http://www.mfw4a.org/.

ment in the countries and the focus of African financial systems on transaction services and short-term finance. It is also consistent with a banking system that focuses on Finance for Market services rather than Finance for Growth services.

African banks do not extend loans equally across sectors. This is not surprising because different economic sectors have different needs for external finance. Even

Figure 2.13   Sectoral Lending Share Relative to GDP Share, 2005–09

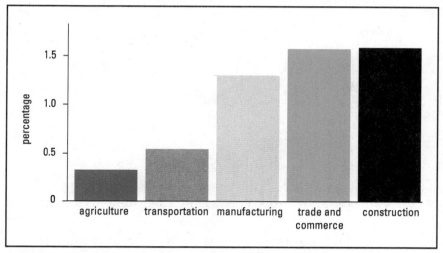

Source: Making Finance Work for Africa (database), Partnership Secretariat, African Development Bank, Tunis, http://www.mfw4a.org/.

within specific sectors, different industries have different financing needs, as documented by Rajan and Zingales (1998) for Canada and the United States. That a specific sector gets less than its "fair" share of bank loans, that is, a lower share in lending than in GDP, may thus be driven as much by lack of demand as by supply constraints.

Figure 2.13 provides interesting insights in that it confirms the anecdotal evidence: the agricultural sector is significantly underrepresented in bank loan books, as is the transportation sector. (We return to the issue of agricultural and, more broadly, rural finance in chapter 3.) The relatively low amount of lending to the transportation sector is somewhat more surprising because one would expect this sector to be able to use its assets as collateral more easily. Manufacturing, trade and commerce, and construction, in contrast, are overrepresented on the loan books of African banks. It is important to stress that the objective is not an equal representation of all economic sectors in bank loan portfolios and in GDP, but these stark discrepancies indicate that more than inherent demand or financing needs are at play in the allocation of loan resources across sectors in Africa.

Concentration and competition

Consistent with their small size, Africa's banking systems are mostly concentrated, and few banks share the small universe of clients. Figure 2.14 presents the Herfindahl index, which is the sum of the squares of market shares; higher numbers thus indicate a more concentrated banking system.[3] Of the countries with a Herfindahl index above 2,000, 50 percent are in Africa, while only a fifth of the countries with

Figure 2.14   Banking Sector Concentration across Countries, 2006

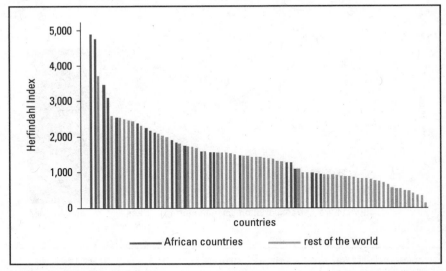

Source: Beck, De Jonghe, and Schepens (2011).
Note: Sample size: 80 countries. HHI index = the Hirschmann-Herfindahl index of the concentration of total assets.

a Herfindahl index below 2,000 are in Africa. The high concentration of African banking systems is also captured by cruder measures such as CR3 concentration measures, that is, the market share of the largest three banks, which, on average, stands at 68 percent. Behind this average is a large cross-country variation. While the CR3 concentration ratio is well below 50 percent in larger financial systems, such as Kenya, Nigeria, and South Africa, it is above 85 percent in Algeria, Angola, Malawi, Mauritius, and Sudan. This concentration can be related to the absolute and relative size of African banking systems. The fixed cost element in banking limits the possibility for a large number of players in markets with a low deposit and lending volume and, accordingly, a small potential customer base for spreading the costs. Similarly, the low income level and limited depth of African financial systems constrain the space for a large number of banks in the banking systems. In recent years, there has been a trend toward consolidation in some banking markets, as regulatory authorities have increased minimum capital requirements. Box 2.3 examines the experience of Nigeria.

Concentration, however, is not the same as competition: even oligopolistic markets can show a certain degree of competitiveness.[4] However, consideration of an indicator of competition provides a similar picture. A comparison across countries of the Lerner index—the ratio of the difference between the market price and the marginal cost of financial services to marginal cost—shows that this indicator of the market power of banks is significantly higher in African countries than in other

Box 2.3 Bank Consolidation: Learning from the Nigerian Experience

The debate on market structure, competition, bank size, and stability has not been settled; rather, it has been reignited by the current global crisis. In the African context, the Nigerian experience provides interesting insights. Before the crisis, the Nigerian banking sector was characterized by a large number of small banks, which taxed supervisory capabilities, and this fragmentation, in turn, coincided with instability. Against this backdrop, the governor of the Central Bank of Nigeria announced, on July 6, 2004, that banks would be required to achieve a minimum capital level of ₦ 25 billion (US$200 million), up from ₦ 2 billion (US$15 million), by December 31, 2005. The increase was intended to help bring about a diversified, stable financial sector that would ensure the safety of deposits, while contributing more to economic development via intermediation. The larger banks were also expected to compete more effectively in regional and global financial systems.

The consolidation occurred along different paths. The largest traditional banks achieved the capital threshold more or less on their own, while other, mostly younger, banks used the consolidation process to make an exponential jump in capitalization often via share issues. The rest of the banks achieved the capital threshold by forming groups. A small number of foreign-owned institutions relied on capital injections from their parent banks, if necessary, to meet the new standard. A careful comparison of these banks (or groups) before and after the consolidation process shows some improvement in cost-efficiency, but no reduction in spreads, suggesting a possible decrease in competitiveness. There was an increase in loans, partly to customers of the banks who used the loans to finance share purchases. There was also regional expansion among Nigerian banks.

The boom ended in a bust, a rather typical end to a financial reform and liberalization episode without the corresponding regulatory upgrade to sustain and monitor bank growth, coordinate among regulators, and ensure proper enforcement. The Nigerian experience also highlights the importance of appropriate corporate governance in terms of regulation and enforcement at the level of the banks and the supervisory authorities. As stated by Dr. Sanusi, the governor of the central bank, "consolidation created bigger banks but failed to overcome the fundamental weaknesses in corporate governance in many of these banks." As a result of special inspections carried out by the central bank in mid-2009, the extent of the buildup of risk and the inaccuracies in financial reporting in the banking system became apparent. Interventions were conducted in nine banks, which were rescued (some through convertible loans) by the central bank; the central bank simultaneously moved to guarantee all interbank transactions and replace senior management and executive directors. These banks not only depleted their capital, but, together, accounted for additional losses estimated at over US$9 billion. There was a flight toward secure assets, including government securities, although there is little evidence that there was a full-fledged credit squeeze. While contemporaneous with the global financial crisis, the Nigerian crisis was homemade, though the global crisis, with the subsequent drop in stock market indexes throughout the world, might have accelerated the onset of the crisis in Nigeria.

The Nigerian experience underlines that rapid changes in market structure have to be carefully monitored and accompanied by the necessary regulatory and supervisory upgrades, as well as proper corporate governance structures. It also drives home the point that consolidation can lead to the too-big-to-fail phenomenon (see the discussion in chapter 5). Through regional expansion, this can have repercussions beyond borders.

Sources: Cull and Trandafir (2010a); World Bank (2010b).

Figure 2.15   Banks' Market Power across Countries, 2006

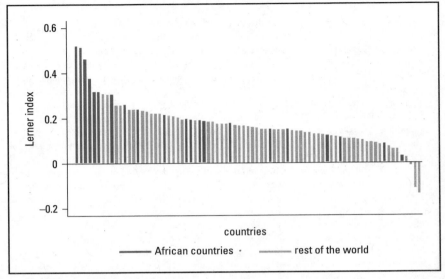

Source: Beck, De Jonghe, and Schepens (2011).
Note: Sample size: 80 countries. The Lerner index is the relative markup of price over marginal cost.

regions. The six countries with the highest markup are all in Africa (figure 2.15).[5] The lack of competition is not only a concern in itself, but has direct negative repercussions for the depth and breadth of financial systems. Higher market power results in higher interest rate spreads and, ultimately, lower levels of bank lending.

The concentration ratios and competition indexes discussed so far consider a country's banking system as one banking market and do not take into account the differences between deposit and lending markets or among different segments within the lending market. Though not captured in such data, anecdotal evidence suggests that deposit markets are typically more competitive than lending markets and that, within lending markets, the blue-chip segment of large domestic and multinational corporations is significantly more competitive than the small and medium enterprise segment. This segmentation of the banking market also has implications for competition across banks, a topic to which we return elsewhere below.

Increasing integration

Africa's banking systems are small, concentrated, and mostly foreign owned. This last has not always been a characteristic. Rather, the ownership structure has undergone significant changes over the past 50 years since independence. At the time of independence, Africa's banking systems were mostly dominated by colonial banks, many of which were subsequently nationalized (or "Africanized," though the re-

Figure 2.16   Foreign Bank Shares across Regions, 1995–2009

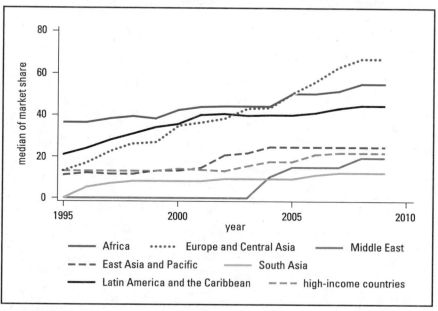

Source: Claessens et al. (2010).

sult—state ownership—was often the same). Structural adjustment and privatization programs in the 1980s saw a return to private ownership among many of these banks, sometimes in favor of the same European banks that had once been the proprietors. Now, Africa is the region with the highest share of foreign-owned banks (figure 2.16), with the exception of the transition economies of Europe and Central Asia. The last 10 to 15 years saw yet another new trend: the transition from international to regional banks (figure 2.17). After the end of Apartheid, several South African banks, most notably Absa and Standard Bank, started expanding throughout the continent. More recently, two West African banks—Bank of Africa and Ecobank—have started expanding throughout Sub-Saharan Africa. Similarly, Moroccan banks started to expand south. Finally and as consequence of the recent consolidation wave in Nigeria, Nigerian banks started expanding throughout West Africa, but increasingly also throughout the rest of the continent (see box 2.3). In addition to an increase in foreign bank ownership, there has thus been a marked increase in the share of regional, that is, African, banks among foreign banks, reaching 45 percent in the median country in 2009, while, in the mid-1990s, such banks had constituted only around a third of all foreign banks and less than 15 percent of total banking assets in the median African country. It is important to note that most international and regional banks have expanded throughout the region in the form

Figure 2.17   Foreign Bank Ownership across the Continent, 1995–2009

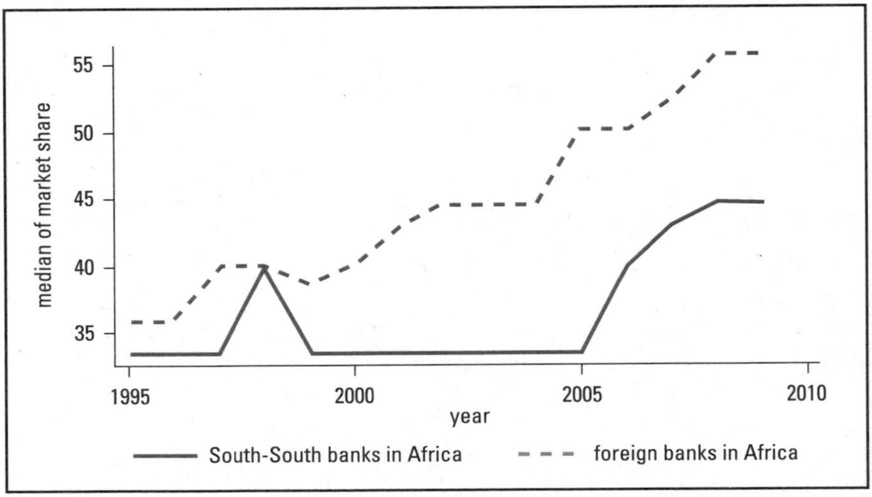

Source: Claessens et al. (2010).

of subsidiaries, which implies higher costs, but can have positive repercussions for supervisors in case of trouble because subsidiaries are somewhat easier than branches (though not perfectly) to ring-fence. We return to this topic in chapter 5.

What has been the effect of the increase in foreign bank ownership on the development, efficiency, stability, and outreach of African banking?[6] Foreign bank entry seems to have several advantages that are specific to Africa: international banks can help foster governance; they can bring in much-needed technology and experience from other regional economies that should translate into increased efficiency in financial intermediation (in the case of South African or West African banks); and they can help exploit scale economies in small host countries. Nonetheless, especially in Africa, with its many small, risky, and opaque enterprises, the dark side of foreign bank entry can become obvious, even more so in countries in which foreign banks have captured almost 100 percent of the banking market. Specifically, the greater reliance of foreign banks on hard information about borrowers as opposed to soft information can have negative repercussions for riskier and more opaque borrowers if foreign banks crowd out domestic banks (for example, see Gormley 2007; Sengupta 2007; Detragiache, Tressel, and Gupta 2008). In addition, there are many factors that can prevent countries from reaping the potential benefits of foreign bank ownership. The presence of dominant government-owned banks can reduce competitive pressures and allow other banks—be they domestic or foreign owned—to earn rents from the inefficiency of government-owned banks, as the example of Kenya in the early 2000s shows. The absence of a sound contractual and informational framework reduces the feasibility of small business lending further. The small size of many financial markets in Sub-Saharan Africa may make foreign banks reluctant to incur the fixed costs of introducing new products and technologies. The small size of many markets also does not allow for the necessary competitive pressure. The result in many African countries has been the concentration of domestic and foreign bank portfolios on government paper and international assets (see above). However, the diversity among the international banks in Africa suggests that there are differential and context-specific variations in the effects. This diversity is reflected in the finding of Čihák and Podpiera (2005) that foreign banks in Tanzania and Uganda lend more and charge lower spreads than domestic banks, while foreign banks in Kenya lend less than their domestic counterparts. This might reflect differences in policies. (The effect of bank market and ownership structure on the depth, outreach, and stability of African banking systems is discussed in more depth in the following three chapters.)

Interest rate spreads and margins

One striking characteristic of banking in Africa is the high interest rate spreads and margins (figure 2.18). True, Africa is not the only region with costly financial intermediation: several Latin American countries also exhibit high spreads. Yet, persistently high margins have been among the top concerns raised by policy makers throughout the region, and closer analysis is certainly warranted. As we argue in the following, these high spreads and margins are mostly caused by the small scale of most African financial systems and the great risks banks still face in most countries.

High interest rate spreads can be seen simply as the complement of shallow financial systems with little depth and breadth, given that countries with more de-

Figure 2.18   Interest Rate Margins across Regions, 2009

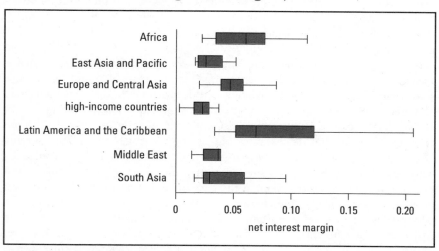

Source: Beck, Demirgüç-Kunt, and Levine (2010).
Note: Sample size: 134 countries. The figure shows the minimum, maximum, and median of the net interest margin. The shaded boxes indicate the interquartile range. Outliers have been omitted (the highest fifth percentile).

Table 2.1   Decomposition of Weighted Average Spreads, All Banks, Uganda, 2005–08

Indicator	2005Q4	2006Q4	2007Q4	2008Q2
Average lending rate	14.66	15.17	15.31	16.72
Average deposit rate	1.57	1.70	2.00	1.97
Spread	13.09	13.48	13.31	14.75
Overhead costs	4.77	4.09	3.47	4.66
Loan-loss provisions	1.17	0.74	1.67	0.72
Reserve requirements	0.17	0.19	0.22	0.22
Taxes	2.01	1.85	1.51	2.51
Profit margin	4.97	6.61	6.44	6.65

Source: Cull and Trandafir (2010b).

veloped financial systems exhibit lower net interest margins. There is one important caveat concerning the interpretation of high spreads in cross-country variation and in within-country variation over time in relation to the outreach of the financial system: higher spreads might indicate the inefficiencies discussed above, but also greater outreach to riskier clients who are more costly for banks.

There are two different ways to analyze spreads and margins: one is to undertake a decomposition of spreads into components; the other is to analyze the relevant underlying bank-, industry, and country-level traits. Another important distinction that is more than semantic is the distinction between spreads and margins, whereby the former refers to the difference between ex ante lending and the deposit rate, while the latter refers to the actual net interest revenue. This is an important distinction on the lending side; the main difference is the lost interest revenue because of loan losses, as well as possible timing issues (that is, the contracted lending rates that affect interest revenues in subsequent periods). While net interest margins are readily available on a consistent cross-country basis, interest rate spread data are much more difficult to find and are mostly inconsistent across countries. We therefore focus on a specific country, Uganda, where detailed data are available across banks and over time for lending and deposit rates at different maturities. Analysis on other African countries has, however, provided similar findings.

The data in table 2.1 illustrate persistently high interest rate spreads, with not only (in real terms) low deposit rates, but also high average lending interest rates. High operating costs are one important factor, while loan loss provisions reflecting loan losses and reserve requirements are rather minor components of the interest rate spread. Perhaps most striking is the high share that profits (and the taxes on profits) constitute in the interest rate spreads. High profits driving high interest rate spreads are, however, consistent with the significant market power of banks in Africa that is documented above. They are also consistent with a high risk premium on banking in Africa that even applies to relatively stable economies such as Uganda. Finally, high profit rates might also be explained—at least in the case of subsidiaries of large multinational banks—by the relatively small scale of operations, which might result in an absolute rather than relative profit target for these subsidiaries.

A second approach is to relate bank-level variations in net interest margins to differences in bank characteristics, such as size, liquidity, and ownership, to industry-level variations in market and ownership structure, and to country characteristics such as the institutional framework and the level of economic development. Table 2.2 shows some of the factors; the data refer to the period 2000 to 2007 (thus, before the onset of the global financial crisis). Estimations of the bank- and country-level factors associated with bank-level variation in overhead costs and computation of the contribution that each of these factors makes to the higher margins and costs in Africa compared with the rest of the world point to size and risk as two of the dominant factors. The small size of African banks can explain 42 basis points of the difference in the overhead costs between African banks and rest of the world banks and 20 basis points of the difference in net interest margins. The deficient contractual framework explains 55 basis points of the overhead costs and 95 basis points of the net interest margins in Africa compared with the rest of the world. Finally, still higher inflation in Africa compared with the rest of the world explains 24 basis points of the higher overhead costs and 23 basis points of the higher net interest margins. Other differences between African and non-African banks can also explain the differences in margins and spreads. The higher capitalization of African banks—a topic to which we return in chapter 5—is positively associated with overhead costs and margins, while the stronger reliance of African banks on (relatively) cheaper sight deposits shave off a few basis points from operating costs and margins. Finally, the higher volatility of banking in Africa (as measured by the variation in the return on assets over the period 2000 to 2007) increases overhead costs and margins, while the higher fee income in Africa raises operating costs and decreases margins.

The variables discussed above are certainly not the only factors influencing margins and overhead costs and might proxy for other important characteristics of financial systems and economies in Africa. Behind the small size of African banks is

Table 2.2 Explaining the Interest Margins and Overhead Costs in Africa

Indicator	Interest margin	Overhead costs
African banks	482	500
Rest of world banks	334	332
Difference	148	168
Contractual framework	95	55
Bank size	20	42
Other bank characteristics	−12	31
Inflation	23	24
Africa residual	23	16

Source: Author calculations using data of Bankscope.

Figure 2.19   Small Scale Comes with High Margins, 2009

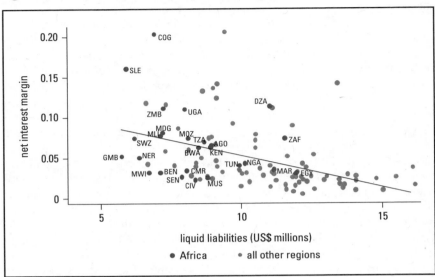

Source: Beck, Demirgüç-Kunt, and Levine (2010).
Note: Sample size: 178 countries. Liquid liabilities are taken in log scale. For a complete listing of 3-letter country codes and the respective country names, see pages xvi–xvii.

the high degree of informality, which results in a small base of potential clientele. The deficient contractual framework is a symptom of larger challenges in the governance agenda of African economies. The high volatility in bank profits reflects the high volatility of African economies. The positive Africa residual might be related to the lack of competitiveness documented above.

Behind these averages are important differences across financial systems within Africa. However, the same factors that explain the differences between the averages in Africa and the averages outside Africa can also explain the differences within Africa. The important roles of scale and the contractual framework are illustrated as examples in figures 2.19 and 2.20 on the aggregate level. The negative relationships between the contractual framework and banking system size, on the one hand, and between net interest margins, on the other hand, hold not only for broad cross-sectional samples of countries, but also within the African continent. The higher efficiency of the contractual framework—here measured by an aggregate meta-indicator of the rule of law (Kaufman, Kraay and Mastruzzi, 2009)—is associated with lower interest margins, as are larger financial systems, as measured by liquid liabilities in U.S. dollars. Net interest rate margins are lower in Mauritius than in Angola partly because of the more effective contractual framework in Mauritius. Similarly, net interest margins are lower in Egypt than in Mali partly as a result of the larger scale of banking in Egypt.

Figure 2.20   Low Governance Comes with High Margins, 2009

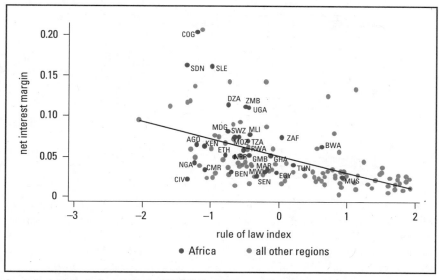

Source: Beck, Demirgüç-Kunt, and Levine (2010); Kaufman, Kraay, and Mastruzzi (2009).
Note: Sample size: 213 countries. For a complete listing of 3-letter country codes and the respective country names, see pages xvi–xvii.

Interest rate spread analysis of a specific banking market also facilitates a deeper analysis of the competition within a system. The analysis of the spreads in the Ugandan banking market provides evidence of segmentation among banks of different ownership (Cull and Trandafir 2010b).

In Uganda, domestic banks show much higher spreads because of the higher lending rates, which most likely reflect a riskier loan portfolio. The comparison between domestic and foreign banks across the different components of the spread shows, however, even more interesting differences. The spread decompositions indicate that domestic banks generate high profit margins from a group of borrowers who repay their loans at a rate that is higher than the rate on the loans of clients of foreign banks. One would expect foreign banks to compete for this clientele, exerting downward pressure on these spreads and profit margins, and, yet, the decomposition of the interest spreads of foreign banks shown in table 2.3 suggests that these banks deal with a different segment of the market. The overhead costs of foreign banks are substantially higher than those of domestic banks (6.0 versus 2.5 percent), and, yet, their spreads are much lower. The relatively high overhead costs and low profit margins for the foreign banks may be consistent with the idea that they deal with a set of blue-chip clients whose projects are more costly to evaluate and maintain. In addition, higher wage costs might add to the costs of the foreign banks, though the higher costs might also result from the propensity of foreign

Table 2.3 Interest Spreads in Uganda: Domestic Versus
Foreign, 2008

Indicator	Domestic	Foreign
Average lending rate	18.44	15.24
Average deposit rate	2.31	1.90
Spread	16.13	13.34
Overhead costs	2.74	6.22
Loan-loss provisions	0.38	1.01
Reserve requirement	0.26	0.21
Taxes	3.34	1.64
Profit margin	9.42	4.26

Source: Cull and Trandafir (2010b).

banks to invest more, including in information technology and technology to develop new products. Over time, these overhead costs might decrease as economies
of scale are achieved and may translate into higher profit margins. Two tentative
conclusions from the simple decomposition exercise are that (1) there is little competitive pressure in the Ugandan banking sector, which is reflected in the persis-
tence of the high interest rate spreads and their determinants, and (2) there is market segmentation between foreign and domestic banks, which is reflected in the
different spread levels and the determinants of these spreads.

Looking beyond banking

The nonbank segments of Africa's financial systems show an even lower degree of
development than banking. This is consistent with the bank-based character of
Africa's financial systems.

Only 21 of the 53 African countries have stock markets, and only a few of these
are liquid. This number does not include Cameroon, Gabon, and Rwanda, which
recently established stock exchanges, but have not yet attracted listings. Few stock
exchanges have histories going back before independence. While most stock exchanges are national, the Bourse Régionale des Valeurs Mobilières, headquartered
in Abidjan, Côte d'Ivoire, caters to the eight-country West African Economic and
Monetary Union. It was expanded from the Abidjan Stock Exchange, which was
created in 1976. Similarly, the Bourse des Valeurs Mobilières de l'Afrique Centrale,
headquartered in Libreville, Gabon, caters to the countries of the Economic and
Monetary Community of Central Africa. Box 2.4 discusses the example of the
Egyptian stock exchange—the Egyptian Exchange—and how the general business
environment and specific policies have influenced its development.

With the exception of the stock exchange in South Africa, African stock exchanges are small as gauged by the ratio of market capitalization to GDP (figure
2.21). African stock exchanges are also dominated by few stocks: the average number of listed companies per 10 million people is around 36 (figure 2.22). This re-

Box 2.4   The Egyptian Exchange

The Alexandria and Cairo stock exchanges, today called the Egyptian Exchange, date to 1883 and 1903, respectively, thus effectively constituting the oldest stock exchange on the continent. Before folding up in 1961 because of the state-sanctioned demise of Egypt's private sector, they ranked together as the fourth largest stock exchange worldwide. Because of the nationalization post-1961, the number of listed companies sharply declined and brokers left their jobs. After a dormancy of 31 years, the stock exchange was revived in 1992 and was the first Arab stock exchange to become a member of the World Federation of Exchanges.

The government took important steps to revive the stock market after its reopening in 1992. First, the foreign ownership of securities was again allowed, which attracted foreign funds into the economy and thus promoted the stock exchange index. Second, arbitration was introduced to circumvent the regular legal system with all its well-known deficiencies. Most critical, however, tax incentives were introduced to attract listings and investors. Tax exemptions on capital gains and dividends for retail and institutional investors were aimed at enticing investors to use their savings in listed equity rather than bank deposits, while exemptions on corporate tax payments were offered for listing firms. Via public offerings, 52 state-owned enterprises were privatized in Egypt.

These incentives led to a rather large boom in listings. Egypt's stock market capitalization reached a staggering 107 percent of GDP in 2007, ahead of countries at similar income levels, such as Colombia, Peru, and the Philippines. However, many firms floated only a small share of their total equity. Feyen (2010) reports that more than 50 percent of firms have free floats of less than 15 percent, and only 5 percent have free floats exceeding 70 percent. This also explains why the boom in listings and market capitalization was not accompanied by a similar increase in liquidity; the turnover ratio, reaching 47 percent in 2007, is similar to the ratios in other middle-income countries.

In 2005, an amendment of the tax law canceled the tax exemption, which led more than 500 companies to delist. More recently, in 2008, in a move to show preference for quality over quantity, the exchange changed its listing rules. The changes were aimed at strengthening governance and improving disclosure among listed companies to enhance market liquidity. This reduced the number of listed companies to 218, down from 550. Trading statistics significantly improved after these changes were implemented. Recently, the exchange also launched Nilex, a trading segment with relaxed listing rules that is expected to facilitate the access of small and medium enterprises to financial markets (see the discussion in chapter 4).

Source: Feyen (2010).

flects the small scale of stock exchanges across Africa and shows the limitations on the use of stock exchanges as funding tools in the host countries. The small number of listed companies also suggests that the concentration among listed companies is high: few companies dominate the market in most African stock exchanges.

Africa's stock exchanges are not only small, but also illiquid. With the notable exception of the exchanges in Egypt, Morocco, and South Africa, Africa's stock ex-

Figure 2.21   Stock Market Capitalization across Countries, 2009

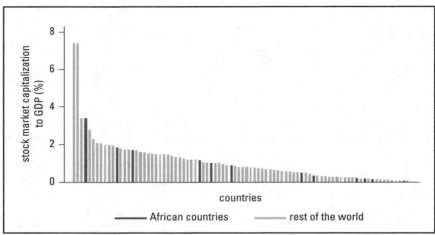

Source: Beck, Demirgüç-Kunt, and Levine (2010).
Note: Sample size: 88 countries. The highest African values are for Mauritius, Morocco, and South Africa.

Figure 2.22   Listed Firms across Countries, 2009

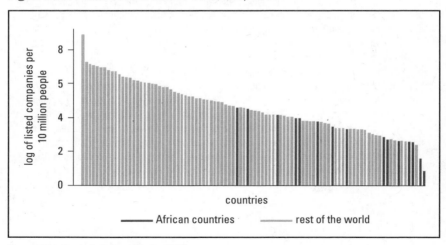

Source: Beck, Demirgüç-Kunt, and Levine (2010).
Note: Sample size: 94 countries. Log scale is used. The highest African values are for Botswana, South Africa, Swaziland, and Zimbabwe.

changes are among the least liquid capital markets across the globe as measured by the ratio of traded to listed stocks (figure 2.23). The low trading levels indicate the degree to which a large fraction of the shares in developing markets is effectively locked up in the strategic stakes of controlling shareholders and not normally avail-

Figure 2.23 Stock Market Liquidity across Countries, 2009

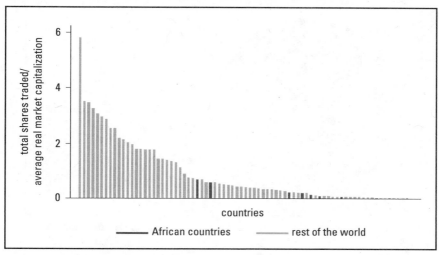

Source: Beck, Demirgüç-Kunt, and Levine (2010).
Note: Sample size: 79 countries. The highest African values are for the Arab Republic of Egypt, Morocco, South Africa, and Tunisia.

able for trading. Given that the positive contribution of stock market development to economic growth derives through liquidity more than size, the low degree of liquidity is indeed worrying and calls into question the role of stock exchanges as drivers of growth (for instance, see Levine and Zervos 1998). We discuss this issue in more depth in chapter 4.

The limited size and liquidity of stock markets are mirrored on the bond side of capital markets. The primary bond markets are small and dominated by government and financial institutions (figure 2.24). Table 2.4 shows that short-term securities dominate most African bond markets as well. Even in South Africa, over-the-counter trading is still prevalent on the debt market (Ambrosi 2009). With the exception of Nigeria and South Africa, no countries have secondary bond markets.

The small size and limited liquidity of African capital markets have many explanatory factors, and we return to the policy implications in chapter 4. Briefly, the nascent character of capital markets is driven by the lack of market culture, high listing costs, the fear of losing family ownership, and inefficient investor protections. The limited success of market segments with relaxed listing rules shows that the development stage of the enterprise population across Africa—few firms are large enough to sustain trading in their stocks—is an important, but not sufficient factor in explaining the small size and low liquidity of African markets. These features make capital markets less attractive as funding instruments for firms or

Figure 2.24 Bond Market Structure in Africa

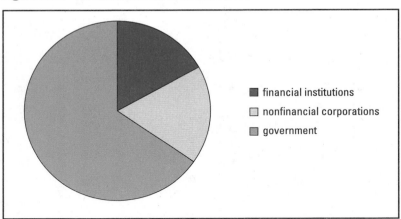

- financial institutions
- nonfinancial corporations
- government

Source: Making Finance Work for Africa (database), Partnership Secretariat, African Development Bank, Tunis, http://www.mfw4a.org/.

Table 2.4 Bond Markets across the Region

	Longest duration, years	Short-term securities/ total securities
Botswana	12	51.1
Ghana	5	35.0
Kenya	15	7.0
Lesotho	10	86.8
Mozambique	—	8.4
Namibia	15	30.0
Nigeria	10	62.7
Swaziland	5	74.4
Tanzania	10	—
Uganda	10	62.1
Zambia	5	63.9

Source: Ambrosi (2009).
Note: n.a. = not applicable. — = not available.

as investment vehicles for personal and institutional investors, resulting in a self-sustaining vicious cycle of low liquidity.

The insurance sector is in its infancy in most African countries as well, as illustrated by the low insurance penetration across Africa (figure 2.25). With the exception of Lesotho, Morocco, South Africa, and Tunisia, insurance penetration is

Figure 2.25 Life Insurance Penetration across Countries, 2008

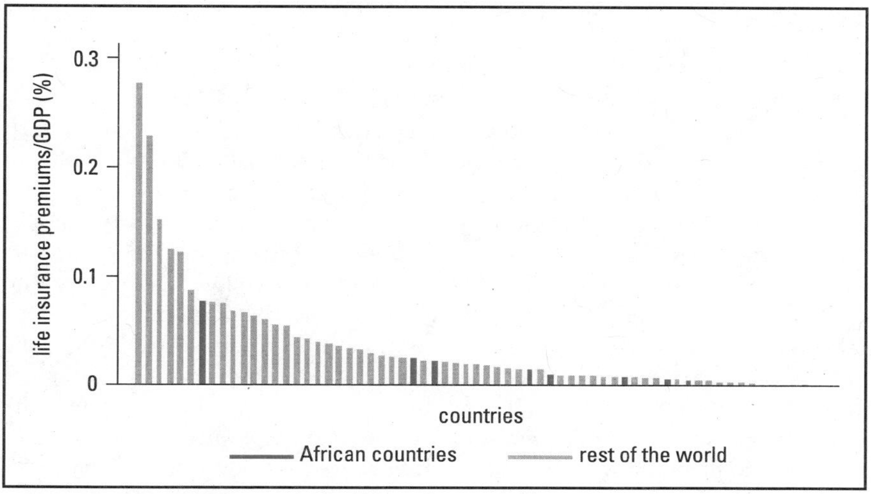

Source: Beck, Demirgüç-Kunt, and Levine (2010).
Note: Sample size: 67 countries. The highest African values are for Botswana, Lesotho, and South Africa.

below 1 percent. In addition, the insurance business is dominated by non–life insurance business lines, such as automobile, health, and industrial insurance policies, while the life segment constitutes less than 30 percent in most countries. This reflects the fact that, in most countries, insurance development is driven by compulsory business lines, such as the motor line. Many countries have fragmented insurance systems characterized by many small, underfunded, and weak companies. The lack of regulatory oversight, including in consumer protection, undermines the development of insurance markets. In many countries, insurance supervision is still undertaken by an office within the ministry of finance, although there is an increasing trend toward a separate nonbank financial institution supervisor. Notable is the development in francophone West and Central Africa of a joint insurance supervisor for 14 countries. In some North African countries (Algeria, Egypt, and Libya), the dominance of state-owned insurance companies may also explain the limited development of the insurance sector. Low incomes explain much of the low insurance penetration; monetary instability and the weak contractual framework contribute as well.

Explaining Financial (Under)Development in Africa

What are the factors explaining the low level of financial development across most African countries and the variation of financial development within Africa? In the following, we discuss several factors, including (in box 2.5) a benchmarking model that takes into account these factors simultaneously.

Size and income level

A first explanation is the small size and low income levels of African economies. (We refer to the scale argument discussed in chapter 1.) At the same time as economic development implies that a larger share of the population is participating in market-based transactions and thus demanding formal financial services, higher incomes imply lower costs and greater skills, resulting in more cost-effective supply. Figure 2.26 shows that, indeed, financial depth increases with GDP per capita. However, we also see that many African countries have even lower levels of private credit to GDP than we would predict based on their level of economic development. This applies to many low-income countries, such as Cameroon, the Republic of Congo, Gabon, and Senegal, but also several middle-income commodity exporters, such as Algeria and Botswana. Closely related to income levels is the share of the population living and working in the informal economy. Because of the documentation requirements, formal financial institutions are less likely to supply services to households and firms in the informal sector, resulting in less supply; by the same token, however, the demand for formal financial services will be lower in the informal sector because of the need to avoid tax payments and regulatory requirements.

Figure 2.26   Financial Development and GDP Per Capita, 2009

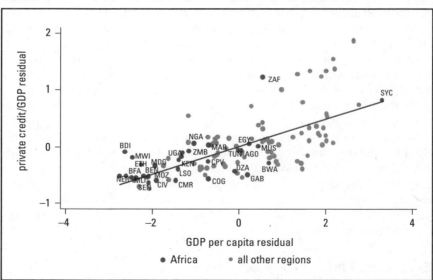

Source: Beck, Demirgüç-Kunt, and Levine (2010); World Development Indicators Database, World Bank, Washington, DC, http://data.worldbank.org/data-catalog/world-development-indicators/.
Note: Sample size: 119 countries. GDP per capita is taken in log scale. For a complete listing of 3-letter country codes and the respective country names, see pages xvi–xvii.

Inflation

Figure 2.26 controls for inflation, which is a second important factor explaining financial underdevelopment. A low and stable rate of inflation provides incentives for financial rather than nonfinancial forms of savings. By providing monetary certainty, it is also conducive to long-term contracting and, thus, long-term savings and investment. The absence of monetary stability is therefore directly related to the volatility that undermines financial contracting. Savers are more likely to entrust their savings for a given interest rate if they can be quite confident of receiving the expected return in terms of real consumption units. Similarly, monetary stability allows investors to compute the return on projects adequately and commit to payments in real terms. Empirical research has shown the relationship between monetary stability and financial development, which also holds for African economies (see Boyd, Levine, and Smith 2001). However, as we discuss in chapter 4, monetary stability is a broader concept than low and stable inflation and is a necessary, but far from sufficient, condition for financial deepening.

Low savings rates

On the resource and deposit sides, aggregate indicators are consistent with the generally low savings rates across the continent. These, in turn, can be explained by the low and volatile incomes and the demographic structure of African populations, which are dominated by young age-groups, high illiteracy rates, and low life expectancy. In some countries, life expectancy has recently decreased again because of AIDS. The median savings rate in Africa is 10.2 percent, which is lower than the rate in all other regions of the world except the Middle East (figure 2.27). It is important to note, however, that there is wide cross-country variation within the continent, ranging from −121 percent in postconflict Liberia to 72 percent in oil-exporting Equatorial Guinea. The low aggregate financial development indicators documented above are also consistent with the high degree of capital flight documented in the literature on Africa. While exact numbers are missing because of the informal methods used to expatriate domestic savings, aggregate data point to Africa as the continent with the largest share of private wealth held abroad (Collier, Hoeffler, and Pattillo 2001). Boyce and Ndikumana (2001) estimate capital flight from 25 low-income Sub-Saharan African countries during the period 1970–96 at US$193 billion, while Ndikumana and Boyce (2008) estimate capital flight from 40 Sub-Saharan African countries during the period 1970–2004 at US$420 billion, making these countries effectively net creditors to the rest of the world.

A rough indicator of the private capital flight is the ratio of offshore to domestic deposits.[7] This is significantly higher in Africa than in other regions (figure 2.28). However, it has been declining significantly in recent years, which may be interpreted as a sign of the increasing confidence of Africans in their domestic financial systems (figure 2.29). Because this indicator is a ratio of offshore and domestic deposits, however, the reduction may be driven as much by a lower return on expatriated savings (which could also be caused by tightened legislation in Europe

Figure 2.27. Domestic Savings across Regions, 2008

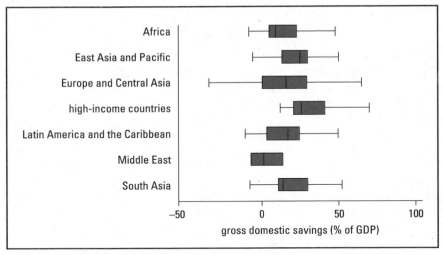

Source: World Development Indicators Database, World Bank, Washington, DC, http://data.worldbank.org/
data-catalog/world-development-indicators/.
Note: Sample size: 161 countries. The figure shows the minimum, maximum, and median of the ratio of gross
domestic savings as a percent of GDP. The shaded boxes indicate the interquartile range.

Figure 2.28   The Ratio of Offshore to Domestic Deposits across Regions, 2009

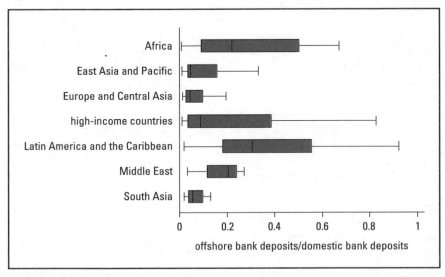

Source: Beck, Demirgüç-Kunt, and Levine (2010).
Note: Sample size: 144 countries. The figure shows the minimum, maximum, and median of offshore to domestic
bank deposits. The shaded boxes indicate the interquartile range. Outliers have been omitted.

Figure 2.29 **The Ratio of Offshore to Domestic Deposits over Time, 1995–2009**

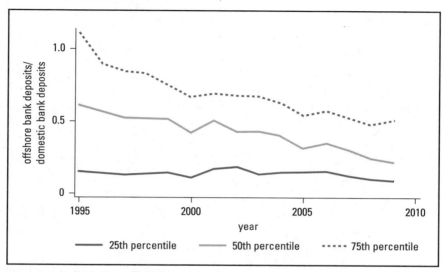

Source: Beck, Demirgüç-Kunt, and Levine (2010).

and other industrialized countries against money laundering) as by the increase in domestic deposits documented above.

Previously, this capital flight could not be offset by private inflows. Until a few years ago, Africa was the only continent in which donor funding exceeded private portfolio funding (Senbet and Otchere 2006). As in almost all other parts of the developing world, however, Africa has benefitted from the global liquidity glut in the form of high capital inflows, though the increase has not been as steep as in other regions, for example Central and Eastern Europe (figure 2.30).

Population density

Population density is another important driver of financial depth, especially within Africa (Allen et al. 2010; Beck et al. 2008). Directly related to scale, a more disperse population is more difficult to serve, especially in the context of Africa and its deteriorated transportation infrastructure. Most African countries have significantly lower population densities than other developing countries (figure 2.31). To illustrate the importance of population density, take the example of Burundi and Zambia. Despite its low income level and an ongoing conflict, Burundi has a ratio of private credit to GDP of almost 20 percent, a higher level than Zambia, which has half the population density, but which has been socioeconomically and politically stable over the past 50 years.

Figure 2.30   Capital Flows across Regions, 2000–09

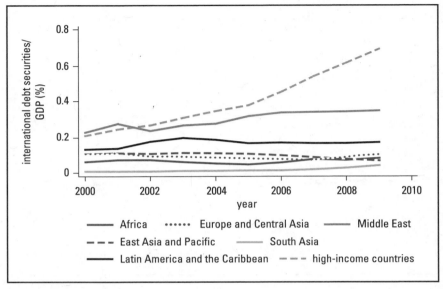

Source: Beck, Demirgüç-Kunt, and Levine (2010).

Figure 2.31   Population Density across Countries, 2008

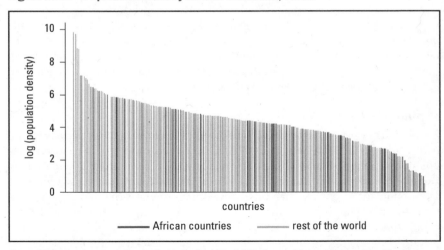

Source: World Development Indicators Database, World Bank, Washington, DC, http://data.worldbank.org/data-catalog/world-development-indicators/.
Note: Sample size: 209 countries. The highest African values are for Burundi, the Comoros, Mauritius, Mayotte, and Rwanda. Log scale is used.

Governance

Financial contracts depend on the certainty of the legal rights of borrowers, creditors, and outside investors and the predictability and speed of the fair and impartial enforcement of these rights. International comparisons have provided ample evidence for the critical role of legal system efficiency and its different elements in financial sector development (for example, see La Porta et al. 1997; Levine, Loayza, and Beck 2000). However, the governance agenda is broader than the contractual framework. Corruption can undermine relationships between banks and customers, as well as between regulators and banks. Political interference can have a negative effect on the optimal allocation of resources.

African economies still face serious governance challenges. Figure 2.32 shows the relative position of African countries in a composite indicator of the rule of law. On a scale that has been normalized to give a worldwide average of 0 and a standard deviation of 1, the median across African countries is 0.73. With the exception of a few middle-income countries, most African countries are below the average of 0. An assessment of the evolution of this indicator from 1996 to 2009, the period for which this composite indicator is available, shows no firm trend toward improvement over these 13 years. Nonetheless, the African countries lagging the most caught up somewhat, as can be seen from the trend in the 25th percentile. It is important to note that this indicator is a relative one, that is, if all countries in the world improve, this would not be picked up by the indicator because, by construc-

Figure 2.32 Rule of Law over Time in Africa, 1996–2009

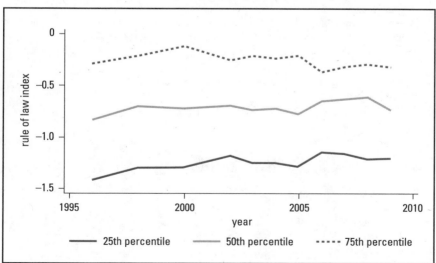

Source: Kaufman, Kraay, and Mastruzzi (2009).
Note: Sample size: 53 countries.

tion, it has a mean of 0 and a standard deviation of 1. So, the statement we can make based on figure 2.32 is that, relative to the rest of the world, Africa has not improved, notwithstanding improvements in the legal system.

Variation in financial sector development across the continent

Box 2.5 shows that there is substantial variation across Africa in the depth, breadth, efficiency, and diversity of financial systems, which we point out throughout this chapter. It is worthwhile recapturing this. The financial systems of most African

Box 2.5   Benchmarking Financial Development

Building on a large literature that assesses the relative importance of different country characteristics in explaining financial development, Beck et al. (2008) construct a benchmarking model that allows a comparison of the actual level of financial development of a country with the expected level also allows the progress of countries to be tracked over time. Deviations of the actual from the expected level of financial development can be explained by country-specific circumstances not captured in the regression model (for example, civil strife) or by the impact of policies that are intentionally not included in the regression model. In its most basic form, the regression model includes the log of GDP per capita to account for the positive relationship between income and finance, as well as the square of the log of GDP per capita to account for nonlinearities in the relationship between income and finance, country size measured by the log of population to capture scale effects, population density to capture the infrastructure costs of outreach, the age dependency ratio to capture differences in savings trends and the demand for financial service products, and dummies for offshore centers, transition economies, and oil-exporting countries.

The level of private credit to GDP has been, on average, at the expected level for African countries (figure a). Figure b, in contrast, shows that the average low-income country in Africa has not achieved the level of financial development expected according to country

Figure a. Private Credit to GDP: Expected Versus Actual across Africa

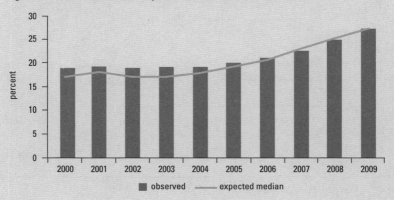

Box 2.5 Benchmarking Financial Development *(continued)*

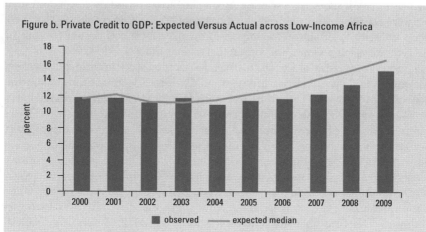

Figure b. Private Credit to GDP: Expected Versus Actual across Low-Income Africa

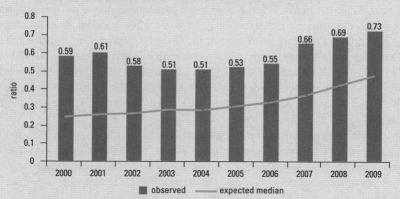

Figure c. Private Credit to GDP: Expected Versus Actual across North Africa

characteristics. Data for North Africa show a persistently higher level of actual financial development than is predicted by the benchmarking model (figure c). The variables in the model contribute to the low expected level of financial development in Africa. The lower incomes in Africa explain 7 percentage points of the lower ratio of private credit to GDP in Africa compared with South Asia. The much lower population density in Africa compared with South Asia explains 14 percentage points of the lower level of private sector lending in the Africa region, while population size, in itself, does not seem to matter much. The higher share of the young population segment in Africa also contributes to a much lower level of financial development compared with other developing regions, such as South Asia.

Source: Beck et al. (2008).

countries essentially consist of banking systems that provide basic transaction and short-term credit services, thus fulfilling the Finance for Markets role, but at high cost. Some of these countries have stock exchanges (see elsewhere above), but these have a limited role, if any, in the impact of finance on the real economy. None of these countries has a significant contractual savings industry.

Several groups stick out from this sketch of a typical African financial system (Alawode 2003). First, there is a group of middle-income countries, such as Egypt, Mauritius, Morocco, and South Africa, that not only have much more developed banking systems, but also exhibit much more diversified financial systems. These countries also have better institutional capacity. However, even within this group, there are important differences. Consumer credit, for example, plays an important role in South Africa, but not in Mauritius, mostly for cultural reasons. A second important group is large low-income countries, such as Ethiopia, Kenya, and Nigeria. The financial systems in these countries do not have the same degree of sophistication. Yet, unlike their smaller low-income peers, they have the capacity to sustain more diversified financial systems, including a diversified nonbank financial sector and capital markets. A third important group consists of commodity-exporting countries. As shown by Beck (2011), financial systems are as susceptible to a Dutch Disease phenomenon as any other part of the institutional framework of countries. Commodity exporters have, on average, less well developed financial systems and banks that are more liquid, more well capitalized, and more profitable, but give fewer loans to firms. Firms in resource-based economies use less external finance, and a smaller share of them use bank loans, although there is the same level of demand as in other countries, thus pointing to supply constraints. A fourth group consists of offshore centers, such as Mauritius, with a segmented financial system.

An additional important difference is that between common and civil law countries, a difference that has been explored in depth by Honohan and Beck (2007). Common law countries—all former British colonies—not only show, on average, a higher level of financial development (private credit to GDP shows a median of 24 percent as opposed to 15 percent in civil code countries), but also have different regulatory approaches. The different profiles of financial systems across countries have implications for the discussions in the following chapters and for the formulation of policy, a topic to which we return in chapter 6.

The Firm and Household Usage of Financial Services

Limited access to enterprise finance

The limited outreach of Africa's financial systems also appears on the user side. Enterprise surveys give a good overview of the obstacles enterprises face and the financing patterns of enterprises. These microlevel data have been used extensively by researchers to understand the challenges faced by enterprises in countries

Figure 2.33   Access to Bank Loans across Countries, 2006–10

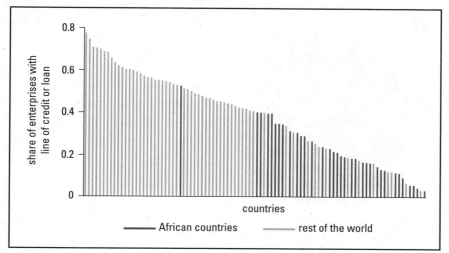

Source: Enterprise Surveys (database), International Finance Corporation, World Bank, Washington, DC, http://www.enterprisesurveys.org/ (accessed in 2010).
Note: Sample size: 94 countries. The highest African values are for Benin, Cape Verde, Malawi, and Mauritius.

in Africa and other developing regions (Hallward-Driemeier and Aterido 2007; Aterido, Hallward-Driemeier, and Pagés 2007). Figure 2.33 shows the limited access to external finance by enterprises in Africa. On average, only 23.1 percent of enterprises have loans or lines of credit, while the corresponding share among enterprises in non-African developing countries is 46.1 percent. This is also reflected in obstacles identified by the enterprises themselves.

The bank-based nature of African finance also becomes clear if one considers the various sources of external financing for enterprises. Figure 2.34 shows that more than 75 percent of the external funding for a cross-section of African countries and enterprises comes from private commercial banks, while less than 12 percent comes from nonbank sources.

In addition, there is limited access to other nonbank sources. We have documented the shallow nature of organized equity and debt markets elsewhere above, but other segments of finance that are prominent in developed countries and many emerging markets of Asia and Latin America are missing in Africa as well. Figure 2.35 shows the limited penetration of private equity across Africa compared with other regions of the world as measured using the ratio of private equity to GDP.

Cost and documentation barriers in deposit and payment services

The high cost of banking affects not only borrowers through high lending interest rates, but also deposit customers through high account fees and high minimum

Figure 2.34   The Bank-Based Nature of African Finance from the Perspective of Users

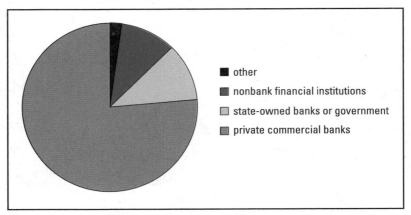

- other
- nonbank financial institutions
- state-owned banks or government
- private commercial banks

Source: Enterprise Surveys (database), International Finance Corporation, World Bank, Washington, DC, http://www.enterprisesurveys.org/ (accessed in 2010).
Note: The figure shows the sources of external funding for a cross-section of African countries and enterprises.

Figure 2.35   Private Equity Penetration across the World, 2009–10

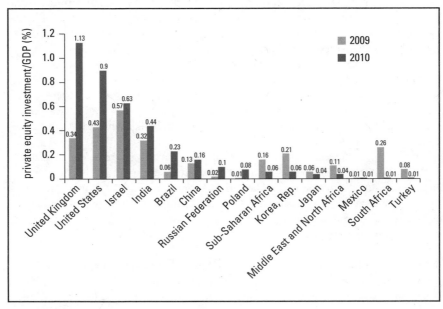

Source: EMPEA (2011).

Figure 2.36 Account Fees across Countries

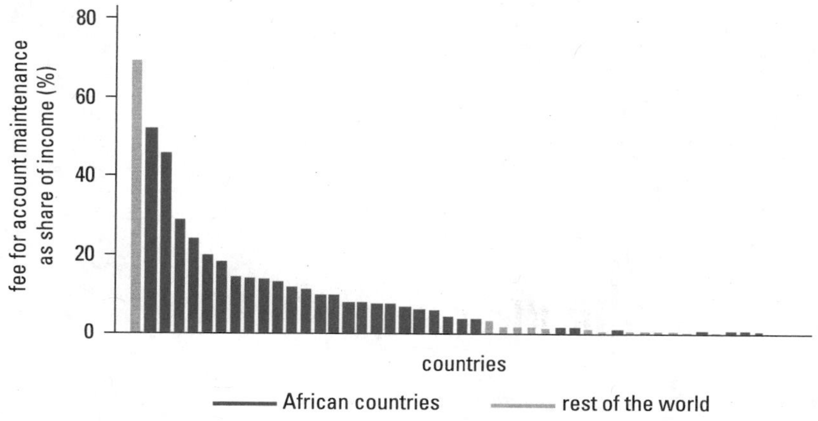

countries

——— African countries ——— rest of the world

Source: World Bank (2009a).
Note: Sample size: 54 countries.

balances. Beck, Demirgüç-Kunt, and Martínez Pería (2008) document the significant monetary barriers that potential bank customers face throughout the developing world, but especially in African countries, in opening and maintaining bank accounts. By themselves and abstracting from other barriers, banking fees can exclude more than 80 percent of a population from accessing formal checking accounts (World Bank 2008a). More recent data collection efforts have confirmed this. Take, for instance, the fees for a current account. They amount to more than 4 percent of monthly income across African countries, compared with less than 3 percent across a set of comparable non-African developing countries (figure 2.36). It is important to stress that these high ratios are driven not only by low GDP per capita, but also by the absolute levels of the fees, which tend to be much higher in Africa than elsewhere. The same holds for specific products, such as debit or credit cards, for which the average annual fee is much higher in Africa (US$12.54) than in other developing countries (US$9.93) (figure 2.37).

Another important barrier for many potential customers in Africa involves the documentation requirements, that is, the number of documents that applicants have to show to open an account (figure 2.38). In countries where few have formal documentation, such as identity cards (which, in some countries, Uganda for instance, do not exist), passports, or driver licenses, where large segments of the population work in the informal economy, and where few have formal residential addresses that they can prove, documentation requirements constitute an often insurmountable hurdle. We return to this topic in chapter 3 to discuss alternative solutions and in chapter 5 to discuss the regulatory implications.

Figure 2.37   Card Fees across Countries

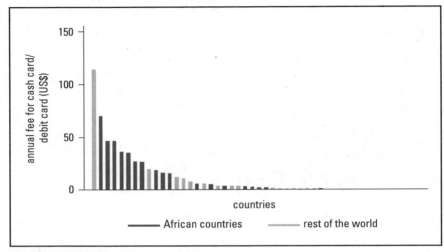

Source: World Bank (2009a).
Note: Sample size: 54 countries.

Figure 2.38   Documentation Requirements across Countries

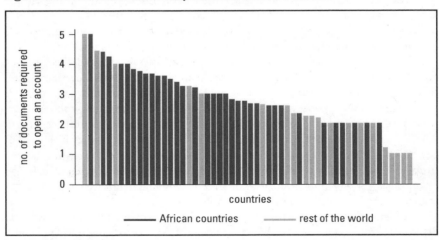

Source: World Bank (2009a).
Note: Sample size: 54 countries.

What explains the high costs of deposit and payment services in Africa compared with the costs in other parts of the world? There are certainly many country-
and bank-level factors that explain these costs. A rigorous analysis unearthing causal
factors will require more data over long time periods, but the initial correlations

reported by Beck, Demirgüç-Kunt, and Martínez Pería (2008) are suggestive. They indicate that cost and documentation barriers are greater in countries in which there is less competition within the banking system and in which there are more stringent restrictions on bank entry and activities. Poorly developed physical infrastructure is, not surprisingly, another critical factor explaining the high costs in many African countries. Finally, a more vibrant media sector that can disseminate information about interest rates and fees is associated with lower barriers. Also, the barriers faced by bank customers are greater if banking systems are predominantly government owned, but lower if there is more foreign bank participation. Larger banks seem to impose fewer barriers on customers, perhaps because they are better positioned to exploit economies of scale and scope. This last finding adds another interesting perspective to the issue of bank consolidation in Africa.

Remittances

The high costs of financial services are also reflected in the costs of transferring international remittances. Figure 2.39 shows remittance costs across corridors, that is, from a specific sending to a specific receiving country, with cost information averaged across the largest formal remittance providers. As the figure shows, corridors that include African countries have significantly higher costs. Beck and Martínez Pería (2011) point to familiar factors explaining the cost variation across corridors. Corridors with a smaller number of migrants and with less competition among providers have higher costs. As in the case of interest margins, this points to a lack of scale and a lack of competition as the dominating factors explaining the high remittance costs in Africa. Beck and Martínez Pería also show

Figure 2.39   Remittance Costs across Countries

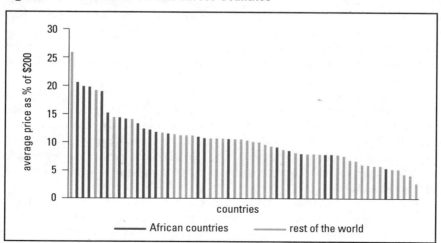

Source: Beck and Martínez Pería (2011).
Note: Sample size: 58 countries. The highest African values are for Botswana, Malawi, Mozambique, and Zambia.

that remittance corridors dominated by banks have higher fees, which emphasizes the need for broadening the institutional landscape. It is important to note that these data only refer to formal remittance services. According to estimates by Freund and Spatafora (2008), at least a third of total remittances are sent through informal channels, such as in-kind or cash transfers, transfers through domestic shops and businesses or social networks, or the underinvoicing of import receipts, commonly referred to as the *hawala* system (literally, in Arabic, bill of exchange, promissory note, or letter of credit). Mazzucato, van den Boom, and Nsowah-Nuamah (2004) show that 65 percent of the remittances going to Ghana are sent through informal channels.

Conclusions

Over recent decades, the financial sectors of Africa have slowly begun to realize their potential to mobilize domestic resources and finance African growth. The aggregate indicators presented in this chapter show only the surface of the much deeper processes and the progress ongoing within African finance. Across the continent, there are numerous examples of finance firmly finding its role as a catalyst in transforming African economies by providing capital and credit to new businesses or supporting the expansion of productive capacity in established firms; by providing cheap and rapid transfer channels for remittances from abroad, within subregions, and from the growing urban centers to rural communities using mobile technology; by offering new products such as weather insurance to help farmers manage climate risks, or equipment leasing to help small enterprises, or using warehouse receipts as security to push financing into agricultural value chains; by providing governments and firms with a reliable and growing source of domestic long-term funding through liquid capital markets; and by supporting low-income households in the more effective management of their lives through microcredit, no-frills accounts, or microhealth insurance. These developments are key transmission channels for growth. For firms, financial development is important in helping promote start-ups, which, at the country level, means growth potential and economic diversification.

However, despite the significant growth in the financial sector, many firms and most households are still excluded from access to financial services in far too many countries. African finance continues to be short term and costly. Although African financial systems have proven reasonably resilient to the shock waves of the global crisis, weak governance and the weak regulatory and supervisory framework explain the fragility in several countries. In the next three chapters, we discuss each of these challenges.

The analysis in this chapter has clearly shown the bank-based nature of finance in Africa, which, to a large extent, is consistent with the level of economic and financial development of the continent. It also goes hand in hand with the limited services, the short maturity of services on both sides of the balance sheet, and the limited competition. Financial services that are provided by other institutions and markets outside Africa are not available in Africa because of the lack of a more diversified financial system. The limited access can be documented on the supply side and on the demand side. In the following chapters, we argue that fostering competition, focusing on new providers to expand the availability of services, and looking beyond the supply-side constraints to the demand-side constraints are critical to deepening and broadening the financial systems in Africa.

Notes

1. For a recent comprehensive discussion on the effects of the crisis on Africa, see Allen and Giovannetti (2011).

2. In addition to the reduction in remittances, there was also apparently some return migration of Africans to their home countries, exacerbating the economic pressures.

3. As an example, a banking system with a Herfindahl index of 2,000 might be a system consisting of five banks in which the banks have equal market shares or in which two banks capture a total of 50 percent of the market, while the other three capture the remainder.

4. Claessens and Laeven (2004) show that there is no significant correlation between concentration and a measure of competition, the H Statistics.

5. These countries are Angola, Ethiopia, Cameroon, Malawi, Morocco, and Sudan. The two African outliers on the right in the figure, which show low levels of market power, are Burkina Faso and Côte d'Ivoire.

6. For a general overview of the literature on the effects of foreign bank entry, see Cull and Martínez Pería (forthcoming).

7. As pointed out by Honohan and Beck (2007), the level of offshore deposits might also arise because of factors unrelated to capital flight, such as use by multinational enterprises or exporters. However, the level of capital flight may be understated by the level of offshore deposits because it does not include capital flight through nonbank channels.

Chapter 3

Expanding Financial Systems

Introduction

The outreach of financial systems in Africa is still extremely limited (see chapter 2). Honohan and Beck (2007) report that, on average, fewer than one in five adults in Sub-Saharan Africa has an account with a formal financial institution. Nonetheless, we have seen lots of innovation in recent years that has led to greater access. Technology has played an important role in this expansion, but so have new actors, such as telecommunications companies. We may also observe a move away from a credit-led inclusion strategy to savings- and payment-led inclusion strategies. These developments put a premium on financial literacy and on an open and adaptable regulatory framework to maximize the benefits.

This chapter takes a fresh look at the access to financial services in Africa and the efforts to expand it. In undertaking our analysis, we have benefited from much better tools to measure the outreach of financial institutions and markets, including information on the geographical and product outreach of financial institutions, the use of financial services by households, and access barriers through documentation requirements. We detail the plethora of innovative efforts and experiences involved in expanding outreach that are ongoing throughout the region, many of which are built on technology.

Our analysis leads us to a somewhat different emphasis than previous analyses. First, we stress more than others the benefits of competition and the consequent financial innovations (without ignoring the risks and challenges) that can help expand the outreach of financial systems. Second, we emphasize the need to look beyond existing institutions and models; innovation often comes from unexpected quarters. Among other steps to enhance outreach and inclusion, this implies that one must look beyond the credit-led approach toward an approach based more closely on payment services. Finally, we would like to push the conversation beyond a purely supply-based analysis toward demand-side constraints, including the limitations in financial literacy.

The chapter opens with a description of the current knowledge about access to finance in Africa, thereby expanding on the discussion in the previous chapter. We then provide a framework—the access possibilities frontier—for the discussion in the remainder of the chapter. Using this framework, we focus on four specific areas: the current providers of financial services and innovative approaches, the role of technology, the role of demand-side constraints, and the role of government and policy reforms. We end the chapter with a focus on two specific areas of concern: rural finance and the finance of small and medium enterprises (SMEs).

What Do We Know about Access to Finance?

In chapter 2, we chronicle the limited outreach to financial services across Africa in comparison with other regions of the world. Most of the indicators—the relative number of branches, accounts, and so on—are proxies for the overall level of financial service use. Detailed numbers on the banked share of populations across all 53 countries of the region are currently not available, though efforts are under way to make progress in this respect (see box 3.1). Recent enterprise and household

Box 3.1   Measuring Access to Financial Services: Recent Advances

Until five years ago, no cross-country data on the outreach of financial systems and few databases at the national level were available. In 2004, the World Bank launched an effort to collect aggregate proxy indicators on outreach by measuring the number of branches, automated teller machines (ATMs), and deposit and loan accounts (Beck, Demirgüç-Kunt and Martínez Pería 2007). These indicators complemented traditional indicators of financial depth, such as the ratio of liquid liabilities to gross domestic product (GDP) and the ratio of private credit to GDP, but it was not until 2010 that the International Monetary Fund started to mainstream these indicators in the International Financial Statistics database by collecting them systematically. In parallel efforts, Christen, Jayadeva, and Rosenberg (2004) collected data on socially oriented or alternative financial institutions with a double bottom line, while Peachey and Roe (2006) collected relevant information on member institutions of the World Savings Bank Association. Using these proxy indicators and other aggregate variables such as GDP per capita and financial depth, Honohan (2008) estimates the share of households with access to formal financial accounts; these estimates are also reported in World Bank (2008a) and Honohan and Beck (2007). Estimates that less than 20 percent of the households in Sub-Saharan Africa have access to formal financial accounts are based on these extrapolations.

Household survey instruments capturing the use of formal financial services are being applied more consistently across countries. The FinScope and FinAccess exercises in southern and eastern Africa and, more recently, in several West African countries allow comparisons across countries, though their primary purpose is the in-depth analysis of the outreach of national financial markets. Such consistent survey instruments and similar questionnaires allow a more rigorous analysis across countries and over time.

Box 3.1 Measuring Access to Financial Services: Recent Advances
       (continued)

Since around 2007–08, a more systematic approach to the collection of cross-country survey-based access indicators has been implemented. Gallup has recently undertaken a household survey in 18 Sub-Saharan African countries. The World Bank, with support from the Bill and Melinda Gates Foundation, is initiating a broad cross-country exercise—the Global Financial Inclusion Survey—by including financial questions in an existing Gallup global poll so as to generate baseline data on financial inclusion levels across 150 countries using samples of 1,000 individuals per country. The survey will be run every three years to measure and track specific data on the use of and access to formal and informal financial services.

It is important to note that these indicators, even the more refined ones, are estimates of access to financial services and not exact numbers because they are based on representative samples and not a census. Comparisons across countries and over time should therefore be treated with caution, and even more care should be applied in making subnational comparisons based on small samples.

A related, but separate data collection exercise is going on to gauge the size and effect of barriers, such as the costs of opening and maintaining accounts and documentation requirements, as discussed in chapter 2. First reported by Beck, Demirgüç-Kunt, and Martínez Pería (2008), such indicators show the substantial barriers in Africa compared with other regions of the developing world and the negative repercussions this has for the use of financial services. Assuming, somewhat arbitrarily, that poor people cannot afford to spend more than 2 percent of their annual income on financial services, the fees on checking accounts alone can exclude more than 80 percent of the population in some African countries, such as Kenya, Malawi, and Uganda, from opening bank accounts.[a] Efforts are under way to expand this exercise to a broader set of countries and financial institutions.

By relating aggregate proxy indicators of banking system outreach and barrier indicators related to cost, eligibility, and geographic access, Beck, Demirgüç-Kunt, and Martínez Pería (2007, 2008) show that financial breadth is significantly, though not perfectly correlated with financial depth indicators. Financial breadth is significantly correlated with the overall level of institutional and economic development, credit information sharing, and the development of physical infrastructure, though less correlated with more detailed indicators of the contractual framework.

These data collection exercises—aggregate cross-country indicators, in-depth country household and enterprise surveys, and supply-side data collection on barriers to access—are complementary and will allow researchers and analysts not only to obtain a better quantitative picture of the access to and use of formal financial services, but also to identify bottlenecks and gaps and, ultimately, the policy areas in which reforms will have the greatest effect. The first attempts at measuring the access possibilities frontier in South Africa have provided additional insights, and, as detailed data collections proceed for other African countries, similar exercises can be undertaken elsewhere.

a. The 2 percent limit is based on unpublished research by the South African Universal Services Agency in the context of a mandated rollout of telecommunications services for lower-income families. Because financial transaction accounts and telecommunications services can be considered network products, similar assumptions on affordability for both types of service seem reasonable.

Table 3.1 The Use of Formal Banking Services across 18 African Countries, 2009

percent of the respondents to the question "Do you have a bank account?"

Country	Yes	No	Demographic profile	Yes	No
South Africa	49	50	Residence		
Kenya	29	70	Urban	28	71
Zimbabwe	28	72	Rural	15	84
Nigeria	23	75	Quintile		
Uganda	21	79	Poorest	11	89
Ghana	19	81	Second	11	88
Rwanda	16	84	Middle	15	85
Tanzania	16	84	Fourth	21	78
Malawi	11	89	Richest	38	62
Zambia	9	91	Gender		
Cameroon	8	92	Men	23	76
Chad	7	93	Women	16	83
Côte d'Ivoire	6	94	Age-group		
Senegal	6	94	15–24 years	15	85
Burundi	4	96	25–39 years	23	76
Mali	2	98	40–54 years	21	78
Congo, Dem. Rep.	1	97	55+ years	20	79
Niger	1	99			

Source: Gallup survey data.
Note: The surveys were conducted in 18 Sub-Saharan African countries in 2009. The data are weighted using adult population estimates for 2008 developed by the World Bank.

surveys on individual countries, however, give us a first indication of the share of households and enterprises that use financial services and thus offer a better picture of who has access to which financial services, even if only in a selected number of countries.

A recent Gallup survey provides aggregate data for 18 African countries, thus representing a third of the countries on the continent (see table 3.1). The data broadly confirm other estimates. They show that the use of formal financial products ranges from 49 percent in South Africa to 1 percent in the Democratic Republic of Congo and Niger. They also show that households in urban areas are more likely than households in rural areas to have accounts, that men are more likely than women to have accounts, and that the use of formal financial services is especially concentrated among the richest 20 percent of the population.

These aggregate survey data give us a reasonably good picture of the use of formal financial services. There is ample evidence, however, that there is widespread use of informal financial services, ranging from moneylenders and deposit collectors over savings clubs to informal financial arrangements among families, friends, and neighbors (Aryeetey et al. 1997). In their financial diaries on a series of developing countries, including South Africa, Collins et al. (2009) document that the poor rely on an array of financial services and financial partners and that the total amount of financial transactions over the course of a year add up to a multiple of incomes over the same period. The financial diary analysis also makes clear that informal financial arrangements are an imperfect substitute for formal financial services, which are out of reach for most of the poor and even parts of the middle class in many African countries. Meanwhile, informal financial services are often unreliable and costly and violate the privacy of customers.

The FinScope and FinAccess surveys in southern and eastern Africa confirm the evidence presented in the financial diaries and elsewhere on the widespread use of semiformal (microfinance providers and cooperatives) and informal financial services. By surveying individuals about a large set of formal and informal financial services and service providers, they give us a good picture of the household use of financial services and the individual characteristics that predict whether someone uses financial services.

Figure 3.1 presents FinScope and FinAccess data on access strands for 12 countries in southern and eastern Africa, that is, the shares of a population that (1) use formal banking services; (2) use formal nonbanking services, but not formal bank-

Figure 3.1   Access to Financial Services across Southern, Eastern, and Western Africa

percent of survey respondents

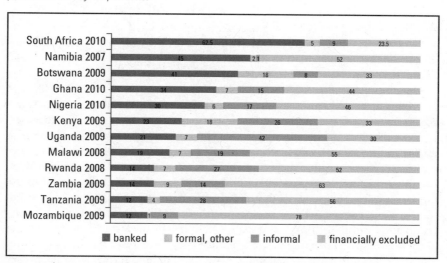

Source: FinScope (database), FinMark Trust, Johannesburg, http://www.finscope.co.za/new/pages/default.aspx (accessed in 2010).
Note: The FinScope and FinAccess survey years are indicated next to the names of the countries.

ing services; (3) use informal services, but not formal services; and (4) are completely excluded from any formal or informal financial service. As we can see, there is wide variation across countries. While, in South Africa, 62.5 percent of the surveyed population uses formal banking services, only 12 percent do so in Mozambique and Tanzania. However, the segments of the population lacking access to formal banking services often use informal or semiformal services. The second strand of financial access—users of formal nonbank services, such as microfinance institutions (MFIs)—accounts for 18 percent in Botswana, but only 1 percent in Mozambique. Finally, the segment of the population with access to informal services, but not formal services (the third strand) ranges from 1 percent in Namibia to 42 percent in Uganda. A large segment of populations are considered excluded from both formal and informal services, though the extent varies significantly across countries, ranging from 23.5 percent in South Africa to 78 percent in Mozambique.

Household survey data do not only allow us to focus on the aggregate numbers, but they do provide a picture of the composition of the banked population (Honohan and King 2009). Univariate comparisons between the banked and unbanked segments of the population according to characteristics and multivariate regression analysis offer insights into the composition of the banked population. One of the most robust predictors of formal financial service use is income (often measured by expenditures): more well off individuals are significantly more likely to use formal services.[1] Education is another strong predictor: the use of formal services increases linearly with educational attainment. Geography measured by rural or urban residence is not as strongly associated with the use of formal services once we control for other household and individual characteristics. Employment status is another important correlate of the use of formal services, while financial literacy, numeracy, and risk aversion are less consistently correlated with the use of formal services. We also find a positive correlation with the ownership of a mobile phone, suggesting that participation in the market economy is related to higher demand for financial services.

One important dimension is gender: across countries, women are less likely to have bank accounts. This is confirmed by the FinScope and Gallup surveys. Is this gender gap caused by discrimination, lower demand by women for financial services, or disadvantages along some other dimensions, for example, education or formal employment? Using FinScope and FinAccess data and controlling for other individual characteristics such as income, education, and formal employment, Aterido, Beck, and Iacovone (2011) find that women are as likely as men to use formal services. This suggests that the narrower coverage of women by banks in southern and eastern Africa is not necessarily caused by lower demand or by discrimination within the financial system, but, rather, by the fact that women are less likely to use formal banking services because they have lower incomes and lower levels of educational attainment and are less likely to hold formal jobs. There may also be a demand dimension given that many women already have indirect access to formal banking services through bank accounts in the names of their husbands.

This is not to downplay the problem of intrafamily resource conflicts, a phenomenon widely documented in the literature (for example, see Goetz and Gupta 1996) or the problem that women in Africa are discriminated against along other dimensions (Hallward-Driemeier 2011). The only country in which there seems to be somewhat of a bias toward women is South Africa, the richest among the nine countries in the Aterido, Beck, and Iacovone (2011) study. Across the nine countries, women are significantly more likely to use informal services, especially in the eastern African countries. In comparing the excluded population of men and women, the authors find that, overall, women are less likely to be excluded from any financial service. It is important to note that these results are for southern and eastern Africa; so, they may not hold for other parts of the continent. However, they point to an important caveat in the exploration of the characteristics of the banked population, that is, one must look beyond univariate correlations to search for the truly restricting household and individual characteristics preventing people from accessing formal financial services.

An analysis of enterprise data leads to similar conclusions. Firms with female ownership participation are no less likely to have loans, and they rely on external finance to fund the same share of working capital or fixed asset investment (Aterido, Beck, and Iacovone 2011). This finding can be explained through a selection bias: women are less likely than men to run sole proprietorships, and firms with female ownership participation are smaller, but more likely to innovate. This conclusion is in line with findings reported in a study on women and entrepreneurship in the North African subregion (CAWTAR and IFC 2007). The study shows that access to finance is not among the three most important barriers facing women entrepreneurs in Tunisia, mainly because of the high level of education of the women entrepreneurs interviewed.

There are undoubtedly a host of legal, social, cultural, historical, and economic traditions, concepts, and practices that account for the varying gender-based differences in access to finance, and this book cannot possibly explore them adequately. In any case, the developmental implications are significant for Africa. Through varying degrees of commitment for policy action, women's contributions to economic development have long been recognized in households, food production systems, and national economies. Increasing women's access to finance is central to expanding their economic and social opportunities and advancing women's rights and, in turn, Africa's broader development prospects.

Household surveys also allow us to track outreach and access to financial services over time, even though the surveys are repeated cross-sectional surveys and not true panels. For example, household data were collected in 2006 and 2009 through the FinAccess surveys in Kenya. A comparison of the two surveys shows an increase in the use of formal financial services, but not at the expense of the use of informal services. It also shows changes in the use of certain financial service providers; in this case, this involved less use of savings and credit cooperatives (SACCOs) and more prominent use of MFIs.

Figure 3.2 Overlap among Users of Formal and Informal Financial Services in Kenya, 2009

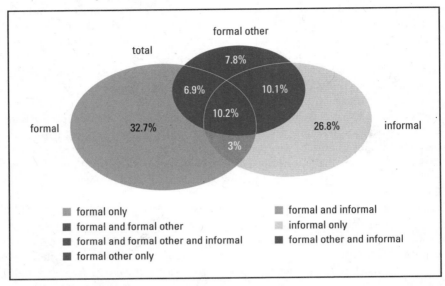

Source: FinAccess (2009).
Note: The figure shows the relative shares of surveyed individuals that use formal or informal financial services or some combination thereof.

Household surveys have also confirmed the findings of previous country-level studies indicating that informal financial service provision is important across Africa. While only 23 percent of the population uses formal financial services in Kenya, more than 50 percent use informal services. Digging deeper, as in the financial diaries, one notices that most individuals use a variety of financial products and providers. Informal financial services are important for large shares of the enterprise and household population, and this will continue to be true. The caricature of the moneylender demanding usury interest rates as representative of informal financial services has to be qualified. Informal financial service providers range from bus drivers who accept remittance payments to rotating savings and credit associations and accumulating savings and credit associations in urban and rural areas. Figure 3.2 shows that there is an overlap among the users of formal and informal financial services in Kenya. The FinAccess survey in 2009 found that over 50 percent of users of formal banking services also used informal financial services.

Formal institutions have also made inroads in areas in which informal providers once dominated. The best example is the domestic remittance market in Kenya, where the introduction of M-Pesa has crowded out informal and other formal delivery channels for domestic remittances (FinAccess 2009). In the FinAccess survey of 2006, a relative (weighted) majority of the people surveyed named specialist money transfer operators as the least risky and most rapid channel for sending remittances, and friends and family as the least expensive and most easily accessed. In 2009, M-Pesa was rated the least risky, the most rapid, and the most easily accessed, but the second least expensive. M-Pesa has not only had an impact on perceptions, but also on remittance flows. The market entry of M-Pesa may explain the increase in remittance flows within Kenya. In 2006, 16.5 percent of the people surveyed reported that they had received a domestic remittance, but, in 2009, the share was 51.8 percent. Similarly, in 2006, 16.9 percent of the people surveyed reported that they had sent a domestic remittance, while, in 2009, the share was 35.3 percent. One can certainly not attribute this increase in remittances exclusively to M-Pesa, but these numbers suggest that M-Pesa has had a positive impact on people's lives and livelihoods.

Broadening Finance: A Reality Check

How realistic is it to expect the formal financial system to reach 100 percent of the population? What are realistic benchmarks and targets in the effort to expand access to financial services? Measuring access to financial services is an important first step. However, to develop policies and targets, benchmarks are needed, and the bottlenecks inhibiting the expansion of access have to be identified.

Access to finance is limited. If African policy makers wish to double the share of populations with access to some type of formal financial service, what has to be done? In the following, we present a framework and identify four areas for discussion and policy reform: the institutions and products that allow African financial systems to expand outreach, the demand-side constraints and solutions, the role of technology, and the role of governments and donors.

To provide an analytical framework for our discussion throughout the remainder of the chapter, we build on the discussion in chapter 1 and introduce the concept of the access possibilities frontier. This frontier is the point of the maximum possible commercially viable outreach of the formal financial system given the technology and the macroeconomic and institutional framework (Beck and de la Torre 2007). This concept allows us to distinguish among the banked, bankable, and unbankable population and provides us with a framework to discuss the bottlenecks impeding efforts to reach the frontier (turning the bankable population into the banked population) and push the frontier outward (turning the unbankable population into the bankable population) (figure 3.3). This concept can also serve as a reality check on the ambition to expand the access to financial services. Finally, it provides a framework to distinguish exogenous trends and developments—such as technology, globalization, and regional integration—and government policies, including regulation.

To understand the limitations to outreach, we first return to the discussion in chapter 1 on the two main barriers that financial institutions face in reaching out to previously unbanked segments of the population: (1) transaction costs and the re-

Figure 3.3   Increasing the Use of Banking Services: A Framework

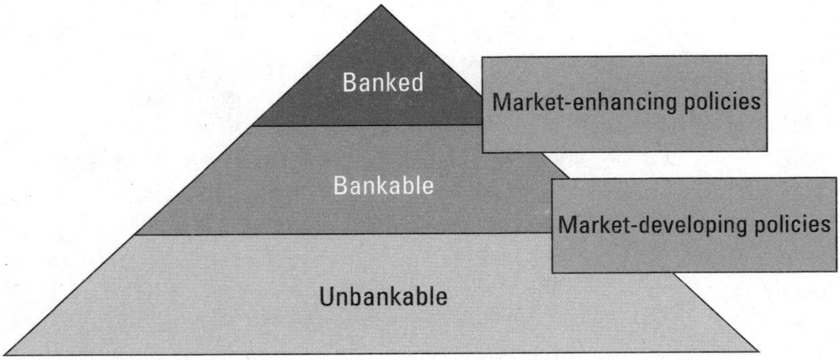

Source: Author compilation.

sulting scale economies of financial services at the level of the user, the institution, and the market and (2) systemic and idiosyncratic risks. To complement these supply-side constraints, we differentiate between economic and noneconomic factors on the demand side that may lead to self-exclusion.[2]

Fixed transaction costs in financial service provision result in decreasing unit costs as the number or the size of transactions increases. Screening and monitoring a borrower entails costs that are, at least in part, independent of the value of the deposit or loan. At the level of a financial institution, fixed costs are crucial; they span a wide range—from the brick-and-mortar branch network to computer systems, legal services, accounting systems, and security arrangements—and are rather independent of the number of accounts or clients. Fixed costs also arise at the level of the financial system, including regulatory costs and the costs of payment clearing and settlement infrastructure, which are, up to a point, independent of the number of institutions regulated. Profitable and sustainable financial institutions have to exploit the resulting scale economies by either sufficiently high-volume transactions or sufficiently high-value transactions. In terms of outreach, this implies a focus on high-volume transactions, thus spreading the fixed transaction costs across a group of customers that is as large as possible. Alternatively, one can look for technologies and products that are not traditional bank products and delivery channels, but that represent a significantly lower fixed cost element.

In addition to costs, the outreach in the supply of financial services, especially credit services, is constrained by risks, especially the default risk (discussed elsewhere above). While financial institutions can influence their costs and risks to a certain degree, they are constrained by state variables, that is, factors that do not change in the short run and affect financial sector activity across the board. These factors might include market size, macroeconomic fundamentals, the available

Figure 3.4   The Access Possibilities Frontier of Payment and Savings Services

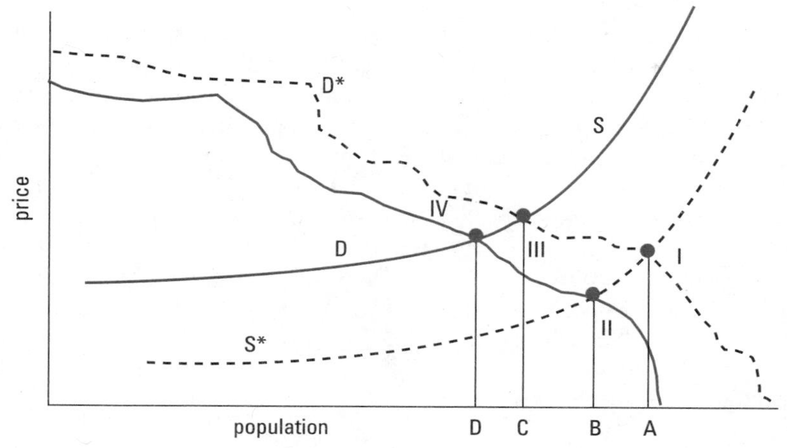

Source: Beck and de la Torre (2007).
Note: See the text for an explanation of the figure.

technology, the average level and distribution of per capita income, and the system-wide costs of doing business that are related, for instance, to the quality of the transportation and communications infrastructure, the effectiveness of the contractual and informational framework, and the degree of general insecurity associated with crime, violence, terrorism, and so on.

Using the concept of state variables allows us to define the access possibilities frontier as a rationed equilibrium, that is, the maximum share of potential clients that can be served by financial institutions prudently. This frontier is a different one for savings/payment services, where the transaction costs are the decisive market friction, and for credit services, where the risk dimension is an additional important friction. Figure 3.4 illustrates the demand and supply for a standardized payment service for which the fee is assumed to be flat, that is, independent of the amount to be transferred. The horizontal axis represents the share of the population (households and firms) engaging in payment and savings transactions, rather than the quantity of service transactions. The population is ordered along the axis starting with agents engaging in transactions that are large in value and number and moving toward agents engaging in transactions of increasingly lower value and number. The downward sloping demand curve D* reflects the willingness to pay and the assumption that customers with a demand for large-value, high-volume transactions have a higher marginal willingness to pay than customers relying on transactions that are few and small. The upward sloping supply curve S* reflects the potential of efficient financial institutions to reach out to a larger share of the population as the fee increases.[3] The intersection of the supply and demand curves (point I) constitutes the access possibilities frontier.

We can use the access possibilities frontier to identify several types of problems in access to financial services and policies to address these problems (see figure 3.4). We denote the maximum commercially viable demand and supply curves by D* and S*, respectively. The intersection of the two, point I, can therefore be seen as the maximum commercially viable share of the population with access to formal payment and savings services. A first type of access problem may arise because of supply suboptimization, whereby financial institutions and markets settle at a point below the access possibilities frontier (curve S, point III). This might reflect, for instance, regulatory distortions or insufficient contestability that lead financial institutions to avoid exploiting all the outreach opportunities fully because of the state variables. We discuss hereafter the need for a diversified landscape of financial service providers so that competition can be increased and the system can be pushed toward the frontier.

A second type of access problem originates in demand. It consists of a number of loan applicants that is too low simply because of the self-exclusion resulting from cultural barriers or financial illiteracy (curve D, point II).[4] Similarly, there might be a lack of demand for payment and savings services because these products may be accessed indirectly through family and friends or avoided for cultural or religious reasons. However, there may also be a lack of knowledge about the advantages of certain financial products or a general aversion to formal institutions. We therefore discuss financial literacy hereafter as an important, though not well-tested policy to address demand-side constraints. A different access problem that can arise mainly in credit markets is associated with excess access, that is, an equilibrium above the access possibilities frontier, whereby loans are granted to a larger share of loan applicants than is prudent based on the lending interest rate and the state variables (covered in chapter 5).

A final access problem involves a prudent access possibilities frontier that is too narrow and thus reaches out to a bankable population that is too small because of deficiencies in state variables relative to countries at similar levels of economic development. We are able to distinguish here between the role of technology in expanding the frontier outward and the role of government policies.

The remainder of this chapter will use this framework to discuss the possibilities for addressing these challenges.

Landscaping the Providers: How to Get to the Frontier

Household surveys have documented a large array of providers of formal financial services. Banks still play a prominent role, but, increasingly, other institutions are emerging, including nonfinancial companies, such as telecommunications companies. As we discuss above, this has been complemented by a large set of different informal financial service providers.

Which institutions can help push the financial system to the frontier? Are specific institutions better than others in serving underbanked segments of the population and helping overcome the market frictions of transaction costs and risk? In the following, we argue that different institutions target different groups and that no single type of institution is the silver bullet. This may change over time as new technologies emerge and market structures change.

Banks

The dominant providers of formal financial services in Africa are still banks, but the universe of banks in Africa today is a diverse one, ranging from large multinational banks with European parents to small domestically owned niche banks. There are also several commercial banks supported by public or private donors, such as OPM in Malawi and the Development Finance Company of Uganda. Rabobank has expanded recently into several African markets based on the cooperative banking experience it acquired in the Netherlands.

One contentious item on the agenda has been the role of foreign-owned banks. Africa's banking systems were dominated by foreign-owned banks before independence. Subsequent nationalizations and indigenization reduced the share of foreign ownership significantly. During financial liberalization in the 1990s, many foreign banks returned, and new foreign banks, especially from South Africa and western Africa, expanded throughout the region. By the early 2000s, almost half of Africa's financial systems were dominated by foreign-owned financial institutions, with the notable exception of North Africa, where banking is still dominated in several countries by government-owned banks. Foreign banks are often accused of cherry-picking the high-end wealthy customers, but their role in outreach has to be qualified: the population of foreign banks is more diverse now than it was 20 years ago. Regional banks from West Africa, especially Nigeria, and from South Africa have often brought competition and new products into domestic markets. The Bank of Africa, a West African bank partly owned by BCME Bank of Morocco, has expanded throughout the continent. In South Africa, Absa (now majority owned by Barclays Bank, but still managed from Johannesburg) and Standard Bank have introduced new technologies and products in the host countries of their subsidiaries.

Banks have grown beyond the concept that microfinance is mainly only a corporate social responsibility and have discovered the bottom of the pyramid as a potential client base. Many commercial banks have therefore progressed past traditional products and delivery channels and recently adopted new products and delivery channels. In The Gambia, Oceanic Bank offers deposit collection services, providing traders and other small-scale businesses with a *condaneh* (or box, in the local parlance) in which they store their daily revenue and which is picked up in the evening by a bank employee. In Ghana, Barclays Bank has piloted an initiative to make microloans to *susu* collectors (a local term of unclear origin that now refers to accumulated money) for onlending to the clients of the collectors. The bank uses the susu collectors as an intermediary to extend loans and mobilize savings to productive rural communities. The susu collectors intermediate on behalf of the bank, conduct appraisals for prospective borrowers, and advise the bank on risky ventures within the communities. Barclays also provides susu lenders with deposit accounts and training sessions. Indeed, Barclays has expanded the program—promoting access through partnerships—to other intermediaries, that is, credit unions and trade associations. Building on this experience, Pesewa Power Trust (PPT), a technology-based susu system, will soon be introduced onto the Ghanaian market. All PPT susu contributors will be issued personal smart cards that register all their micropayments. PPT susu collectors will also wear PPT uniforms and have a smart card collection device for easy identification.

Commercial banks have also initiated cooperative efforts with MFIs or directly started them. One successful example is the partnership between Ecobank and ACCION International in Cameroon that was formed in April 2010. Both partners have launched EB-Accion Microfinance to provide microcredit and savings products to currently unbanked Cameroonians (Ecobank 2010). Ecobank also supports 200 MFIs on the continent in wholesale loans and other products (ACCION 2011). Absa has moved into South Africa's microfinance market and, in partnership with CompuScan, built Microfinance Enterprise Service Centers, which are freight containers functioning as rural mobile lending outlets. To reach rural and remote areas, the centers are fitted with third-generation mobile telecommunications, general packet radio service, and satellite connectivity that are linked to CompuScan's South African credit bureau database. Prior to the rollout, Absa, together with Fin-Mark Trust, invested a lot of effort in understanding the market for microfinancial products in general by learning from ICICI Bank, in India, and the scope of South Africa's market potential in particular. In Morocco, Banque Populaire du Maroc has, since 1999, operated a microcredit subsidiary, Fondation Banque Populaire pour le Micro-Crédit, which acquired, in 2009, the Fondation Zakoura, one of the leading players in the market. In the Arab Republic of Egypt, service companies, a new category of microfinance providers, are acting as agents for banks in the provision of microfinance services.

The importance of government-owned commercial banks has declined in recent years mostly because of the privatization process. The initial fears that the privatizations in favor of large multinational banks would lead to a decrease in outreach have not been confirmed across the board, but neither have the hopes that the privatizations would lead to a wide-scale increase in outreach and competition. Experiences in Tunisia, Uganda, and Zambia have shown that careful privatization of these institutions can increase efficiency and stability, while not reducing outreach. In Uganda, the largest government-owned bank, Uganda Commercial Bank, which was also the largest bank in the system, was successfully privatized (after an initial failure at privatization) to the Standard Bank of South Africa. Although an agreement not to close any branches was in place for only two years following the sale of Uganda Commercial Bank, Standard Bank kept all branches in place and even opened new ones. It also introduced new products and increased agricultural lending (Clarke, Cull, and Fuchs 2009). Similarly, the privatization of the Tunisia-based Banque du Sud in favor of Attijari Wafa Bank and the rebranding of Banque du Sud as Attijari Bank led to a 78 percent expansion of the bank's network and the development of a range of new products within five years of the privatization. The case of Zambia National Commercial Bank, which was privatized in 2007 in favor of Rabobank, based in the Netherlands, shows how a formerly wholly state-owned financial institution can branch out, establish agency arrangements with local partners (gas stations, post offices), and introduce mobile phone technology to facilitate low-cost transactions in an effort that holds promise to increase the bank's deposit base substantially and convey a healthy demonstration effect among private banks.

The example of Uganda, however, also shows that privatization and foreign bank entry is not a panacea for increasing efficiency and competition in a banking system. Beck and Hesse (2009) find that there was no significant impact of privatization and of increased foreign bank participation on interest rate spreads, and Cull and Trandafir (2010b) show that the Ugandan banking system is segmented (see the discussion in chapter 2).

If privatization is not feasible, the turnaround of such institutions by external management teams can also be successful under the proper conditions. Such a turnaround would rely on the franchise value of the large network and customer base, while leveraging private expertise. The example of the National Microfinance Bank of Tanzania has been heralded as a success story (Dressen, Dyer, and Northrip 2002). Government-owned banks that focus completely on deposit services, such as postal savings banks, have a safer record in terms of fragility than government-owned commercial banks, though they often suffer from poor service quality. Nonetheless, some of these institutions have been at the forefront in expanding access, such as in Morocco, where the transformation of postal savings banks has helped increase the access to financial services.

Development finance institutions (DFIs) are more important in financial terms than government-owned commercial banks. While it is more difficult to obtain hard data because DFIs are not subject to central bank supervision, country reports suggest that there is a substantial number of such institutions in many countries of the continent. The evidence on the success of these institutions is mixed, however. We return to this topic in chapter 4 and in our discussion of rural finance below.

Microfinance and cooperative institutions

Over the past decade, MFIs have become an important segment of the financial system in terms of outreach if not also in volume. One of the advantages of microfinance is nimbleness, responsiveness, and its ability to adapt to environments, including in conflict-affected areas. MFIs have traditionally targeted women, who

Table 3.2   Total Borrowers, Depositors, and Penetration Rates, 2008
totals and percent

Indicator	Africa	North Africa	East Africa	Southern Africa	Central Africa	West Africa
Population below national poverty line	420,758,767	30,637,572	87,304,988	70,162,168	63,983,852	168,670,188
Total borrowers	9,250,759	2,205,769	3,750,164	1,089,481	285,394	1,919,951
Penetration rate, borrowers	2.2%	7.2%	4.3%	1.6%	0.4%	1.1%
Total depositors	17,324,291	41,961	8,799,457	2,131,460	736,994	5,614,419
Penetration rate, depositors	4.1%	0.1%	10.1%	3.0%	1.2%	3.3%

Sources: Author calculations based on Mix Market (database), Microfinance Information Exchange, Washington, DC, http://www.mixmarket.org/data-center; World Development Indicators Database, World Bank, Washington, DC, http://data.worldbank.org/data-catalog/world-development-indicators/; World Factbook (database), Central Intelligence Agency, Washington, DC, https://www.cia.gov/library/publications/the-world-factbook/#.

make up a significant proportion of the poor and suffer disproportionately from poverty. As discussed elsewhere above, women face an array of barriers to access in the formal banking system.

Until 2008, the sector experienced impressive growth in outreach and operational self-sufficiency. However, the crisis affected the attempt of microfinance to expand. Food and fuel price increases and a severe financial and global economic contraction exerted severe strain on MFIs across Africa in 2008 so that growth was slowed significantly. Since the onset of the crisis, MFIs have generally not expanded their client base, instead concentrating on trusted, known borrowers. Despite the crisis, however, there has been less volatility in returns, and fewer MFIs are incurring significant losses than was the case in 2007 (MIX and CGAP 2010). MFIs have been also facing more difficulties in raising funding as credit spreads widened and the resources from donors became more scarce (MIX and CGAP 2010). In international comparison, however, Africa has fared better than other regions and was already showing signs of recovery in 2009, while the East Asia and Pacific region and the Eastern Europe and Central Asia region experienced negative growth rates during that year.

The sector's resilience in the face of the crisis is laudable. Nonetheless, Africa is still relatively underserved by MFIs compared with other parts of the developing world, and most of the institutions are focused on urban rather than rural areas. At the end of 2008, MFIs in Africa reported that they were reaching 9.2 million borrowers and a significantly larger number of depositors, 17.3 million.[5] Both numbers, however, are below the 20 million microfinance clients in Bangladesh. With considerably more borrowers than the Eastern Europe and Central Asia region and the Middle East region, these numbers still bring Africa's penetration rate among borrowers (relative to the population living below the national poverty line; see table 3.2) to only 2.2 percent, which is significantly lower than all other regions

Figure 3.5 Total Borrowers and Depositors across African Subregions, 2000–09

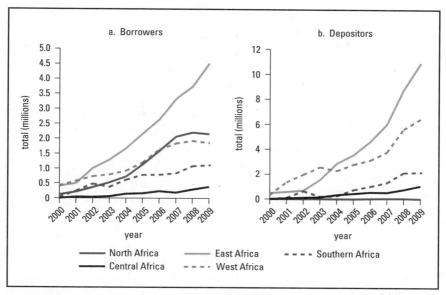

Source: Mix Market (database), Microfinance Information Exchange, Washington, DC, http://www.mixmarket.org/data-center.

Note: All figures provided by Mix Market represent trends because not all MFIs in a country report to the database.

aside from Eastern Europe and Central Asia.[6] The depositor penetration rate is somewhat higher, at 4.1 percent.

The penetration rates vary greatly across the continent. While borrower penetration rates are 7.2 and 4.3 percent, respectively, among North and East African MFIs, Southern, Central, and West African MFIs deliver loans to only 1.6, 0.4, and 1.1 percent, respectively, of the population living below the national poverty line. Among depositors, East African MFIs have a penetration rate of 10 percent, while MFIs in West and Central Africa reach only 1.2 and 3.3 percent of the poor, respectively. Southern and North African MFIs reach even fewer poor depositors: only 3.0 and 0.1 percent, respectively. This variation is remarkable given that all subregions started out at a similar level in 2000 in terms of the numbers of both borrowers and depositors (figure 3.5). For example, East African MFIs did not experience depositor growth spurts until 2002, but then grew significantly through the crisis and beyond (figure 3.5, chart b). Meanwhile, North African MFIs have seen little growth in depositor penetration over the past 10 years, which is a result of restrictions they face on deposit collection. The differing penetration rates between the credit side and the deposit side reflect the contrast in the models for MFIs across the subregions. Thus, North African MFIs focus on credit provision, while MFIs in other subregions focus on deposits (table 3.2 and figure 3.5).

Figure 3.6   Borrower and Depositor Growth Rates and Average Loan and Deposit Balance, 2005–09

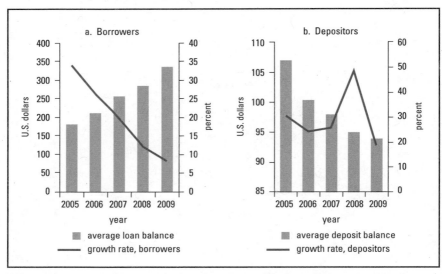

Source: Mix Market (database), Microfinance Information Exchange, Washington, DC, http://www.mixmarket.org/data-center.
Note: All figures provided by Mix Market represent trends because not all MFIs in a country report to the database.

This underlines another interesting development on the African continent: while borrower growth rates slowed for the five years to 2009, depositor growth rates accelerated, except for 2009 (figure 3.6). A comparison across regions shows that, in 2008, the depositor growth in Africa was only paralleled by the Middle East, leaving all other regions far behind; some, such as East Asia and the Pacific, experienced negative growth rates. In 2009, the declining growth rates were in line with other regions, apart from East Asia and the Pacific, which had recovered slightly from the negative growth rate in the previous year. Depositor growth rates within the region have been persistent in recent years, and, with the notable exception of North Africa, all subregions increased their depositor base from 2007 to 2008. While depositor growth accelerated in the five years to 2009, the average deposit decreased consistently, falling another 1 percent from 2008 to 2009. While borrower growth rates decreased, average loan balances increased. This rise and fall was consistent in Africa over the period. One assumption is that, because MFIs were not expanding their client base, they were able to grant higher loan balances to their current clients. Simultaneously, existing clients may have been more in need of larger loans because of the higher food and fuel prices and other effects of the crisis.

Among borrowers, women make up the majority, consistent with the original goal of MFIs to target women as a disadvantaged group. On aggregate, since 2007, women borrowers account for around twice as many borrowers as men on the continent. Looking at the median MFI, however, we see a different picture: in 2009, only 52 percent of the borrowers were women.

Early on, African MFIs shifted toward an individual lending model and away from the microcredit model implemented by Muhammad Yunus in Bangladesh that initially focused on group lending. Indeed, MFIs in West Africa never used the latter model in the first place.

There is a large variety of institutions offering different products and targeting different clients. One may observe throughout the continent different ownership and organizational models, including the cooperative model, the model based on nongovernmental organizations (NGOs), and the microbank model. There are also different sources of funding for MFIs, ranging from donor funding to commercial funding, funding through the savings of members (in the case of cooperatives), and government funding, in Ethiopia for example. While most of these institutions were originally set up to provide credit only, some of them have started offering other financial services, including deposit services. Notably, MFIs in West Africa offered both savings and credit services from the beginning, though this was limited to members. Several countries have introduced a regulatory framework to support deposit-taking MFIs, a topic to which we return in chapter 5.

The increasing focus on deposit services is also reflected in the funding structure of MFIs. Even though the funding sources for microfinance around the world have become increasingly diverse, including an array of crossborder flows, local funding remains the key source for growth in the African context (MIX and CGAP 2010). In international comparisons, African MFIs have been generally successful in mobilizing deposits: deposits reached 57.3 percent of overall funding in 2009 (figure 3.7). During the financial crisis, the institutions that relied more on deposits as their main funding source fared better. A large share of the deposits across different MFIs are voluntary deposit accounts rather than compulsory savings. According to the Microfinance Information Exchange and the Consultative Group to Assist the Poor, the structural composition of funding varies strongly by type of organization (MIX and CGAP 2010). Deposits are an important funding base for credit unions and bank MFIs, while NGOs are substantially more dependent on grants and wholesale borrowings as a source of funding. Across all regions, Africa has the lowest rate of borrowings as a source of funding, at 23.4 percent in 2009. In recent years, private financiers, including banks, have come to play a more important role in funding compared with donors, especially in North Africa. Donor funding is, not surprisingly, also unevenly distributed, with a heavier focus on low-income countries (MIX and CGAP 2010).

The discussion on the merits of the commercialization of microfinance—which has become personalized in the debate between Muhammad Yunus and the Mexican microlender Compartamos—centers on the interest rates that microfinance borrowers should be charged. Should they be commercially viable or subsidized? The discussion can be easily politicized, as the recent experience in Andra Pradash

Figure 3.7   The Funding Structure of African MFIs

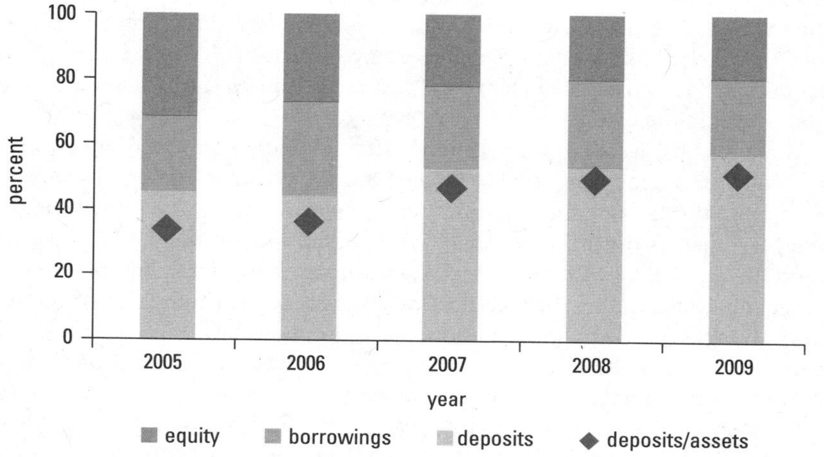

Source: Mix Market (database), Microfinance Information Exchange, Washington, DC, http://www.mixmarket.org/data-center.
Note: All figures provided by Mix Market represent trends because not all MFIs in a country report to the database.

in India shows. While the debate has not yet touched Africa on a wide scale, commercial microlenders—nonbank financial institutions that mainly provide consumer loans at high interest rates—have been shunned by the microfinance community in South Africa.

The mantra upon which microfinance is built—reaching out to the poor—has also been the main challenge of microfinance. A consensus has developed that the poorest of the poor do not really benefit from microfinance services, but need other support. Over time, the challenge has therefore become to reach the poor with products that will yield the best possible outcome. Much research has been conducted to determine the products that might be most beneficial to the poor. The initial focus on credit services has been questioned in the literature and by practitioners. The analysis of financial diaries carried out by Collins et al. (2009) has shown that the poor lack appropriate savings instruments and credit facilities. The experiences reported by the authors suggest that savings and credit may be interchangeable in the minds of the poor, the only difference being that large expenditures—such as weddings, funerals, or emergencies—are possible at the end of the contract period in the case of savings, while, with credit, they are possible at the beginning; meanwhile, both equally involve regular payments over time. Recent evidence from Kenya shows that enterprise development can, indeed, be fostered through the provision of credit, but also through the provision of more effective savings instruments. Through a field experiment in rural Kenya, Dupas and Robinson (2009) show that access to savings accounts had a substantial, positive impact on the levels of productive investments among market women and, within six months, led to higher incomes. Their findings imply that a significant fraction of women entrepreneurs have difficulty saving and investing as much as they would like and therefore represent a potential clientele for formal savings products even if these offer negative interest rates. Intrahousehold conflicts and time-inconsistency problems—short-run impatience (high-discount factors in the near future) and long-run patience (low-discount factors in the far future)—prevent many poor households from saving despite the inherent demand for savings products. Learning from informal arrangements such as rotating savings and credit associations, MFIs have therefore developed deposit collector services and savings commitment products for their clients, including limited access to savings until a target amount has been reached (Ashraf et al. 2003).

A major challenge facing MFIs in Africa is the need to move beyond urban areas toward rural areas. Data on a few selected countries clearly suggest that, in most countries, MFIs still operate mainly in urban areas. In Tanzania, for example, only 1 percent of the rural population saves with MFIs, while 7 percent of the urban population fits this category (Napier 2011). In Nigeria, 208 of the country's 901 microfinance banks are in Abuja and Lagos, while two of the northern states, Jigawa and Katsina, have only 12 microbanks between them despite a combined population of 10 million (Napier 2011). In this respect, MFIs face the same challenges as other financial institutions, including banks: especially physical infrastructure deficiencies make outreach costly. MFIs in Africa face higher cost barriers than MFIs elsewhere. The average ratio of overhead costs to assets is 22.5 percent, compared with 17.4 percent in non-African developing countries.[7] High staff salaries have been one of the main costs. The ratio of the average salary to gross national income per capita is nearly three times higher in Africa than in other regions. Significant competition among MFIs and from banks, as well as the lack of an ample qualified labor force, may be one of the reasons for the high operating costs and staff salaries (MIX and CGAP 2010). Moreover, the ratio of borrowers per staff member has not increased in recent years. The high operating costs are also driven by the high costs of processing, monitoring, and collecting payments, which reflects not only infrastructure deficiencies, but also demand constraints and the substantial level of information asymmetry.

In overcoming these cost constraints, MFIs have made gains by using technology, especially cell phone–based technology. Particularly in countries where mobile banking (or m-banking) is already available, examples abound. Tujijenge Tanzania, an MFI in Tanzania, has made the repayment of individual loans via M-Pesa mandatory below the threshold of US$1,800. In Kenya, various MFIs offer the possibility of loan repayments through M-Pesa for individual loans, but also group loans. Deposit-taking MFIs such as Faulu Kenya allow their customers to deposit through M-Pesa. In Malawi, MFIs have used biometric technology, based on a physiological characteristic (fingerprint, face, eye iris, or retina) or behavioral characteristic (speech or signature) to identify customers. Preliminary evidence has shown that this can help increase repayment rates, especially among borrowers with ex ante high risk profiles (Giné, Goldberg, and Yang 2010).

It is rather difficult to jump-start a microfinance industry through a licensing window or some other special regulatory process. A regulatory framework helps mainly at a later stage. In Uganda, for example, the push for a regulatory framework to support deposit-taking microfinance banks arose from within the MFI industry, which realized that the industry could not grow and become viable without proper regulation. The need for a special regulatory framework for MFIs so as to encourage market entry has to be balanced with the concern about regulatory arbitrage, that is, institutions choosing to adopt this form to avoid more burdensome bank regulations. Forcing MFIs to focus on specific sectors or regions can backfire. Meanwhile, donor support facilitated the establishment of a significant microfinance industry in Madagascar, though the sustainability of this industry will have to be managed carefully through a gradual withdrawal of the support.

MFIs can suffer from excessive ambition that translates into significant, but poorly managed growth. For instance, several MFIs in Morocco recently implemented extensive growth strategies to increase their market shares, but they did not accompany this growth by assembling appropriate human and information technology resources. This led to significant pressure on the microfinance industry. In attempts to jump-start microfinance, donors sometimes provide too many resources to MFIs without also providing the necessary capacity to absorb these resources. The example of Crédit Mutuel of Guinea shows how this can backfire. This was the largest MFI in the country until it had to be shut down in the early 2000s because it had lent excessively without proper screening or monitoring systems after it had received substantial resources from donors, including the French Development Agency and the World Bank.

SACCOs, which are member-based financial institutions that lend and take deposits, are an important player in many African countries. In many countries, these institutions function in the semiformal arena: they are registered by an authority (such as the ministry of cooperatives), but are not formally supervised as banks are. The cooperative model is based on the cooperative movement in Central and Western Europe (Austria, France, and Germany) that has often been credited with the almost universal access to financial services in these countries, including access to credit among farmers, thus helping rural areas develop. Donors have tried to implement this concept in developing countries, including in Africa. Local circumstances, however, have to be taken into account. Countries with communities having deep roots and little migration offer themselves to this kind of initiative, while countries or regions with large migration flows and less tightly knit community links may be less appropriate. A similar argument can be made to defend the idea that group lending as a lending model is less attractive in Africa than elsewhere.

In most countries, these institutions suffer from a limited skill base and a lack of capacity. Apex institutions, supported by donors through technical assistance, can help overcome these barriers. The Co-operative Bank of Kenya was, for a long time, considered a success story, but it has recently experienced problems in governance. In Rwanda, the cooperative network of the Union des Banques Populaires du Rwanda was initially established with technical support from the Swiss government, but suffered from financial and operational deterioration in the wake of the conflict in Rwanda, and its management has recently been taken over by Rabobank.

Looking beyond existing institutions

The variety of institutions in a financial system is often a function of the overall size of the system, but also the overall degree of competitiveness and contestability of the system. Even small financial systems such as the system in Uganda can support a variety of financial institutions. Often, the push to expand the frontier comes from unexpected directions. In Kenya, Equity Bank transformed itself from an underperforming building society into an innovative bank and is now the largest bank in the country in terms of clientele. It did this by offering new delivery channels, such as mobile branches, by targeting a new clientele, and by focusing on the quality of service delivery. More recently, it launched M-Kesho, which is an advanced mobile financial product offered by M-Pesa (Safaricom, a leading mobile operator) and Equity Bank. In Rwanda, one bank is offering payment services to SACCOs through mobile branches on trucks.

Regional integration has become an important driver of new providers and products around the continent. As documented in chapter 2, the share of regional banks has increased significantly in recent years. One example is the expansion of Kenyan banks into Uganda following the lifting of a moratorium on new bank licenses in Uganda and in expectation of the establishment of a free trade area in East Africa.

Increasingly, new delivery channels beyond brick-and-mortar branches are being tested. The transaction accounts mentioned elsewhere above are often linked to a preference for the use of less costly ATMs rather than branches. Mobile branches located on trucks that deliver financial services to remote areas have become a popular delivery channel. Another promising example includes agency agreements, a model favored in several Latin American countries. Through these agreements, banks offer financial services through third-party agents, such as stores or post offices. Agency agreements offset several supply- and demand-side constraints simultaneously. First, they address the scale diseconomies involved in the provision of financial services to small communities of customers with a need for small-scale transactions because they allow financial services to be bundled with other products and services and reduce the fixed costs of a full-fledged branch. Second, they reduce cultural and social barriers to the access to branches by large population segments. Kenya has recently put in place the necessary regulatory framework. Most countries in Africa, however, do not yet allow such arrangements.

New products have been tested to facilitate the inclusion of the unbanked population in the banked population. On the deposit side, simple transaction accounts have been offered. In South Africa, following moral suasion, if not outright pressure by the government, the Mzansi basic account initiative was launched by banks in 2004 to provide affordable banking services to the unbanked, but bankable population. Although the pricing structure differs from bank to bank, the Mzansi basket includes a bundle of basic services on a monthly basis at no monthly fee and with no switch fees, such as free electronic deposits, two ATM withdrawals, two cash deposits, one balance enquiry, one debit order, one rejected debit order, and one money transfer. By the end of 2007, there was a substantial shift in the geographical distribution of the footprint of the Mzansi account: major geographical regions had experienced decreases, while significant gains were being achieved in more remote provinces. Almost 52 percent of all the new accounts were previously unbanked customers. It thus appears that the Mzansi account is gaining acceptance especially among black women between the ages of 25 and 54. However, the results have not all been positive. A staggering 44 percent of all accounts remained inactive. The jury is therefore still out on the sustainability of the account as originally designed. Although highly praised for bringing the unbanked into the financial sector, its ability to keep them is less clear, perhaps because of brand consciousness or cost-related issues. Likewise, in 2008, Banque Centrale Populaire put in place a similar low-income banking program in Morocco that was called Al Hissab Chaabi (popular account). For DH 9 (approximately US$1) per month, clients are offered a bank account, a debit and payment card, a mobile service, a monthly bank statement, and free counter operations. As of April 2010, Al Hissab Chaabi had helped 193,000 formerly unbanked individuals gain access to banking services.

On the lending side, salary loans have become a popular form of consumer lending. This model builds on a formal agreement between a company and a lender to deduct repayments for a loan directly from the salary of the borrower. It seems a good technology to avoid the key problem of contractual deficiencies and reduce the transaction costs for lenders. There is a critical downside, however: the overindebtedness to which such agreements can lead. We return to the topic in chapter 5 under the heading of consumer protection.

Islamic finance

Islamic finance is a relatively new addition to the set of financial providers and products in most African countries, even though the first African Islamic Bank was created in the 1960s in Egypt. There are five principles that differentiate Islamic finance from conventional finance. Three of these are negative principles: the prohibition on *riba* (usury, which is generally defined as interest or excessive interest), the prohibition on *gharar* (risk or uncertainty, which is generally defined as speculation), and the prohibition on financing for illicit sectors in Sharia (such as weapons, drugs, alcohol, and pork). The other two principles are positive: the profit- and loss-sharing principle and the principle that all transactions have to be backed by a real economic transaction that involves a tangible asset. Despite the implication of the term, Islamic finance is not restricted to Muslim customers. Islamic financial products can be offered by Islamic banks and conventional banks through specialized windows.[8] It has been popular in the Middle East and some Asian countries for many years and has expanded to Africa in recent years.

Currently, 20 of the 53 African countries have Islamic institutions, including a total of 42 Islamic banks, plus numerous conventional institutions offering Sharia-compliant products through Islamic windows. There are 32 insurance companies offering Sharia-compliant insurance (*takaful*). In contrast, only three countries (Egypt, The Gambia, and Sudan) have issued Sharia-compliant government bonds known as *Sukuk* (legal instrument, deed, check, which is generally defined as financial certificate). Islamic finance is mainly found in countries with a significant Muslim population, such as The Gambia, Kenya, and Sudan (which has a completely Islamic financial system in the north), and North Africa generally. Some of the related institutions have been supported by the Islamic Development Bank, based in Saudi Arabia, through resources and technical assistance. Providing resources can be important not necessarily because of a lack of funds, but because of the constraint that both sides of a balance sheet at an Islamic bank (or Islamic window) have to be Sharia-compliant.

Despite the presence of a large Muslim population, the development of Islamic finance in North African countries has not been as rapid as one might have expected. There are several factors behind this outcome. First, for the most part, North African countries, along with a large part of Muslim Asia, follow a less conservative interpretation of Sharia relative to Gulf countries. In Egypt, for example, Al Azhar University has stated that riba should be defined as excessive interest and not interest per se. Second, for a long time, banking customers in North Africa have preferred conventional banks for their transparency on interest rates and the cost of transactions. The openness of North African countries toward the rest of the world meant that banks preferred to align with the practices of Western banks. Furthermore, given their structure, the average cost of a similar banking service has generally been higher for Sharia-compliant instruments than for conventional instruments. While this additional markup has been easily accepted among the wealthy Gulf population, it has been more difficult to accept among less well off North African clients. A final factor behind the slow emergence of Islamic finance may be found in the political will to avoid religious tensions or risk the perception that conventional banks are unlawful because an Islamic bank has been authorized.

The emergence of Islamic finance will certainly pose regulatory challenges (Sole 2007). Regulators have to become familiar with and stay current on the Sharia compliance of the Islamic financial products offered in their jurisdictions and on the accounting and auditing standards of Islamic institutions. The equity-like nature of some Islamic finance instruments increases the risk-taking incentives for Islamic banks, which might require more intensive monitoring by supervisors. Islamic finance also poses problems of financial literacy in terms of transparency. In Islamic finance, the interest rate structures of conventional banking are often replaced by fee structures. While, at first glance, this may be easier for clients to understand, it raises the challenge of disclosure.

An important issue that is beyond the scope of this chapter and this book is the effective difference between Islamic banks and conventional banks. Recent analysis by Beck, Demirgüç-Kunt, and Merrouche (2010) finds few significant differences in business models across Islamic and conventional banks. This is based, though, on rather crude indicators derived from financial statements. Consistent with this finding is the observation that Islamic finance in northern Sudan is rigorous in complying with the no-interest rule, while Islamic finance in Malaysia, a sophisticated financial system, resembles conventional banking.

In the long term, a large-scale expansion of Islamic finance would involve the creation of parallel structures for bond markets, discount windows, and so on. Given the current resource and skill constraints in many African countries, it seems unlikely that this can occur outside the largest markets, such as Kenya, Nigeria, or South Africa, and it is questionable that this should be a priority among policy makers and donors.

The ultimate question—the extent to which the provision of Sharia-compliant products can expand the banked population—is still open. On the one hand, such products might overcome the reluctance of religious households and entrepreneurs to use formal financial services. This population segment, however, is probably small in most African countries. On the other hand, the main barriers laid out above—cost and risk—are also present in Islamic finance, so that Islamic banking is unlikely to help push the frontier outward. Islamic finance seems to offer the chance to attract additional resources from the oil-exporting countries of the Middle East. However, most African countries face an intermediation constraint, but not a resource constraint.

The jury is still out, but the experience of the past few years suggests that the share of Islamic finance in overall intermediation will continue to increase across the continent; however, it will help deepen and broaden the financial system only at the margin and will not be a game changer.

Demand-Side Constraints

We have discussed supply constraints extensively, but there are also important demand-side constraints, that is, characteristics that can prevent households and individuals from accessing formal financial services.

One way to explore demand-side constraints is to consider the information provided by household surveys. FinScope and FinAccess survey users about their experiences with banks and nonusers about the reasons why they do not use financial

Figure 3.8   Asking Potential Users in Kenya about the Barriers to Access

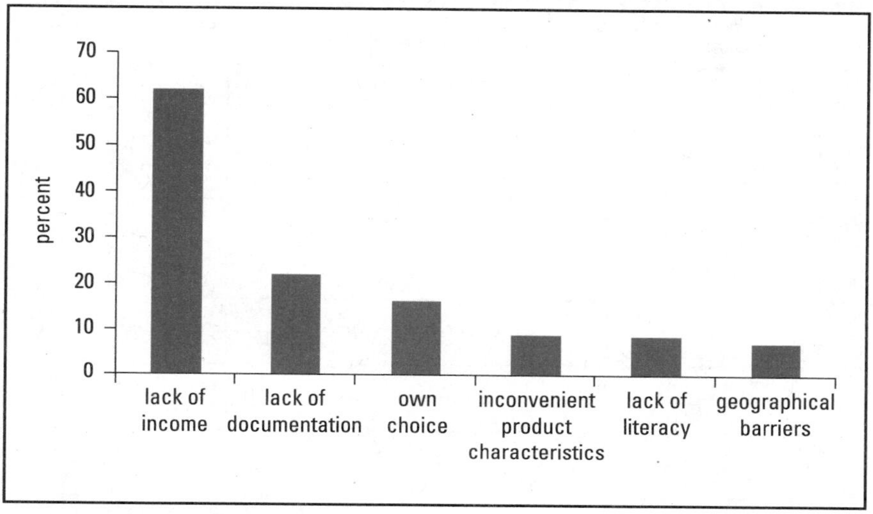

Source: FinAccess (2009).

services (FinAccess 2009). These questions are typically open ended; so, the surveyed have to state the reasons without being offered formulated responses. Figure 3.8 reports the reasons reported by interviewees in Kenya to explain why they do not use formal banking services. At the top of the list is the lack of stable, regular income. Inadequate products (for example, products that are too costly) and the lack of the necessary documentation are often cited as important, while the lack of demand is rarely the most important reason. Reasons related to literacy and the lack of knowledge about products account for another important factor (see elsewhere below). Overall, this points to three of the main barriers we discuss in this chapter: the large segment of the population that is currently unbankable, the supply constraints related to the significant documentation requirements and product and geographical barriers, and the demand-side constraints.

The lack of formal income sources is an important constraint to participation in the formal economy, including conventional banking. Conversely, the lack of formality and the small size of transactions pose important barriers to banks in reaching out to such customers. Semiformal and informal providers seem much more appropriate. Nonetheless, mobile payment providers are much more likely to be able to reach out to this segment because they have much lower fixed costs and do not rely on a threshold transaction volume for each customer, but, rather, the overall volume; they thus follow a high-volume strategy. The barriers related to the lack of the necessary documentation are harder to overcome, especially in light of the recent trend to formally register subscriber identification module (SIM) cards. Overall, however, the profile of the unbanked population points to transaction ser-

Table 3.3   The Awareness of Microfinance across African Countries, 2009
percent of the respondents to the question "Are you aware of any institution/company in your community helping people with microfinancing, that is, helping people like you to obtain small loans, with interest, for a business?"

Country	Yes	No, not available in my community	No, never heard of it
Malawi	65	29	7
Uganda	63	30	7
Kenya	57	29	14
Senegal	56	29	13
Tanzania	47	40	13
Rwanda	46	40	13
Chad	38	51	10
South Africa	38	34	28
Ghana	37	43	18
Mali	36	51	13
Cameroon	36	36	28
Niger	33	59	8
Nigeria	31	43	17
Zambia	30	53	14
Burundi	25	59	15
Côte d'Ivoire	18	65	18
Congo, Dem. Rep.	16	61	22
Zimbabwe	15	46	39

Source: Gallup survey data.
Note: The surveys were conducted in 18 Sub-Saharan African countries in 2009. The data are weighted using adult population estimates for 2008 developed by the World Bank.

vices as a more promising entry point for financial institutions and to technology as a promising delivery channel.

A simple lack of awareness about the availability of financial services may also be an important barrier. A recent Gallup poll across 18 African countries showed that, on average, only 36 percent of the surveyed are aware of the existence of MFIs in their communities: 18 percent had never heard of MFIs, and the remainder claimed to have heard of them, but said that MFIs were not available in their communities (table 3.3). Obviously, this also points to the lack of availability. Perhaps more worrisome is the fact that the awareness increases with income and is greater among men than among women, though the latter are often targeted by MFIs. This suggests that MFIs are not reaching their target clientele or may not be able to reach as far down-market as they would like.

There is a general trust issue. Overcoming the mistrust of financial institutions might be easier in the case of transaction services, where the intertemporal nature of financial services is reduced to a few minutes, especially in m-banking, than in the case of savings or credit services, where the result can only be seen after months or even years.

Financial literacy has been an increasingly important topic among policy makers and donors in recent years. It is important to distinguish between financial literacy (or knowledge), that is, awareness and knowledge about the existence and functioning of specific services and products, and financial capability, that is, good financial decision making. Financial capability includes managing resources well, knowing how to evaluate and compare different financial products and services, and demanding one's rights if necessary. Box 3.2, on the next page, describes some of the related efforts across the region.

Do financial literacy programs help? It is hard to establish causality, but randomized evaluations have provided some evidence. A recent financial literacy training program in Indonesia targeted selected unbanked households. It sent half of them invitations to a free financial literacy seminar two to three hours in length (Cole, Sampson, and Zia 2010). While the program had no effect on the general population, there seems to have been a significant impact on the likelihood of unschooled and financially illiterate households to open bank accounts as a result of the program. Additionally, a financial literacy program delivered over several weekly sessions seems to be more successful than a single session of a few hours. Monetary incentives offered for opening accounts seemed more successful than education programs, at least in the short run. In Uganda, women microentrepreneurs were offered business development and literacy training (McKenzie and Weber 2009). The training led many entrepreneurs to keep separate business and personal accounts, specify the salaries they would draw each month, and draft budgets they would monitor. However, this effect was concentrated among women with some university training. The lesson from these two experiments seems to be that targeted literacy programs are more promising than general programs and that programs have to be adjusted according to feedback from participants. It is important to stress that these are preliminary findings. Significantly more research and analysis are needed to explore the sorts of programs and the targeted population groups that may be appropriate. It is certainly easier to improve the basic awareness of financial concepts and financial attitudes. Measuring the long-term impact of financial literacy programs on behavior requires longer-term analysis.

There is a more general demand-side issue: Which financial service does the currently unbanked population segment in Africa need most? As we discuss above, the poor use a large portfolio of informal financial services, including credit (moneylenders), savings (susu collections or rotating savings and credit associations), and payment services.

Technology: The New Silver Bullet?

Africa has been at the forefront of mobile financial services.[9] In 2002, Celpay, a specialized provider linked to mobile network provider Celtel, started a business-

Box 3.2   Financial Capability Programs

There are many types of financial literacy programs, ranging from widely distributed to targeted efforts and efforts using different media and different channels. The following are a few examples from across Africa.

Drama, music, and dance. Drama and role plays, accompanied, sometimes, by music and dance, can help bring to life issues of personal finance. In Uganda, the Association of Microfinance Institutions of Uganda has used music, dance, and drama to reinforce other means of communications in finance. This channel was chosen because it is the most highly appreciated means of communication within communities and because it reflects local culture: knowledge is traditionally passed from one generation to another through storytelling.

Exhibitions, road shows, and gathering points. In South Africa, where many people use local transportation to go to work, brief education messages on personal finance are transmitted via radio, television, and compact discs at some of the main taxi (minibus) stands and train stations and in vehicles. These infomercials typically contain music, as well as education messages on personal finance. In addition, roving trailers and stages, with live sessions by trained facilitators, are used at taxi stands and train stations. In South Africa, the national credit regulator runs the Borrow Wisely Campaign after Christmas. The campaign includes broadcasts from shopping malls at which prizes are given to shoppers who answer personal finance questions correctly.

Mass media. In Africa, mass media has long been used to communicate health-related messages and educational content. Now, these tools are being used for financial capability outreach. In Kenya, for example, a popular soap opera, *Makutano Junction,* has received funding to include financial literacy messages in the story lines. They are using content developed by the United States–based NGO, Microfinance Opportunities. The content was created for classroom-type instruction, but is now being modified for mass media. In Uganda, rural radio, including call-in shows during which local experts respond to the questions of callers, has been found to be a cost-effective means of reaching large numbers of rural people, particularly because, taken together, these shows are presented in a range of local languages. Listeners can identify with callers who have similar profiles and may be facing similar issues. In Tunisia, radio commercials have been used to educate people on the benefits of holding and using payment cards instead of cash.

Source: Miller (2011).

to-business payment service in Zambia, and, in 2005, First National Bank started a similar service in South Africa, though limited to existing customers. In 2007, Safaricom started M-Pesa in Kenya, which had more than 10 million registered customers, or 40 percent of Kenya's population, by June 2010 and a business volume of US$400 million per month, or 15 percent of Kenya's GDP. Most countries in Africa have a mobile payment service provider by now, although the penetration has not reached the same level in other countries as in Kenya. These service providers are building on the wide success of mobile network providers across the continent that are leapfrogging more conventional technologies because of the poor state of landline telephony in Africa. According to Aker and Mbiti (2010), the total number of mobile phone subscribers in Africa rose from 16 million in 2000 to 488 million in 2010, covering effectively two-thirds of the population. These payment networks are also referred to as second-generation models of mobile financial services.[10] Rather than building on the existing payment infrastructure, these providers had to build their own infrastructure, including a large agent network where customers could exchange electronic money for cash. The second-generation model of mobile financial services has also introduced new players into the financial system, at least in some countries.

Mobile phone banking offers two critical advantages over other delivery channels. First, it relies to a greater extent on variable rather than fixed costs, which implies that even customers who undertake small and few transactions are viable or bankable relative to banking through conventional channels. Second, trust can be built much more easily by reducing the risk from the customer's and the provider's viewpoint. By overcoming these two major barriers, mobile phone banking can help push out the access possibilities frontier to cover a large share of the adult population. By overcoming these barriers, mobile phone banking can change the economics of retail banking (Mas and Radcliffe 2010).

There has been a lot of speculation about the factors behind the success of M-Pesa in Kenya and whether it can be replicated elsewhere. Conditions were conducive for Safaricom to reach the necessary scale as rapidly as it did; these conditions may not be available for replication in other countries. First, Safaricom had a high market share in mobile telephony (75 percent), which gave it the necessary network advantage in allowing its customers to reach friends and family with payment transfers. This strong market position also allowed it to attract customers and cash-in/cash-out merchants rapidly, as the usefulness of the system was obvious. In Tanzania, for example, where Vodacom has a 40 percent market share, M-Pesa managed to attract only 280,000 customers in the first 14 months, compared with 2.7 million in Kenya during a corresponding time period (Napier 2011). Second, the demographic structure of Kenya has helped because of the migration flows toward Nairobi and the necessity to transfer money on a regular basis. Third, Safaricom managed to overcome the challenges of scale and network effects through a massive start-up marketing and investment effort, thus avoiding the subscale trap. A final positive factor was the open regulatory environment that allowed a nonbank company to offer financial services.

Beyond the question of how easy it is to replicate the success of M-Pesa elsewhere on the continent, there seem to be two important lessons of this success for the ongoing discussion on how to expand the outreach of formal financial systems. First, the success of M-Pesa and the spread of similar products and services around the continent might indicate a shift away from a credit-led inclusion approach, the hallmark of the original microfinance movement—which saw credit as the only

Table 3.4   The Regulatory Framework for Branchless Banking in Selected Countries

Indicator	Angola	Malawi	Mozambique	South Africa	Zambia
Domestic branchless banking regulatory framework					
Nonbank-based branchless banking model permissible?	Restrictive	Unclear	Permissive	Transition[a]	Permissive
Outsourcing to retail agents permissible?	Restrictive	Transition[a]	Permissive	Permissive	Permissive
Regulator and policy maker perspectives on outsourcing	Restrictive	Transition[a]	Permissive	Permissive	Permissive
Electronic money services	Transition[a]	Unclear	Permissive	Transition[a]	Permissive
Effect of AML and CFT[b]	Restrictive	Transition[a]	Permissive	Transition[a]	Permissive
Regulatory framework for crossborder transactions					
Who can offer them?	Restrictive	Restrictive	Restrictive	Transition[a]	Permissive
Transaction limits?[c]	Restrictive	Restrictive	Permissive	Transition[a]	Permissive
Identification requirements	Restrictive	Restrictive	Permissive	Restrictive	Permissive

Source: Data of the Consultative Group to Assist the Poor and the World Bank.
a. Transition = in between or in transition.
b. AML = anti–money laundering. CFT = combating the financing of terrorism. Information on the effects of AML and CFT for Angola is incomplete.
c. The transaction limits in South Africa are restrictive for Postbank, but not so restrictive for banks.

barrier between the poor and entrepreneurship—toward a payment-led inclusion approach (Mas and Radcliffe 2010). Such an approach can have several advantages over the credit-led approach. It addresses people's most immediate needs, that is, the need for safe, rapid payments. There is also a potential for scaling that is not necessarily available for credit because there is no need for large resources within such an approach. Finally, focusing on transaction services rather than credit services also seems consistent with the overall level of financial development, which is more highly focused on transactions. It therefore fits well with the Finance for Market approach. This transaction-led rather than credit- or savings-led approach toward inclusion does not downplay the importance of other financial services; rather, the issue is: Which service should one start with and which delivery channel should one use?

The second important lesson revolves around the fact that innovation can come from an unexpected quarter, a conclusion we discuss in the previous section. Given the limited competition in banking in Africa because of the small size of banking systems in most African countries and given the limited development of nonbank financial institutions in Africa, it is important to find alternative financial service providers. This does not mean that there should be an open-door regulatory environment to permit all and sundry to offer deposit-taking services. Rather, it means that there should be an open regulatory environment with regard to new providers and new products that might increase outreach and competition within the financial system.

The state of development of the information and communication technology infrastructure and the legal framework in countries has a lot to do with the regulatory attitude and approach toward mobile technologies, especially among nonbank sources, as a recent study of southern African countries shows (table 3.4). Countries not only have different regulatory regimes in relation to the potential for m-banking, they are also at different stages in the development of m-banking facilities; thus, m-banking is widespread only in South Africa, though its use is also expanding for commercial users in Zambia.

The challenge will be to use the network created by mobile financial services to make the transition from payment services to other services. The recent introduction of M-Kesho in Kenya is a first step in this direction. M-Kesho is a savings account offered by Equity Bank that provides only electronic transaction functionality, that is, money can be transferred in and out either via the customer's M-Pesa account or an account with Equity Bank. Eventually, Equity Bank hopes to offer both credit and insurance services via this delivery channel. In Ghana, MTN, a mobile network operator, is planning to offer life insurance products for the low-income market.

More recently, there has also been a push to integrate mobile payment systems across borders. Celtel's network project in East Africa is the world's first borderless (or unified) phone network. It offers subscribers in Kenya, Tanzania, and Uganda free roaming facilities across borders with airtime charged in local currencies.

While the dominance of Safaricom in the cell phone market has facilitated the success of M-Pesa, concerns have arisen about this dominant market position. Exclusivity agreements with agents can become effective entry barriers for new suppliers. Eventually, the shift to an interconnectivity model might be required, whereby (as in railway services) the infrastructure and the transfer services are separated. Another challenge is the decision whether to allow stand-alone mobile payment service providers or bank-based solutions. Kenya has selected the stand-alone solution, while many other countries have preferred a bank-based solution or a solution that centers on a telecommunications company that acts in cooperation with a bank (box 3.3). One size certainly does not fit all. The Kenyan solution was possible because of the market dominance of Safaricom and the desire to induce more competition from outside the banking system. Banking systems that face significant competition from within the sector may prefer the bank-based solution. In middle-income countries that are already reasonably well banked and have the related infrastructure, the bank-based model may also be more appropriate.

As an alternative to an activist regulatory approach to sharing infrastructure, such as agents, a shift to third-generation mobile financial services can help overcome problems of scale and competition. The third-generation model implies the existence of access to Internet via mobile phones. Two technical aspects would

Box 3.3   Examples of Transformative Technology-Based Products

Bank-based models

Wizzit is a joint venture between an independent provider and the South African Bank of Athens. Its services are based on the use of mobile phones to access bank accounts and conduct transactions, in addition to a Maestro debit card that is issued to all customers upon registration. Wizzit has partnered with the South African bank Absa and the South African Post Office, which act as banking agents and allow Wizzit customers to deposit funds at any Absa or Post Office branch.

MTN Banking is a joint venture between mobile network operator MTN and Standard Bank that allows customers to obtain immediate access to their bank accounts at anytime they wish using cell phones, MobileMoney MasterCard, and the Internet. They can withdraw cash from any ATM in South Africa and also make balance and statement inquiries using cell phones. MobileMoney account holders can make person-to-person payments.

Hello Money is now offered in Botswana by Barclays Bank, in partnership with Orange and Mascom. It supports a full range of retail and business banking services that are already offered to its customers and allows customers to make transactions such as account inquiries, fund transfers, bill payments, mobile recharges, and checkbook and statement requests.

Nonbank-based models

Zap was launched in Kenya, Tanzania, and Uganda in February 2009 by Zain Mobile, in partnership with leading international banks, enabling Zain and bank customers to use mobile phones to withdraw cash or pay for goods and services, school fees, and utility bills, including electricity and water; receive money from or send money to friends and family; send money from and receive money to their bank accounts; top up their or someone else's airtime; and manage bank accounts. More than 10 million people are using the service, and Zain expanded Zap to Niger and Sierra Leone and, in the context of a full commercial pilot, also expanded to Malawi.

Mikemusa mobile is a pilot mobile, wallet-based money transfer service that aims to cater to Zimbabweans in diaspora. Customers can access the service online and open m-cash accounts. They can load funds onto their m-cash accounts through direct bank-to-bank online payments (suitable for customers with online banking facilities) or direct bank cash deposits; this is most suitable for customers without bank accounts or online banking facilities.

Mobicash Payment Solutions (Pty) Ltd, trading as MobiPay, is Namibia's first mobile payment solution. It was licensed and authorized by the Bank of Namibia in August 2010. Customers must first register free of charge before depositing money with Mobicash Payment Solutions. The actual cash is either deposited with the company's bank account or with the company's agents across the country. Customers would then use their cell phones to access the money for transactions, which may include the purchase of airtime, electricity payments, the transfer of money to other persons, and payment for goods at shops.

Note: In nonbank-based models, unlike in bank-based models, it is not mandatory to have a bank account.

make this a promising route. First, this can lead to a reduction in costs. Second, the Internet can serve as a shared platform for different providers of payment services, such as PayPal. The initial applications have enjoyed high take-up rates, for example, MXit in South Africa. However, there are also risks involved with this next generation of mobile payment service, most prominently the risk of viruses. This might also have implications for supervision and even monetary policy.

In summary, electronic banking can change the economics of retail banking. It can help push out the possibilities frontier substantially because it reduces the fixed cost component of financial service provision. Pushing out toward the new frontier, however, requires that one also overcome other constraints, such as the lack of financial literacy and awareness, and might require a new regulatory approach. There are two major challenges. One involves shifting from transaction services to other financial services, that is, to use the initial mobile payment services as entry points rather than as end points in the effort to extend the outreach of the financial system. The other challenge is to minimize the problems associated with scalability, which might require a large market share and competition. Contestability—that is, openness to competition from new providers and new products—can go a long way in this direction.

Pushing Out the Frontier: The Role of Governments and Donors

The right mix of institutions, competition, and generally open systems can allow a financial system to push toward the frontier. However, for most African countries, this frontier is still narrow. How can the frontier—the share of the bankable population—be pushed out at the level of households and enterprises? This brings us back to a long-term agenda item: institution building.

Contractual institutions—laws, the courts, collateral registries, and so on—have long been at the top of the agendas of policy makers. The modernist approach focuses on the ability of borrowers to use fixed assets, such as land or machinery and vehicles, as collateral and on the existence of the infrastructure necessary to establish sound lending practices. The creation of a sound and effective contract enforcement mechanism is an important part of the long-term institution building agenda; we return to this in chapter 4. Are there more short- to medium-term solutions that can help push out the frontier and address the challenges of competition and the demand-side constraints?

Credit registries have been heralded as a major policy tool to push financial systems toward the frontier by providing more competition and allowing more entrepreneurs and households to become part of the bankable population. Djankov, McLiesh, and Shleifer (2007) assert that credit registries are better than the reform of the contractual framework as a tool for deepening financial systems, and Honohan and Beck (2007) highlight credit registries as a useful tool. What can we expect from the introduction of credit registries?

Credit registries that provide easy, reliable access to client credit history and both negative and positive information can dramatically reduce the time and costs necessary to obtain such information from individual sources and thereby reduce the total costs of financial intermediation. Through credit reporting, borrower quality becomes much more transparent, which benefits good borrowers and increases the cost of defaulting on obligations, thus providing a disciplining tool. It helps borrowers build up credit histories—reputation collateral—and thus eases the access to credit. Credit registries are especially important for SMEs because the creditworthiness of SMEs is generally more difficult to evaluate, and SMEs typically are less visible and transparent relative to large enterprises. Many cross-country studies have found that countries with effective credit registries possess deeper and broader financial systems (see, for example, Jappelli and Pagano 2002). Does this also hold over time, that is, comparing individual countries before and after the introduction of credit registries? There is, indeed, evidence of a useful effect on the stability of banks and on the access to credit by enterprises, though little of this evidence is on African countries.[11] There is specific evidence for countries that have introduced credit registries and have seen improvements in the access of enterprises to credit (Brown, Jappelli, and Pagano 2009).

While credit registries have often been praised as an important policy tool, one has to be realistic about what can be achieved and about the related time frame. Negative information sharing will lead to the more effective screening of borrowers by lenders through access to information, which, in the first instance, may generate a reduction in access rather than an expansion. However, only through the inclusion of positive information can one achieve a buildup in the reputation capital of existing borrowers that might have an effect on competition, though this will only be felt over time rather than immediately. At the outset, this positive impact will affect the existing borrower population and cause an expansion of the frontier to the previously unbanked population only by fostering stronger competition among the participants in the credit registry, thus forcing some of the participants downmarket. Here, the type of information on which the registry can draw is critical. In general, the broader the sources the registry can draw on (utility companies, trade registries, and so on), the larger the share of enterprises that will be captured and that can potentially benefit from such a registry by proving their good borrower status. In this context, the connection to information from MFIs seems crucial. While the borrowers targeted by such institutions are often different from those targeted by banks, growing microenterprises that formalize into small enterprises will, at some point, want to access bank credit as they become too large for MFIs. It is at this stage that a credit registry can help them. All these possible effects, however, should not be expected immediately, but over the medium term, that is, in three or more years.

There has been an important debate about the private versus the public model in credit registries. While the private model has the advantage of being able to draw on data from many different sources, it is typically a voluntary arrangement. Moreover, it can be exclusive to certain groups of financial institutions, thereby under-mining competition within the banking system and fostering segmentation in the financial system. Meanwhile, the public model, which is usually hosted at the central bank, has the advantage of being compulsory. In many cases, however, it is limited to credit information from banks themselves and refers to loans above a certain threshold, while focusing on negative information only.

As in the case of many items on the policy agenda, the space for action by policy makers varies significantly across Africa. Larger countries, such as Egypt, Kenya, and Nigeria, can afford several competing credit registries, while small countries cannot. Even where there are competing credit registries, however, it is important that they truly compete with each other, rather than representing separate segments of a financial system, as in the case of Nigeria. This entrenches the segmentation of the banking system rather than fostering competition.

Egypt offers an interesting example. In Egypt, the central bank recognized its capacity constraints and encouraged the banking sector to set up its own credit registry, I-Score, which could then also draw on data from the central bank's credit registry. Expansion toward the MFI segment is now being considered. Similarly, in Morocco, through a private-public partnership, private banks are building a data platform that is ultimately controlled by the central bank, but which may be ac-cessed by any private credit registry. Some of these experiences would certainly be useful for other countries farther south as long as they always take into account the capacity constraints of small markets.

There are also potential benefits associated with regional arrangements in credit registries. Sharing the fixed costs of setting up and running such a registry can thereby be spread across more users, which, if passed on to the end users of the registry, makes the registry more cost-effective. Furthermore, as the economies in subregions, such as East Africa, become better integrated and as more, even smaller enterprises expand across national borders, a broader supranational information base becomes important. However, in this case, a consistent legal foundation must be created as a basis for information sharing across borders and to ensure the com-patibility of different models.

The lack of proper identification cards in some African countries is a challenge. Biometric identification can help solve this problem, though there are cost con-cerns. Given the absence of a national identification system, Uganda has introduced biometric identification in the context of the establishment of a new privately man-aged credit registry.

The Role of Government: Looking beyond Institution Building

While governments continue to play a major role in pushing financial institutions toward the frontier and pushing the frontier outward, the role of governments in access to finance has changed significantly in recent decades.

Government entities acting as financial service providers, especially in the retail trade and in credit services, have failed almost everywhere in the developed and developing world. In contrast, the role of government in the policy arena has increased and is no longer limited to macroeconomic stability and long-term institution building. In this context, it is important to discuss the role of DFIs. While they have failed in providing retail credit, they can have a key role in alleviating supply-side and demand-side constraints.

Another area of possible policy intervention is affirmative action to push financial systems toward the frontier through moral suasion or the legislative and regulatory process. The example of South Africa and its financial charter is insightful in this context, although the dictum "one size fits all" certainly does not apply here because similar policies may not be feasible in poorer and smaller countries in Africa, as Honohan and Beck (2007) point out. Furthermore, there is a fine line between moral suasion and political interference, as the recent example of Uganda has shown. In early 2006, frustrated by the insufficiency of earlier attempts to raise access to financial services, the Ugandan government announced that each district should be serviced by at least one financial institution. In those districts where no financial service provider was in operation, the government mandated the establishment of SACCOs to be supported through payment services and other services supplied by the poorly managed government-owned Postal Savings Bank. Similarly, in Nigeria, the government put in place the Small and Medium Enterprises Equity Investment Scheme, which obliges banks to set aside 10 percent of their profits for equity investment in SMEs. The experience was not successful. As of September 2005, only about 27.5 percent of the resources set aside by 82 banks had been utilized (Abereijo and Fayomi 2007).

Beyond institution building, governments have a critical role in ensuring competition and in designing regulation in a manner compatible with the goal of outreach. We discuss these in the following.

Encouraging competition

Competition is an important area for government action. However, this entails a sophisticated approach that has to balance (1) the need for innovation, (2) the need to avoid market dominance by new players who rapidly gain market share in new products, and (3) the need to reduce the risks of fragility. To illustrate, we return to the topic of mobile financial service providers.

Its monopolistic position in the cell phone market and its anticipation of monopolistic rents encouraged Safaricom to launch M-Pesa.[12] The possibility of entering the market without regulatory restriction certainly helped. However, the dominating market position represents a concern in terms of market development going forward, and mobile payment services might raise previously unknown risks. A dynamic approach is therefore called for, whereby regulatory authorities—in this case, banking and telecommunications regulators—have to follow market development closely and react flexibly.

As Porteous (2010) clarifies, the pricing and access conditions imposed by telecommunications companies in regard to third parties such as banks can affect the willingness of the latter to offer such services. Meanwhile, by charging high rates, banks can impede the access to payment systems by companies offering mobile payment services. The banks thereby similarly erect barriers to competition. These issues call for close coordination between bank and telecommunications regulators.

Allowing the entry of sound and reputable service providers into financial systems is critical for innovation and for the objective of broadening access to finance in Africa. Data on license applications and approvals across Africa's banking systems are worrisome given that more than a third have been rejected for numerous reasons in recent years. While this might simply be a symptom of a lack of reputable and experienced financial service operators in Africa, it does raise concerns about competitive barriers.

Another lever to increase competition is more transparency, which can be created by, for example, forcing financial institutions to publish their service fees in major newspapers. Currently, only 18 countries in Africa have such a requirement.[13] It is important to stress that publishing by itself is not sufficient to ensure transparency; the publication of fees on comparable products and the distribution of the information properly are paramount.

In certain instances, the authorities might have to force financial service providers to cooperate rather than compete with each other, especially in financial sector infrastructure, such as payment systems. One striking feature of African financial systems is the lack of interconnection among ATM and point-of-sale networks across banks. More than half the countries on which data are available have more than one payment card switch, which is highly cost-inefficient given the small scale of most African financial systems. Similarly, relative to other countries, African countries show, on average, lower interoperability scores for ATM systems and point-of-sale systems (World Bank 2008b). Even where there is interoperability, participants face high fees. Central banks, in carrying out their payment system oversight responsibilities, have to ensure that the balance between competition and cooperation is a healthy one. As a public good, key payment system infrastructure such as this should meet public policy concerns by, for example, allowing fair and competitive access to retail payment infrastructure. This would also entail ensuring that different types of institutions, be they banks or nonbank entities, provide payment services and promote fair access, thereby establishing a level playing field in the market. In most African countries, access to payment services is limited to banks, which gives banks a competitive advantage over other financial service providers.

Governments have to act with caution, however. Thus, in 2008, for example, Bank of Ghana introduced a national retail switch (eZwich) to which all banks had to connect. While banks obliged, few cards were issued, mainly because of the high cost of the technology and because the switch is not interoperable with other bank-level networks. Box 3.4 presents another example, in Malawi. The lesson from these

Box 3.4   Malswitch

Malawi has made great progress in the modernization of its payment system, but its decision to invest in a proprietary smart card payment system technology has been costly and has inhibited its ability to achieve an interoperable platform with a broad base of participation by issuers and acquirers. Keen to establish a shared retail payment system platform, the Reserve Bank of Malawi (RBM) invested, in 1999, in a nationwide payment service provider called Malswitch. (The provider is owned by RBM and the government. The respective ownership shares are 99 and 1 percent.) Malswitch operates the real time gross settlement system on behalf of RBM, while the Electronic Check Clearing House participates on behalf of other banks. The smart card system has off-line capabilities, as well as biometric identification facilities. It was thus intended that the system should reach a wider customer base than traditional payment instruments, including in unbanked rural areas.

RBM hoped that the commercial banks would subsequently subscribe to the Malswitch smart card technology and compete on products rather than infrastructure. After 11 years, this aspiration has not materialized. Banks found the selected technology expensive and invested in alternate open platforms, which are governed by open standards that allow interconnection and interoperability with existing payment system platforms. Today, the Malswitch smart card is still not interoperable and is inconsistent with best practice and user needs. Furthermore, the advances in technology since Malswitch was introduced and the proprietary nature of the technology have made Malswitch additionally unattractive to the private banking sector.

While RBM was right in seeking to champion a public good for the banking sector so as to attract the significant transaction volume required to lower average transaction processing costs, good practice today requires private sector ownership and management of such shared retail payment system infrastructure. In this way, banks could collectively make all key decisions affecting the infrastructure, thereby demonstrating a good balance between cooperation and competition.

experiences is that the authorities have a critical role in ensuring cooperation in infrastructure, but the private sector has to be closely involved in technical design. Another important dimension is the increasing trend toward SIM registration, that is, implementing the documentation requirements for acquiring a SIM card. This increases the costs for customers and mobile telephony companies, with potentially negative repercussions on efforts to broaden access to cell phones and mobile payment services. However, it also seems to offer an opportunity if the documentation requirements for opening bank accounts and registering SIM cards can be harmonized and linked, thus lowering the documentation requirements for bank accounts, at least at the regulatory level.

Fostering innovation

Providing the necessary environment for innovation is essential, but nurturing it is much more difficult. Innovation funds and innovation challenges, possibly financed and sponsored by donors, might help. M-Pesa was partly financed by a challenge fund sponsored by the U.K. Department for International Development. The recent G20 SME Finance Challenge included several winners who focused on Africa.

Another important step in pushing the financial sector toward the frontier is the reduction of information hurdles. Throughout this chapter, we refer to and use household-level data produced through the FinScope and FinAccess databases. These databases are useful not only for analysts and researchers, but also for financial institutions that are considering expanding their outreach. Identifying the geographical and sectoral gaps in financial service provision can be helpful for financial institutions that want to expand. Identifying gaps in the outreach of financial institutions can also have a demonstration and incentive effect. In South Africa, the private banking sector has supported such studies, while governments and donors have financed such studies in other countries given the limited buy-in so far by private financial institutions, though these institutions should have a strong incentive as well.

Avoiding a regulatory bias against outreach

Regulations are important in safeguarding finance and ultimately protecting the beneficiaries and users of financial services. Burdensome regulations, however, restrict the outreach of financial institutions (box 3.5). Regulatory constraints prevent

Box 3.5   Financial Innovation: The Opportunities and Risks in Expanding Outreach

New providers and new products represent opportunities to push the financial system toward the frontier and push out the frontier. The discussion in this chapter shows the powerful effect that competition and the ensuing innovation can produce. Partisans of the modernist approach have the tendency to focus on new laws and regulations to enable new providers and products. Partisans of the activist approach would like the government to take a more active role in introducing new products. Both sides seem too eager in their respective drives. First, M-Pesa was introduced in Kenya well before any regulations on m-banking. Islamic banking works in South Africa without the accompanying regulations because regulators apply the same rules in spirit to Islamic banks and to conventional banks. Second, innovations are mostly introduced by private players; perhaps these are not always commercially oriented, but they have a clear vision of long-term sustainability. An open policy approach is therefore called for that adopts an initial caveat emptor attitude toward financial innovation.

This should not imply that regulatory authorities stand by silently as the financial system is changed through innovation. On the contrary, the success of M-Pesa and the possible dominance of the mobile payment market by Safaricom show the need for an active regulatory approach to prevent the potential entrenchment of a monopolist, while excesses in payroll lending show the need for an active approach to consumer protection to avoid overindebtedness on the household side and financial fragility on the supplier side.

microfinance from exerting the maximum effect. In Morocco, for example, MFIs are treated as nonprofit organizations, a rule that prevents them from diversifying services and funding sources beyond the original donors. Similarly, maximum lending thresholds limit the business of MFIs. As they are implemented in many African countries, interest rate ceilings have an even worse effect because they price microcredit providers out of the market (see the discussion in chapter 5).

At a more individual level, regulations on anti–money laundering and on combating the financing of terrorism (AML-CFT) are important, but they can also restrict access to financial services, thereby constraining outreach. The need to make AML-CFT regulations as access-friendly as possible is recognized by specialists (Hernández-Coss et al. 2005). To accomplish this, one must ensure that the requirements are based on risks and that they therefore do not impose excessive rules on documentation and verification on low-income customers who access services that have limited scope for abuse. Regulatory authorities should engage with financial service providers to design the services needed by the poor, such as basic bank accounts, in such a way that they can be safely offered without triggering concerns about AML-CFT. Thus, for example, South Africa lowered the documentation barriers on basic financial products subject to monetary limits and certain other conditions, including that clients be natural persons, South African nationals, or residents and that the transactions be domestic. Such documentation requirements are also relevant in agency agreements so that they guarantee the right of nonbank staff to open accounts and verify identities, as well as receive and make cash payments even under the AML-CFT regime. Otherwise, the outreach of this important delivery channel will not be effective.

Even more important than focusing on the supply-side constraints of regulation is to formulate regulations so as to address demand-side constraints. South Africa has taken an active approach to curbing excesses in consumer lending through the National Credit Act in 2007 by requiring lenders to undertake affordability tests before granting credit. By curbing consumer credit, this law (which also covered the establishment of a national credit regulator) may well have prevented the buildup of a consumer credit bubble, as we have seen in several industrialized countries. We return to this topic in chapter 5.

Facilitating regional solutions

Beyond developing national markets, African policy makers also need to look at regional solutions. Developments on the continent are such that there are tremendous incentives for expanding access to finance through the rapid, but safe launch of domestic and crossborder branchless banking, accompanied by appropriate protections for customers and the financial system. The immediate motivations include current migration patterns, regional remittance flows, and trade patterns (Stone et al. 2009).

In Africa, there is a complex mix of skilled and unskilled migrants. While most migrants in the region are men, there is an increasing pattern of the feminization of migration in the region. Migrants typically use cash as they cross borders and have to go through numerous hurdles to obtain the relevant documentation to access banking services in their new places of residence. Internal migration is also widespread and is linked to rapid urbanization. Internal migrations have greatly contributed to the enlargement of the informal sector within countries. Rural-urban migration has also resulted in many geographically split households, with important implications for the demand for m-banking.

The infrastructure for transferring remittances among African countries remains rudimentary. The means of sending remittances relied on by crossborder and internal migrants include banks and other formal financial intermediaries, post offices, money transfer operators (for example, Western Union and Moneygram), and the hand transport of cash (personally or through an agent such as a friend, a relative, or a taxi driver). The informal channels are inextricably linked with the informal nature of migration in the region, with important consequences for the relative ease and security of money transfers. The relatively high costs of sending remittances through the formal financial sector are also an important factor in determining patterns of demand (Maimbo et al. 2010; Maimbo and Ratha 2005).

Informal crossborder trade is the main potential source of demand for crossborder m-banking services. Individuals cross borders to sell small amounts of goods—informal street traders, for example. While these informal traders are not strictly migrants, some studies describe them as among the most entrepreneurial and energetic of contemporary migrants. One study noted that informal traders who cross borders are mostly women (70 percent). Thus, informal crossborder trade may be closely linked to the feminization of migration.

Despite the importance of crossborder migration, remittances, and trade patterns, the financial architecture for facilitating these processes remains hindered by regulatory constraints. Financial sector development policies and products have focused on facilitating large-value payments within national borders and pay little attention to innovations in small-value payment systems whether domestic or crossborder.

From a regional regulatory perspective, in addition to the recommendations above regarding the development of national markets, it is important that policy makers recognize and address the fact that countries still have (1) different regulatory regimes in relation to the potential for m-banking in general and for crossborder m-banking in particular and (2) are at different stages in the development of m-banking facilities. Countries need to accelerate the process of harmonizing the licensing and supervisory framework for mobile money to facilitate private sector–led technological solutions, many of which will benefit national markets.

From Agricultural Credit to Rural Finance

Throughout the developing world, rural finance, especially agricultural credit, has always been the troubled child in the financial family. Considered costly and risky, it is often avoided by commercial lenders, who leave the field to cooperatives, donor-supported MFIs, and government-owned DFIs.

The conditions in Africa exacerbate the difficulties that agricultural and rural finance faces. The four characteristics of African economies described in chapter 1 that make financial service provision more challenging in Africa apply even more so to the rural sector in Africa.

- *Scale:* Dispersed populations and deteriorated road infrastructure make financial service provision through normal delivery channels prohibitively expensive. Deficient energy supply and, thus, the need for generators, as well as the lack of a reliable landline phone system, increase the costs of providing banking services through traditional delivery channels. In some countries, the difficult security situation drives costs up additionally.

- *Informality:* Informality is typically more prominent in rural areas, where there are few formal residential addresses or land titles and little formal employment except government jobs. Competing systems governing land rights, that is, the overlap between modern land law and traditional land assignment systems, make the use of land as collateral difficult for traditional lenders.

- *Volatility:* Agricultural products face high operational and price risks, and, given the monoculture of many farms and regions, risk diversification is not possible for lenders. There is also significant price volatility both seasonally, but, even more, also over multiyear cycles.

- *Governance:* The provision of subsidized credit through government-owned financial institutions has undermined the culture of credit, and commercial lenders are often reluctant to enter the market. Repeated debt forgiveness by government-owned institutions causes borrowers to confuse loans with grants. In addition, the agricultural sector in most countries is subject to substantial government intervention. Unlike in most developed countries, however, such intervention does not always favor agriculture. This makes agricultural finance more challenging.

These four characteristics of rural areas in Africa mean that the challenge of overcoming scale diseconomies and managing risk is more difficult for financial service providers. As we discuss below, technology can be as powerful a game changer in rural finance as elsewhere. Critically, competition is important to attract new providers, new products, and new delivery channels to rural areas. Demand constraints, including the lack of financial literacy and business development, but also nonfinancial supply constraints, such as lack of access to markets, loom large in agriculture and in rural areas more generally.

In discussions of agricultural and rural finance and in seeking to attain the general objective of expanding access to financial services to previously unbanked segments of the rural population, one should distinguish among target groups, which partly overlap in terms of the concepts of Finance for All, Finance for Markets, and Finance for Growth introduced elsewhere above. Specifically, one should make the important distinction between cash crop producers, who sell their produce on markets and thus need a large array of financial services, including transaction, savings, and credit services, and staple crop producers, who, in many cases, are subsistence farmers with limited resources and little scope for becoming customers of formal financial institutions. Furthermore, the focus long ago shifted from agricultural credit to a much broader set of financial needs, including the link with nonfinancial corporations, such as input providers and produce purchasers, as well as links with informal financial services providers (see World Bank 2005; Coates and Hofmeister 2010). This reflects the fact that agriculture is, for large parts of the rural population, only one of many income sources.

The market gaps in agricultural credit—documented in chapter 2—led most African countries in the 1960s and 1970s to establish development banks and DFIs that focused on agricultural credit, including, in many cases, extension services. These entities were often supported by donor institutions, including international financial institutions. The performance of these entities has generally not been effective, which reflects an overreach in activism in light of governance deficiencies. Nonperforming loans and little, if any, additionality effect—that is, loans accruing to borrowers that have access to commercial bank credit—undermined the financial performance and economic impact of these entities. Governance challenges, including political interference in the credit allocation process, politically motivated debt forgiveness, corruption, and even incompetence, further damaged the sustainability and efficiency of these entities.

In response to the negative experience with government-managed or government-sponsored agricultural banks, donors and governments have moved away from retail lending in agriculture. The challenge of financial service provision to agriculture and to rural areas continues to exist, however, and it is here that the promise of modernism has not been realized. The good news is that, in recent decades, new products and delivery channels have been developed, new players have entered the market, and new partnerships have emerged. As in the general effort to expand access, there is no silver bullet for the problem of access to finance in rural areas; there will be many small solutions that help push rural finance to the frontier and move the frontier outward. In the following, we discuss some of these innovations and link them to the general theme of this chapter.

Value chains: utilizing existing relationships to expand formal finance

One promising way to overcome the limitations imposed by information asymmetries and the lack of collateral is to use value chains as entry points for financial institutions. Value chain finance, or buyer and supplier finance, is important throughout the economy, but especially in agricultural finance, given the predetermined time periods between sowing and harvesting (box 3.6). Financial relationships related to the value chain are most effective if the value chain is clearly defined, such as the value chain between input providers and farmers or between farmers and wholesalers. Well-structured value chains allow an opening for value

Box 3.6   Examples of Value Chain Finance

Perhaps one of the best examples of short-term trade credit for agricultural producers is the cocoa value chain in Ghana. Cocoa is a huge industry in Ghana, and the purchase of the output from producers is dominated by a market of private sector companies (licensed buying companies or LBCs) with licenses to sell to the state-owned marketing monopoly.

LBCs routinely provide significant amounts of short-term credit to producers for the purchase of the required inputs (for example, fertilizer and pesticides) before the growing season. In return, the cocoa growers commit to selling the resultant cocoa harvest to the LBCs at an agreed price. The capital and interest are repaid to the LBCs through the proceeds of the sale, and the balance goes to the farmer.

Similarly, credit can also be provided by the input supplier. In another example from Ghana, one of the country's largest suppliers of fertilizer and other agricultural inputs furnishes supplies on credit to members of a major cocoa growers association, with repayment due following the harvest.

A bank in Ghana had a large local supermarket as a customer. The supermarket was keen to expand its sales of horticultural produce from local producer groups, but the supply of the produce was unreliable and limited. It wanted to improve the supply chain by making formal arrangements with producer associations to provide an agreed quantity and quality of produce for an agreed price in return for helping to prefinance the horticultural production. Rather than relying on its own balance sheet, it approached the bank with a view to helping with a credit line of its own.

In Mozambique, small farmers have established self-managed outgrower schemes with the assistance of the international program of the Cooperative League of the United States of America. The program established a two-tier structure of producer organizations and their regional associations. The producer organizations serve as the intermediary between the individual farmer and the agribusinesses and other processors that provide short-term production credit and purchase the output. The producer organizations provide extension services to help the farmers improve their methods and the quality of the produce; they also provide storage and transport facilities. While outgrower schemes are well established, particularly in the cotton and tobacco sectors, more loosely organized marketing arrangements are prevalent in the cashew, groundnut, sesame, sunflower, and maize sectors. At the end of 2002, the program had established over 840 producer organizations involving approximately 26,000 farmers. Repayment had reached 96 percent. The program has since been handed over to OLIPA, a local NGO.

Source: GIZ (2010).

chain financing, whereby smallholders can leverage the reputation and collateral of large input providers or large clients for their products.

By using their balance sheets to strengthen existing value chain finance arrangements or to help arrange new ones and contribute their expertise and resources, the financing of a value chain can constitute an important entry point for banks into agricultural finance (box 3.6). DFIs can play a key role by providing platforms for the value chains and bringing together other actors.

Value chain finance can have important benefits for a bank. First, the intermediary firm—be it the buyer of the produce or the seller of the input—has close links with producers at the grassroots, which allows the bank to overcome the constraints of scale and asymmetric information. Second, the intermediary firms are more well placed to make sure that the finance is spent by the borrowers on productive inputs rather than diverted to activities that may not guarantee repayment. The buyer and supplier financing arrangements rely on stable and professional relationships between producers and intermediary firms. To some extent, it is beneficial if the intermediary firms are in a position of power on the market relative to the producer, and the implications of a breach of loan covenants by the producer in terms of subsequent difficulty in sourcing alternative suppliers or buyers, such as side-selling, are therefore clear. This sort of sanction is usually more obvious to producers than the more ambiguous threats of legal actions by banks in costly and ineffective legal systems.

The challenge for the financial institution is to agree on an appropriate credit line and terms and conditions in line with the market risk profile and competitive conditions. It needs to develop a simple and streamlined credit process for the intermediary firm, ideally with a basic application form that the intermediary can use to score the proposed customer in keeping with the agreed credit policy. One of the simplest mechanisms is to mandate that producers receive the payments for their produce in a dedicated account held with the bank (which is particularly easy in the case of supplier finance) from which repayments can be automatically deducted. This also represents a cross-sell opportunity for the bank and a way of increasing the formality of producer financial activity. However, it might also be useful to link a rural-based cooperative or a microbank into the relationship. A major factor of differentiation among value chains is the presence of a strong agribusiness player at some point in the value chain. This increases the overall credit standing of the chain and its participants from the viewpoint of the financial institution. Credit enhancement can also take place through credit guarantees, a topic that is treated more generally in chapter 4.

Looking for collateral

One major problem facing lenders in rural areas is the lack of collateralizable assets. Land can often not be used as collateral, given the dominance of traditional land law or the impossibility of reselling land in a tight-knit community. In several countries, land cannot be owned by foreigners, which makes the use of land as collateral problematic for foreign-owned banks. Secure property rights, however, are also important for other transactions such as the rental or sale of land. Reforms in this area encompass a large number of actions, ranging from legal, sometimes constitutional changes to the establishment of land registries and enforcement mechanisms. One has to be realistic about the outcomes of such actions, however. Traditional land customs and cultural trends will make the application of modern land law infeasible in many rural areas of Africa. This is one of the best examples of modernism reaching its limits.

An alternative used with increasing success is warehouse receipts for crops. Under this arrangement, commoditized produce (for example, wheat, coffee, cocoa, or maize) is deposited in a warehouse by the owner, and a receipt is issued that stipulates the quantity, quality, and type of produce deposited. The warehouse receipt would generally be negotiable, meaning ownership is transferable, which makes it quite suitable for collateral purposes. Financial institutions have therefore been willing to extend loans against this security in the appropriate environment. From a financial perspective, the product is a simple one, but it does require some fundamentals to be established. It is essential that good physical warehousing facilities are available so that all parties to the transaction can be confident that the produce is well protected and secure. There must also be high levels of trust among the players, particularly the assurance that the warehouse operator will not release the produce to any party other than the owner (that is, against the presentation of the warehouse receipt). The inspection and grading services must also be reliable to ensure that the produce is of the precise type, quantity, and quality stipulated. The legal environment must be supportive of the bank's right to realize security quickly and unilaterally in the event of default, usually by selling the warehouse receipt to a third party, and, thus, there must also be a vibrant secondary market for warehouse receipts. There is nothing particularly complex about these components, but they must all work together in a fairly flawless way.

Warehouse receipts tend to be a slightly awkward product for small producers. They rarely have the volume of produce that makes such an operation cost-effective. However, they are suitable for higher levels of aggregation, such as agricultural cooperatives. They are also only suitable for certain types of produce, that is, produce that is highly commoditized and can therefore be reliably and consistently graded, for which there is a clear and open market price, and that is not highly perishable. Warehouse receipts are especially useful for short-term finance. For similar reasons of market volatility, banks will typically only extend a relatively modest proportion of the market value of a warehouse receipt.

Assets such as equipment and machinery can also be financed through leasing, which can help free up working capital over the medium term. These arrangements usually work best when a bank acts closely with a supplier of agricultural machinery and equipment. They usually also work best with assets that enjoy a vibrant secondary sales market. The legal environment has to be appropriate because the bank must be able to seize and realize collateral easily and quickly in the event of default. One of the reasons for the popularity of leases in developed markets has usually been the favorable tax treatment and the potential to treat them as off–balance sheet items for accounting purposes. Leasing and other asset finance solutions have huge potential for African agribusiness and for other parts of the economy, as we discuss elsewhere below under the heading of SME finance. It remains to be seen how much value these solutions will offer directly to the smallest producers, but, given the right circumstances, they certainly have potential.

Looking beyond smallholders and credit

Our focus so far has been on the extension of credit to agricultural and other activities in rural areas, mostly short term. As in other sectors, however, there is also a lack of equity finance in rural areas. Few agribusinesses are sufficiently large to list on a stock exchange or issue debt instruments; private equity thus seems more promising. We return to the theme of private equity providers in the next chapter in discussing the challenge of more long-term finance for African economies, but private equity seems even more difficult in agribusiness than in other sectors. First, agriculture is much more heterogeneous than other sectors in terms of products and markets, meaning that it is more costly for private equity funds to undertake market research and specialize. Second, information asymmetries are typically larger in agriculture, and monitoring is made more difficult because of the distances. Third, as much as in other sectors, there is often a lack of exit options for private equity financiers.

Looking to other financial services and beyond finance

While the emphasis of policy makers was for a long time on agricultural credit, the debate has more recently broadened from agriculture to rural areas generally, given that the incomes of a large share of the population in rural areas does not depend exclusively on agriculture. The debate has also broadened from credit to financial services more generally, given the financial needs of the rural population (and the urban population); one has to consider the entire array of products, from short-term trade credit to long-term investment credit, but also beyond credit to savings and payment products, as well as insurance services.

Technology can be especially useful in rural areas. However, one has to be realistic in terms of which technology is the most cost-effective, given the higher costs of financial service provision mentioned above. One case in point is the Dowa Emergency Cash Transfer Program (2006–07) of Opportunity International Bank of Malawi. The bank set out with the objective of helping the poor in remote, drought-stricken parts of the Dowa District to purchase food. To enable the related cash transfers, the bank employed off-line smart cards developed by Net1 Aplitec. The system was supposed to match funds deposited at the bank with the identity of each approved recipient established by the smart card at enrolment. To deliver the cash payments, 11 paypoints were introduced that were serviced by a van equipped with ATMs to read smart cards and with fingerprint readers to authenticate each recipient biometrically before payment. The project increased the outreach of financial services in Dowa: 45 percent of the recipients were still using their bank accounts in 2009 (Pickens, Porteous, and Rotman 2009). And yet, during the project, 80 percent of the funds were used to purchase food, indicating that the poorest had a rather low need for transactions outside the government-to-person payments.[14] Despite being effective, the smart card technology was expensive, taking up 23 percent of the overall cash that was put into the project, but that was supposed to reach the poor. Furthermore, because the technology was expensive and proprietary, the project could not be scaled up. Pearson and Kilfoil (2007) conclude that the smart card could have been replaced by a substantially cheaper technology: magnetic stripe cards.

Index-based weather insurance is a relatively new product that allows smallholder farmers to hedge against risks stemming from natural disasters, such as drought or flood. The policy pays out only if a publicly observable index, such as rainfall, passes a certain threshold. Such an instrument allows insurance to be provided against one of the most important sources of volatility and risk for agricultural producers. The principal advantage relative to traditional insurance policies is that individual insurance cases do not have to be followed up by the insurance company. The challenge, meanwhile, is to identify an index that is closely related to the actual variation for the individual producer and to have sufficient time series available to compute appropriate thresholds for insurance payout and actuarially fair premiums.

Recent experience with the introduction of such a product in Malawi offers valuable insights (Giné and Yang 2009). First, the marketing of index insurance is critical for the take-up of such a product. Teaching smallholder farmers the advantages of such a product and the payout structure is important; designing the product in a way that pays out relatively often in the first few years can increase acceptance. Linking such a product to credit provision can constitute a win-win proposal for borrowers and lenders, though borrowers might be reluctant to pay extra given the limited liability of many agricultural loans.

Another useful innovation is the application of radio frequency identification technology to monitor the movement of livestock so as to ensure there are no fraudulent insurance claims. This reduces the premium cost and also increases access to finance by the livestock owners.

It is important to look beyond the financing constraints for agricultural producers. While the observation of a lack of finance has often led to the conclusion that limited access to finance is the binding constraint on agriculture, this may not be the case. First, there may be serious demand-side constraints in the form of missing bankable projects. Second, agriculture faces an array of constraints, including the transportation problems associated with bringing produce to market. As much as in other sectors, business development services are important in agriculture.

Institutions for rural finance

There is an increasing variety of players in rural finance in Africa. While microfinance has been traditionally limited to urban areas, more and more donor-financed and donor-supported institutions are pushing out toward rural areas, partly because the urban MFI market is maturing. One challenge faced by MFIs catering to clients with income streams dominated by agriculture is the high risk and seasonal volatility of revenues. The solution requires lending based on anticipated crop production rather than current cash flows. It also involves longer loan periods and bullet payments rather than regular, frequent repayments. Risks related to price volatility and natural disasters have to be taken into account by the lender and priced appropriately. One important set of institutions in rural finance are community-based institutions, especially in connection with banks.

With the new approach to rural finance, the role of government has changed from direct lending through DFIs or agricultural loan quotas imposed on commercial banks to a more policy-oriented wholesale function. By the 1990s, it had become clear that most of the activist market-replacing approaches, such as interest rate caps, direct lending by government-owned institutions, lending quotas for private institutions, and credit forgiveness, were not working. However, reliance on market forces alone has not proven successful either. Some governments responded by establishing dedicated institutions with different mandates combining agricultural extension services and financial services. In Malawi, the government went further and established a plethora of government institutions and programs (box 3.7, on the next page).

In summary, the analysis of financial service provision in rural and agricultural finance is consistent with other themes and messages in this book. As in the case of SMEs in other sectors, there is a dearth of equity and new institutional forms to fill this gap. Rural finance in general and agricultural finance more specifically need a variety of different institutions for different services. The analysis of rural finance also underlines that we need an increased focus on services and users that looks beyond institutions providing credit, as well as on the needs of users in rural areas, whose livelihoods may not be linked to agriculture, but who, in any case, require an array of financial services.

Our analysis of agricultural finance emphasizes that one size does not fit all. Different countries specialize in different crops, mostly because of climate factors, and, for historical reasons or because of the crops, have different organizational structures in agriculture (that is, microfarms, smallholders, and agribusinesses) and in rural financial institutions. Different forms of financing and innovations in finance are therefore appropriate for different countries.

SME Finance: Continuing Challenges

It is by providing financial services to firms with good growth opportunities that the financial sector has its main impact on African economies, helping them to grow and converge to the high-income levels of advanced economies. However, it is not so much the overall level of credit, but, rather, the allocation of credit to the most creditworthy that matters. Firms look toward banks and other financial institutions for an array of financial services, including payment, deposit, and insurance services. However, it is through the external financing function that financial institutions and markets play their most important role.

Box 3.7 Malawi: Development Finance Institutions

The Malawi Rural Finance Corporation (MRFC) was established in 1993 following the collapse of the Small Holder Agriculture Credit Administration. MRFC began operations in October 1994 using the former rural extension service offices of the Ministry of Agriculture and Irrigation that had belonged to the Small Holder Agriculture Credit Administration. The Malawi Savings Bank was incorporated in 1994 as a successor to the financial services arm of the Malawi Post Corporation, then known as the Malawi Post Office Savings Bank, which was established in 1911 to mobilize rural savings. Other government programs include the Malawi Rural Development Fund, which was established in January 2005 to increase access to finance among low-income groups in rural communities; the Small Enterprise Development Organization of Malawi, which has been focusing on a crop marketing loan scheme and a group lending facility; and the Development of Malawi Enterprises Trust, which was established in 1979 and focuses on business advisory services but also provides limited loan services for small enterprises.

Some programs achieved a modest measure of success. For a long time, government ownership of the Malawi Postal Services savings accounts increased public trust in the banking system, leading to more savings and a deeper rural financial market. MRFC had 200,000 loan customers in 2002 and an estimated 293,600 in 2003, making it one of the largest lenders to smallholder farmers in Sub-Saharan Africa. Today, it has 120 field offices, 20 supervisory offices, 6 branches, and the head office. Malawi Savings Bank currently has a network of five branches and 35 agencies. All its branches have dial-up internet connectivity, an improvement over their previous manual processes. Its deposit base grew from MK 1.8 billion in 2005 to MK 3.8 billion in 2007. With a minimum account opening requirement of only MK 500, it is able to attract deposits at the lower end of the market.

Overall, however, the performance of government-owned financial institutions and programs has not been stellar. By 2004, the loan portfolio of Malawi Savings Bank (around US$1 million) was heavily concentrated in a few companies (42 percent was lent to one borrower). Although performance has improved more recently, the bank is not maximizing its full potential. At the MRFC, collection on loans fell from 90 percent in 2004 to 80 percent in 2005 and 74 percent in 2006. MRFC's income has also been impacted by the fall in Treasury bill rates and competition in the SME lending market from the National Bank and the National Building Society. Furthermore, because MRFC does not have a banking license and is not part of the payments system, its operations are restricted, and it cannot engage in regular revenue generating financial intermediation activities. MRFC also has problems in managing information flows within its network.

The size gap

One striking characteristic of financial underdevelopment is the limited access of firms to external funding, be it debt or equity. While most firms—even in Africa and even the small ones—have access to deposit services and thus payment services through banks, the picture on the credit side is different. Moreover, alternatives to banking credit are few and far between. Few firms are listed, and, among those that are, even fewer have used the possibility to issue corporate bonds. This reduces the

Figure 3.9   The Size Gap in Corporate Finance and in Deposit Services

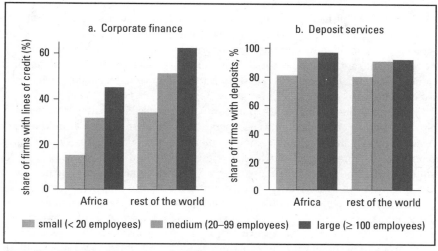

Source: Enterprise Surveys (database), International Finance Corporation, World Bank, Washington, DC, http://www.enterprisesurveys.org/ (accessed in 2010).
Note: Sample size: 90 countries.

financing choices of firms to retained earnings, funds from family and friends, and supplier credit. Cross-country comparisons have, in addition, shown that there is a size gap in corporate finance: small firms have more difficulty accessing external finance than medium-size firms, which, in turn, have a more difficult time accessing external finance than large firms. This size gap in corporate finance is greater in financially less well developed countries. Not surprisingly, therefore, this size gap is larger in African countries than in other developing countries, while the size gap in deposit services is about the same in Africa as in non-African developing countries (figure 3.9). The other striking observation is that, across all firm size groups, the average use of deposit services is as great or even greater in Africa, while access to credit is significantly less in Africa. We find a similar variation across firms of different ages: firms that have been established more recently receive significantly less external finance than older firms (also reflecting a survivor bias). Across all firm age-groups, however, African firms are less likely to have a loan or credit.

The financing of SMEs continues to pose significant challenges not only for African financial systems. It is important, however, to distinguish among the small enterprises that have different financing needs and different profiles. A large share of the enterprises in Africa consists of informal microenterprises that have been established because of a lack of alternative economic opportunities. Because these firms are not able to produce formal financial accounts or formal guarantees, it is hard to see this segment of the enterprise population becoming bankable over the medium to long term, at least not for credit services. They seem a natural target group for microcredit institutions and rely more heavily than other enterprises on informal finance providers. A second segment consists of medium-size enterprises that are well established and, often, export oriented. In most cases, they have access to bank finance, but struggle to gain access to equity finance, including through financial markets. Finally, there are small formal enterprises, some of which may possess significant growth potential. These firms—often referred to as the missing middle—are usually too big to use MFIs, but not sufficiently formal or well established to use banks.

The International Finance Corporation–World Bank Enterprise Surveys (used also in chapter 2) provide additional insights into the financing structure of enterprises of various sizes and the constraints enterprises face.[15] Small firms consistently report greater financing obstacles relative to medium and large enterprises, as do younger firms throughout the developing world. The limited access of firms to external finance can be explained by constraints on both the supply side and the demand side. Banks typically impose high collateral and documentation requirements, citing information barriers and deficiencies in the contractual framework, as well as poor applicant capacity in preparing clear business plans. There is a tendency toward cash and personal guarantees because land and machinery are more costly to use as collateral given the deficiencies in the legal system, collateral registries, and the court system. Audited financial statements are a sine qua non for most banks, though they are not a sufficient condition for banks to grant credit. Finally, there is a tendency toward short-term credit for working capital rather than medium- to long-term credit for fixed asset purchases, as documented in chapter 2.

Most small firms and even many medium-size firms face significant hurdles in complying with bank requirements in collateral and documentation. Moreover, the related opportunity costs may be substantial given the high cost of finance and the other costs of formality that the business environment imposes. Accordingly, it is not surprising that banks often explain their high liquidity with reference to the lack of bankable projects, while firms complain about the lack of financing for investment projects. Policy has to address the market frictions that drive this spread between supply and demand.

An important area in this context is accounting and auditing standards. Most African countries have weak accountancy professions, partly because of the weak education and training programs in accountancy and auditing practices and partly because of the weak oversight institutions. This calls for capacity building and development, but also for assistance with institution building. Beyond these important issues, however, is the question of whether standard accounting rules are too much of a burden or even necessary for SMEs. There seems to be a need for the development and implementation of simplified accounting standards for microenterprises and for SMEs. This still leaves open the issue of the acceptance of proper financial reporting and the costs this involves among enterprises. Only if enterprises see the benefit of increased access and the lower cost of external finance will they be willing to incur these costs. Financial literacy and business development services can help to a certain extent in this area.

Bank finance: relationship versus transaction lending

In the absence of a functioning contractual and informational framework, banks have found alternative mechanisms to manage credit risk and ensure repayment. Where no credit registries exist, information about existing borrowers is exchanged informally among bank executives, which is only feasible in small and concentrated banking systems based on old boy networks that, in turn, strengthen the oligopolistic nature of the systems. Especially in the case of smaller enterprises, there is a tendency toward relationship lending (Berger and Udell 1996). Long relationships between a financial institution or even a specific loan officer and the borrower allow problems of information asymmetry and, thus, risk to be overcome. Relationship-based lending, however, might be more costly, moving the equilibrium away from the access possibilities frontier discussed above. Recently, the more nuanced view has been put forward that large banks and foreign banks, relative to other institutions, can have a comparative advantage at financing SMEs through arm's-length lending technologies, such as asset-based lending, factoring, leasing, credit scoring, and centralized organizational structures (see Berger and Udell 2006; de la Torre, Martínez Pería, and Schmukler 2010).

The debate on relationship-based versus transaction-based lending techniques also has implications that affect whether institutions can cater cost effectively to SMEs. Relationship lending might be more readily done by small, community-based financial institutions, while transaction-based lending is more cost effectively done by large financial institutions that can exploit the necessary scale economies implied by investment in technology. In many developing countries, this debate has an additional dimension because smaller banks are often owned by domestic shareholders, while large financial institutions are often foreign owned. Using data for 91 banks across 45 countries, Beck, Demirgüç-Kunt, and Martínez Pería (2011) find that foreign banks are more likely to use transaction-based lending techniques and more centralized business models relative to domestic banks. However, they also show that foreign banks do not tend to lend less to SMEs relative to other banks. It thus seems that both relationship-based and transaction-based lending techniques are appropriate for SME lending and that domestic and foreign-owned banks can cater to SMEs.[16]

Expanding into the SME segment often requires a new approach and attitude as a bank in Nigeria demonstrates (World Bank 2010b). After bringing in international expertise, the bank launched new products targeted specifically at SMEs. It scrapped its Commission on Turnover, which effectively penalized customers for growing their deposit accounts. It began charging its SME customers a tiered fixed rate for banking (capped at ₦6,000 per month), which quickly resulted in the rapid growth of the bank's SME loans. The bank then introduced a peripatetic system of quarterly seminars where SMEs gathered to hear various success stories and gain valuable information and expertise from SME bankers and other business leaders. The bank introduced an entrepreneur's guidebook and launched a business club where SMEs could network and develop valuable business relationships. In Egypt, meanwhile, Banque Misr has targeted the SME segment by allowing lending to SMEs to be conducted in a completely different way relative to corporate lending. This included hiring young graduates as loan officers without the preconceptions of experienced loan officers in terms of risk assessment. Taking a page from microfinance, Banque Misr introduced step-up loans, allowing SMEs to take out increasingly larger loans upon the full repayment of previous loans (Napier 2011).

Beyond an increasing focus on transaction lending as opposed to relationship lending, there have been other innovations in SME financing. Several regional banks, including Absa and Standard Bank, have started using psychometric assessments as a viable low-cost, automated screening tool to identify high-potential entrepreneurs and evaluate risk and future potential; these have proven successful in initial pilot tests.

Looking beyond bank finance

Leasing can be a prominent instrument for SME financing. Leasing is a contractual arrangement whereby one party (the lessee) can use, for a defined period of time, an asset owned by a second party (the lessor) in exchange for periodic payments. Several arguments may be put forward to explain why supporting the leasing industry is important for Africa. First, collateral requirements have been well documented as one of the main impediments that prevent African SMEs from accessing the traditional forms of financing needed to acquire machinery and equipment. Leasing is backed by cash flows from assets, and its applications are often assessed based on a project's capacity to service lease payments. Accordingly, businesses and entrepreneurs that are denied traditional banking and commercial credit because of their lack of credit histories and inability to provide sufficient guarantees can find a new financing alternative in the leasing market. This could also bring more businesses into the formal sector (IFC 2009). Second, leasing allows businesses to avoid tying down resources, which should reduce pressure on their financials and free resources for other purposes. It also translates into lower barriers against starting a business or upgrading existing facilities, which should promote entrepreneurship and the acquisition of new technologies. New equipment is likely to reduce maintenance costs and increase productivity. Additionally, unlike bank credit, leasing directly provides the asset, instead of the financial resources needed to acquire the asset, which reduces the possibility of diverting funds from the intended purpose. Leasing contracts involve less paperwork and more relaxed credit requirements as well, which lead to shorter waiting periods relative to bank loans. According to a review of the leasing sector in Tunisia, funding could be offered in periods as short as 24 hours (MAC SA 2010). Reduced waiting times allow companies to respond quickly to business needs without having to lose important transactions.

Despite these advantages, the African leasing market is still in its infancy, representing a tiny 1 percent share of the world leasing volume (White 2009). Where they exist, most leasing markets in Africa are small and underdeveloped; annual leasing volumes do not exceed US$500 million. Even in larger African markets, such as Egypt, Morocco, Nigeria, South Africa, and Tunisia, which exceed this threshold, penetration rates—measured as the ratio of the annual leasing volume to GDP—are below 2 percent, compared with ratios above 3 percent in many markets in Central and Eastern Europe (White 2009).

Most leases are finance leases, reflecting the limited development of the leasing market in Africa, given that operating leases usually develop at a later stage relative to finance leases. Another feature of African leasing markets is the dominance of banks and bank-related operators. In Ghana, bank lessors sourced more than 75 percent of the new leases in 2007 and held 65 percent of the market share, while five of the six leasing companies operating in Morocco are backed by banks (Naouar 2009; APSF 2010). In Tunisia, of the 10 leasing companies, the major shareholders of 8 are banks (MAC SA 2010). Such ownership structures could potentially threaten the potential of leasing to service SMEs; experience shows that banks offering leasing through internal units tend to target large-ticket, low-risk clients (IFC 2009). The African leasing market also continues to be centered on the provision of financing for vehicles. In Rwanda, vehicle financing represented 65 percent of total leasing activity (IFC 2007). Similarly, in 2009, vehicle financing accounted for 46 percent of lease financing in Morocco (APSF 2010), while the Equipment Leasing Association of Nigeria recently disclosed that commercial vehicle leasing represents the bulk of leasing business in Nigeria. This is driven to a large extent by the availability of a thriving secondary market for such products. The sectoral distribution of leasing activities also reflects the structure of local economies. For instance, in 2009, oil and gas captured more than 45 percent of the lease transactions in Nigeria, while construction and transformative industries received 48 percent of the lease financing in Morocco.

Leasing thus has large potential, but there are important regulatory impediments. There are taxation issues concerning sales or value added taxes and the deductibility of asset-related depreciation costs. Inefficient repossession systems also limit the leasing activities in a number of countries. This includes lengthy court procedures for asset repossession, the absence of implementation bodies, and a lack of capacity in the juridical system. The average length of time taken by the courts to issue repossession orders in Egypt in 2005 has been estimated at around one month (Nasr 2008). As noted by Al-Sugheyer and Sultanov (2010), the requirement to register the leasing contract, not the leased asset, in countries such as Egypt adds no benefit and may prevent leasing companies from entering the market if the incurred cost is prohibitively high. The lack of capacity in the juridical system to handle commercial cases was also identified as a challenge for the leasing sector in Rwanda (IFC 2007). Similarly, in Kenya, once two-thirds of the price has been paid by the lessee, the lessor has no right of repossession (Kapchanga 2010).

The scarcity of funding is an additional challenge that leasing companies need to address in Africa. Leasing companies depend on external funding from donors and wholesale borrowing to fund their operations. Funding availability and cost could prevent them from competing with banks and threaten their financial viability. This may explain why the leasing market is still dominated by banks.

Similarly, factoring—the discounting of sales receivable—is attractive for small suppliers of large creditworthy buyers because it does not rely on information about the borrower, but rather on the obligor (Klapper 2006). Under a factoring contract, the factor purchases the seller's accounts receivable, with or without recourse, and assumes the responsibility to collect repayments. Originally limited to domestic contracts, international factoring has become popular because it eases the credit and collection burden of international sales on exporters. Several African middle-income countries have factoring industries, though these are focused on domestic rather than international factoring. Like leasing companies, factoring companies can only function within a legal framework governing these transactions, but rely to a lesser extent on the contractual framework of a country so that they can help push a financial system toward the frontier of SME lending, even if this frontier is too low. Development finance institutions can have an important role in jump-starting this industry, as shown by an example from Mexico, described in Box 3.8.

A key constraint on bank finance is the lack of equity in enterprises. Significant leverage can prevent enterprises from pursuing more debt so that a lack of equity rather than a lack of debt is the binding constraint. At a more general level, equity can be a potentially beneficial financing source for enterprises in their early years and for enterprises with a profile of high risk. Yet, there are few, if any, instruments and vehicles for equity finance available in most African countries, as we discuss in more depth in chapter 4.

Increasingly, equity funds that specialize in SMEs are appearing across Africa. Business Partners International Kenya SME Fund is a private fixed-life fund established in 2006 that invests in the equity, quasi-equity, and debt of Kenyan SMEs and has been successful in ultimately attracting external financing from donors and private sources. Several Aureos Capital Funds focusing on East, West, and South Africa have also been set up with support from donors.

Demand-side constraints

While supply constraints are important in the access of SMEs to finance, the demand-side constraints should not be underestimated. Table 3.5 presents data from the Enterprise Surveys to explore the various categories of banked and unbanked enterprises in Africa and in non-African developing countries. A first remarkable result is the small number of African enterprises that have taken out loans. Perhaps even more striking is the fact that only 23 percent of the African enterprises without loans have applied for a loan, compared with 40 percent in non-

Box 3.8   NAFIN's Productive Chains

Nacional Financiera (NAFIN) is a Mexican development bank created in 1934 to provide commercial financing. NAFIN is mostly a second-tier bank, lending 90 percent of its portfolio to banks. In 2001, NAFIN launched an online system, *cadenas productivas* (productive chains), to provide reverse factoring services to SMEs. NAFIN's online system is important because small businesses, lacking access to bank credit, frequently face difficulty financing the production cycle, and most buyers usually take between 30 and 90 days to pay their accounts payable. NAFIN's online system helped breach the 60-day liquidity gap. NAFIN's factoring program has been successful, extending over US$9 billion in financing since its inception in September 2001 and brokering more than 1.2 million transactions, 98 percent by SMEs.

Once a supplier delivers goods to the buyer and issues an invoice, the buyer posts an online negotiable document equal to the amount that will be factored on its NAFIN Web page. Participant financial institutions that are willing to factor this particular receivable post their interest rate quotes for the transaction. The supplier can then access this information and choose the best quote. Once the factor is chosen, the discounted amount is transferred to the supplier's bank account. The factor is paid directly by the buyer when the invoice is due.

NAFIN developed, produced, and marketed the electronic platform. To participate, all financial institutions must use NAFIN's second-tier funding to provide credit through the system. For this service, NAFIN does not charge a fee; instead, it covers its costs using the interest it charges on its loans.

To reduce information problems, in the NAFIN case, it is the buyer who posts the accounts payable on the online system (reverse factoring), thus reducing risk. The financial institutions (factor) only need to assess the creditworthiness of the buyer, which is frequently a large firm. Hence, it is the buyers who invite suppliers to join their chains and the online system. This reduces principal-agent problems by effectively outsourcing screening to the buyers, who have an informational advantage relative to financial intermediaries. All transactions are carried out on the electronic platform, reducing transaction costs, increasing speed, and improving security. The online system also increases transparency because all banks can access historical information on the performance of suppliers, which helps them establish a credit history.

NAFIN's experience suggests that, to foster competition through this type of intervention, it is necessary to facilitate the participation of all financial intermediaries and avoid giving preferential access or other advantages to larger banks or public institutions. Furthermore, a significant advantage of factoring, especially in developing countries, is that it does not require good collateral laws, but only the legal ability to sell or assign accounts receivable.

NAFIN's initial participation has been important as it helped foster innovation. If a private financial institution would have invested in a like online system, it would have had little incentive to let other financial institutions participate and thus compete. The initial investment in the development of a large retail sales staff and promotional resources to reach firms and establish the productive chains has been central.

Source: de la Torre, Gozzi, and Schmukler (2008).

Table 3.5 Enterprise Credit Demand: Comparing Africa with Non-African Developing Countries

Area	Do you have a loan?	
	Yes	No
Africa	22.44	77.56
Rest of the world	47.59	52.41
		⇓

Area	Did you apply for a loan?	
	Yes	No
Africa	22.82	77.18
Rest of the world	40.01	59.99
		⇓

Reason	Why didn't you apply?	
	Africa	Rest of the world
No need for a loan	40.80	64.44
Application procedures are complex	17.96	6.51
Interest rates are not favorable	16.74	12.48
Collateral requirements are too high	9.55	5.18
Size of loan or maturity are insufficient	2.25	1.68
Informal payments needed to obtain bank loan	5.69	1.75
Did not think loan would be approved	6.92	6.42
Other	0.10	1.54

Source: Enterprise Surveys (database), International Finance Corporation, World Bank, Washington, DC, http://www.enterprisesurveys.org/ (accessed in 2010).

African developing countries. The reasons given for not applying also show interesting differences. The share of enterprises that cite the lack of demand is significantly lower in Africa (41 percent) than in non-African developing countries (64 percent), suggesting that lack of demand is less of a problem in Africa than elsewhere. There are two interpretations of the high interest rates (17 percent in Africa versus 12 percent in non-African developing countries) as a reason for not applying. On the one hand, the return on investment in projects may be too low. On the other hand and more in line with the high interest rate spreads noted in chapter 2, the cost of credit may impede the use of bank finance. Even more striking as a reason for not applying is the difference in application procedures. Among nonapplicant enterprises, 18 percent in Africa cite this as a reason for not applying, compared with 6.5 percent in non-African developing countries. Collateral requirements also seem more of an impediment in Africa than in other regions of the developing world (9.5 versus 5 percent), as does the need for bribes (5.7 versus 1.8 percent).

It is important to stress that financing is only one of the many obstacles that African enterprises face in their operation and growth. As indicated in figure 3.10,

Figure 3.10 Business Obstacles in Africa and Elsewhere

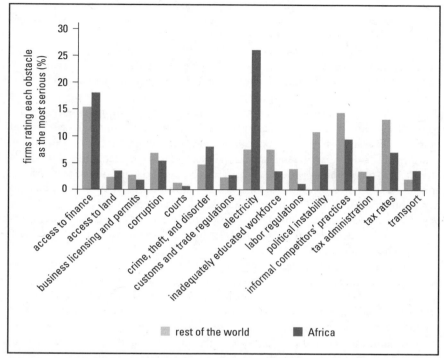

Source: Enterprise Surveys (database), International Finance Corporation, World Bank, Washington, DC, http://www.enterprisesurveys.org/ (accessed in 2010).
Note: Sample size: 90 countries.

African firms report greater obstacles than firms outside Africa in financing, but also in access to land, customs and trade regulations, transport, and, most strikingly, electricity. This points to the deteriorated physical infrastructure that African enterprises have to deal with, as well as the deficiencies in the broader regulatory environment.

Conclusions

The access landscape and the agenda are diverse in Africa. Relative to a few years ago, we have a much better picture about the demand and supply of formal and informal financial services across Africa. Having better data also allows us to benchmark countries and to formulate targets for policy. The framework of the access possibilities frontier allows us to disentangle the challenges in the expansion of outreach. Specifically, we have distinguished among (1) constraints that prevent the financial system from reaching the maximum commercially viable outreach and (2) demand-side constraints that depress the effective demand for financial services and the possibilities for pushing out the frontier, which is too low, through (3) technology and (4) government policies.

The analysis of these challenges and the possible solutions leads us directly to the three main messages of the book. First, allowing competition within banking systems and from outside banking systems will foster the necessary financial innovation to push the financial system toward the frontier and exploit the opportunities that new methodologies, products, and technologies offer. An increased focus on competition, however, has critical repercussions on regulation and government policy in general. Fostering competition implies a more open regulatory mind-set. This might require reversing the usual timeline of legislation-regulation-innovation among new players and products and adapting a more try-and-see or test-and-see approach, as applied by regulators in Kenya with respect to M-Pesa. It also means expanding traditional infrastructure, such as credit registries and payment systems, beyond banks. However, it might also imply a more activist, hands-on government approach to force financial institutions to share infrastructure, such as payment systems and credit registries.

Fostering competition and openness toward new services and products is directly related to the second main message: focusing on services rather than existing institutions and markets. A focus on expanding the provision of payment, savings, and other financial services to previously unbanked segments of the population might mean looking beyond existing institutions, products, and delivery channels, such as banks, traditional checking accounts, and brick-and-mortar branches. It might also mean a new approach to inclusion by moving away from the credit-led approach toward a savings- or transaction-led approach.

Our third message—focusing as much on demand constraints as on supply constraints—refers mainly to financial literacy programs for households and enterprises and the need to address nonfinancial constraints, especially among small enterprises and in rural areas.

The options for expanding the access to financial services and the opportunities for governments to implement policies to enhance access vary across country groups, as we see throughout the chapter. Competition is more difficult to achieve in small financial systems, be they small because of low-income status or because of small country size. Yet, dominance of the mobile phone market is more likely in small economies, so that it might be easier for a new provider to achieve the necessary scale. In small financial systems, it is more important to allow for competition from all possible providers. There is a premium in these economies on increasing competition through crossborder providers. In countries with high shares of government ownership in financial systems, such as in North Africa, a stronger role for the private sector can be helpful. There seems to be little relationship between country size and the extent to which governments and donors can address demand-side constraints. However, sophistication might vary. In middle-income countries such as South Africa or the countries in North Africa, the focus is on the various options, while, in low-income countries across most of Sub-Saharan Africa, the focus is on the use of financial services in general. This is certainly an area where one size does not fit all.

Technology can be a game changer throughout the continent, but its impact is larger in some countries than in others. It is especially important in countries with disperse populations so that traditional delivery channels are more costly than elsewhere. It can also be more important in countries at lower levels of financial and economic development so that it can help financial systems leapfrog.

Notes

1. Typically, individuals are likely to give more accurate responses on their expenditure patterns than on their incomes.

2. For the following, see Beck and de la Torre (2007) for a more in-depth discussion.

3. We can derive a similar curve for credit services, though with the complication that the price, that is, the interest rate, is endogenous. Rather than focusing on the overall population of potential borrowers, we therefore have to focus on the universe of loan applicants, that is, the supply constraints. See Beck and de la Torre (2007) for a more detailed discussion.

4. Note that a key problem in emerging markets may be a lack of investment projects that deserve financing based on the expected return. While this is a relevant problem, it is not a problem of access to finance.

5. The data used in the analysis are taken from the latest surveys and reports of the Consultative Group to Assist the Poor (CGAP) and the Microfinance Information Exchange (MIX) (for example, see Pickens, Porteous, and Rotman 2009; CGAP and World Bank 2010; Kumar, McKay, and Rotman 2010; MIX and CGAP 2010). While this is the most comprehensive data set available on MFIs, there is a caveat related to the fact that only MFIs who reported to MIX and CGAP are taken into consideration in the surveys, meaning that data may not be as comprehensive as one might expect. Yet, MFIs that report to MIX and CGAP are often market leaders and control a large share of the microfinance market. The statistics are therefore an acceptable reflection of the development of the microfinance market.

6. The lending penetration rate represents active borrowers as a percent of the population living below the national poverty line. The savings penetration rate represents depositors as a percent of the population living below the national poverty line.

7. It is important to note that these averages are based on data of the Microfinance Information Exchange, which represents a (supposedly higher-quality) subset of MFIs throughout the developing world.

8. Islamic products have to be offered through specialized windows that must, in theory, rely on resources that are ring-fenced because the source of the resources and the use of the resources have to be Sharia-compliant, that is, assets and liabilities must match.

9. For the discussion in this section, see Porteous (2010).

10. First-generation models of m-banking were launched in the late 1990s mostly in European countries as additional delivery channels for financial services for existing customers. This approach is referred to by Porteous (2010) as an additive approach rather than

the transformative approach of second-generation models of m-banking that target the previously unbanked in Africa.

11. For the positive effect of credit information sharing on stability, see Houston et al. (2010); for the effect on the financing constraints on firms, see Galindo and Miller (2001).

12. Even stronger may have been the incentive of the expectation of cross-selling because mobile payment revenues appear to constitute a miniscule share of Safaricom's overall revenue stream.

13. Making Finance Work for Africa (database), Partnership Secretariat, African Development Bank, Tunis, http://www.mfw4a.org/.

14. See Pearson and Kilfoil (2007). The results of this study have also been published in Bankable Frontier Associates (2008).

15. Enterprise Surveys (database), International Finance Corporation, World Bank, Washington, DC, http://www.enterprisesurveys.org/.

16. This is consistent with evidence from the transition economies, where foreign banks quickly went down-market after their entry (De Haas and Naaborg 2005).

Chapter 4

Lengthening Financial Contracts

Introduction

Chapter 3 documents the scale of the problem of limited and costly access to finance. This chapter focuses on an area of finance in Africa that is particularly challenging in many countries across the continent: long-term finance. Long-term finance is crucial for Africa's economic development. The ability of financial systems to transform short-term claims into long-term assets is a key ingredient of Finance for Growth. It is this aspect of finance that transforms African economies: by supporting the expansion of the productive capacity of established firms, by financing productive investments such as equipment leases especially for farmers, and by financing infrastructure such as power, roads, and housing, financial deepening improves Africa's investment and business environment.

Despite recent encouraging innovations in banks, contractual savings institutions, and the capital market, the lengthening of financial contracts remains a challenge for financial systems across Africa. In areas where progress has been made, the progress is not yet at a rate at which it can significantly affect the scale of the financing deficit on the continent. The challenge for policy makers thus consists of scaling up current initiatives that are succeeding or showing promise; tapping new long-term funding sources, especially domestic sources; and working on long well understood constraints to long-term finance, namely, macroeconomic instability and weak institutions.

This chapter provides examples of long-term funding gaps in infrastructure, housing, and firms. It describes the current landscape of providers of long-term resources and offers policy options for expanding long-term finance. In discussing policies, we take a similar approach as in the previous chapter on expanding access: we distinguish between policies that help Africa optimize the current possibilities to expand long-term finance and policies that expand the frontier of long-term finance. It is important to keep in mind that, as in expanding access, there is no silver bullet for enhancing long-term finance in Africa. The legislative and institution building agenda, including the establishment of reliable commercial courts, efficient property registries, and procedures for facilitating public-private partnerships (PPPs), is substantial and will take a long time to realize. It is therefore important to address this challenge through multiple initiatives and to pursue them consistently over time. Only with significant confidence in the financial system will investors and households seek longer-term savings instruments and financial institutions for longer periods. In this regard, this chapter is demonstrative and not exhaustive of the challenges and potential solutions for long-term finance in Africa.[1]

Africa's Long-Term Financing Gap

There are various ways in which we could demonstrate the scale of Africa's long-term financing gap, but, for illustrative purposes, this chapter focuses only on three areas: infrastructure, housing, and firm finance.

The infrastructure finance gap

The deficit in the availability of long-term financing is most evident in the state of infrastructure across the continent. Even if we take into account Africa's income level, the continent still lags behind other developing regions of the world and this holds back per capita GDP growth by 2 percentage points each year (see table 4.1). Electricity outages, deteriorating roads, and the poor provision of water and sanitation networks are too common in many countries. Africa's total installed power generating capacity is estimated at the equivalent of the capacity of Spain. Infrastructure services are twice as expensive in Africa as in other parts of the world because of diseconomies of scale and the lack of competition among providers. Transportation costs in Africa are more than twice the corresponding costs of the BRIC countries (Brazil, the Russian Federation, India, and China) in part because the relatively sparse road networks are poorly maintained (World Bank 2010a).

Table 4.1   Infrastructure: Comparing Africa with Non-African Developing Countries

Indicator	Africa	Non-African developing countries
Road density, kilometers per 100 square kilometers of arable land	7.22	127.11
Electricity production, megawatts per million population	398.00	2,475.00
Share of population with access to water, %	66.95	85.33
Share of population with access to improved sanitation facilities, %	34.67	70.14

Source: World Development Indicators Database, World Bank, Washington, DC, http://data.worldbank.org/data-catalog/world-development-indicators/.

The cost of addressing Africa's physical infrastructure needs is estimated at US$93 billion per year, some 15 percent of Africa's gross domestic product (GDP).[2] About two-thirds of this amount is needed for greenfield and rehabilitation investments, and the other one-third is needed for the maintenance of existing infrastructure (Foster and Briceño-Garmendia 2010). This infrastructure gap, however, varies greatly by country type: it is greater in landlocked and sparsely populated countries. While there are substantial needs across sectors, more than 40 percent of the estimated spending is for power infrastructure. This reflects the particularly large physical deficits in this sector relative to other sectors such as transportation, telecommunications, and water. However, there remains a paucity of long-term resources available for investment in Africa's infrastructure to facilitate private investment in these key sectors.

Current spending on infrastructure is around US$45 billion per year; two-thirds is sourced domestically, while one-third is financed externally through private, public-private, multilateral, or bilateral development partners, such as China and India (see elsewhere below). Because of the recent financial crisis, which resulted in limited fiscal space in Africa, but, even more so, in the developed world, the funding base for infrastructure has been reduced. There is thus a greater focus on finding new funding sources.

How can the sizable infrastructure gaps in Africa be filled? As this chapter shows, there is an increasing array of financing options for infrastructure. Most infrastructure financing has traditionally come from the public sector, either from national governments or multilateral or bilateral development partners. However, addressing Africa's chronic infrastructure shortfall is as much about improving efficiency as about raising more finance. Fiscal pressures have mounted because of the global financial crisis, and redressing the region's infrastructure shortfall has become more challenging than ever.

The main difficulty for many countries is often not the lack of financing, but rather the limited capacity to absorb infrastructure-related development aid and private investment. With a few exceptions, there is a serious lack of capacity to generate credible long-term strategies, policies, and programs for infrastructure finance. The lack of transparency and efficiency in bidding processes, the shortage of qualified financial skills for drafting and negotiating long-term financial contracts, and the absence of mechanisms for holding governments accountable for investment decisions limit the scale and pace of financing transactions for infrastructure. When public-private transactions have occurred, political constraints have often been an issue, especially for utilities such as water, where the sociopolitical resistance to staff reductions and to raising tariffs to cost-covering levels has often been underestimated. Not surprisingly, the overall balance of private participation in infrastructure finance has therefore fallen short of expectations (Jerome 2008). Overall, private participation in infrastructure finance has occurred mostly in transportation and telecommunications, while energy is a distant second.[3]

The housing finance gap

Demand for housing, especially in urban areas, continues to rise across the continent as Africa rapidly urbanizes.[4] Yet, the ratio of outstanding mortgage debt to GDP remains low, averaging around 10 percent, which compares with 50 percent for Europe and 70 percent for the United States (see figure 4.1). Excluding South Africa, the ratio for Africa falls to 8 percent. Excluding the North African countries reduces the ratio to only 1 percent for Sub-Saharan Africa. In those Sub-Saharan African countries in which formal mortgage markets exist, such as Burkina Faso, Ghana, Nigeria, Tanzania, and Uganda, the number of loans is rarely more than a few thousand, and these loans are often limited to the wealthiest segment of the population. External financing for housing thus eludes the vast majority of the African population.

Rapid urbanization and the lack of financing for private housing and public infrastructure impede any long-term planning processes, which, in turn, explains the lack of urban planning, the poor utility connections, and the poor transport links that can be observed across the continent. These factors also explain, in large measure, why over 50 percent of the urban population in Africa lives in slums.

The need for additional housing, however, varies significantly across Africa. Cross-country differences in population growth and internal migration point to

Figure 4.1   The Size of Mortgage Markets in Africa

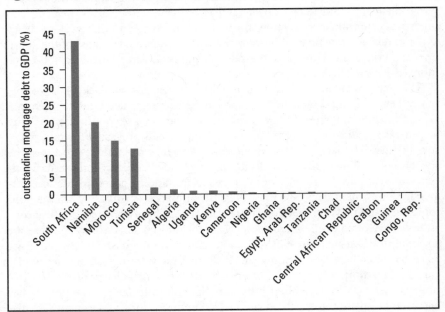

Source: Walley (2010).

important variations in additional housing needs over the next 40 years. For example, in Nigeria, which is rapidly urbanizing, 550,000 new houses are required in cities, but only 144,000 in villages. Contrast this with Kenya, which requires, on an annual basis, only 65,000 new urban dwellings versus 136,000 new rural dwellings. Across the continent, almost the entire housing need will be urban by 2050. Even within the context of the current macroeconomic constraints and the demand and supply barriers, a growing, though still small segment of the African population could afford mortgage finance, as we discuss in box 4.1, in which we calculate an access possibilities frontier for housing finance.

Because of the low level of development of many housing finance markets in Africa, the direct impact of the financial crisis was limited. However, the conservative nature of much of the lending that resulted from the crisis meant that the longer-term development prospects of housing finance were negatively affected. Prior to the crisis, some banks had ambitious plans for expansion across Africa, as well as plans for raising the ratio of capital to debt. Subsequently, banks with a strong presence across the continent scaled back their expansion plans, although they still have a positive long-term outlook on Africa.[5] Alongside the expansion plans, there had been tentative signs that some banks would look to international capital markets such as the Eurobond market to fund some of their balance sheet growth. These plans, which would have provided banks with the longer-term funding required for products such as housing finance, were put on hold in the wake of the crisis (Walley 2010).

Firms' long-term finance gap

For firms, term finance is equally acute, especially for local small and medium enterprises (SMEs). Large multinational firms in Africa have access to finance from outside the continent, from parent companies, from domestic banks in local markets keen to keep large corporate entities on their books, or from foreign banks, often with mandates to accompany multinational firms outside their home countries. Local firms do not have these options, and, if funds become available, tenure is limited. In a survey of tenures in Cameroun, Côte d'Ivoire, Ghana, Kenya, Nigeria, and Senegal, Shendy, Kaplan, and Mousely (2011) find that, in most countries, 95 percent of loans are for five years or less. Similarly, available data suggest that, although firms in North African countries have made progress accessing longer financing contracts, mainly at the level of medium-term maturities, long-term financing remains limited in the region. Data from bank loans across five selected countries show that long-term credit is scarce (figure 4.2).

Optimizing the Current Possibilities for Expanding Long-Term Finance

More recently, there has been an increase in the entry of new institutions, instruments, and products, which allows one to hope that Africa may be turning the

Box 4.1   The Housing Finance Frontier: An Approximation for Africa

Calculations can be made on future housing needs that can be supported by commercial finance for housing. There are two principal determinants over the long term that dictate housing need. These are the net population growth rate and the level of internal migration, which is, essentially, the urbanization process whereby villagers leave their homes in rural areas and move to the cities. This is a simplified model, but it also must take account of the average household size in rural and urban areas. The household size is used where data are available, and, where data are not available, the African average is used, which is 4.79 people per household in urban areas and 5.28 people per household in rural areas. This changes depending on cultures and relative levels of wealth and is also likely to change over time, but these factors are not accounted for in the model. This methodology can be put to use with United Nations population data to predict housing requirements over the next 50 years. The results for Africa as a whole are shown in figure a.

Figure a. Annual Housing Needs in Africa, 1955–2050

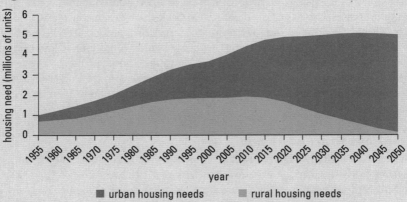

urban housing needs ■   rural housing needs ■

On the supply side, one has to take into account several factors. Based on the average interest rate, one can compute the most cost-effective maturity of a mortgage. Using the average price of a house, mortgage conditionality (based on interest and maturity), and a self-financing ratio of 20 percent, one can compute the average monthly mortgage costs. Assuming a maximum ratio of mortgage payment to income of 40 percent and using income distribution data, one may compute the share of the population that can afford commercially viable mortgages from formal financial institutions. On average, this provides one with a cut-off point for mortgage affordability among the richest 2.9 percent of the population across Africa (with large variations across countries). This translates into six million mortgage loans. Assuming an average loan of US$50,000—half the average loan amount in South Africa—yields a total mortgage market across Africa of US$300 billion, or 18 percent of GDP, almost twice the size of the current mortgage market. Behind these aggregate numbers are large variations across countries in the housing finance frontier.

Sources: Walley (2010) based on author calculations; STATcompiler (database), Measure DHS, ICF Macro, Calverton, MD, http://www.statcompiler.com/; World Urbanization Prospects: The 2009 Revision Population Database, UN Population Division, UN Department of Economic and Social Affairs, New York, http://esa.un .org/wup2009/unup/index.asp.

Figure 4.2 Bank Loan Maturities in Selected Countries, 2008

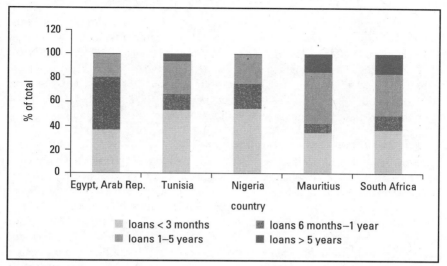

Source: Data of Bankscope.

corner on this challenge. In commercial banking, innovations in the use of specialized products and instruments are enabling banks and specialized lenders to extend the maturity of their long-term financing instruments. Also, the recent renewed interest in development banks has highlighted the need for appropriate governance structures that shield these banks from political interference. In the following, we offer a summary discussion of these trends.

Commercial banks

Although commercial banks dominate the financial system in Africa, their participation in long-term finance remains limited. A number of reasons account for the limited tenor that banks are willing to provide. First, banks are plagued with a structural asset-liability mismatch. Although banks are highly liquid, their liquidity is largely financed by short-term deposits (discussed in chapter 2). Underdeveloped corporate bond markets are one factor inhibiting the ability of banks to cover their asset-liability mismatch. Second, an underdeveloped government bond market inhibits the development of the yield curve benchmarks necessary for commercial banks to price long-term debt in local currency.

Despite these constraints, Shendy, Kaplan, and Mousely (2011) find that there are some exceptions: some local commercial banks find ways to overcome these challenges and provide long-term finance. For example, in Nigeria, the Lekki-Epe Express Toll Road, which reached financial close in 2008, was able to mobilize a 15-year loan from Stanbic's IBTC-Nigeria in local currency for ₦2 billion (US$13.4 million) at a fixed interest rate of 13.9 percent and with a moratorium on principal repayments for four years. The deal was also supported by other local banks, namely, Diamond Bank, Fidelity Bank, First Bank, United Bank for Africa, and Zenith Bank, which provided a total loan value of ₦9.4 billion (almost US$63 million) for a tenor of 12 years.[6] In Senegal, the Dakar-Diamniadio Toll Road reached financial close in November 2010. The concessionaire Eiffage was able to tap into a local credit line at a Senegalese bank that provided approximately US$10 million, with a 13.5-year tenor and a fixed interest rate of about 10 percent. This amounts to 10 percent of the total debt of the project. Similarly, the Kenyan Equity Bank has been the single largest financier in a syndicated loan to Rift Valley Railways.

Development banks and specialized lenders

State-owned financial institutions, particularly development banks, have returned to the spotlight of public debate. Concerned because of the lack of notable progress in increasing access to long-term finance, policy makers are discussing the efficacy of the role of development banks. African countries have had differing relationships with state financial institutions over the last couple of decades. In some, such as Malawi, there has been an active state-led interventionist approach to financial sector development until recently. In others, such as Mozambique and Zambia, there has been a more liberalized private sector–led model. In yet others, such as Ethiopia, the government continues to dominate the sector.

For decades, the debate on the rationale for state intervention in the financial sector has centered on market failures, such as lack of information, which are more prominent in some sectors, as discussed in chapter 3. In this case, direct state participation would be warranted to compensate for market imperfections that leave socially profitable (but sometimes financially unattractive) investments underfinanced.

Take the example of housing finance. Where commercial banks have feared to go in the past, state housing banks have often sought to bridge the gap. Many African countries have such banks, including Cameroon (Crédit Foncier du Cameroun), Gabon (Compte de Refinancement de l'Habitat du Gabon), Mali (Banque de l'Habitat), Rwanda (Caisse Hypothécaire du Rwanda), and Tanzania (Tanzania Housing Bank). Almost without exception, these institutions have failed in their mission to expand access to housing finance. Many have also required large bailouts from the government when they became insolvent. The reasons for the failures are repeated across the institutions and include poor management, political interference, and a perception by borrowers that they are receiving grants rather than loans, with little consequence if they do not repay. The concern related to state housing banks is the displacement effect they have on the private sector. There are certainly exceptions, as the case of the Banque de l'Habitat in Tunisia shows (box 4.2). There, the major difference with Sub-Saharan housing banks relates to the Tunisian bank's access to retail savings.

Some African countries have opted to establish specialized single-purpose nonbank mortgage lenders, or monoline lenders, most notably, the Arab Republic of

Box 4.2 The Role of the Housing Bank in Mortgage Finance in Tunisia

In its social and economic policies, the Tunisian government has assigned a top priority to access to housing and has taken an activist stance. Banque de l'Habitat (BH) was established in 1989 as successor to a failed savings bank (Caisse Nationale d'Epargne Logement) to provide financial solutions in the housing sector. BH's mandate includes savings mobilization, prefinancing for real estate developers, and the provision of diversified mortgage loans to individuals through savings-based loans and direct loans. Unlike many housing banks in Sub-Saharan Africa, it is thus primarily a savings bank. In 1992, BH was authorized to extend its loans to all economic sectors and was listed on the Bourse de Tunis, though the government kept a majority shareholding of 58 percent. During the early 1990s, BH was the only bank authorized to offer mortgage loans in Tunisia, but, after the liberalization in 1998, private banks were allowed to enter, and, over time, BH's market share dropped significantly, to only 22 percent in 2008. Today, the bank is the major player in low-end housing finance, given that it is the only bank authorized to offer the classic housing savings plan, which pays the highest savings deposit rate, benefits from an exemption from the withholding tax on savings-for-housing accounts, and allows clients to enjoy subsidized interest rates on loans. In 2003, the financing of social housing projects represented almost 80 percent of BH interventions. This contrasts with private commercial banks, which mainly serve the upper part of the market. One of the success factors of BH is thus the more numerous subsidies and privileges it has received relative to private institutions in the housing segment.

Despite the success of BH and the overall situation on the mortgage market in Tunisia, serious constraints remain. There is a large disparity in the quality of the housing stock between urban areas and rural areas, mainly in the northwest and center-west regions. While official statistics suggest that supply meets demand and significant progress has been made on the financing side, affordability remains an issue, mainly among low-income households. There seems to be an oversupply among upper-income and upper-middle-income groups and a shortage among lower-income groups. This is corroborated by the global property guide, which shows that demand for houses in Tunisia is mainly driven by the middle class and that house prices range from TD 450 (US$320) to TD 1,700 (US$1,215) per square meter. These prices are high relative to the minimum wage, which does not exceed TD 251 (US$180). Relying mostly on retail saving accounts, BH faces funding constraints. Its loan-deposit ratio is above 1, plus it has maturity risks: deposit rates are fixed, while lending rates are tied to the interbank market rate. The current levels of interest rate risk exposure and maturity mismatch remain manageable, but the latter will need careful follow-up, especially in light of the political unrest that the country experienced recently and the potential negative effects of this on the real economy.

Egypt, which has mortgage finance companies; Kenya, which has housing finance companies; Nigeria, which has primary mortgage institutions; and South Africa, which has financial service providers specializing in mortgage lending. Typically, these institutions have a narrow banking license limiting their activities and, in particular, restricting deposit collection. This means that they are usually reliant on wholesale funding on the liability side of their balance sheets. This type of institution was especially vulnerable during the crisis because its funding costs rose to a much greater extent relative to lenders with a deposit base. One response has been a consolidation in the financial sector as banks acquired specialist mortgage businesses or started up their own. This is the case in Egypt (where a number of mortgage finance companies have been acquired by banks), Kenya (where Savings and Loan was acquired by Kenya Commercial Bank), and Nigeria (where banks have been setting up Project Management Institute subsidiaries to carry out their mortgage lending business). This bank-subsidiary model allows specialization in mortgage lending and may attract some regulatory benefits, but it avoids the funding downside because banks can rely on a stable retail depositor base.

Meanwhile, for private and government financial institutions, the constraints to the development of mortgage markets are not restricted to problems within the financial sector. A major constraint for housing finance is the contractual framework, because high fees and difficult registration processes—that might involve additional informal fees—constitute a large hurdle to the formal recognition of property ownership (figure 4.3). Land laws in many countries still put restrictions on private ownership, and the infrastructure for property transfer is cumbersome, which makes the use of land as collateral difficult. Registries are often in a dismal state and are frequently based on handwritten records, which means the systems are open to abuse and corruption. Furthermore, government approval is often necessary before land can be transferred; this is the case, for example, in Malawi. Stamp duties and fees are another major hurdle. In Nigeria, for instance, the consent fee

Figure 4.3   The Cost to Register a Mortgage or Transfer a Title

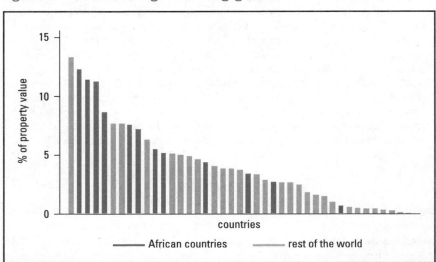

Source: World Bank and IFC (2008).
Note: Sample size: 43 countries.

(the governor has to agree to a land transfer) amounts to at least 15 percent of the land valuation, and total stamp duties, registration fees, and other levies can add another 30 percent. Yet, there are many exceptions; thus, Rwanda and Zambia have continued to strengthen their already well-functioning property transfer systems.

Development finance institutions: continuing challenges and unclear mandates

While many development finance institutions (DFIs) have been established and have good objectives, the activities of DFIs have often resulted in unintended consequences in terms of the credit culture of beneficiaries and the interest of the private sector in investment in the financial sector. Experience worldwide suggests that, despite the apparent advantages of government intervention in the effort to broaden access to credit, the public provision of banking services has generally not been successful in developing countries. La Porta, Lopez-de-Silanes, and Shleifer (2002) find a close association between government ownership and lower levels of financial development, less credit for the private sector, wider intermediation spreads, greater credit concentration, slower economic growth, and recurrent fiscal drains.

Even today, as governments revisit the role of development banks, the performance of these banks remains suboptimal. African DFIs, on average, perform poorly. They show low levels of profitability, with a 2.4 percent return on average assets, and high levels of loan impairment, with a 15.8 percent ratio of impaired loans to gross loans (figure 4.4). These are only some of the indicators of poor performance. For many of these banks, the problems of yesteryear persist, including political interference, the lack of capacity, and the lack of economies of scale.

This is not to say there are no success stories, but they are few and far between. In a survey by the International Monetary Fund covering 100 institutions in 25 countries, a third of these institutions reported losses over three years, and a third reported nonperforming loans greater than 10 percent, while capital injections were common as banking crises led to fiscal crises (Brooks 2006). Despite the limited number of success stories, DFIs, even poorly performing ones, have been tenacious survivors. There are more than 60 in Africa. Meanwhile, in Mali, Tanzania, Zambia, and many other countries, specialized state-owned banks have remained stagnant; they are largely illiquid and deliver few services, and their solvency is precarious and conditional on support from governments (Honohan and Beck 2007). Looking specifically at specialized DFIs that focus on the provision of housing, Hassler and Renaud (2009) distinguish among three types. Most of the funds for the first type are deposits, as in Algeria (Caisse Nationale d'Epargne et de Prévoyance) and Tunisia (Banque de l'Habitat). These banks, which are typically savings banks, have a strong funding foundation and the ability to offer a wide range of banking products. The second type typically consists of specialized banks without a large deposit-collection capacity that raise funds on bond markets, as in the case of Morocco (Crédit Immobilier et Hôtelier). The third type consists of

Figure 4.4   The Profitability and Loan Impairment of African Development Banks, 2009

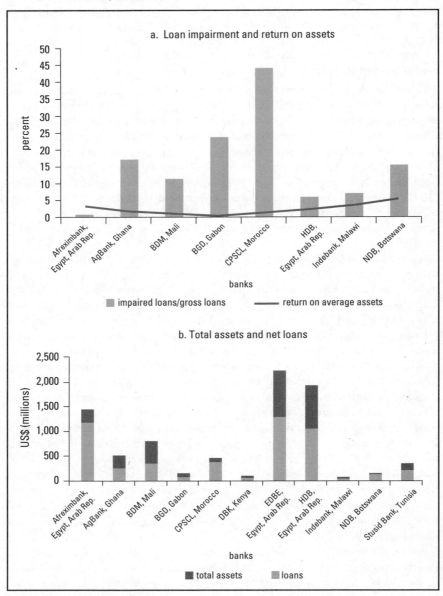

Source: Author calculations.
Note: The data are valid as of December 31, 2009.

banks that are largely funded by public finance sources, such as mandatory savings or wage taxes, central bank facilities, or government grants and loans. This model is rare, but it has been used, for instance, in Cameroon (Crédit Foncier du Cameroun).

The limited success of DFIs—except where they can rely on a large retail savings base—calls into question the current business model of these entities. Rather than their current focus, policy-oriented and wholesale financing tasks seem more appropriate (see below). Such tasks could range from managing partial credit guarantee funds, discussed below in this chapter, to facilitating value chain finance arrangements in agriculture, managing investment funds that are provided by donors, and serving as conduits to private commercial banks acting as ultimate lenders. Caisse de Dépôt et de Gestion (CDG), in Morocco, is an example of a para-governmental entity that helps deepen the financial system. It collects funds from pension and provident funds, as well as insurance companies, and invests in listed and nonlisted companies. The CDG Group is the largest institutional investor in Morocco and a major player in funding development and social programs. It participates in private sector enterprises and investment on international stock markets (mainly France). CDG has also been supporting the private equity industry, including through its investment in Averroes Fund I, a €30 million (around US$42 million) fund of funds targeting the Mediterranean region.

Many refer to the success of the Development Bank of South Africa (DBSA), which is one of the four state-owned development banks in the country. Its main objective is to facilitate financing and technical assistance among companies and municipalities, principally for infrastructure funding. It also provides financing to large infrastructure projects in neighboring countries. DBSA's taxable profits go to DBSA Development Fund, a subsidiary of DBSA, of which the main objective is to provide support to low-income municipalities through grants, the deployment of technical expertise, training, and the identification of projects. Rudolph (2009) concludes that DBSA's success can be primarily attributed to the bank's sound corporate governance structure. The presence of an independent and qualified board of directors, professional management, and the South African Treasury as an active shareholder have contributed to the bank's strong corporate governance practices. Furthermore, the lack of financial dependence on government funding has strengthened the asset-liability management functions of the bank.

Rudolph (2009) observes, however, that DBSA has faced challenges. Because its taxable profits go to DBSA Development Fund, DBSA has two conflicting objectives: financing infrastructure projects in middle-income municipalities and generating revenues to fund the operations of DBSA Development Fund. Although requiring a minimum return is a desirable objective, the goal of maximizing profits (with the purpose of funding DBSA Development Fund) may intensify the investments of the bank in commercially oriented projects that are not necessarily consistent with social objectives.

To help avoid a repetition of the disappointing performance of development banks in the 1970s and 1980s, Thorne and du Toit (2009) identify six dimensions of success, namely: an enabling environment; a mandate; regulation and supervision; governance and management; financial sustainability; and performance assessment. Development banks need a climate of macroeconomic stability without too many microeconomic distortions. They must be integrated into the financial system and operate along commercial lines, with a flexible mandate. They should do this without competing with the private sector, but, rather, they should aim to develop the private sector. They should also operate autonomously, while ensuring that they adhere to their mandate. Sound governance and management may be the single factor most likely to determine the success of a development bank. To align incentives, it might also be advisable for governments to capitalize new (or restructured) development banks adequately and then limit additional fiscal support to ring-fenced noncommercial activities undertaken on behalf of the state. Governments should also put in place arrangements for development banks to be assessed on a regular basis against an agreed set of financial and social or developmental objectives.

Guided by the principle that government intervention should support rather than distort incentives for the private sector provision of financial services, however, our preference remains for a reorientation and possible restructuring of existing state-owned financial institutions toward more wholesale long-term financing activities. Given the limited success of the direct provision of financial services by government-owned financial institutions and the promise that the use of technology and agent agreements holds for the expansion of access, government-owned financial institutions will be able to maximize more effectively their impact on financial sector broadening by providing assistance as second-tier rather than first-tier financial institutions.

For many countries, policy makers would be better served by refocusing the primary engagement of governments in the financial sector on policy formulation and wholesale lending activities, while leveraging the private sector to lead in the retail delivery of financial services, including long-term financial services. A holistic review and restructuring of current government institutions and programs could yield substantial economies of scale and reduce the current contamination of private sector–led efforts to increase access to financial services. Rather than establishing a new program each time a government prioritizes a particular sector, region, or activity, policy makers ought to consider focusing on using a single agency or institution to prepare and draft the eligibility criteria for the program and then tender the retail implementation of the program to interested institutions. All bank and nonbank financial institutions would be eligible to bid for the tender. By leveling the retail financial sector landscape in this manner, the government would increase the involvement of the private sector in the delivery of commercially sustainable long-term financing programs in the country.

Contractual savings: pensions and insurance funds

To the same extent that there is a renewed interest in development banks, there is also a persistent interest in unlocking the funds held by pensions and insurance firms and using them for long-term investments. Because of its long-run liabilities, this segment of the financial sector has the potential to play an important role. However, as discussed in chapter 2, the contractual savings sector in Africa is even more underdeveloped than the banking systems. Insurance sectors across the continent are mostly focused on non–life insurance business lines, with the notable exception of several southern African countries, where life insurance products are popular for, among other reasons, tax motives. Few countries on the continent have private pension funds; the majority rely almost exclusively on public funds in the form of pay-as-you-go funds or social security funds. An important feature of African pension funds is the limited coverage of the working population, though important variations exist across countries. While the coverage rate used to exceed 80 percent in Libya and Tunisia, it is 3 percent in Niger. We discuss below the insurance and pension industry in turn.

As shown in chapter 2, insurance sectors across Africa are small in depth and breadth, and most insurance sectors are dominated by the shorter-term non–life insurance business lines, while life insurance products such as mortality or savings products are less popular. In addition to the country factors discussed in chapter 2 that explain the limited financial sector development, demographic characteristics also play an important role. High mortality reduces the incentive to save through life insurance policies, but also makes the pricing of such products more difficult and less attractive for consumers. The small populations in most countries mean that the pooling and diversification of risks are more difficult. There are other important demand-side constraints, including low savings rates, the lack of awareness and financial literacy, and the lack of trust in insurance companies because of fraudulent practices and the shortage of consumer protections.

Many insurance sectors on the continent are characterized by a large number of small, locally owned, often undercapitalized companies with low levels of expertise and insufficient economies of scale that are unable to offer attractively priced products or professional levels of service. Consistent with the short-term nature of non–life insurance lines of business, insurance companies are mostly purchasers of short-term financial instruments. However, limited supply, lack of skills, and governance deficiencies would prevent the life insurance segment from maximizing its positive role even if there were demand for more long-term financial instruments.

The lack of long-term assets is particularly problematic for life insurance companies, which offer products with a payout many years after policy commencement, such as whole life or universal life contracts and long-term savings plans. Long-term investment assets offering attractive rates of return are seldom available, particularly because there are generally severe restrictions on investing assets outside a country. As a result, the returns from life insurance products are frequently unattractive. Because of the short-term nature of their insurance contracts, such as automobile insurance and fire insurance, non–life property and casualty insurance companies are not as affected by the unavailability of long-term asset classes. Non–life insurers need to keep most of their funds, such as cash and fixed interest, in liquid form. However, even non–life insurers are not immune and are affected by the general lack of liquidity in government bonds, for which there is rarely a secondary market, and, hence, bonds need to be held to maturity. In addition, stock markets are frequently underdeveloped; stocks are thinly traded; and stockholdings are therefore generally illiquid. Thus, it is not uncommon for a smaller insurance company to advise its clients that valid insurance claims will not be paid for some months, until such time as the company sells a longer-term investment asset, after which it will have sufficient liquidity to pay the claim. This problem arises when an insurer invests in virtually any investment asset class other than cash, given that the illiquidity of stock markets, real estate investments, and even bond markets does not allow insurance companies to convert investment assets into cash in a timely fashion to pay insurance claims and policyholder benefits.

Similarly to the life insurance sector, the private pension industry in most African countries is small. With the exception of larger or middle-income common law countries, such as Botswana, Mauritius, and South Africa, but also Kenya, such funds are rare for the same reasons life insurance business is limited. In Kenya, over 1,000 occupational pension schemes are licensed and are required to outsource asset management to independent, registered fund managers and hire independent custodians to ensure the full segregation and safe custody of the assets of sponsors. Most of these schemes, however, are underfunded and suffer from risk concentration on both sides of the balance sheet. Botswana has seen impressive growth in occupational pension schemes only over the past 10 years or so, and the schemes now reach 40 percent of the formally employed population.

The pension sector in many African countries is still dominated by obligatory, state-owned pension schemes administered by national social security parastatals. Among pension funds, 7 percent are privately managed in Africa, compared with 16 percent worldwide.[7] Coverage is, however, mostly limited to the formally employed. There is a large variation in funding structures. In Uganda, the pension fund for civil servants is financed through the general budget, while, in Botswana, after the reforms around 2000, there is a fully funded, defined contribution scheme. Prefunding can have critical advantages, including an increase in the national savings rate and opportunities for international risk diversification.

Overall, the pension funds in Africa suffer from absent or weak investment guidelines, as well as limited capacity to implement investment strategies. Large parts of pension fund investments, whether private or public, are in real estate, short-term bank deposits, or government securities, while a limited, though increasing percentage is invested in equity (table 4.2). An even smaller share is held in corporate bonds. However, even if one wished to invest pension funds in corporate bonds, there might not be enough available in the domestic market, an issue to

Table 4.2 Pension Fund Portfolios
percent

Country	Cash and deposits	Fixed income	Shares	Land and buildings	Other
Egypt, Arab Rep. (2008)	26.82	69.28	2.07	0.39	1.44
South Africa (2006)	5.01	8.70	23.32	0.49	62.48
Zambia (2005)	15.00	27.85	17.83	23.57	15.75

	Fixed income	Equity		Real estate		
Ghana (2008)	46.00	42.60		11.40		

	Government debt	Listed equities	Government equities	Real estate	TPS[a]	Other
Kenya (2009)	13.00	50.00	1.00	29.00	5.00	2.00

	Fixed income	Equity	Real estate
Uganda (2009)	70.00	10.00	20.00

Sources: For Egypt, South Africa, and Zambia: data of the International Organization of Pension Supervisors; for Ghana: data of the Social Security and National Insurance Trust; for Kenya: data of the Retirement Benefits Authority; for Uganda: World Bank (2009b).
a. TPS = Tenant Purchase Scheme.

which we return below. The participation of some pension funds in African bond markets is also limited because of restrictions on the exposure of funds to this asset class or to investments outside the country; this is the case, for instance, in Egypt. In Nigeria, savings are managed by separately licensed private investment managers, who are also severely restricted in investment across asset classes and generally cannot invest outside the country. There may be macroeconomic reasons for restricting investments to the country of origin; however, this approach also restricts potential investment returns. The need to diversify away from government securities and real estate alone is reflected in the investment guidelines of the International Social Security Association (ISSA 2004).[8]

Recently, several countries have undertaken comprehensive pension reforms. These reforms might eventually result in a more important role for this sector in providing funding for long-term investment and growth. There is a significant trend toward greater autonomy among social security organizations, notably in Côte d'Ivoire, Gabon, Ghana, Kenya, Nigeria, Senegal, Tanzania, and Uganda. In many countries, the challenge lies in being able to tame the role of the government, even in the presence of a technically sound pension sector regulator. Autonomy is not the sole requirement for good governance. Moreover, it is sometimes associated with high administrative costs and excessive staffing levels. However, it helps in creating an environment for more accountability and a framework that can ensure proper governance.

In June 2008, the Social Security Regulatory Act was passed in Tanzania. It defines a framework to distribute the supervision of schemes between the Bank of Tanzania and a new social security regulatory authority. Ghana has also moved forward by creating the National Pensions Regulatory Authority following passage of the National Pensions Authority Act in January 2010. For both agencies, it remains to be seen whether they will follow the widely accepted principles that supervision must be independent, money managers must be professional, and audits must be external, thereby enhancing their investment activities, but the potential is there.

In Kenya, the pension sector has experienced a significant improvement in performance since the establishment of the Retirement Benefits Authority, which resulted in the introduction of investment guidelines and a shift to private portfolio managers. The returns from privately managed pension funds have been strong since these reforms. In contrast, the government-controlled National Social Security Fund remains unreformed and has a long history of low returns. Moreover, it operates outside the Retirement Benefits Authority Act. (For example, it is not subject to the related investment guidelines, and it relies on internal portfolio management rather than outside professional money managers.) An argument could therefore be mounted that government-controlled pension managers, like all other managers, ought to be subject to the same enforcement measures associated with the stringent guidelines.

The lack of alternative domestic investment opportunities for insurance and pension funds raises the issue of how necessary it is that a portion of the funds be invested abroad. Many countries on which data are available show a bias toward domestic funds; Botswana is one notable exception. Yet, investing a proportion of their assets abroad allows pension funds to reap the benefits of diversification and offers greater investment opportunities, given the dearth of such instruments in most African markets. In addition, investment quality would be significantly improved. Few African assets are investment grade as defined by Standard & Poor's and Moody's; even the sovereign risk of many Sub-Saharan countries does not qualify as investment grade. This is particularly important for insurance companies: international requirements call for the use of more than 90 percent of available funds in investment grade assets. Investing a portion of funds outside the home country would thus present the management of insurance companies with an opportunity to upgrade investment quality, improve returns, and acquire the ability to match long-term liabilities with commensurate long-term assets.

However, permitting the management of insurance companies and pension funds to invest outside the home country has drawbacks. First, insurance company and pension fund management may not have sufficient expertise to make appropriate international investment decisions. Second, foreign investment could become a mechanism whereby funds are transferred outside the reach of policyholders.

Investing outside the country therefore requires safeguards. Rigorous checks and balances would need to be introduced through significantly stepped-up corporate governance requirements, supported by improved regulation. This would likely include criminal penalties for directors and managers who abuse their authority. Regulators would need to build their expertise in investment matters, improve their market surveillance, act upon alerts from early warning systems, and rigorously enforce compliance with regulations. Investing abroad also introduces an additional element of volatility related to exchange rate movement and other possible sources of risk. Regional integration could help in this case, especially across countries with similar economic structures and stable, if not fixed exchange rates, such as in the currency unions of Central Africa and West Africa.

For pensions and insurance, there is an urgent need to undertake reforms in such areas as risk diversification, solvency, consumer protection, and taxation. Capacity building among regulators and financial literacy programs for policyholders are essential. Insurers are short on training and experience, and gaps in regulatory coverage persist. To ensure effective corporate governance, it is vital that insurance companies and pension funds have appropriate risk management processes in place. Insurance and pension regulators need to deploy risk-based supervision methodologies and thereby make use of sound oversight and supervision. In the case of the pensions industry, a separate implementation body and external evaluators for the overall process need to be considered (box 4.3).

Capital markets: a limited role

Long touted as essential to unlocking the long-term potential of finance by providing a trading platform for equities, stock exchanges have been the must-have institution of a modern national financial system. Yet, for decades, stock market capitalization has remained low in Africa and represents, as of 2009, only 2 percent of world market capitalization. As we discuss in chapter 2, markets in Africa have low levels of liquidity, with the exception of the Johannesburg Stock Exchange. As stated by a market practitioner, "an entire year's worth of trading in the frontier African stock markets is done before lunch on the New York Stock Exchange."[9]

To revitalize, many stock markets in the region have undertaken regulatory and institutional reforms, such as a relaxation of the restrictions on foreign investors. All African stock exchanges now allow foreign participation (Allen, Otchere, and Senbet 2010). Governments have also tried to use tax incentives. In Tanzania, for example, equity-issuing companies face a reduced corporate tax rate for a period of three years if at least 35 percent of the equity is issued. Efforts have been made to reduce the transaction costs as well, including the taxation of capital gains. While tax incentives can increase the number of listed firms, it will not necessarily translate into enhanced liquidity in the market, as indicated by the example of Egypt, which recently abolished some tax subsidies.

However, the capital markets in the region still face severe challenges. Some capital markets are constrained by outdated practices and inefficient listing procedures and trading mechanisms, such as manual systems, the lack of a regulatory framework, and an inefficient market information dissemination process, though most African stock exchanges have now shifted to an electronic rather than manual trading system. Governments continue to try to make their markets more cost-effective by working with development partners on (1) market development strategies to

Box 4.3   International Labour Organization Best Practice Guidelines for Board Members in Africa

An investment committee should be established concentrating on investment policy, strategy, monitoring, and evaluation (see figure a). Because the board needs to monitor investment policy and strategy on an ongoing basis, it is important that board members receive training to be able to evaluate and pass judgment on the investment committee's reports.

Figure a. Administrative Bodies of a Social Security Scheme and Their Control Mechanisms

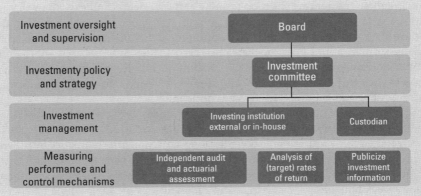

Investment committees are different from investing institutions. The investing institution may be the administering body or a separate institution dealing only with investment management. It can be separate, but in-house, or it might be completely outsourced to professional money managers. Three more entities are necessary to contribute to achieving the best results from pension fund investments: a custodian, an external auditor, and an external actuarial assessment body. A custodian should be appointed for the assets, including to hold the documents and prove the ownership of the assets. This can be an independent firm, the central bank, or the ministry of finance. The renewal of an independent firm's contract should be based on performance. An external auditor who is free from political interference and independent of all internal bodies should be appointed by the board to carry out annual audits of the scheme. The same should be true of the actuarial assessment body. Its task will be to report findings to the board. In the extreme case that the future expenditures of a scheme are not covered by reserves and no remedial action is taken by the board, the actuary body should also make a report directly to parliament.

To improve performance, control mechanisms need to be employed on a regular basis as well, that is, performance assessment, compensation mechanisms, information systems and processes, risk management procedures, and regular reviews of expert advisers and any contractual arrangements. To help ensure accountability and good performance, a suggestion of the International Labour Organization is to publicize the relevant information on investments—such as the associated objectives, policies, and strategies and the performance of investments—in the annual report, but also throughout the year in press releases on the organization's website.

Source: ILO (2010).

increase listings, especially listings of upcoming medium-size enterprises; (2) capacity building among staff in the industry as a whole, including brokers and regulators; (3) education campaigns for relevant stakeholders and the general public that are aimed at informing the general public on long-term investment opportunities and risks and at informing firms about the benefits of listing on stock markets; and (4) reform in investor protection laws and corporate governance codes. The evidence of sustained success is still mixed at best, however.

Another option is secondary trading boards, such as exist in Botswana (introduced in 2001 as the Venture Capital Board and dedicated to helping firms that are looking for start-up capital), as well as in Egypt and South Africa. These make lower demands on issuers in terms of listing fees, track record, size, reporting requirements, and float, or the minimum number of shareholders. They thereby try to attract medium-size companies, for which the regular conditions are too burdensome. While these markets have facilitated the access of firms to stock markets, their limited success suggests they can only partly solve the problem of the access to finance. Box 4.4 describes the experience with a secondary board in Egypt. In Kenya, the introduction of a secondary trading board led to a switchover among companies from the main board to the secondary board to avoid the more onerous

Box 4.4   The Experience with a Secondary Board in Egypt: Nilex

Nilex is a second-tier market initiated by the government in 2007 to offer funding to SMEs. By offering relaxed listing rules, Nilex is meant to attract promising companies that cannot comply with the listing rules of the regular market. Nilex is currently functioning as a market segment of the Egyptian Exchange, but will be spun off once it reaches a critical size. So far, companies listing on Nilex cannot thereby benefit from any tax exemption.

While trading on Nilex started fairly recently (in June 2010), 16 companies were already listed on the market as of September 2010, and 4 are close to initial public offerings. On average, the listing process takes two months, but can be fast-tracked to two weeks if a company has a complete application. Candidates for listing operate in various sectors, including real estate, agribusiness, and manufacturing.

So far, companies have not been keen to list on Nilex for the following reasons: (1) fear of losing control by complying with enhanced disclosure requirements, (2) limited resources to pay listing fees, and (3) lack of understanding of the benefits of listing and of the need to pay listing fees. Nilex listing fees are set at LE 0.5 for every LE 1 million of paid capital, with a maximum of LE 25,000 per year. To tackle the listing fee problem, exchange authorities are working closely with several governmental and professional bodies to subsidize part of the listing costs. For example, the Industry Modernization Center bears at least 90 percent of the listing costs for industrial companies. Candidates must select a nominated advisor from a list prepared by the exchange. Nominated advisors are expected to help the company restructure its operations, comply with Nilex requirements, and assist in the listing process by playing the underwriter role.

Source: Feyen (2010).

listing and disclosure requirements on the main board. The switch therefore had only a limited overall effect on trading.

But even more cost-effective domestic stock exchanges will be constrained by the limited firm and investor universe of their respective host economies. Most small economies in Africa are too small to sustain a liquid stock exchange. Moving toward regional models or cross-listing arrangements are viable alternatives in this context. One route is toward regional stock exchanges, as in the case of the Abidjan Stock Exchange, which was expanded to become the Bourse Régionale des Valeurs Mobilières to allow enterprises from throughout francophone West Africa to list, or the Bourse des Valeurs Mobilières de l'Afrique Centrale, on which companies and states of the Economic and Monetary Community of Central Africa are encouraged to list. However, as of December 2010, of the 39 companies listed on the Bourse Régionale des Valeurs Mobilières, only six are not Ivorian and, of these, only Niger has more than one listed company. Similarly, with the exception of the International Finance Corporation bond issue, all issues on the Bourse des Valeurs Mobilières de l'Afrique Centrale were made by the government of Gabon or Gabonese firms (Banque de France 2009). The harmonization of regulations, trading systems, and tax regimes can be an important first step toward the regionalization of stock exchanges, but also in facilitating cross-listings.[10] The three stock exchanges in West Africa (Côte d'Ivoire, Ghana, and Nigeria) are in talks to establish uniform rules, regulations, and operational procedures. An alternative to regional stock exchanges is to allow cross-listing, which permits enterprises to tap additional investor communities and encourages more liquid trading of the shares of enterprises, thereby increasing the efficiency of the price-finding process (Pagano et al. 2001).

Yet, even under the best-case scenario, with the implementation of all the necessary regulatory reforms and all the cost problems solved, one has to be realistic about what to expect in terms of stock market development. The experience in Latin America, but even in Western Europe has shown that it is difficult to sustain liquid stock exchanges in smaller economies (box 4.5).

Given experiences in other regions, it is unrealistic to expect stock exchanges across Africa to flourish. The modernist approach would hold that financial services per se matter, not where or by whom they are delivered; this would mean that listing on foreign exchanges would be a good solution, for example, on the Johannesburg Stock Exchange. However, this would only help the largest enterprises in each country and might even increase the listing threshold, given the potential additional listing and transaction costs of listing abroad rather than at home. It might also pull liquidity away from small stock exchanges, exacerbating the small exchange curse (Levine and Schmukler 2006).

Corporate bond markets across Africa are also small and illiquid. They are limited in many countries by cumbersome regulatory structures. Rather than focusing on disclosure, most African countries impose a complex approval process. Rather than allowing the market to assess the financial viability of bond issuers and the risk of the securities, regulators feel compelled to undertake this assessment on

Box 4.5   Capital Markets in Latin America

In Latin America at the beginning of the 1990s, high hopes for capital market development in emerging markets had catalyzed the debate about reform and action to address financial liberalization, the establishment of stock exchanges and bond markets, and the development of a regulatory and supervisory framework. The associated expectations that were thus built up were not met: Latin American countries, despite their reform efforts, greatly underperformed relative to East Asia and the G7 countries.

A couple of explanations can help shed light on what went wrong in the Latin American experience. One explanation ascribes the failure to a combination of impatience and the insufficient implementation of reform. Because reform efforts materialize only long after the initial steps, policy makers have to be patient in harvesting the fruits that they have planted. Instead, the claim has been put forth that some key reforms were not initiated, while other reforms were often implemented in an incomplete or inconsistent fashion. Appropriate laws and regulations were approved, but not duly implemented or adequately enforced. The policy advice that follows from this is to forge ahead persistently with reform and be patient. The reform efforts should seek to improve the enabling environment for capital markets, enhance market discipline through greater competition, upgrade the regulatory and supervisory framework for securities markets, and address problems in key areas, such as accounting and disclosure standards, corporate governance practices, and securities trading, custody, clearing, and settlement systems.

The second explanation ascribes the underperformance to mistakes in sequencing the reform. This view contends that, before the application of capital market reforms, other reforms are necessary, such as the achievement of a minimum threshold of institutional strength in the legal and regulatory framework, supervisory capacity, accounting and disclosure standards, and so forth. Hence, whether the Latin American countries will be successful in building capital markets will depend on their clarification of the sequencing issues.

A recent paper by de la Torre, Gozzi, and Schmukler (2007) finds that stock market development in the region is below what could be expected, given the economic and institutional fundamentals. There is a particular shortfall in market capitalization, trading, and capital raising. The authors believe the two explanations offered above are complementary to their gap analysis. A forward-looking reform agenda has to take into account the intrinsic characteristics of developing countries, in particular their small size, lack of diversification opportunities, weak currencies, and prevalence of systemic risk. The first point that should be considered is whether a given country can sustain an active domestic market for private sector securities. Furthermore, any reform agenda on capital markets should be part of a broader reform agenda that is embedded in an all-encompassing financial development agenda.

Source: Based on de la Torre, Gozzi, and Schmukler (2007).

behalf of market participants, which leads to inefficiency (because incentives are not aligned), but also opens the door to arbitrary decisions and corruption. Furthermore, some regulators require credit guarantees before issuing bonds, and this has also led enterprises to consider bonds unaffordable. For instance, the supervisory authority of the Bourse Régionale des Valeurs Mobilières, the West African regional market, requires private companies to offer a guarantee equal to 100 percent of the issue value (interest, plus capital). This approach has been adopted to ensure that only companies with high-quality credit (or a guarantor) can issue debt. However, the result has been a de facto requirement for expensive guarantees, which add as much as 100–200 basis points to the cost for the issuer. The complex approval process for bond issuances also implies a long process of up to six months (in Kenya and in Senegal), which constitutes another hurdle for enterprises accessing corporate bond markets. In all these cases, there is a clear misalignment of objectives. The regulatory philosophy represented by the rules is appropriate in dealing with equities to protect small investors, but it is misplaced in dealing with institutions given that these can be expected to have access to professional investment advice and services.

High issuance costs are another impediment. In Kenya, issuance fees for corporate bonds have historically ranged from 3–4 percent compared with 1–2 percent for bank loans (World Bank 2003). In Nigeria, issuance fees in 2004 were over 6.0 percent, of which 1.8 percent went to regulatory authorities and the exchange, around 2.5 percent went to financial intermediaries, and another 1.5 percent went to fees for professionals and marketing. This turns a corporate bond issue into a financing tool of last resort. Costs are also high on the secondary market. Thus, in Nigeria, secondary market trading of corporate bonds involves fees of 3.75 percent, including 2.75 percent as a broker fee and 1.00 percent as a fee for the regulator and the exchange (World Bank 2007b).

In general, fixed income instruments are geared toward institutional investors, who have the capacity to operate in a disclosure-based framework. The requirement that corporate bonds need to be traded on exchanges shuts down a channel for introducing liquidity into the market. The one-off nature of the issuance of corporate bonds, combined with the small average size of issues, introduces a major liquidity constraint on this type of instrument. In this situation, the negotiation of the instrument by dealers and institutional investors in the over-the-counter market is the predominant practice around the world. Private placements can reduce the overall costs of a bond issuance because it shortens the time it takes companies to access the market.

The rather restrictive supervisory approach to issuers of stocks and bonds has been detrimental to the development of these markets in Africa. This observation is consistent with broader cross-country evidence that public enforcement contracts do not foster stock market development, but that laws mandating disclosure and facilitating private enforcement through liability rules benefit stock market liquidity (La Porta, Lopez-de-Silanes, and Shleifer 2006).

Tapping International Markets

As a source of finance, global investors have an important role to play in Africa. By investing through banks, contractual savings institutions, and capital markets in Africa, they not only provide finance for investment projects, but they also have the potential to increase and improve the intermediation capacity of financial systems. In this section, we discuss the sources of long-term finance in Africa associated with international financial markets. One is private equity funds, and the other is sovereign wealth funds (SWFs). Both of these include African funds, as well as non-African funds that invest in Africa. Affecting both, but especially the latter, is the changing global environment and the increasing role of Brazil, China, India, and other emerging markets in Africa. A final opportunity is diaspora bonds, which we discuss in box 4.8 elsewhere below. While we see the possibilities for raising funds with such an instrument, we remain rather skeptical in the case of countries in Africa.

Private equity funds

Where organized exchanges are too expensive, more private structures might be helpful. While equity funds have acquired a somewhat bad reputation in Europe, especially in the aftermath of the global financial crisis, equity funds could be an important part of the corporate finance solution in Africa (box 4.6).

In Africa, private equity is becoming a growing part of the financial sector, especially for long-term finance. In the boom years of 2006 to 2008, private equity funds raised in Sub-Saharan Africa amounted to approximately US$6.4 billion, while those invested reached US$7.6 billion. Similarly, a survey shows that North African countries raised at least US$1.6 billion in 2008 (ANIMA Investment Network 2008). Nonetheless, Africa still attracts only a small fraction of global equity funds, although there are promising trends (EMPEA and Coller Capital 2010). There is a growing number of seasoned and regionally experienced fund managers, an increasing number of investment opportunities (because of the improving macroenvironment, sustained growth, and significant regulatory reforms), and, critically, improving exit opportunities.

Although the financial crisis dented the market, there are clear signs of recovery. Fund-raising in Sub-Saharan Africa through 2010 reached US$1.5 billion, surpassing by far the 2009 total of US$964 million (figure 4.5). Following the financial crisis, the recovery of fund-raising momentum was stronger in Sub-Saharan Africa than in many other emerging markets, including China, India, and Russia, and was comparable with the robust performance in Latin America. In contrast, private equity investment activity tells a modest tale: investments with known transaction values accounted for US$631 million in 2010, the lowest level in emerging markets (EMPEA and Coller Capital 2010). This suggests that bullish fund-raising efforts are not being met with an equally bullish pipeline of transactions.

South Africa continues to be the main fund-raising hub and investment destination. Most funds operating in Sub-Saharan Africa have a panregional focus; these represent approximately 75 percent of the funds raised in both value and number from the beginning of 2009 through mid-2010 (figure 4.6). However, the market is slowly shifting away from generalist pan-African funds because fund managers are increasingly looking to specialize and develop a comparative advantage within an extremely diverse region. In terms of single-country focused funds,

Box 4.6   Private Equity Funds: The Benefits and Experience in Africa

The benefits of private equity funds can be assessed from different perspectives. At the macrolevel, private equity can catalyze structural changes through support for new economic sectors and by fostering industrial innovation (Kortum and Lerner 2000). It can help reduce unemployment rates, mainly among skilled workers, and spur overall employment growth (Fehn and Fuchs 2003; Belke, Fehn, and Foster 2003). Bernstein et al. (2009) show that industries with private equity investments grow more quickly in production, value added, and employment, while exhibiting more resilience to industry shocks. Conversely, opponents of private equity argue that these funds are return driven and that they reflect no hesitation to destroy jobs, ultimately jeopardizing global economic welfare in exchange for higher returns. According to this view, private equity funds are, at best, not value destroying, but certainly not value creating. In support of this view, Davis et al. (2008) report no differences in employment growth between their control group and manufacturing companies that are backed by private equity, and they report a higher level of job losses in businesses that are backed by private equity and that are operating in the services and finance sectors. Similarly, Lerner, Sørensen, and Strömberg (2008) find no significant difference in the quantity of patenting in the years following private equity investment. Most of this research, however, refers to cross-country samples or samples outside Africa, thus allowing few inferences on the expected effects of an increased role of private equity in Africa.

The employment and sales growth rates reported on random samples of exited deals in Morocco, South Africa, and Tunisia support the perception that businesses backed by private equity funds grow more rapidly and create more jobs than those without private equity fund support. South African businesses that were backed by private equity funds grew their sales by 20 percent, outperforming companies listed on the Johannesburg Stock Exchange and companies included in the all share index by 2 and 6 percent, respectively (SAVCA and DBSA 2009). Similarly, these companies backed by private equity funds reported employment growth rates significantly superior to the regional rates, which were estimated at almost 3 percent for North Africa and Sub-Saharan Africa. The involvement of private equity funds in African businesses seems to foster innovation as well. For instance, SAVCA and DBSA (2009) show that 69 percent of companies backed by private equity funds have introduced new products and services. According to the same report, the annual growth rate of research and development in these businesses was 7 percent, sevenfold the rate reported among companies listed on the Johannesburg Stock Exchange over the same period.

The value added of private equity funds can include more than the financing. A randomly selected sample of deals shows that private equity funds provided targeted businesses with valuable guidance that catalyzed improvements in their corporate governance structures and reporting standards. They also managed to strengthen management teams by leading to the replacement of entrenched managers, investment in training, or assistance in the recruitment of missing skills in the management team. This is consistent with the findings of Bloom, Sadun, and Van Reenen (2009) that businesses backed by private equity have superior management practices relative to family, private sector, and government ownership structures. The randomly selected sample also shows that private equity funds often introduce investee companies to strategic partners, including suppliers, clients, and acquisition targets which facilitate their expansion. Obviously, these simple comparisons cannot be interpreted in a causal sense because private equity funds will most likely invest in more promising industries and businesses, but the comparisons supply suggestive evidence that there is space for private equity in Africa to improve resource allocation and foster growth.

Box 4.6   Private Equity Funds: The Benefits and Experience in Africa *(continued)*

Private equity can generate benefits to the enterprises in which they invest, but this is also a profitable business proposal. As the head of one major global equity fund recently said, "the highest returns are in Africa." Data on the realized returns from deals made by private equity funds are difficult to collect because funds are reluctant to disclose information about their gains. Nonetheless, the limited data available suggest that African businesses deliver attractive returns to private equity funds. For instance, a recent survey published by the Moroccan Private Equity and Venture Capital Association reports average internal rates of return of 26.9 percent for 26 deals of private equity investors in Morocco (AMIC and Grant Thorton 2010). The highest rate is reported for deals involving development capital investments (33.3 percent). Several reports by the Emerging Markets Private Equity Association include data about internal rates of return for 62 deals and the realized multiplier for 25 deals (EMPEA 2011; EMPEA and Coller Capital 2009, 2010). This information is schematized in figure a. The average internal rate of return for deals exited between 2005 and 2010 was 55.4 percent if the 972 percent internal return on resources is included that is reported by Citadel Capital on its investment in ASCOM Geology & Mining in Egypt, which appears as an outlier, and 40.16 percent if this return is excluded.

Figure a. Average Internal Rate of Return and Multiplier by Exit Strategy

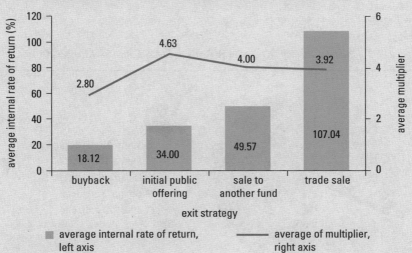

average internal rate of return, left axis

average of multiplier, right axis

South Africa is the market leader, accounting for 17 percent of funds by value, followed closely by Nigeria, at 10 percent. In North Africa, Egypt and Morocco are leading the markets. Most private equity markets in North Africa outside of these countries remain modest, but new funds are emerging. Over the last decade, the average size of deals among private equity funds in Africa increased significantly. For instance, the sale by Citadel of its ownership in Egypt Fertilizers Company was the first subregional private equity deal to break the billion-dollar mark.

Figure 4.5   Sub-Saharan Africa: Private Equity Fund-Raising and Investment, 2006–10

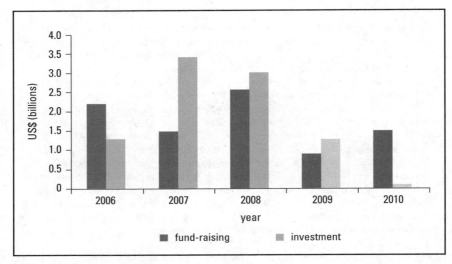

Source: EMPEA and Coller Capital (2010).
Note: The data for 2010 are year to date.

Figure 4.6   Private Equity Investment Activity, Sub-Saharan Africa, 2009–10

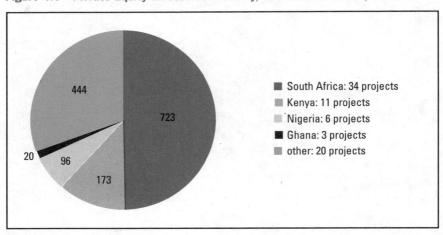

Source: EMPEA and Coller Capital (2010).
Note: The data for 2010 are year to date. Values are US$, millions.

The private equity model in Africa seems to target mainly well-established medium-size enterprises at the top end of the market. This is corroborated by survey data of ANIMA Investment Network (2008), which finds that there is a lack of seed and venture capital money compared with the equity investments in leveraged

Table 4.3 Risk Premiums for Private Equity Funds Worldwide
percent

Emerging market country, region	2008	2009	Increase in risk premium
Brazil	6.9	6.4	–0.5
China	6.3	6.4	0.1
India	6.1	6.4	0.3
South Africa	6.4	7.0	0.6
Latin America, excluding Brazil	6.7	7.5	0.8
Middle East	6.5	7.3	0.8
North Africa	6.7	8.0	1.3
Central and Eastern Europe, including Turkey	5.0	6.4	1.4
Russian Federation, Commonwealth of Independent States	6.9	8.4	1.5
Sub-Saharan Africa, excluding South Africa	6.7	8.4	1.7
Other emerging Asia	—	7.3	—

Source: EMPEA and Coller Capital (2009).
Note: The figure reflects the perceptions of limited partners (investors in private equity funds) of the risk premiums required for emerging market private equity funds relative to developed-market buyout funds.
— = not available.

buyouts and the expansion of investee companies in North Africa. Similar conclusions can be drawn from a study on Kenya (FSD Kenya 2008). The study found that, in 2008, US$40 million of the US$200 million of venture capital available in the country targeted early-stage SMEs. In addition, larger countries with a rising middle class, such as Egypt, Nigeria, and Tunisia, are more attractive to private equity funds given the potential for consumer goods industries.

Notwithstanding these positive trends, the main obstacles continue to be the limited interest of financiers in investment in private equity funds targeting Africa and the excessive risk aversion of investors toward Africa (table 4.3). Investors in Sub-Saharan Africa north of the Limpopo River demand some of the highest risk premiums, and risk premiums in the North African countries are only slightly lower. Investor behavior reflects the lack of an institutional track record because most of these funds are first-generation funds, as well as the perception that political risk remains high in Africa relative to other regions of the world (figure 4.7). For instance, well-publicized cases such as the tensions over the Jubilee oil field that pitted the government of Ghana against private equity–backed Komsos Energy are likely to damage the frail confidence of private equity investors in African markets. Furthermore, poor governance structures and inadequate research coverage make the identification and assessment of potential investment targets a challenge for private equity funds. Another key challenge for equity funds is the limited local access to debt coinvestment.

In addition to the perceptions of high risk, the industry suffers several specific challenges in Africa, most of them related to the institutional environment in which the industry operates.

Figure 4.7   Factors Deterring Limited Partners from Investing in Africa and Latin America

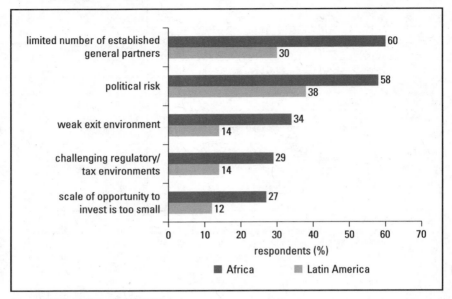

Source: EMPEA and Coller Capital (2010).
Note: Limited partners are investors in private equity funds. General partners are private equity fund managers.

First, the lack of scale affects private equity in three ways. Most private equity funds in Africa are small, which, by construction, excludes investments from several institutional investors, including SWFs. These funds usually have large investment tickets and strict exposure limits dictated by their risk management guidelines. For instance, if an SWF has an average investment ticket amounting to US$80 million and an exposure limit to a single investment of 20 percent, only private equity funds larger than US$400 million will be eligible. The size of investment opportunities also limits private participation. On any number of measures, the size of many firms is small; many are family owned and reluctant to bring in third-party management participation, which is essential for private equity. Finally, many of the markets make exit challenging. The highly illiquid stock exchanges and the limited availability of domestic funds severely limit the range of exit options for most private equity firms.

Second, there are many domestic regulatory constraints. For instance, current regulations in Morocco preclude insurance companies from using their regulated reserves instead of their equity to invest in risk capital entities that are not structured as *organismes de placement en capital risque* (OPCRs, venture capital investment funds). Insurance companies are also required to report their investments at accounting value rather than market value, which reduces their appetite to invest in private equity structures.[11] Furthermore, Law 41–05 offers tax incentives to OPCRs, but requires such institutions to hold at least 50 percent of their resources in SMEs with annual turnover inferior to DH 75 million. The SME definition is being reviewed to reflect current market practices, and the 2011 Finance Act eliminated this minimum allocation rule, but the rule remains a problem because OPCR status is still conditional on compliance with it.[12] Additionally, current regulations on foreign exchange preclude private equity funds domiciled in Morocco with less than three years of operation from investing outside the country.[13] Similarly, Tunisia requires local private equity providers to invest at least 50 percent of their resources in priority sectors or regional development zones and upgrade programs, while investors in such vehicles are required to lock their investments for at least five years to benefit from tax exemptions.[14]

Third, there remains only a limited participation of contractual savings institutions. In Tunisia, domestic private equity markets are dominated by bank-controlled providers. These operators tend to favor applications made by the existing clients of banks and often adopt prudent investment strategies that are not always consistent with the purposes of banking. Financial institutions control 75 percent of the capital of fund managers in Morocco as well as slightly over 31 percent of the funds under management in South Africa (AMIC and Grant Thorton 2010; KPMG and SAVCA 2010). One of the investors in an equity fund may be contractual savings institutions, which have only a limited choice on organized capital markets. Yet, the contribution of pension funds and insurance companies seems to be small. For instance, they contribute less than 10 percent of the total venture capital funding in Kenya (FSD Kenya 2008). Most African countries restrain pension funds' and insurance companies' investment share in equity, which significantly reduces the potential resources available to African private equity funds. However, as noted elsewhere above, there is a trend toward the revision of investment guidelines. In September, Nigeria's National Pension Plan released draft regulations that would allow pensions to invest up to 5 percent of their portfolios in private equity funds targeting Nigeria.

Fourth, there are also ownership and foreign exchange barriers to foreign private equity funds. Some countries still restrict foreign ownership. Algeria imposes a 49 percent limit on foreign ownership, with the exception of importing companies, which must have a minimum of 30 percent of local participation (Deloitte 2011). The borrowing levels of foreign-controlled companies are restricted in South Africa (Bowman Gilfillan 2009). In Ethiopia, foreign investment is prohibited in the telecommunications, financial, transportation, and retail sectors. Even where there are no ownership restrictions, few African countries have fully convertible currencies, and a large number of them do not allow free profit repatriation for private equity and venture capital providers. In addition, several African countries have volatile currencies that cannot be properly hedged given the lack of instruments or the poor liquidity of the available instruments. Local currency volatility could result in a dramatic decline in a fund's performance.

Fifth, there are also taxation-related barriers across the continent. First, there is a double-taxation issue because investment revenue is taxed both at the fund and the ultimate investor level. Even if this may be addressed in individual countries, there is a lack of double-taxation treaties among African countries. Another issue related to some African tax regimes is the application of the value added tax on management fees or carried interest. Fund managers are subject to a 20 percent value added tax on management fees in Morocco. These taxes increase the cost of doing business significantly. Often, disparities in tax treatment make other asset classes more attractive. Today, most international private equity funds are based in Mauritius for tax purposes. Moreover, they also benefit from the fact that Mauritius offers both a common law framework and a civil law framework, a stable business environment, and a well-developed financial services industry.

Lastly, in the aftermath of the financial crisis, Europe and the United States are enacting new rules aimed at regulating nonbank financial institutions and enhancing the stability of their financial systems. These rules are expected to make fundraising for private equity funds targeting Africa more challenging and expensive. For instance, the European Union's Directive on Alternative Investment Fund Managers will make it more costly for non-European Union–based private equity funds to market their funds to European investors. Similarly, new registration requirements with the U.S. Securities and Exchange Commission will increase the cost of doing business for non-U.S. funds that have more than 15 United States–based investors, U.S. resources in excess of US$25 million, and at least one office in the United States (PEI 2010). Thus, the Volcker Rule, which is expected to become effective in July 2012, precludes banking entities—both U.S. and non-U.S. banks with a U.S. branch or agency—from investing in or sponsoring private equity and hedge funds (Clifford Chance 2010). The increased burden resulting from this regulation will reduce the amount of resources available for investments in private equity in Africa and raise the cost of managing private equity funds targeting Africa, ultimately translating into lower returns to investors and new limits on their appetite to invest in Africa.

Despite these challenges, private equity funds in Africa are growing and are expected to play a more significant role in the future. Multilateral and regional DFIs are increasingly using them as a complementary way for more cost-effective investment and support for private sector firms in Africa. In 2009–10, the African Development Bank invested in 13 private equity funds targeting Africa; as of September 30, 2010, its investments in private equity funds represented 10 percent of its private sector active portfolio. Similarly, the International Finance Corporation launched the SME Ventures Program, which aims at establishing venture capital funds in several International Development Association countries, including the Central African Republic, the Democratic Republic of Congo, Liberia, and Sierra Leone. The Development Bank of Namibia has established a private equity fund focused on SMEs.

The performance of the public-led versus private-led model has not yet been explored in Africa. Nonetheless, recent evidence reported in Brander, Du, and Hellman (2010) based on a sample of 126 countries suggests that a PPP model, whereby the government invests in independently managed funds that also rely on private investors, leads to better results in terms of value creation and innovation compared with either a public-led model or a private-led model.

Sovereign wealth funds

Another potentially significant source of long-term funding is SWFs with strategic interests in Africa. These include funds in China, India, and the Middle East that have become important players in African infrastructure projects. The appetite of SWFs in Africa is growing for minerals and raw materials, as seen in China's successful efforts to lock up deals in the oil and gas sector, but they also provide substantial funding for transport infrastructure. SWFs from the Middle East are active in the physical and social infrastructure sectors. One can expect these trends to continue in the near future, though they may slow as some of the SWFs restructure portfolios and investment strategies damaged by the global financial crisis. SWFs experienced considerable losses as a result of the crisis, but remain active in the exploration of infrastructure opportunities in Africa. For instance, the 2008 annual report published by the Central Bank of Libya shows that revenues from the Libyan Investment Authority's long-term investment portfolio dropped from US$687.3 million in 2007 to US$63.5 million in 2008, mainly because of the financial crisis.

As of December 2009, African SWFs had US$114.3 billion in assets under management. This was much less than their Middle East peers, which held assets amounting to US$1.4 trillion (figure 4.8). The regional distribution of SWFs dis-

Figure 4.8 The Size of Sovereign Wealth Funds, December 2009

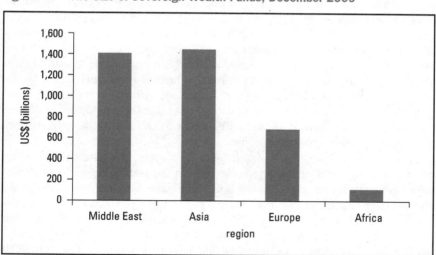

Source: Data of the Sovereign Wealth Fund Institute.

plays a predominance of the Middle East (43 percent), followed by Asia (36 percent) and Europe (18 percent).

Africa counts 15 SWFs. More can be expected, especially in countries with recently discovered oil (box 4.7).[15] Meanwhile, in 2006, Chad canceled its Fund for Future Generations. Among the five largest African SWFs, four are sourced from oil and gas revenues, and one from diamonds, minerals, and other natural resources. It must be noted, however, that the collection of data on the existence, holdings, and institutional arrangements of SWFs in Africa remains a challenge. This explains why there is also a limited literature on the activities of these funds.

In the case of Africa's development process, one has to make the important distinction between the role of domestic wealth funds—the task of which is mainly to manage a nation's natural wealth and stabilize the income stream from this wealth, thereby avoiding the well-documented Dutch Disease phenomenon—and the role of non-African SWFs.

Let us first discuss the role of domestic SWFs in managing Africa's natural wealth. Domestic SWFs can have a critical role in avoiding the Dutch Disease phenomenon that result from an appreciation of the real exchange rate, thus crowding out non–resource-related economic activities. They can prove to be efficient fiscal stabilization instruments by facilitating intergenerational transfers and creating higher risk-adjusted returns that allow savings in fiscal resources. For most African countries, such stabilization needs are twofold. In the short term, African countries need to smooth their expenditures in a context of volatile commodity prices to avoid the challenges in macroeconomic management resulting from revenue instability. In the long term, African countries need to protect themselves against the declines in revenues resulting from the depletion of nonrenewable commodities. This means that SWFs might still invest in financial markets and systems to pursue long-term stabilization objectives. They can also help avoid problematic privatizations and the looting of national wealth, as has happened so often already on the continent. Unlike the management of reserves by central banks, which is usually limited to investments in European and U.S. sovereign fixed income securities, SWF holdings are expected to be more diversified and could be structured to maximize the risk-adjusted investment returns that are not necessarily pegged to the dollar. Stabilization funds help insulate African economies from bullish and bearish cycles driven by commodity price swings and ensure fiscal stabilization. A final, less discussed, purpose of domestic SWFs can be to enhance overall transparency and governance throughout the economy.

However, the available data suggest that African countries have been regularly using their SWFs to close budget deficits rather than keeping resources to implement countercyclical macroeconomic policies or future long-term and intergenerational stabilization. For instance, Nigeria paid US$6.8 billion out of the Excess Crude Account to state governors in 2008, while Sudan has almost wiped out its Oil Revenue Stabilization Fund to meet increased expenditure commitments (Ahmed 2010). Additional drawdowns of US$12 billion in 2009 and US$7 billion in 2010 almost entirely depleted the fund. Algeria has also been using its stabilization fund

Box 4.7   Sovereign Wealth Funds

SWFs are government-owned investment vehicles managed by a government entity or external managers on behalf of a sovereign state primarily to serve medium- to long-term economic and financial objectives. They have emerged as a potential solution for the active management of the large stocks of foreign reserves that several countries have accumulated by exporting commodities and other goods and services. There is considerable controversy about the relative merits of SWFs and their value added. Often citing the experience of Norway, the International Monetary Fund and the World Bank are increasingly advocating the creation of SWFs in resource-endowed economies, arguing that they can help foster economic growth and prosperity for current and future generations. Proponents of SWFs also point out that these vehicles can help stabilize the global financial system by providing crossborder liquidity in times of financial turmoil. Other observers, meanwhile, are expressing serious concerns that SWFs would endow governments with too much power, which could edge the global economy away from liberalism and impede market forces and competition. This argument is strengthened by empirical evidence suggesting that state-owned companies often operate less efficiently than private firms.

The first African SWFs were established in 1993 in Botswana (the Pula Fund) and Ghana (the Minerals Development Fund). Currently, Africa counts 15 active SWFs, which are, for the most part, relatively small compared with their peers in other regions of the world (such as Asia and the Middle East) in terms of the size of assets. The two exceptions are the Libyan Investment Authority (LIA) and the Algerian Revenue Regulation Fund, which rank among the largest 15 SWFs worldwide in size.

The LIA is the largest and most active Africa-based SWF, although the political unrest in Libya has created uncertainty about its future. It was created in December 2006 by a decree of the Comité Populaire Général and started its activity on June 2007 with US$50 billion in assets under management. The aim of the LIA, which currently manages about US$70 billion in assets, is to create a durable source of revenue and reduce Libya's dependence on oil

Figure a. The Geographical Distribution of Libyan Investment Authority Investments in Africa by Region

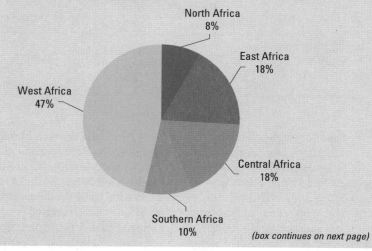

(box continues on next page)

Box 4.7   Sovereign Wealth Funds *(continued)*

exports. It invests both domestically and internationally either directly or via its subsidiaries. The bulk of LIA's investment in Africa, however, is undertaken by the Libyan African Investment Portfolio, which was created in February 2006 and has around US$8 billion in assets under management. Its subsidiary, the Libyan African Investment Company, is present in 30 African countries, where it invests mainly in real estate and hotels (it owns 22 hotels in 15 African countries). The Libya Oil Holding Company (formerly Tamoil), another subsidiary of the LIA, runs gas stations in 16 African countries.

In terms of the regional allocation of LIA's investments in Africa, a sample of 98 deals shows that West Africa stands out as the largest beneficiary, with a share of 47 percent (figure a). East Africa and Central Africa each attract 18 percent of total investments. In terms of the sector allocation of these investments, the largest fraction is allocated to restaurants, hotels, and motels, followed by real estate and infrastructure (figure b).

Figure b. The Sectoral Distribution of Libyan Investment Authority Investments in Africa

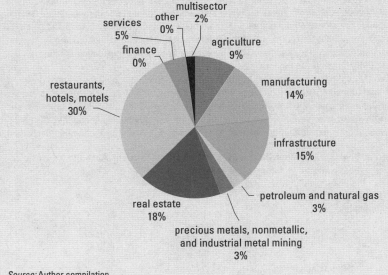

Source: Author compilation.

to repay public debt and reduce fiscal deficits. Similarly, between November 2008 and March 2009, Mauritania withdrew US$45 million from its Fond National des Revenus des Hydrocarbures, leaving a balance of US$34 million as of March 2009. São Tomé and Príncipe withdrew US$11.9 million in 2006, US$1.7 million in 2008, and US$1.2 million in 2009, leaving its fund with US$9.9 million at the end of 2009. This represented 12 percent of the US$77.8 million received by the country as an oil signature bonus. Such statistics suggest that African governments kept spending, while also accumulating resources in their stabilization funds, which may potentially result in zero net savings. This raises concerns about intergenerational equity and long-term fiscal and macroeconomic sustainability, especially in a context of external shocks. The implication of such behavior is that African SWFs will have limited resources for long-term stabilization purposes and even less for savings for future generations. Accordingly, the role of SWFs as long-term investors in Africa can only be marginal if current practices are maintained.

Additionally, data suggest that most African SWFs are investing their resources mostly outside Africa. For instance, Asfaha (2007) reports that Chad invests the proceeds from its natural resources abroad, while article 6.6 of the Oil Revenue Management Law in São Tomé and Príncipe prohibits the use of the National Oil Account for investments in São Tomé and Príncipe or in companies controlled by São Tomé and Príncipe nationals (Albin-Lackey et al. 2004). According to the São Tomé and Príncipe oil revenue law, the National Oil Account is to be held at the U.S. Federal Reserve. Similarly, Belaicha, Bouzidi, and Labaronne (2009) argue that half of Algeria's foreign currency reserves have been invested in U.S. sovereign bonds and deposits and tier-one banks. Botswana invests only in rated securities, which excludes all Sub-Saharan African countries except South Africa.

Over the past decade or so, Africa has also become the target of investment by non-African SWFs. Some governments are creating development funds (the China-Africa Development Fund established by the China Development Bank) or investment companies (Dubai World Africa) entirely dedicated to Africa.[16] Nonetheless, Africa's share in foreign SWF investments remains relatively negligible. Many SWFs, including African funds, are discouraged by the high risk of investment in Africa. According to recent research published by TheCityUK (2010), an independent membership body that promotes the financial and professional services industry based in the United Kingdom, Africa receives less than 5 percent of worldwide SWF investment flows. Similarly, as of December 2009, of 8,300 companies in which the Norway SWF held equity investments, only 144 (corresponding to 1.74 percent) were African, and these companies were concentrated in only three countries, namely, Egypt (32 companies), Morocco (8 companies), and South Africa (104 companies).

Such investment strategies are justified by the weak governance and significant volatility of African economies. Unfortunately, investment risk in Africa is still perceived as high, which hinders the continent's attractiveness as a target for African SWF money. This brings us back to the sequencing issue. African countries would have to reform governance structures and communicate more about the returns and risk profile of financial markets and institutions in Africa before SWF money would follow.

Foreign SWFs could have a striking effect on the amount of investment received by Africa. Statistics published by TheCityUK show that SWFs were managing US$3.8 trillion in assets globally as of December 2009. The Organisation for Economic Co-operation and Development expects assets under SWF management to reach US$5 trillion in 2010 and US$10 trillion by 2015. Investing 1 percent of current SWF resources in Africa would channel up to US$29.7 billion in foreign investment to the continent.

As with all foreign direct investment (FDI), however, there are also risks for receiving countries. First, high and volatile capital inflows, albeit with less volatility for SWFs, can lead to asset boom-and-bust cycles, especially in small countries with small and illiquid capital markets. Second, destabilization can result from SWF involvement in the banking sector, where these funds can distort the credit allocation process to favor home country businesses (Heyward 2008). Third, large reverses in SWF flows resulting from profit repatriation or asset reallocations also involve currency transactions that might affect the exchange rates of African countries, as was observed during the early stages of the financial crisis.

The Changing Global Environment: Tales of Dragons and Elephants

Among the options available for tapping international finance, none is more noticeable than the BRIC countries, particularly China. China, India, and several Gulf states have been increasingly investing in Africa. This investment has come after a decade-long trend toward increased trade between middle-income emerging markets and Africa (map 4.1). This must also be seen in light of the increased demand for natural resources by emerging markets, notably the BRIC countries. There are other complementarities between these large emerging markets and Africa that likewise explain the increasing cooperation. China and India, for example, bring expertise from the construction sector and from their recent experience in building large infrastructure. Chinese construction firms are globally competitive, and they have won a large number of civil works contracts financed by the African Development Bank and the World Bank (Foster et al. 2008). Furthermore, both countries have a growing need for natural resources for their rapidly expanding manufacturing sectors and want to diversify their large financial resources away from U.S. Treasury Bonds. They have increasing food needs as well because of growing populations and increasingly scarce arable land. Chinese finance is often invested in large-scale infrastructure projects, with a particular focus on hydropower generation and railways. Currently, more than 35 African countries are engaging with China on infrastructure finance deals. The biggest recipients are Angola, Ethiopia, Nigeria, and Sudan.

The China-Africa economic ties experienced a great leap forward after the first triennial Forum on China-Africa Cooperation, held in Beijing in October 2000. Bilateral trade and Chinese FDI in Africa grew about fourfold between 2001 and 2005. This was accompanied by a major influx of Chinese enterprises and workers in the region. The natural resource exports of Sub-Saharan Africa to China grew exponentially, from slightly more than US$3 billion in 2001 to US$22 billion in 2006. Foster et al. (2008) estimate that Chinese financial commitments to African

Map 4.1   Trade Links between the BRIC Countries and Africa, 1980–2009

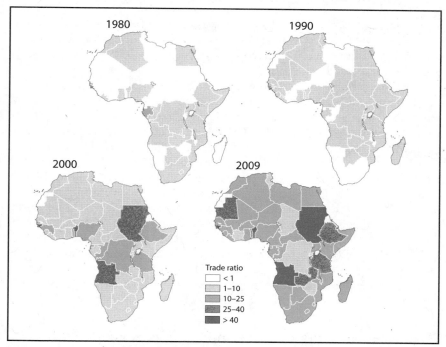

Source: Direction of Trade Statistics (database), International Monetary Fund, Washington, DC, http://elibrary-data. imf.org/FindDataReports.aspx?d=33061&e=170921 (assessed in 2010).
Note: The figure shows the ratio of the total BRIC trade with Africa to African trade with the world.

infrastructure projects rose from less than US$1 billion per year in 2001–03 to around US$1.5 billion per year in 2004–05 and reached at least US$7 billion in 2006, China's official "Year of Africa," before trailing back to US$4.5 billion in 2007. Chinese infrastructure finance has been widespread across sectors, from oil to hydropower and transportation. However, in the period through 2007, there was a geographical concentration. Over 70 percent of the finance went to only four countries: Angola, Ethiopia, Nigeria, and Sudan.

A typical arrangement is for the Chinese investment entity, whether private or state-owned, to form a joint venture with the local African state-owned enterprise. This has been the pattern set, for example, in the Democratic Republic of Congo, the Republic of Congo, Gabon, and Zambia. Chinese FDI flows typically involve investments by Chinese contractors that are funded through bilateral loans from the Export-Import Bank of China to the government of the beneficiary country. This accounted for 92 percent of recorded Chinese investment projects from 2001 to 2007. This leaves little room for African banks to become involved in the funding of the projects. Increasingly, the China-Africa Development Fund has gained importance. While, previously, China Eximbank lent mostly to state-owned Chinese enterprises, it has recently also opened up its coffers to private Chinese enterprises. This has resulted in the Angola mode, or resources for infrastructure, whereby repayment of the loan for infrastructure development is made using natural resources.

What drives China's interest in Africa? According to Cheung et al. (2011), the determinants of China's engagement in Africa are similar to the determinants of traditional FDI: the search for new markets and follow-up on trade links, as well as natural resources, especially oil. Unlike Western countries, Chinese FDI is less influenced by concerns about the risk of political instability or corruption and therefore flows to countries where Western investors often do not dare to invest. China has also started creating special economic zones, such as in Mauritius and in the Chambishi copper belt region in Zambia. India has followed suit, using the Export-Import Bank of India. Similarly, several Arab countries have invested in African infrastructure projects. The finance from Arab donors is channeled through special funds or development agencies, such as the Islamic Development Bank, the Arab Bank for Economic Development in Africa, the Kuwait Fund for Arab Economic Development, the OPEC Fund, and the Saudi Fund.

Another possible option for raising international finance for the benefit of Africa is represented by diaspora bonds, which we analyze in box 4.8.

Pushing toward the Frontier and Beyond: A Long-Term Agenda with Tricky Shortcuts

Lengthening financial contracts in Africa requires that policy makers address the structural bottlenecks that inhibit the issuance of longer-term contracts. To this end, there is a need to (1) increase the diversity of domestic sources of long-term finance and (2) promote an appropriately diverse range of long-term financial products and services. As in the case of expanding access, we can distinguish among several layers of policies for lengthening contracts. On the first level are market-developing policies, that is, policies that help create the necessary conditions for long-term funding flowing to and staying in Africa, as well for long-term financing tools and products to emerge. While far from sufficient, these policies are necessary. Most prominently among them are policies aimed at the contractual framework and macroeconomic conditions, including price stability and the development of long-term sovereign bond markets.

These policy reforms seek to unlock substantial additional sources of long-term finance through currently existing, but underdeveloped segments of financial systems, including pensions, insurance, and capital markets. While a boom in contractual savings cannot be expected in the short term (because of demographic and income factors), a stronger role for insurance companies, pension funds, and mutual funds should be fostered. Such reforms should also seek to encourage new

Box 4.8 Diaspora Bonds

A diaspora bond is a debt instrument issued by a country or, potentially, by a subsovereign entity or by a private corporation to raise financing from its overseas diaspora. India and Israel have raised US$11 billion and US$25 billion, respectively, from their diaspora abroad (Ketkar and Ratha 2010). The people of the diaspora usually have more information about their country of origin than other foreign investors. These bonds are issued often in times of crisis and frequently at a "patriotic" discount. Unlike international investors, the people of the diaspora tend to be less averse to convertibility risk because they are likely to have current and contingent liabilities in their home countries. Furthermore, they usually have a strong desire to contribute to the development of their home countries and are therefore more likely to purchase diaspora bonds.

The stock of the Sub-Saharan African diaspora is estimated at about 16 million, with 5 million in high-income countries. Assuming that members of the Sub-Saharan African diaspora earn the average income of their host countries and save a fifth of their incomes, their annual savings would be more than US$28 billion. Most of these savings would come from African migrants in the countries of the Organisation for Economic Co-operation and Development, where a third of the Sub-Saharan African diaspora is located, because of the larger income differentials. In an alternative scenario, if the Sub-Saharan African diaspora were assumed to earn only half the average per capita income in the host countries and save a fifth of their incomes, the annual savings of the African diaspora would still be over US$10 billion. Presently, the bulk of this savings is invested outside Africa. African governments and private corporations can potentially tap into these resources by issuing diaspora bonds. Diaspora bonds can also provide an instrument for the repatriation of Africa's flight capital, estimated at more than US$170 billion (see chapter 2). Diaspora bonds could potentially raise US$5 billion to US$10 billion annually by tapping into this wealth.

While the size of the potential market for diaspora bonds is impressive, it may be difficult for most unrated Sub-Saharan African countries that are characterized by high risk to issue such bonds. Some of the constraints that Sub-Saharan African countries may face in issuing these bonds include weak and nontransparent legal systems for contract enforcement; a lack of national banks and other institutions in migrant destination countries, which can facilitate the marketing of these bonds; and a lack of clarity on regulations in the host countries that allow or constrain people in the diaspora in the investment in such bonds (Chander 2001; Ketkar and Ratha 2010). Finally, the diaspora of African countries is typically dispersed across various host countries, constituting small communities, which makes fund-raising more costly and more difficult.

Source: Based on Ratha, Mohapatra, and Plaza (2008).

providers and more competition, for example through equity funds. More urgent, however, is the need to explore alternative methods for intermediating pension recourses transparently.

On a second level are market-enabling policies that take the current environment as a given and try to maximize the absorption and intermediation of existing resources in the financial system. These policies should be focused on competi-

tion—encouraging the entry of new providers—and the removal of regulatory restrictions, as discussed in the case of equity funds above. However, they may also
imply the application of market-friendly activist approaches that try to crowd in
private providers. Most prominently among these have been partial credit guarantee funds as risk mitigation instruments.

Macroeconomic stability

Most African countries have made enormous progress in macroeconomic stability
over the past 20 years. Chart a in figure 4.9 shows the median inflation rate across
African countries, while chart b in figure 4.9, shows the standard deviation of inflation, computed over five-year rolling averages. Behind these medians, however, are
some rather large outliers, such as Zimbabwe.

External debt has been reduced substantially across Africa, often because of the
heavily indebted poor countries initiative. In the case of commodity exporters, the
reduction has also been caused by commodity price increases. The privatization of
loss-making state-owned enterprises can also contribute to an easing of fiscal pressure and thus reduce the crowding out effect. However, many countries in Sub-
Saharan Africa still depend heavily on donor flows. Although Mozambique, for
example, benefited from debt relief under the heavily indebted poor countries initiative in 2001 and the multilateral debt relief initiative in 2006, the budget for 2008

Figure 4.9   Inflation and Inflation Volatility, 1990–2009

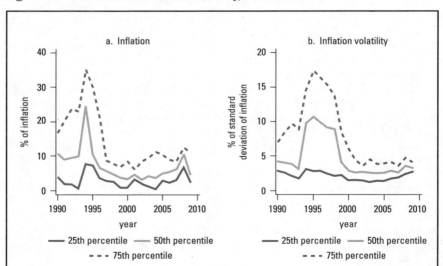

Source: International Financial Statistics (database), International Monetary Fund, Washington, DC, http://elibrary-
data.imf.org/FindDataReports.aspx?d=33061&e=169393 (accessed in 2010).
Note: Sample size: chart a: 35 countries; chart b: 32 countries. The number of countries indicated represents the
situation following the balancing of the data set.

projected external funding of 55 percent from various bilateral and multilateral donors. In large part because of Mozambique's success in implementing public financial management reforms, a substantial proportion of external assistance takes the form of direct budget support.

Despite the sustained macroeconomic stability in many African countries, the yield curve is still steep in most countries, if it exists at all. This can be explained by the high risk premium on long-term resources, which, in turn, is caused by political uncertainty and uncertainty about the willingness of governments to meet longer-term commitments, and which is also reflected in the illiquidity of long-term capital markets. The effective management of government debt—often seen as a purely technical area, but extensively discussed by Honohan and Beck (2007)—can make an important contribution to the creation of a yield curve and also help flatten it. As confidence in markets improves and issuing costs fall, the issuance of longer-term bonds, for example for infrastructure, can also help establish a yield curve. Interest rates might have to be adjustable, however, until confidence is created in long-term, stable macroeconomic management. A yield curve is a necessary, though far from sufficient condition for private market participants to lengthen their financial contracts. Having a benchmark curve allows easier pricing so that banks and other financial institutions may establish prices. Benchmark curves can also help reduce the risks in refinancing.

An important aspect of the management of macrostability is the challenge of tending to the Dutch Disease phenomena that arise from large inflows of capital through aid money, revenues related to commodity exports, or—least likely in the case of most African countries—portfolio inflows. If such inflows are mostly spent on import goods, a more relaxed approach can be considered, while an increase in the demand for domestic goods and services can easily result in inflationary pressures. For natural resources, there are SWFs, as we discuss above. Similar problems, however, can arise from aid surges if they are not absorbed properly in the domestic economy. Here, the domestic financial system has a critical role in terms of absorbing such funds.

Institution building

As discussed above, financial institutions in Africa, as in other parts of the developing world, face significant hurdles in the screening and monitoring of borrowers, that is, in choosing creditworthy borrowers and projects and in ensuring repayment, especially for long-term transactions. This points to the critical role of the contractual and informational framework, as well as appropriate corporate governance structures.

The informational framework, most importantly accounting and auditing standards, are critical to long-term transactions. This might enable banks to undertake what Berger and Udell (2006) refer to as financial statement lending, at least for medium-size and larger firms. The reliability of cash flows for a long-term investment can be a viable form of collateral if there is confidence in the financial statements that have been produced.

While many countries in Africa have taken the first step in advocating for the use of international financial reporting standards, at least for enterprises above a certain size, as well as for financial institutions, more work remains to be done. The emergence of a number of strong national accounting associations and professions on the continent is a welcome development for the industry.

Reforms in the contractual framework and corporate governance are another important item on the long-term agendas of policy makers throughout the region. There have been advances, though much slower than hoped by the modernists. These agendas comprise a large number of elements, ranging from changes in legal codes to changes in the court systems and building and reforming property and collateral registries. Recent reforms have been promising. In 2010, Ghana created a unified registry for movable property and now requires any secured credit agreement covering an amount of about US$350 or above to be registered in the collateral registry. In recent years, Rwanda has significantly upgraded company law and related legislation, strengthening minority shareholder rights and disclosure requirements for companies. The 16 member countries of the Organization for the Harmonization of Business Law in Africa have started reviewing the Uniform Commercial Act (see World Bank and IFC, various).

Regulatory and legal reforms

Beyond the ongoing challenges of macroeconomic stability and the proper management of international capital flows, as well as the long-term tasks of building a contractual and informational framework, there is also an array of more immediate, short-term steps that governments can take to push financial systems toward the frontier of long-term finance.

One area is the regulatory framework for various segments of financial systems. As we discuss above, there are many regulations that, for the sake of stability, restrict the engagement of banks in long-term finance, but that, for the sake of usefulness for financial stability, might also be questioned. Loan concentration ratios—typically defined relative to capital—can be restrictive in terms of the scale of lending. In Africa, concentration ratios are defined at relatively high levels, at 20 percent or more in most countries. Exceptions are Ghana, where it is only 10 percent in the case of unsecured lending, and Tanzania, where it is only 5 percent for unsecured loans. Having to lend 60 percent of a portfolio to borrowers who are eligible for refinancing by central banks, as is still formally the case in West Africa, can also increase the cost of lending for banks and limit the borrower universe.

The legal and regulatory framework, including adjustments in tax codes, might be necessary if the leasing industry is to take off. Similarly, stamp duties and restrictions contained in legal codes concerning the sale of claims to third parties can limit the extent to which factoring is used as a financing instrument. Likewise, regulatory restrictions on the operations of domestic and international equity funds, as well as concerns about taxation, can limit the extent to which equity funds enter markets, as we discuss above.

An important and often overlooked challenge is the demand side. In chapter 3, we discuss the extent to which demand-side constraints can limit the expansion of the banked population; such constraints can also hold back the access to and use of credit services by enterprises, especially small and medium-size firms. Turning investment into bankable projects requires business planning and development skills that many entrepreneurs lack, but can be taught. Furthermore, even if the financing constraints are eliminated, enterprises across Africa face a plethora of constraints related to market and government failures that have to be addressed in the context of a broader reform of the business environment. African enterprises feel more constrained about various dimensions of the business environment relative to enterprises in other regions of the developing world. One should not downplay the importance of finance, but it is not necessarily always the binding constraint.

Beyond easing regulatory restrictions, addressing demand-side constraints, and fostering competition, governments across the continent have tended to favor more activist instruments in seeking to foster lending to underserved segments of the enterprise universe. Directed lending through commercial or development banks has not helped in most instances. A more indirect method is partial credit guarantees. Because these have become the intervention tool of choice among many donors and governments, we discuss the experience a bit more in depth below.

Public-private partnerships

We discuss the benefits, elsewhere above, that PPPs can create by closing infrastructure gaps. In most countries, however, the legislation on such partnerships remains confusing. How and with whom should one start negotiations? With the line ministry or the ministry of finance? Do the competitive clauses of national procurement laws apply to all PPP transactions? There is weak capacity in the public and private sectors in the management of such partnerships, and there is an opaque bidding process. PPPs in infrastructure have therefore not been used in Africa to their full potential or even to the same extent as they are used in other developing regions.

The donor community has initiated and invested in a number of funds aimed at attracting private financing for infrastructure projects in the form of PPPs. For their part, governments across Africa are making a concerted effort to harness this source of long-term finance by strengthening the legal and regulatory framework for PPP transactions. In Zambia, for example, the government has recognized that it has limited resources to embark on all the infrastructure development projects on its wish list and is actively working to improve the PPP environment. In December 2008, the government approved a policy framework for the implementation of PPPs. A central unit has been established at the Ministry of Finance and subunits in line ministries, including the Zambia Development Agency. The legal and regulatory framework has been approved by Parliament.

For countries such as Zambia to strengthen their pipelines for PPPs substantially, more work is required to ensure that the PPP legislation enacted by parliaments and the accompanying regulations issued by ministerial statutory instruments are conducive to a wide variety of PPP transactions, support national PPP agencies in acquiring the relevant technical skills and financial resources to act as effective PPP transaction facilitators on behalf of the government, and ensure that all relevant public and private stakeholders in PPP transactions have a clear, established process for facilitating such transactions in a coordinated and complimentary manner.

An important mechanism for increasing the appetite for PPPs for longer-term infrastructure projects is represented by risk mitigation instruments, to which we turn next.

Risk mitigation instruments

Over the years, some specialized instruments have been developed to mitigate the effects of specific risks. In housing, for example, mortgage liquidity facilities help lenders obtain long-term funds to finance their retail mortgage portfolios. This is a popular model that many francophone African countries have adopted in the form of *caisses de refinancement hypothécaire*, which is based on a similar institution in France. Such institutions exist, have existed, or are planned in Egypt, Gabon, Nigeria, Rwanda, South Africa, Tanzania, and the countries of the West African Economic and Monetary Union. The basic concept is simple: mortgage lenders are allowed to use their mortgage assets as collateral for loans from a centralized bond issuer. The bond issuer or liquidity facility is typically owned by the banks that use it for refinance purposes and is therefore a sort of mutual organization providing a service to members. The institution gains its strength from a strong capital base and careful lending, which is secured by mortgage assets as collateral.

Lenders can use a mortgage liquidity facility in two ways. First, it can be used as a direct source of long-term funds to help overcome the maturity mismatch, or, second, it can be used as a backup in the case of liquidity problems. Because the facility acts as a safety net, a lender is able to make better use of short-term deposits in the knowledge that any liquidity imbalances can quickly be overcome by presenting mortgage assets to the liquidity facility in exchange for long-term funds. Essentially, this allows banks to refinance their mortgage loans if they are in trouble. During the crisis, this was a function undertaken by a number of central banks to support mortgage markets in the absence of a mortgage liquidity facility.

Requiring borrowers to save for a period as part of the qualification for a mortgage as an alternative risk mitigation instrument is not a widely developed housing financing scheme in Africa. Such a scheme represents a significant opportunity, especially in markets where lenders are unable to obtain the credit histories of borrowers. The requirement allows lenders to verify the capacity of borrowers to save regularly and meet mortgage payments, and it helps borrowers build up a mortgage deposit and equity in the property. In Nigeria, the national housing fund mechanism requires a potential borrower to save for six months before becoming eligible to access a loan. This is a closed savings scheme, that is, the savings determine the eligibility of borrowers for loan disbursement. The six-month savings period qualifies many more potential borrowers than can be serviced by the

Figure 4.10   The Effects of Guarantees on Loan Maturity

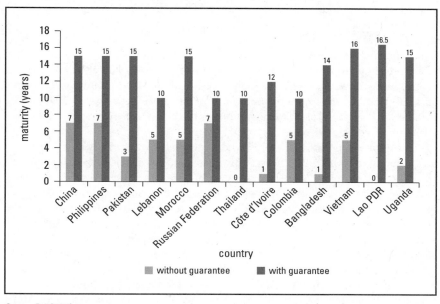

Source: Fall (2010).

fund, which is therefore fundamentally unsustainable. In Kenya, meanwhile, investment in housing bonds allows borrowers to build up the necessary equity for home purchases. The government actively encourages this scheme by providing tax concessions to savers. A similar scheme exists in Uganda, although without the tax break.

One way to foster long-term financing is credit-enhancement through guarantees, such as an infrastructure guarantee facility (figure 4.10). Mitigating risk means protecting projects against arbitrary interference by regulatory agencies, including preventing tariff adjustments commensurate with cost increases caused by exchange rate movements. The partial risk guarantee against regulatory default that the World Bank granted for the concession of Uganda's electricity distribution company, for example, played a key part in attracting private investors (see Mazhar 2005; Nyirinkinda 2005). In the case of guarantee facilities, these are managed most effectively by independent private managers selected through a competitive process. DFIs can also use specific structures to mitigate the risks of commercial loans. This is the case, for instance, of the A/B loan structure that is offered by the African Development Bank and that extends the bank's privileges to commercial investors.[17]

African Trade Insurance (ATI), an initiative established by the Common Market for Eastern and Southern Africa in 2001 with financial support from the World Bank, is an example of a regional African institution that offers risk mitigation instruments.[18] The ATI offers political and credit insurance for transactions involving ATI-member countries. Participating states are liable for any loss triggered by violations of their commitments toward the ATI. Such violations would also trigger default with respect to the World Bank, thereby enhancing the deterrence effect of the ATI insurance. Given ATI's regional shareholding, ATI products have a stronger deterrent effect than the guarantees offered by national export credit agencies. The ATI has been providing political and credit insurance to facilitate the financing of several infrastructure projects. These projects have included mainly power plants and information and communication technology infrastructure. As of December 2009, only 10 percent of ATI exposure to political risk was represented by infrastructure projects.

An important policy tool to foster lending to the enterprise sector in general and, notably, to SMEs and other disadvantaged groups has been partial guarantee schemes. These schemes exist on a private basis, but governments and donors have been aggressively pushing to establish partial credit guarantees to overcome the limited access of SMEs to bank credit. Partial guarantees can help overcome the lack of collateral of most SMEs, but issues of appropriate pricing, funding, and institutional structure are important. Although such schemes could be run on a self-sustainable basis, they often involve significant subsidies and contingent fiscal liabilities to cover losses. While it is difficult to compute such costs ex ante, it is even more difficult to measure the benefits, which would be partially captured by additionality, that is, the share of borrowers that would not have gained access to finance if the partial credit guarantees had not been available. There are only a few rigorous impact assessments of such schemes, and evaluations are urgently needed given the popularity of this policy tool.[19]

As discussed by Honohan (2010), private credit guarantee schemes can emerge for three main reasons. First, if the guarantor has informational advantages over the lender, this can help overcome information asymmetries and improve access to borrowing or reduce the related costs of financing for certain borrower groups. Requiring guarantors for new borrowers was one of the pillars of the success of the cooperative banking movement in Germany and other European countries in the 19th century (Ghatak and Guinnane 1999). Second, guarantee schemes can help diversify risk across lenders with different sectoral or geographical specializations. As created in several European countries, cooperative central banks serve to insure individual cooperatives that are heavily invested in specific regions or sectors. Third, guarantee schemes can emerge to exploit regulatory arbitrage if the guarantor is not subject to the same regulatory requirements as the lender. The recent growth in guarantee schemes in China might derive from such regulatory arbitrage (Honohan 2010).

Coordination failure among private parties and first-mover disadvantage could prevent private providers from entering the market for credit guarantees or prevent lenders from pooling resources for such a scheme and thus justify government intervention (de la Torre, Gozzi, and Schmukler 2008). This can be seen as one major reason why most guarantee funds in Africa are, today, publicly financed and often even operated publicly. Another reason for the popularity of the schemes is the limited resources that are needed up front, leaving potential liabilities to a much later stage.

The important assessment criteria are additionality and sustainability. How many creditworthy borrowers who previously did not have loans have been included because of the scheme? This requires not only an assessment of the additionality effect in itself, but also an assessment of the creditworthiness of the additional borrowers. The other important criterion is financial sustainability. The design of the scheme can be critical in reaching these two goals. While there has not been a rigorous research effort on the optimal design of such schemes, there has been quite a lot of discussion.

A first important design element is eligibility. Targeting the scheme on specific sectors, specific geographical areas, or firms of a specific size can help maximize the additionality effect. Targeting that is too specific, meanwhile, may increase the bureaucratic costs of running such a fund (for example, verification costs) thus limiting take-up. It might also limit the overall economic effect.

The coverage ratio is a second important design feature that can impact both additionality and sustainability. Retaining part of the risk with lenders can increase their incentives to assess and monitor borrowers properly and thus reduce loan losses. Too low a coverage ratio might reduce the value of the guarantee and dampen take-up. Too high a coverage ratio could incentivize lenders to excessive risk taking. Important to note is that the impact of the coverage ratio on lender incentives might vary with the informational advantage of the lenders. If guarantors have an informational advantage over lenders, then the coverage ratio that is sustainable might be higher than the coverage rate that would be sustainable under a scenario in which the informational advantage lies with the lenders. One interesting example in this context is the Small Businesses Credit Guarantee Fund of Chile, known as Fogape, which was launched to auction available guarantee amounts. In this case, lenders bid on the loan shares that are to be guaranteed. Bankers who bid for coverage of lower shares than the maximum allowable have their requests filled; others are rationed. In practice, the auctions have meant that primary lenders retain between 20 and 30 percent of the risk (Benavente, Galetovic, and Sanhueza 2006; Bennett, Doran, and Billington 2005).

The pricing structure is another important feature, especially for the sustainability of the fund both under the revenue aspect, that is, recovering the costs of the fund, but also in terms of providing proper incentives for lenders. If fees are too high, lenders might be reluctant to use the fund, and it can also cause good customers not to be included in the guarantee scheme that would have received funding otherwise. If fees are too low to maximize the additionality effect, the fund might not be sustainable. Critically, the fee structure should influence the incentives of lenders to screen and monitor properly.

The payment structure is a fourth important design feature. Prompt payments can increase trust in the system and, thus, the use by lenders. However, delays in payments until after a threshold of recovery efforts by the banks has been reached can be important in enticing lenders to monitor borrowers properly. Delaying payments until all legal recourse has been exhausted, however, might be too extreme, especially in countries with weak legal recovery processes. A staggered reimbursement schedule might be more appropriate, such as in Morocco and Tunisia, where 50 percent is paid once the claim is presented, followed by the remainder once the legal process has been exhausted.

Another item is the approach to operational management. Individual loan-level guarantees involve guarantee agencies in the screening stage to review eligibility (that is, whether potential borrowers are within the target group of the private credit guarantee), but also risk profiles (that is, whether the level of credit risk associated with specific borrowers is within adequate limits). In this approach, lenders will usually first approve the loans and then seek a guarantee approval on behalf of the borrowers. Alternatively, the portfolio model allows lenders, at their discretion, to assign guarantees to higher risk loans or targeted borrowers (that is, SMEs) and inform the guarantors after loans are approved or the loans default. While the loan-level approach might allow for more careful screening and risk management, it is also more costly for the credit guarantee fund. A hybrid approach would allow the guarantees to be extended to portfolios of loans up to a limit, after which additional loans would be screened by the guarantee fund.

Beyond the details of the design features, there is the more general issue of the relative roles of the private sector, the government, and donors. The assignment of responsibilities among government, the private sector, and donors might be important in creating the incentives so that lenders screen borrowers properly. Funding of the scheme through the proper pricing of the guarantees and by limiting government funding to setup costs might be important in giving lenders the proper incentives to monitor borrowers, avoid excessive risk taking, and, thus, minimize loan losses. Credit risk assessment by private parties rather than government bureaucrats can help improve the quality of the risk decisions and, again, minimize loan losses. Similarly, loan recovery by lenders rather than the government can maximize recovery because lenders typically have more information about the borrowers and potentially stronger incentives to recover loan resources.

Conclusions

This chapter documents the enormous long-term resource needs of Africa, but also the increasing number of sources for long-term finance. Beyond commercial banks, development banks, capital markets, and other traditional sources, there is an increasing variety of nonbank financial sources that are gaining ground in Africa, including private equity funds and SWFs, and various financial instruments such as corporate bonds and partial risk guarantees. This chapter briefly touches on some of the central themes important in efforts to achieve improved long-term finance. It also demonstrates that Africa can find new and more well managed providers and new products and delivery channels of long-term finance. This will mean, however, that governments must play a facilitating rather than a market-replacing role. We advocate an appropriate regulatory touch in organized capital markets that also fosters regional integration and cross-listing arrangements. We argue for a stronger role for more private arrangements wherever organized markets are too costly and cumbersome, including a stronger role for private equity funds. Ultimately, this will help (1) attract more long-term resources to Africa and (2) intermediate these resources more effectively.

The main messages in the analysis offered in this chapter are consistent with the overall messages of the book. Competition among different providers can prove critical in the provision of the resources and products necessary for long-term finance in Africa. As in chapter 3, looking beyond banking is important for firm finance, but also for other areas of long-term finance, including infrastructure and housing finance. Looking at the necessary services and, thus, beyond existing institutions and markets is critical in expanding long-term finance: looking beyond national capital markets to regional solutions and looking beyond organized exchanges to private solutions. Consideration of the demand-side constraints implies looking at nonfinancial constraints, as well as business development services. The ultimate goal is to turn investment into bankable projects, where *bank*able is broadly defined.

As in the case of the effort to expand access, policy recommendations have to be tailored to country circumstances. Larger or middle-income countries will have an easier time attracting international funding and can support a larger number of institutions, including capital markets. In the case of smaller and low-income countries, more emphasis has to be placed on linking to international markets and pushing for regional integration. Postconflict countries and countries with traditionally heavy government intervention in financial systems should have governance reform at the top of the policy agenda.

Notes

1. We are not able to go into depth on many issues that we touch upon in this chapter. For more on infrastructure finance, refer to Sheppard, von Klaudy, and Kumar (2006) and Foster and Briceño-Garmendia (2010); for pension reform, refer to Stewart and Yermo (2009).

2. See Ndulu (2006) on the importance of closing this gap for the sake of Africa's growth performance.

3. For a detailed discussion on PPPs in infrastructure in Africa, see Shendy, Kaplan, and Mousley (2011).

4. For the following, see Walley (2010).

5. See "Africa's Banking Boom: Scrambled in Africa," *Economist*, September 18, 2010.

6. The full structure of the deal is such that the relative share of total senior debt and equity were 77.79 and 22.52 percent, respectively. The total senior debt package is as follows: ₦11 billion (Stanbic IBTC and Standard Bank London: 39.29 percent of the total debt package), ₦9.6 billion (African Development Bank), ₦9.4 billion (a syndicate of Nigerian banks), and ₦3.5 billion (standby debt from Nigerian banks). A mezzanine debt of ₦5 billion was provided by the Lagos state government, in addition to ₦5.318 billion in shareholder loans and ₦1 billion in standby equity.

7. Egypt, Ghana, and Nigeria have privately managed pension funds, but only for their mandatory schemes.

8. According to these guidelines, there should be no minimum level of investment in any asset, in particular in government debt. Social security funds should not be a means for governments to finance deficits.
- The investment strategy should set quantitative restrictions on the maximum levels of investment in different asset classes.
- The investment strategy should not permit holding more than a specific proportion of the total market value of the assets of a particular industry or enterprise.
- Investments in some types of assets may be forbidden (for example, unguaranteed loans or unquoted shares).
- A list of admitted (or recommended) assets could be applied based on the investment quality of the assets.

9. John Niepold, quoted in Christy (1998); see also Moss, Ramachandran, and Standley (2007).

10. In West Africa, the fiscal advantages offered through bonds issued in the zone do not equally benefit all bondholders within the region.

11. Direction des Assurances et de la Protection Sociale, February 2011.

12. "Capital risque: L'assouplissement de la réglementation préconisé," *L'économiste* (Casablanca), 3446, January 17, 2011, http://www.leconomiste.com/article/capital-risquebr-l-assouplissement-de-la-reglementation-preconise.

13. Current regulations on foreign exchange in Morocco authorize companies domiciled in Morocco to invest outside the country and to repatriate revenues. This is subject to several conditions, including (a) the investment aims at developing and consolidating the activities of the company and (b) the company has been operating for a minimum of three years. This second condition prevents newly established funds domiciled in Morocco from making investments outside the country.

14. Association Professionnelle Tunisienne des Banques et des Etablissements Financiers, http://www.apbt.org.tn/fr/htm/fichespratiques/sicar.asp (accessed February 3, 2011).

15. In 2004, Nigeria established the Excess Crude Account to store profits from oil sales so as to insulate the Nigerian economy from boom-and-bust cycles in commodity prices. The country is expected to launch the Nigerian Sovereign Investment Authority to stabilize macroeconomic fundamentals, accumulate savings for future generations, and develop critical infrastructure.

16. Introduced in 2007, the China-Africa Development Fund is essentially an equity fund, investing in Chinese enterprises with operations in Africa in agriculture and manufacturing industries, infrastructure (electric power and energy, transportation, telecommunications, and water), and natural resources (oil, gas, minerals).

17. An A/B loan may be split into one or more senior components and one or more subordinate components. The borrower is the same, and the collateral is the same, but the treatment of each loan component may be structured differently.

18. Current member states are Burundi, the Democratic Republic of Congo, Djibouti, Eritrea, Gabon, Ghana, Kenya, Liberia, Madagascar, Malawi, Rwanda, Sudan, Tanzania, Uganda, and Zambia.

19. See Lelarge, Sraer, and Thesmar (2010) for an assessment of the credit guarantee scheme in France and Larraín and Quiroz (2006) for Chile. See Beck, Klapper, and Mendoza (2010) for a survey of credit guarantee schemes around the world.

Chapter 5

Safeguarding Financial Systems

Introduction

The global financial crisis has put financial stability back onto government agendas around the world. The crisis has exposed weaknesses in the way national and international financial markets and national and crossborder banks are regulated and supervised, and the international community has responded through concerted efforts to strengthen international supervisory and regulatory standards. Many of these efforts have repercussions in Africa. Their adoption across the continent should be guided by the different needs of individual African financial systems relative to systems in industrialized and advanced emerging markets.

The themes of this chapter are closely linked to the main messages in chapters 3 and 4. We stress the importance of competition in the banking system and the financial system at large. However, this also poses additional challenges for regulators and supervisors. The recent Nigerian experience of widespread and systemic fragility linked to (though not necessarily caused by) rapid changes in market structure and the capital structure of banks shows that regulators and supervisors have to develop the capacity to follow such changes carefully. It also shows that increased competition has to be accompanied by improvements in governance. Similarly, expanding financial service provision beyond banking poses additional challenges to regulators and supervisors. This means not only the challenges in the supervision of insurance companies and pension funds, but also the coordination between bank and telecommunications regulators, a topic we touch upon in chapter 3. It also requires an open and flexible regulatory and supervisory approach that balances the need for financial innovation with the need to be alert to the emergence of fragility in new forms. Finally, to the same extent that addressing demand-side constraints is important in expanding outreach toward the access possibilities frontier, demand-side constraints have to be dealt with to keep the financial system from moving beyond the sustainable frontier and to avoid overindebtedness and abuse on the individual level and financial fragility on the aggregate level.

This chapter takes a fresh look at the challenges represented by the need to safeguard finance in Africa and is informed by the recent crisis experience, but also Africa's own experience with fragility and by solutions adopted across the continent and in other developing and emerging markets. Overall, our approach is guided by the principle that finance should be safeguarded for the ultimate users. Thus, our goal is not to resolve the problems of banks for the sake of banks and not to foster the regulation of exchanges to prevent the failure of brokers and dealers. Rather, our goal is to protect the ultimate beneficiaries, that is, investors and customers. In the case of sophisticated investors, we follow the recommendation by Honohan and Beck (2007), who adopt a caveat emptor approach. For the bottom-of-the-pyramid users of financial services, we stress the need for more effective consumer protection. As the objectives of deeper and broader financial systems are being realized, appropriate regulation and supervision are becoming more important.

This chapter is organized to reflect the three main messages of the book. After discussing the stability of the financial system, we turn to the challenges in bank regulation and supervision in a rapidly changing environment of increased competition and a continuing trend toward globalization, but also toward crossborder banking within the region and the reform discussion in the context of the G20 process. We then discuss the expansion of the regulatory perimeter beyond banking in light of our discussion on expanding the financial system beyond banking. The regulation of insurance companies, pension funds, and capital markets has traditionally been weak, while the regulation and supervision of microfinance institutions (MFIs) have undergone significant changes in large parts of the continent in recent years. We argue for a risk-based approach that focuses on more rigorous regulation of those segments that manage the savings of unsophisticated savers. Finally, we turn to the users of financial services, especially small savers, and advocate an increased focus on consumer protection.

Stability: We Have Come a Long Way

African financial systems have come a long way in terms of financial stability. The 1980s and 1990s saw a series of costly banking crises, both systemic and nonsystemic.[1] In 1994, at the height of widespread bank fragility, countries in Africa, from the Arab Republic of Egypt to South Africa and from Cameroon to Kenya, were suffering systemic or nonsystemic banking crises. Beginning in 2000, this fragility subsided across the continent. Between 2000 and 2007, Laeven and Valencia (2008) report no single systemic crisis in Africa (figure 5.1). As Honohan and Beck (2007) discuss, African banking crises of the late 20th century were distinct from banking crises outside Africa because they were mostly caused by governance problems at the bank level and at the regulatory level or simply by bad banking practices. This

Figure 5.1   Systemic Banking Crises in Africa, 1980–2009

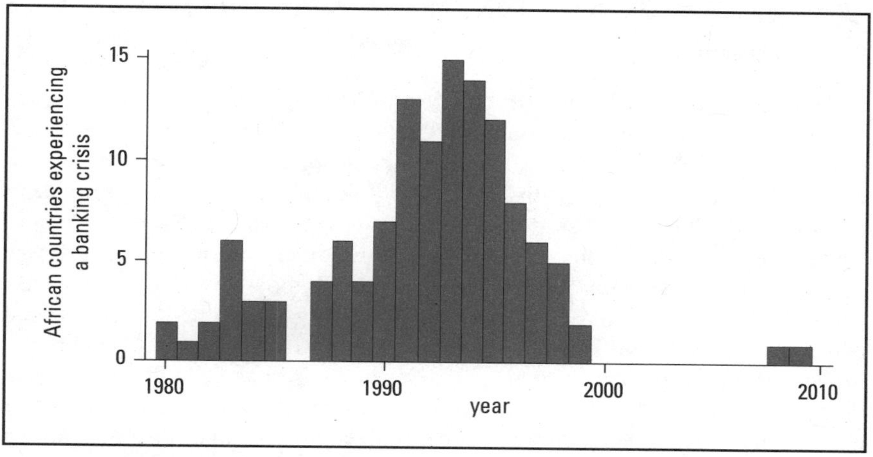

Source: Laeven and Valencia (2008).

is true of countries in which the banking systems were dominated by government-owned banks, but also of countries with predominantly private banking systems, no matter if these were local banks or foreign banks (for example, Meridien BIAO and the Bank of Credit and Commerce International).

Governance continues to be a major challenge in banks and regulatory entities in some countries, though important steps have been taken in most. In some instances, privatization has helped by reducing the conflicts of interest that public authorities face because they are owners and supervisors of the same institutions, though, in other instances, the process was not smooth and, at first, exacerbated misgovernance and fragility and, subsequently, had to be renegotiated. The privatization process in Mozambique, Tanzania, and Uganda in the 1990s, for example, was undermined by governance challenges leading to insider lending and looting, often by politically connected insiders, which forced the respective governments to renationalize the institutions before a successful second round of privatization could be undertaken. In Nigeria, internal bank governance deficiencies were at the core of the recent crisis, as we discuss in chapter 2.

Improving asset quality and capitalization are the two dimensions in which African banking systems have made the greatest progress over the past two decades. It is partly because of this progress that Africa has weathered the recent crisis. The traumatic experience with bank fragility in the 1980s and 1990s explains the rather conservative bias of bank regulators and supervisors across the continent toward stability. Today, most African banking systems are stable and well capitalized. They also have a good level of liquidity. (Indeed, sometimes, the liquidity is excessive to a degree that undermines the ability of the systems to intermediate efficiently.)

Nonetheless, there is still hidden or silent fragility in several Central and West African countries. Among the smaller financial systems, Togo has several banks with a high level of nonperforming loans and insufficient capital-asset ratios, and 50 percent of the banking system is effectively in distress, a result of governance deficiencies and political and economic turmoil over the past two decades. The banking crisis in Togo illustrates how banking systems may suffer from a deterioration in public finance. Similarly, there are undercapitalized banks in the Democratic Republic of Congo, a consequence of political and economic turmoil. In Côte d'Ivoire, a large number of banks, mostly local or regional, faced difficulty in 2008, generally related to the accumulation of public sector arrears, loans to risky sectors, and governance problems. The government took control of three banks and recapitalized them. In Ghana, systemic distress is concentrated in state-owned banks and a number of small, locally owned banks that face liquidity problems because of their dependence on the public sector and wholesale funding. Similarly, in the West African Economic and Monetary Union (UEMOA), many banks do not comply with prudential norms and are subject to potential shocks stemming from the heavy involvement of the governments in economies throughout West Africa. In addition to governance weaknesses, the lack of an appropriate bank resolution framework prolongs the distress and exacerbates the overall costs, a point to which we return below.

Figure 5.2 shows the significant capitalization of African banks. Even in their unweighted version, capital-asset ratios are well above 8 percent. The ratio of regulatory capital to risk-weighted assets is more than double the 8 percent given by the Basel capital adequacy ratio and has even increased during the recent crisis. Raw capitalization ratios and risk-weighted capitalization ratios are thus highly conservative. Given the characteristics of African banks and their host economies that we discuss in previous chapters, especially the high volatility African lenders face, it might be argued that a conservative bias in capitalization is appropriate.

A comparison of the liquidity of African banks over time shows similar trends, as we discuss in chapter 2. In general, African finance is liquid, with limited maturity risk. There has been limited exposure to derivative products and securities with high price volatility on bank balance sheets, partly because of the lack of well-developed financial markets and partly because of the conservative approach of African regulators. The simplicity and conservative bias of bank balance sheets minimized contagion during the crisis. This is symptomatic of the low level of financial development, which also, however, prevents the financial system from fulfilling a growth-enhancing role.

The stability focus is on banking because of the vulnerability of banking based on the maturity mismatch and because of the dominant role of banking within the financial systems of Africa. Nonetheless, it is worthwhile to discuss other segments of finance as well. The insurance sector is characterized across the continent by undercapitalized institutions, poor governance structures, poor payout records, and a weak regulatory framework. In countries where they exist, pension funds are

Figure 5.2   The Capitalization of Banks: Delevering during the Crisis, 2005–10

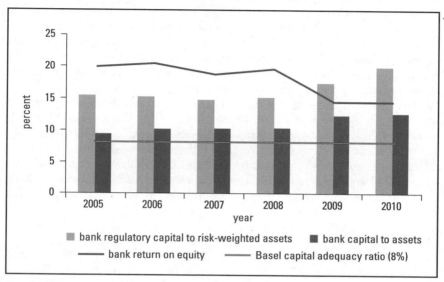

Source: IMF (various).

often underfunded, have poor governance structures, and are poorly regulated, as we discuss in chapter 4. While this is a different kind of fragility given that, with a pension fund, there is no implication of the risk of a run, the fragility of pension funds has a direct impact on long-term growth because the resources of the pension funds are not being allocated to the most effective use, as we discuss in chapter 4. While there is no immediate risk for the overall financial system and the economy at large, the misallocation creates long-term, contingent fiscal liabilities.

Bank Regulation and Supervision: New Challenges in a Changing Environment

Although we advocate the expansion of the financial system beyond banking, this sector is and will continue to be the most important part of financial systems across Africa for many years to come. In addition, the regulatory and supervisory focus is on banking rather than on other segments of the financial system. This is so be-. cause of the sector's vulnerability to runs given the maturity mismatch between assets and liabilities, because of the close interconnection through the interbank market and payment system and the consequent risk that a single bank failure could spark systemic distress, and because of the role of banks as the creators of private information about borrowers in the economy. For the overall financial system and the real economy, these externalities make bank failures much more damaging than fragility in other parts of the financial system.

However, the environment in which banks are operating is changing, even in Africa. First, there is increased competition from within and from outside the banking sector. As we discuss above, increased competition has many advantages; however, it also implies greater uncertainty and risks, which have to be properly managed. This puts a premium on improved governance in the banking system (as in the financial system at large; see below), as well as on supervisory upgrades. Second, in an increasingly global financial system and given the prominent and still increasing presence of multinational banks, but, recently, also regional banks, Africa's financial systems and economies will become more interconnected and subject to more external shocks that have to be properly managed. Third, the international regulatory reforms put forth by the Financial Stability Board and the Basel Committee have direct and indirect repercussions for Africa. Africa needs to be careful to manage the process of adopting similar standards for its own markets, a subject to which we return in chapter 6.

From a regulatory to a supervisory upgrade

Over the past decade or so, there has been a significant strengthening of the regulatory framework in various African jurisdictions. Reviews and subsequent reforms of banking sector legislation have been undertaken in a number of countries. Many countries have complemented legislative reforms with an overhaul of the corresponding regulations. However, there are still deficiencies in the regulatory framework, especially as regards the independence of supervisors, risk management, and the resolution capacity of supervisors, as we discuss below.[2]

One way to measure the adequacy of the regulatory and supervisory framework is the Basel Core Principles for Effective Banking Supervision (BCPs). These cover 30 areas of bank regulation and supervision on which countries are being assessed by their peers in other countries, often in the context of joint International Monetary Fund–World Bank financial sector assessment missions. One should bear in mind that different assessors apply different grading principles; nonetheless, it has been reported that, on average, the 16 African countries for which the BCPs have been assessed were largely or fully compliant with only 20 of the 30 principles. Among the important principles that pose a challenge in the effort at compliance are BCP 1.2 (the independence, accountability, and transparency of bank supervisors), BCP 7 (the risk management process in bank supervision), BCP 18 (the abuse of financial services), and BCP 23 (the corrective and remedial powers of supervisors) (BCBS 2006). The median ratings for these were materially noncompliant (figure 5.3). Looking beyond banking to other segments of the financial sector, we see that there is still a striking lack of a sound, best practice regulatory framework in the insurance and pension fund industries in most African countries.

Focusing on compliance with international best practices is an important part of the modernist agenda for building financial markets. How important is the

Figure 5.3   The Median Basel Core Principle Assessment across Africa

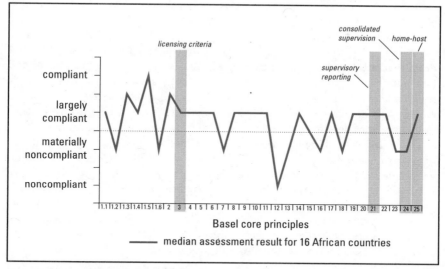

Source: Fuchs, Losse-Müller, and Witte (2010).

adoption of these principles in explaining the stability of the financial systems in the region? Cross-country comparisons have shed doubt on the usefulness of the BCPs in predicting stability across countries. Demirgüç-Kunt, Detragiache, and Tressel (2008) find no significant relationship between most of these principles and banking system stability, with the notable exception of BCP 21, which measures the quality of supervisory reporting. Countries in which banks have to report their financial data regularly and accurately to regulators and market participants have banks showing greater financial strength. None of the other BCPs is significantly associated with bank stability. This does not mean that peer review of the regulatory and supervisory framework is not important. Rather, it means that one has to look beyond adherence to the principles to the actual implementation and functioning of bank supervision. One also has to consider the root causes of widespread financial fragility in the 1980s and 1990s, which, as pointed out by Honohan and Beck (2007), lie mostly in governance failures in the public sector and in the private sector. These failures led to credit boom-and-bust cycles. The most recent example, Nigeria, also points to weak governance within financial institutions and markets as a core cause of fragility.

Weak supervisory capacity and the lack of regulatory independence

Pervasively weak supervisory capacity and the lack of regulatory independence are at least as important as gaps in the regulatory framework in explaining fragility. In many countries, licensing and closure decisions are still vested with ministries of finance rather than bank regulators, which gives rise to a risk of political interference in these critical decisions, as well as delays in early intervention in the case of fragile and weak banks. In most African countries, supervisory resources are limited, including qualified staff and the availability of analytical tools and skills. Supervisory processes focus on compliance with regulatory standards, but are not set up to identify and manage the changing risks in banking systems. In addition, the ability to monitor risk at the institutional and systemic level is hampered by insufficient quality in data and reporting processes. These deficiencies weigh even more heavily in an increasingly globalized world, in which most African countries host banks from developed countries, but also from other African countries.

The UEMOA Banking Commission, for example, lacks sufficient power to enforce corrective measures in cases of noncompliance with regulations, a situation that political authorities have only recently started to address. Ill-suited regulations, such as the regulation on preapproval of loan applications, are often ignored, which undermines supervisory discipline. To ensure certainty and supervisory discipline, one would prefer that such outdated regulations be dropped and the focus be shifted to the consistent enforcement of meaningful regulations.

While most supervisory authorities still use the Basel I capital regime (with notable exceptions, such as Mauritius and South Africa), the large majority plans on implementing the Basel II capital requirements. In the recent Making Finance Work for Africa survey, all responding countries across Africa, except Angola, Eritrea, and Lesotho, indicated their intention to implement, though many have not yet set a date.[3] Given the complexity of Basel II, it is surprising that its adoption is so high on the agenda of regulators in Africa. African regulators offer a variety of reasons why they want to adopt Basel II, although adoption is not mandatory outside the member states of the Basel Committee on Banking Supervision. Specifically, they are concerned that Basel I is beginning to be perceived as an inferior standard by international investors and that African markets may be penalized by international market participants or that African banks will eventually be denied access to foreign markets if they do not comply with the latest Basel standards. According to a Financial Stability Institute study (FSI 2004), the main driver among nonmember countries of the Basel Committee on Banking Supervision to move toward Basel II is the fact that foreign-controlled banks or local subsidiaries of foreign banks operating under Basel II expect regulators in low-income countries to adopt the framework as well. Whether or not these concerns are justified, they have accelerated the diffusion of the Basel accords not only in Africa, but across the developing world.

South Africa was one of the first countries on the continent to introduce the full-fledged version of Basel II, pillar 1, in 2008, leaving it up to banks to decide which approach to use for capital calculation, though their choice is subject to approval by the supervisor. Even so, most domestic banks opted for the standardized approach, in addition to the minimum Tier 1 capital ratio of 7.0 percent and the minimum total capital ratio of 9.5 percent. The latter includes a 1.5 percent systemic requirement on top of the internationally agreed minimum capital ratio of

8.0 percent that was imposed to adjust international capital standards to an emerging market environment.

Implementing the full-fledged version of Basel II beyond the simplified standardized approach carries significant costs for banks and regulators alike. However, even choosing the standardized approach can be problematic because of the low penetration of credit ratings across the continent and the disadvantages unrated companies (typically small or informal sector companies) would face in accessing credit at affordable terms. Building up supervisory capacity (including staff training), new processes, and the substantial investments in information technology infrastructure is beyond the budgetary scope of many regulators in low-income African countries. The development of their own internal rating systems might be easy for subsidiaries of larger international banks, but it is a steep hurdle for smaller domestic banks, thus creating an additional competitive barrier. Importantly, as long as supervisory capacity remains low, Basel II does not provide an adequate framework for enhancing financial stability in African countries. Because of the lack of preparedness among authorities to supervise the use by banks of highly sophisticated risk models effectively, moving beyond the simplified standardized approach could result in a de facto loss of supervisory power and would therefore be counterproductive.

The crisis and new international reform proposals offer a valuable opportunity to revisit the regulatory and supervisory landscape in Africa and to look at the priorities for the continent. Caution is called for, however. In defining the regulatory and supervisory reform agenda in Africa, policy makers need to assess carefully the costs and benefits of implementing international standards. Rather than applying the standards wholesale, a more successful alternative might be appropriate sequencing and cherry-picking among the building blocks that correspond to the regional implementation environment and risks.[4]

The new Basel III standards developed by the Basel Committee on Banking Supervision are meant to incorporate lessons learned from the financial crisis. Most of the proposed measures are of limited immediate relevance to African banking sectors because the weaknesses they address are largely a result of regulatory philosophies and market practice in developed markets. This does not signify that they are irrelevant in the effort to enhance the regulatory framework in the future, but it does signify that they are of limited practical application today. First, Basel III outlines various measures to raise the quality, consistency, and transparency of the regulatory capital base and focuses largely on the definition of Tier 1 capital. In most African countries, bank capital structures are a relatively straightforward composition of common shares and retained earnings and, thus, already fulfill Basel III quality requirements. Second, measures to improve the risk coverage of the capital framework for counterparty credit risk will have little immediate impact because African bank activity in derivatives, repurchase agreements, and securities financing is limited. However, they should be included in the regulatory approach of African jurisdictions going forward because they might become relevant as financial markets deepen. Third, given the high levels of liquidity in most African markets, global minimum liquidity standards imply little change for African banks. However, given the lack of data quality and the system constraints in Africa, more basic approaches, such as the simple ratio of customer loans to deposits seen in some low-income countries, appear more appropriate and easier to implement. Care would need to be exercised to balance prudent liquidity controls with the risk of excessively constraining loan growth and the consequent economic develop-ment. Finally, a leverage ratio, currently under supervisory monitoring, may offer an important safeguard for all low-income jurisdictions, especially those that are in the process of introducing Basel II. However, in practice, the leverage of African banks is significantly less than the suggested standards.

Finally, the addition of a layer of macroprudential regulation, as proposed in the Basel III framework, is viewed by most regulators in Africa as a key challenge. Macroprudential oversight is meant to address systemic risk as opposed to bank-level idiosyncratic risk, the focus of microprudential regulation. Perhaps the most prominent example is the cyclical provisioning for loans. As attractive as these cy-clical requirements are from a theoretical viewpoint, they seem much more diffi-cult to implement in low-income or even most middle-income countries than in countries of the Organisation for Economic Co-operation and Development. They are technically challenging, and, if regulators get them wrong, capital adequacy lev-els become out of tune with risk. With the exception of a few countries, the devel-opment of macroprudential supervisory capacity is in its infancy. Most central banks do not have dedicated financial stability units. The additional resource de-mands are considerable, particularly in skills, training, modeling, technology, and data. In addition, macroprudential supervision requires a cultural shift from a pas-sive rules-based supervisory approach to active risk management. Regulators may lack the legal authority for intervening on the basis of macroprudential factors (rather than institution-specific factors). Regulators need to work with govern-ments to determine how far they are prepared to intervene in the event of a buildup of systemic risk.

Despite these difficulties and independent of the need to adhere to new interna-tional standards, the development of a macroprudential supervisory capacity is crucial to most African supervisors. It is generally agreed that macroprudential su-pervision is a function that all regulators must address, but it imposes a range of new demands that many regulators are unable to meet. It requires new cross-cutting skills combining macroeconomic analysis and regulation, new modeling techniques, data collection and analysis, and practical criteria for triggers and inter-ventions. The development of international standards on tools and measures to monitor macroprudential risks could inform similar exercises by African regula-tors that are adjusted to the existing resource and data constraints.

Minimum capital requirements

Throughout the book, we discuss the diseconomies of scale arising among small banks in terms of expanding outreach and lengthening contracts. An additional

Box 5.1   Competition and Stability

In chapters 3 and 4, we emphasize the positive impact that competition can have on deepening and broadening. However, more competition can certainly also bring about more fragility. What have the academic literature and recent examples taught us about the relationship between competition and stability?

Theoretical models have made contrasting predictions about the relationship among bank concentration, competition, and stability. On the one hand, bank concentration may enhance market power and result in high profits, which provide a buffer against adverse shocks and increase the franchise value of a bank, thus reducing the incentives for bankers to take excessive risk (Marcus 1984; Keeley 1990). On the other hand, proponents of the concentration-fragility view argue that market power might result in higher interest rates, which, in turn, provide incentives to borrowers to take higher risks (Boyd and de Nicoló 2005).

Closely linked to the market structure and fragility debate is the issue of bank size. On the one hand, larger banks can diversify more readily so that banking systems characterized by a few large banks tend to be less fragile than banking systems with many small banks (Allen and Gale 2004). Furthermore, a few large banks might be easier to monitor than many small banks. On the other hand, policy makers are more concerned about bank failures if there are only a few large banks. Larger banks in a concentrated banking system could also increase the risk of contagion, thus creating a positive link between concentration and systemic fragility.

Cross-country evidence shows that more concentrated banking systems are less likely to suffer systemic fragility; at the same time, competition also contributes to greater stability (Beck, Demirgüç-Kunt, and Levine 2006; Schaeck, Čihák, and Wolfe 2009). Bank-level evidence provides conflicting evidence on the impact of competition and concentration on stability. This emphasizes that market structure is not the same as competition and that idiosyncratic bank fragility and systemic distress are far from perfectly correlated. However, there also seems to be significant cross-country variation in the relationship between competition and stability; the effect of competition depends on the regulatory framework, the market structure, and the potential herding behavior by banks (Beck, De Jonghe, and Schepens 2011). This puts the emphasis back on the regulatory and supervisory framework.

In summary, competition is not detrimental per se for bank stability, nor does a more concentrated banking system necessarily imply less competition and more stability. It is critical, however, to adjust the regulatory and supervisory framework to changing market structures. The governance of financial institutions is as important, including ownership structures and cash-flow rights, as well as the accountability of senior management for risk decisions and the financial statements to which they agree (Caprio, Laeven, and Levine 2007; Schaeck et al., forthcoming; Beltratti and Stulz 2009).

dimension is whether concentrated banking systems with larger banks can also be considered more stable. Box 5.1 discusses the evidence. Nigeria dramatically increased minimum capital requirements a few years ago to create larger banks (see chapter 2, box 2.3) and other countries are following this trend. The evidence discussed in box 5.1 and in previous chapters points to potential gains in the efficiency and stability of the financial system from such a consolidation. However, consolidation can result in more aggressive risk taking by the banks that have now become larger and are seeking to exploit their too-big-to-fail status; in any case, their failure will exert more stress than the failure of small banks on the resolution framework. In addition, the consolidation process might have a negative impact on access, especially for customers of small niche banks. Meanwhile, the impact of consolidation on efficiency, stability, and access will depend on the implications for competition of a more concentrated banking system. At higher concentration, it is even more important to have an open, contestable financial system that allows for competition from outside the banking system, including from nonbank financial institutions such as leasing companies, equity funds, and also mobile phone companies.

Thus, consolidation can create important scale economies in African financial systems. However, the consolidation process has to be accompanied by the necessary changes in the regulatory and supervisory framework, and greater contestability through the nonbank provision of financial services has to be assured.

Bank resolution: the missing component

The weakest point in the financial safety net in most countries across the developing and developed world continues to be the lack of effective resolution systems, crisis management tools, and implementation, where this is present at all. Effective resolution systems rely on the capacity to intervene in a failing bank in time to prevent economic damage and contagion. Effective crisis management tools rely on the capacity to coordinate a response to a crisis when it occurs. The recent crisis and the often bungled attempts of the countries of the Organisation for Economic Co-operation and Development to deal with their failing banks have put this issue high on the agenda. There are two main dimensions to the problem: one on the domestic level and one on the regional or international level.

Few countries in Africa have a separate bank resolution framework, and, in most countries, either supervisors or courts can intervene in banks. Even in South Africa, supervisors have to obtain approval from the minister of finance to intervene in a bank. Immediate intervention is not possible: there is a delay of 30 days, during which time the bank can argue against intervention. This hinders supervisors in intervening decisively, expediently, and effectively. In Tanzania, meanwhile, regulators can intervene in a failing or noncompliant bank without the involvement of the policy sphere or courts. The resolution framework includes a prompt corrective action procedure and provides for a large number of options, including private solutions and the possibility of mergers and acquisitions supported by the regulator. In Ghana and Kenya, the central bank has the power of intervention, but the legislation does not include provisions for specific resolution techniques. The lack of legal clarity in terms of the power of intervention and, more critically, the lack of a clear framework for resolving weak banks undermine not only market discipline, but also supervisory independence with respect to banks.

The banking crisis in Togo illustrates this point. The slow resolution of the crisis points to the ineffectiveness of the mechanism for managing banking crises within

UEMOA. The UEMOA Banking Commission does not have the necessary powers to intervene in failing banks and shares many of its responsibilities with national ministries of finance, which is of special concern given the increasing dominance of regional banks. Specifically, the banking law authorizes the chairman of the commission to call for market solidarity or to request shareholder assistance in the event of a banking crisis. The provisions of the law, however, are not binding on shareholders, and any action is thus based on the chairman's power of persuasion. The national ministries of finance have the power to appoint a temporary administrator and to lodge an appeal with the UEMOA Council of Ministers against any license revocation decision. The appeal suspends action until the council reaches a decision.

The main challenges in the domestic agenda thus include the lack of an appropriate legal framework to deal with failing banks. Dealing with failing banks can often only be accomplished under the provisions of the general bankruptcy law, which, as discussed in box 5.2 in more depth, is not sufficient. A common feature of the special resolution regimes is that, provided certain trigger conditions are met, they allow the supervisor to overrule shareholders during the preinsolvency stage. In turn, this allows for good-bank–bad-bank solutions, whereby a set of liabilities and a corresponding set of high-quality assets are transferred to an acquiring bank (a purchase of assets and an assumption of liabilities if this occurs directly; otherwise, a bridge bank is used). This permits a transfer of the systemically relevant parts of the bank, while the remainder can be liquidated. It also allows for continuity. The advantage relative to a scenario in which no special bank resolution regime is in place is that the decision for the authorities to intervene is no longer a binary one (that is, save the entire institution, or do not intervene). It thereby serves the public interest of financial stability at minimum overall cost to taxpayers.

Related to the more general point on supervisory capacity above, many African countries also lack the capacity to deal with failing banks. This concerns not only supervisory skills, but also the financial resources that might be needed to fill potential capital shortfalls. This has often led to regulatory forbearance, which deepens fragility. As we discuss below, this problem can be exacerbated by the presence of subsidiaries of large multinational banks and the fact that many regulators are not independent of ministers of finance or other government institutions in their decision making. Moreover, the legal framework often limits regulatory discretion in two important regulatory decisions: licensing and the corrective and remedial powers of supervisors to intervene in failing banks.

The recent Nigerian experience in responding to bank failures and several self-assessments by other African countries have highlighted the need to establish and rehearse effective crisis response mechanisms and bank resolution procedures before such events occur. Several countries in the region have undertaken holistic reviews of the crisis management and bank resolution framework, such as Malawi, Mozambique, and Zambia. They have strengthened the resolution framework through the adoption of prompt corrective action mechanisms, the development

Box 5.2   Bank Resolution

The three basic functions of banks in any market economy are to (1) provide payment services; (2) pool society's savings, thereby transforming short-term liquidity into long-term investment; and (3) screen and monitor borrowers and investment projects. These three functions result in (1) the need to belong to a network of financial institutions, (2) the risk of a maturity mismatch and liquidity shortages in the case of shocks such as bank runs, and (3) the creation of private information. The failure of a financial institution results in negative externalities beyond the private costs of the failure to shareholders, management, employees, depositors, and borrowers. It also imposes external costs on other financial institutions and the economy at large. This gap between the private and the social cost of bank insolvency by itself justifies the establishment of a special insolvency regime for banks. Specifically, the three characteristics discussed above can be mapped to three problems that lead to the external social costs arising from bank failure, as follows: (1) the *domino problem* that is created because banks belong to a network: the failure of one institution can easily result in the failure of other institutions despite the sound fundamentals of these other banks; (2) the *hostage problem* that results from the maturity mismatch and the incapacity of banks to satisfy the liquidity needs of all its customers in the case of a bank run, which, in turn, might lead to contagion effects throughout the financial system; and (3) the *refrigeration problem* that results from the deterioration in lender-borrower relationships occurring because of the loss of information after the institution fails. These problems require swift attention, which cannot be provided through the regular insolvency regimes for corporate insolvencies. Such a special framework with clearly defined rules is also necessary to avoid a classical time inconsistency problem among regulators: while it is optimal ex ante to deny the possibility of a bailout so as to instill market discipline, it is optimal ex post to focus on reducing the social costs of bank failure.

In the absence of a proper bank resolution framework, authorities are often left with two ways to deal with failing banks: make them undergo regular bankruptcy procedures or bail them out. Implementation of the first option exacerbates the problems described above because it can lead to bank runs, contagion, and the destruction of private information. Implementation of the second option creates perverse incentives for banks to take aggressive risks. Any gains realized from this risk taking accrue to the banks, and any losses are socialized through the bailouts. The objective of a bank resolution framework is to create options so that bank regulators can minimize the costs imposed by bank failures on the rest of the system, while reducing moral hazard because bankers are encouraged to be too aggressive in the face of risks. Such options may include a supervisory-driven merger of a weak bank with a strong bank or a purchase-and-assumption technique, where the good part of a failing bank's assets (the purchase portion), together with some of the liabilities (the assumption portion), is transferred to another bank, while the remainder of the assets, together with residual liabilities, is sent through the liquidation process. If such options are not available because of the absence of purchasers or because the failing bank is too large, a bridge-bank option may be considered. This involves establishing a temporary bank to administer the deposits and liabilities of the failed bank.

However, bank regulators do not operate in a vacuum. They are part of an overall institutional and political framework. Their objectives might not coincide with those of taxpayers,

Box 5.2 Bank Resolution *(continued)*

who ultimately have to pay the bill for bank failures. Imposing certain rules on supervisors in terms of when and how to intervene (in the form of a framework for prompt corrective action) and certain rules on which resolution option to choose (for example, the least cost rule in the United States) can help structure the bank resolution framework in a way that the incentives of supervisors become better aligned with the incentives of taxpayers and the objectives of an effective and sound financial system.

of crisis management plans for large, systemically important banks, and the introduction of coordination mechanisms within central banks and ministries of finance. Proper procedures need to be established by African authorities to define efficient information-sharing, analysis, decision-making, and internal and external communications processes, as well as appropriate mechanisms to fund bank resolution. The various responsibilities can be described in detail in interagency memorandums of understanding (MOUs) on crisis management, which should contribute to preventing coordination failures, facilitating timely exchanges of key information, ensuring coordinated communications among institutions, markets, and the public, and, in general, strengthening overall contingency planning for financial crises. Acute time pressures and severe shortages of information are common during banking crises.

One size does not fit all. In some financial systems, for instance in West Africa, a current task is the restructuring and possible privatization of weak or failing government-owned banks, while other countries should focus on implementing a structure to deal effectively with potential failures of private banks.

A dimension in which quick progress could be made is fire drills, simulation exercises, and contingency plans. Fire drills can hone the necessary capacities of supervisory staff. They can also help expose shortcomings in the current legal bank insolvency framework and thus influence reform in the bank resolution system. Fire drills can also highlight the need to prepare contingency plans for major bank failures or a systemic banking crisis. A contingency plan should include previsions for the necessary human resources; the legal background; the lines of communication with other institutions, government authorities, and foreign supervisors; and action plans for the response to major bank failures or a systemic crisis. Contingency planning should include all relevant national authorities, including the supervisor, deposit insurance authorities, and finance ministries, as well as other relevant agencies (such as international agencies, foreign supervisory authorities, and so on). Scenarios such as a takeover by competitors inside or outside the domestic banking system should also be part of contingency planning. Well-prepared and realistic contingency plans allow regulatory authorities to be proactive rather than reactive in a crisis. Simulation exercises can be used to test the adequacy of contingency plans.

Contingency planning is especially important in countries with a history of exercising forbearance, whether because the owners of distressed banks have been politically influential or because governments have shown fear that bank closures and the attendant job losses and disruptions among bank customers would be politically and economically unpopular. In addition to economic forbearance and political forbearance, Maimbo (2001) argues that, in some cases, a third kind of forbearance—bureaucratically institutionalized regulatory forbearance—may be more prevalent. In a study of the regulatory and supervisory process in Zambia, he finds that this type of forbearance was not only embedded in the formal and informal administrative policies and procedures for effecting legislative and supervisory sanctions, but also appeared to be part of the organizational culture of decision making within the regulatory agency.

The efficient resolution of failing subsidiaries of foreign banks is often both more challenging and more critical, especially in many smaller economies in Africa, where such banks often have a dominating position.[5] It is more challenging because bank supervisors in host countries often lack the necessary information to be sufficiently prepared for a failure event. In addition, given the nature of bank balance sheets, the asset-liability composition and, thus, the liquidity and equity positions of banks can be changed within hours in favor of the parent and at the expense of the subsidiary. While the idea of stand-alone subsidiaries has been offered as an option against these risks, such firewalling would also take away the advantages of multinational banks in terms of scale economies and the use of joint platforms. Bank of Africa, Ecobank, First Rand, and Standard Bank, four important regional banks throughout the continent, have centralized their group functions for treasury and liquidity management, group audit, large credit authorization, and electronic data processing (Lukonga 2010). Contingency plans can thus be especially useful in the context of subsidiaries of multinational banks. Such plans would also entail making the corporate structures of these banks more transparent. In an additional phase, it might even be worthwhile to require subsidiaries of multinational banks to undertake their own contingency plans, that is, plans on resolving the subsidiaries on a stand-alone basis if the need arises. This is similar to the idea of instituting living wills that has been floated in Europe and North America for large, systemically important financial institutions.[6]

A role for deposit insurance?

A critical issue in a bank resolution framework is access to the necessary resources to resolve failing banks. Recent reforms in the bank resolution framework in Latin America have put deposit insurance at the center of the resolution of weak banks to align incentives across the financial safety net and provide resolution authorities with appropriate resources. Can the Latin American experience be transplanted to Africa? Most countries in Africa currently have no deposit insurance scheme, and, over the past decade or so, more and more empirical evidence has pointed to the pitfalls of moral hazard associated with deposit insurance (Demirgüç-Kunt and

Kane 2002). Thus, by reducing the incentives for bank depositors and creditors to monitor and discipline banks (although one has to remain skeptical of the ability of small-scale depositors to assess the risk profile of banks in the first place) and by institutionalizing the liability of governments, banks are more likely to follow their natural instinct of taking an aggressive stance toward risk (given that they only participate in the upside but not the downside of this risk), especially in the presence of a weak supervisory framework. The argument that an explicit deposit insurance is better than an implicit guarantee because it limits this guarantee does not necessarily hold in reality, as the case of Bolivia has shown. Bolivia's financial system is small and not well developed, somewhat similar to many African financial systems, and the introduction of explicit deposit insurance led to increased risk taking by banks (Ioannidou and Penas 2010). However, there is much anecdotal and practitioner evidence that the existence of a deposit insurance scheme can help in the reform or establishment of a proper and incentive-compatible bank resolution scheme; Bolivia is, again, the example (see Bolzico, Mascaro, and Granata 2007). There thus seems to be a trade-off between ex ante and ex post efficiency in the use of deposit insurance as part of the financial safety net: it raises the incentives for aggressive risk taking, but serves as an effective instrument in resolving failing banks. There also seems to be path dependence in the sense that, where certain institutions and structures already exist, it is best to maximize their usefulness, while, in countries in which they do not exist, it is easier to start afresh with optimal structures.

Would the introduction of deposit insurance to improve the efficiency of bank resolution be practical in the context of small, low-income African countries? Given the limited number of banks and the often limited human resources, it seems that the introduction of a deposit insurance scheme with the primary purpose of establishing an incentive-compatible bank resolution scheme would be costly. Also, bank runs are much less common in Africa than elsewhere. The failure of a single bank, not even the largest, would exhaust the fund, and diverting staff to the establishment and administration of a deposit insurance scheme might draw necessary resources from bank supervision. However, where deposit insurance already exists, transforming it from a pay-box scheme into an integral part of failure resolution, as is happening in Kenya and Uganda, might enhance efficiency and crisis preparedness. This might include assigning regulatory powers to the deposit insurer, along with access to supervisory information, the right to require additional and intensive on-site and off-site supervision, and participation in the intervention decision. It would help align incentives because deposit insurers would then have the incentives, but also the tools to minimize the losses of the insurance fund. As with so many other discussions throughout the book, we see that one size does not fit all: the structure of the ideal financial safety net is a function of the development, structure, and size of the relevant banking system.

Alternatives to deposit insurance are available. Given the significant liquidity of most banks in Africa, the investment of liquidity in the central bank or government papers, earmarked to reimburse small depositors in the case of failure, could be useful. Most banking systems in Africa impose high liquidity requirements on banks, plus high reserve requirements; so, such an arrangement would be easy to implement.

Another lesson from the European crisis is that crossborder issues of deposit insurance must be addressed. This is especially the case with respect to branches because these are supervised by the respective home countries and may or may not be covered by the deposit insurance schemes of these countries. Such arrangements have led to problems within Europe, as the case of Iceland has shown. Almost half the countries in Africa that responded to the recent Making Finance Work for Africa survey on the regulatory framework (see elsewhere above) allow foreign banks to enter through branches. In reality, however, foreign bank entry through branches is rare in Africa because most multinational or regional banks establish subsidiaries. Even where the regional integration of bank supervision might facilitate a regional resolution framework, such as in West Africa and Central Africa, bank regulators insist that foreign banks must enter each country through subsidiaries rather than branches.

Regional crossborder supervisory cooperation

Another important dimension in bank resolution is the crossborder dimension, an area where the recent European experience can be insightful. Crossborder supervisory issues are increasingly important among African regulators, especially in light of the fact that, by the end of 2009, there were at least 20 banks of African origin with crossborder operations in four or more countries (Lukonga 2010). The home countries ranged from Morocco to Mauritius, Nigeria and South Africa. The effective supervision of crossborder financial institutions requires close cooperation between the respective supervisors in the home countries of the institutions and in the host countries of the subsidiaries. This is also a key issue in advancing consolidated supervision.

Recent reforms in the international supervisory architecture have focused on the constitution of colleges of supervisors for all banks with international operations. The representation of African supervisors in these supervisory colleges remains a weak point given the current asymmetry of the size of operations of large international banks in developed markets and in most African markets. For example, the activities of an international banking group in Africa may make up only a small part of the total balance sheet of the group, but they may be of disproportionate systemic importance in African countries. This asymmetry introduces an inherent complication in the design of college arrangements, namely, that African supervisors have a great interest in being included in the supervisory college, but may be overlooked by the home supervisors under a biased view of efficiency and effectiveness. To these issues may be added the substantial money and time costs required for relatively scarce qualified senior personnel in low-income countries to travel to and attend meetings in distant locations.

Closer to home, the emergence of regional banks headquartered in African jurisdictions requires close cooperation among banking supervisors across the region. African home supervisors have begun championing regional college agreements and bilateral MOUs to facilitate the cooperation process. Restrictions on the sharing of banking information to protect confidentiality need to be loosened to enable proper communication among regulators.

The recent European experience suggests, however, that colleges of supervisors and MOUs are necessary, but not sufficient tools for coordination in cases of idiosyncratic or systemic fragility. MOUs are legally nonbinding documents, and, even within a college of supervisors, it is the home country supervisor who makes the final decision. MOUs are therefore not as crisis proof as is commonly assumed prior to a crisis. Moreover, given the asymmetries in information and capacity, the position of African supervisors will be weak with respect to home country supervisors in Asia or Europe. Closer to home in the case of regional banks, there might be more room for cooperation given the relative size of host and home country operations, and there might be more balance in capacity and skills. More political will might be necessary, however, in pursuing regional financial integration in the regulatory framework and in achieving supervisory cooperation so as to avoid the mistakes of Europe.

How can the limitations of the traditional crossborder bank resolution framework be overcome? As discussed above, the major challenge is the gap between the ex ante and ex post objectives of the resolution framework, the objectives of reducing aggressive risk taking ex ante and of avoiding the negative repercussions of bank failure ex post. A complicating factor in crossborder bank resolution is that costs have to be distributed in an incentive-compatible way, which is almost impossible ex post because decisions have to be made quickly (Goodhart and Schoenmaker 2009). Ultimately, this points to living wills, an idea that is being increasingly adopted across developed financial markets. Living wills are drawn up by the banks themselves and lay out how to wind down large crossborder banks. Combined with international contingency plans and ex ante binding resolution cost-sharing plans, living wills can create, ex ante, adequate incentives against excessive bank risk taking, but also provide a blueprint for dealing with large failing crossborder banks in the region.

And market discipline?

Allow us one quick remark on the debate on market discipline versus supervisory discipline. The obvious failure of market discipline during the recent crisis can be attributed to the moral hazard generated by the Bernanke-Greenspan put, although other explanations such as mood swings or externalities have also been put forward (de la Torre and Ize 2009). In addition, the absence of markets in many low-income countries leads observers to the conclusion that there is no room for market discipline in the financial systems of these countries. As Caprio and Honohan (2004) do, we argue that there is sufficient room for market discipline because of the pres-

ence of large depositors (often expatriate or donor accounts) and the limited resources of governments to bail out large banks (even if the latter may be small in
global comparisons). In addition, the relatively small business community and the
less-sophisticated banking business in Africa make monitoring and information
collection and dissemination easier. While strengthening supervisory capacity and
discipline seems important, fostering market discipline, where possible, can be
critical. One option would be a greater role for equity markets where they exist.
Encouraging large and listed banks to float a greater share of their equity can lead
to share prices that reflect the risk taking of management more accurately. Another
instrument is the strengthening of auditing standards so that auditors are liable for
the financial statements they have agreed to and ensure accountability with regard
to shareholders and supervisors.

Market discipline is essential in addressing the challenges of governance. The
discussions throughout the book, but especially in the context of recent banking
crises across Africa, point out the severe governance challenges at the core of fragility. Corporate governance in banks is especially important, given that many previous crises in Africa have been caused by governance challenges. Moreover, the
expansion of Africa's financial systems can only be achieved if the governance
challenges in nonbank financial institutions, including MFIs and cooperative institutions, are also addressed.

Governance is as much an issue of legal rules as it is an issue of enforcement.
Most of the bank regulators that responded to the Making Finance Work for Africa
survey reported that they have regulations on related party lending and disclosure
requirements of directors and controlling shareholders about their business interests involving related party relationships or potential conflicts of interest with
banks. This begs the question about the enforceability and enforcement of these
rules. Similarly, as discussed in chapter 3, many cooperative institutions suffer from
weak governance structures.

Entrenched political elites tend to use financial systems for their own financing
purposes. However, the problem in governance goes beyond direct government
ownership. It involves cross-ownership between the financial and the nonfinancial
corporate sector and, most importantly, connections among politicians, regulators,
and financial institutions that result in noncommercial lending decisions associated with high risks and, thus, contingent and, often, realized losses. Privatization is
not a panacea in this context, but only a first step, as the experience in several countries in East Africa and southern Africa mentioned above has shown.

One method is to induce more competition into the system. Certainly, one size
does not fit all. Advances in governance through competition and the media is
more easily achieved in larger and middle-income countries than in smaller or
low-income countries. Encouraging openness and competition is widely seen as
effective in dealing with this type of governance challenge. Foreign bank entry and
strategic private foreign management can be effective in tackling problems associ-

ated with the political capture of the financial sector, while contributing to a buildup in technical expertise.

Equally important is ensuring that there is a measure of effective self-discipline within institutions. Self-regulation, whereby a bank voluntarily monitors its own adherence to legal and ethical standards, is far preferable to enforcement of these standards by outside regulators. To this end, there has been a lot of governance work aimed at making boards of directors more effective. The reports of the King Committee on corporate governance in South Africa, led by former High Court Judge Mervyn King, have been influential in setting the direction of codes of corporate practice and conduct in Africa. The latest report, King III, builds on the spirit of the December 1992 Cadbury Report, which was published in the United Kingdom and which was the first in-depth statement on corporate governance and a model for sound practice worldwide for dealing with the division of responsibilities among top management to ensure that the decision-making power is not delegated to one person alone (IODSA 2009). On governance, King III is based on principles and accepts that there is no one size fits all in the solutions to corporate governance issues. Instead, it encourages firms to tailor standard corporate governance principles as appropriate to the size, nature, and complexity of their organizations. For banks in Africa, this message is especially relevant given the diversity of strategies for overcoming Africa's unique challenges.

Looking beyond Banks: How to Regulate Which Segments of the Financial System

Contractual savings institutions and capital markets

The regulation of insurance companies and pension funds has often been neglected, especially when financial sector supervision has been housed in ministries of finance with small staffs, a weak regulatory framework, and no supervisory powers. As we argue in chapter 4, the lack of proper regulation and supervision is an important, though not necessarily the decisive factor in explaining the underdevelopment of these segments of financial systems across most of Africa. Similarly, severe governance challenges plague these segments. As important as capital and governance regulations are, consumer protection regulations seem especially conducive to increasing the public's trust in these institutions. Fortunately, this has recently started to improve. Regulatory and supervisory functions have been moved to central banks or to dedicated nonbank regulatory agencies, as in the case of Botswana and Zambia.

The lack of proper regulation and supervision can be a drain on the development of capital markets. As we discuss in chapter 4, however, in the case of Africa, it is, overly burdensome licensing and issuing requirements that seem to be holding back the development of the market. As shown in a broad cross-country sample of countries, transparency and disclosure standards are more important than the existence of strong supervisory entities (La Porta, Lopez-de-Silanes and Shleifer 2006).

Another reform suggestion in the recent postcrisis debate has been the idea of extending the regulatory boundary, that is, extending financial sector regulation and supervision to nonbank financial corporations such as private equity funds. This reform push has been influenced by the recent crisis experience that brought to light the large shadow-banking sectors outside regulatory oversight in many developed financial markets. This has led to recommendations that capital funds be supervised and that market oversight be more stringent, including requiring standard products to be traded over the counter on organized exchanges. The purpose of such a step would be to supply supervisors with better information and early-warning signals, as well as to throw sand into the gears of rapidly moving global financial markets by increasing trading costs. Would the implementation of such recommendations fit the African reality?

The trend toward the extension of the regulatory perimeter conflicts with the lack of the necessary human and financial resources in many low-income countries, but also with the transaction costs that the expansion of regulation would generate in the emerging components of the financial system, such as certain over-the-counter markets and capital funds. More generally, the decision to regulate and supervise a segment of the financial system has to take promissory intensity into account. This is determined by (1) the likelihood that a financial contract cannot be honored, (2) the problems faced by consumers in assessing the creditworthiness of a financial service provider, and (3) the impact of the breach of a contract (Quintyn and Taylor 2007). This promissory intensity, in turn, has to be balanced with the costs of regulation for users, providers, and the economy at large, and the systemic risks must be weighed against the long-term benefits of the development of these segments of the financial system (Honohan and Beck 2007). A caveat emptor approach, whereby the weight of the responsibility for monitoring lies on sophisticated investors rather than supervisors, might therefore be more adequate for segments of the financial system that are being used by such investors.

This caveat against expanding the regulatory boundary indiscriminately certainly does not exclude strengthening the regulation and supervision of the insurance and pension fund sectors, which are still rudimentary in many countries of Africa, or the risk-based expansion of regulation and supervision to MFIs or savings and credit cooperatives (SACCOs). In a nutshell, expanding the regulatory net to include nonbank financial institutions that serve households with less financial exposure might be more important than expanding it toward products and markets mostly used by more educated and sophisticated segments of the population.[7]

The bottom of the pyramid: prudential regulation where appropriate

One of the areas experiencing the most rapid changes over the past decade or so has been the regulation of institutions that serve the bottom of the pyramid. Many African countries have introduced some kind of special regulatory framework for

MFIs or are in the process of doing so. In a third of the countries in Africa, meanwhile, MFIs still either fall implicitly or explicitly under the banking or nonbank financial institution regulatory framework or are left out completely.

One important issue is the failure of nonregulated or poorly regulated bottom-of-the-pyramid institutions, such as SACCOs. As we have seen across the world (for example, in Albania and Colombia), the failure of such institutions can lead to bank runs and the loss of trust in all financial institutions among large parts of the population, but also to social and political unrest. On a more general level, the failure of an MFI has potentially an even bigger impact on people's lives than a bank failure. While concerns about a domino effect are usually unjustified because MFIs and SACCOs feature only limited interconnectedness and size, the number of savers affected by a failure can be considerable.

A question many countries across the continent have been struggling with is whether microfinance or cooperative institutions should be regulated and supervised to the same extent as banks. A global consensus has developed around the idea of extending prudential regulation and supervision only to deposit-taking institutions, while avoiding "burdensome prudential regulation for nonprudential purposes, that is, purposes other than protecting depositors' safety and the soundness of the financial sector as whole" (Christen, Lyman, and Rosenberg 2003, 3). While, for a long time, deposit taking was limited to banks, more and more countries have loosened this restriction and created a regulatory framework for deposit-taking MFIs or community banks. In some cases, regulation has followed reality because many SACCOs in East Africa are already taking deposits not only from their members (as they are allowed to do), but also the broader public through front-office facilities. This creates serious concerns if the broader public does not understand the difference between banks and such bank-like financial institutions, expecting the same regulatory oversight and protection. Introducing a formal regulatory framework for such institutions, however, without complementing this by the necessary supervisory structure can backfire. This can be exacerbated if a deposit insurance scheme for such institutions is introduced before their financial situation and viability have been assessed, resulting in potentially high fiscal liability and, even worse, a loss of trust in bank supervision if the authorities do not follow up on their commitments.

Deposit-taking MFIs can certainly benefit from reporting requirements and absolute minimum capital standards that are less strict than those applying to banks; however, they may need more stringent requirements in terms of capital and liquidity ratios. An argument can be made that higher capital-adequacy ratios should be required among MFIs because their loan portfolios are typically more geographically and sectorally concentrated and, for this reason, tend to be more volatile. Rules, such as limits on unsecured lending as a ratio of equity, should not be imposed on MFIs because most, if not all microlending is uncollateralized. It is important not to impose overburdening activity or geographical restrictions on such institutions because this might undermine their viability. Similarly, the regulation of MFIs is expensive for supervisory agencies, given the fixed costs. There is thus a trade-off between the goal of inclusion and the goal of stability. However, there are ways to alleviate this trade-off. Unnecessary regulatory burdens, such as excessive loan documentation or excessive branching requirements, should give way to simpler reporting requirements and ownership diversification rules that do not represent barriers to investment in MFIs by nongovernmental organizations. Member-based financial institutions, such as cooperatives, might also benefit from reduced supervision, especially if the supervisory authorities can rely on well-run, well-governed, and appropriately regulated and supervised apex institutions. A separate question is whether a special regime is needed for deposit-taking MFIs. The example of Uganda, which introduced a regulatory framework for deposit-taking MFIs a few years ago, might be rather depressing because there are currently only two institutions under this regime. However, such an assessment does not take into account the contestability aspect of this option with regard to a growing MFI or a new entrant.

The transition process from credit-only to deposit-taking institution is a tricky one. Allowing credit institutions to start collecting deposits requires that the new institutions first submit to a careful process of vetting and screening. Are they sufficiently viable and profitable? Do they have the proper management information systems? Can they bear the regulatory burden? Does a license to take deposits entail a certain promise from regulators? It is therefore important to be open toward the public about the implications of such a license in terms of security and guarantees.

MFI regulation can be both restraining and enabling and can help low-end financial institutions push toward the access possibilities frontier. Yet, regulation that is too lax can also provide perverse incentives to move beyond the frontier by allowing too many unqualified providers into the market or by giving support to disreputable providers.

The supervisory structure: two is a party; three is a crowd?

An important discussion in recent years has revolved around the organizational structure of financial sector supervision.[8] Across the world, the advantages and shortcomings of various models—separate supervisors for each segment, unified supervisory agencies, or a functional approach involving separate prudential supervision and supervision of business conduct—have been discussed. Traditionally, bank supervision has been carried out by central banks, with the exception of UEMOA, the Economic and Monetary Community of Central Africa, and other francophone countries in which bank supervision is housed in a separate entity. The supervision of other financial institutions and markets, including capital market supervision and insurance and pension fund supervision, has often been carried out through ministries of finance. Even today, countries as diverse as Algeria, Madagascar, and Mauritania supervise insurance companies through the ministries of finance. The latter arrangement, however, has often been plagued by the limited skill base and the lack of independence. Several countries have therefore undertaken the establishment of specialized insurance and capital market supervisors in recent years. Specifically, Egypt, Mauritius, and South Africa have introduced financial service boards for nonbank financial service providers to streamline rules regulating these industries and supervise institutions with multiple financial nonbanking activities, while Ghana and Kenya have separate insurance supervisors. Another discussion concerns the issue of who should supervise deposit-taking microfinance and cooperative institutions. The majority of countries rely on supervision by the same institutions that supervise banks, though not necessarily under the same regulatory framework. In Kenya, deposit-taking MFIs are supervised by the Central Bank, which also supervises banks, while SACCOs are supervised by a separate entity.

In each of these cases (insurance companies and capital markets, as well as MFIs), there are arguments in favor and arguments against using the same entity to supervise nonbank financial institutions and banks. On the one hand, bank supervisors have accumulated the necessary supervisory expertise and skills, as well as the necessary reputation, which might be especially critical in the early stages of the supervision of a new segment of the financial system. This might be particularly important in countries with a limited skill base. On the other hand, the supervision of nonbank financial institutions and markets often requires a separate skill set. This also applies to MFIs. Moreover, there are concerns about competition because bank supervisors might dominate other types of supervisors and favor the banking segment of the financial system over other segments.

While the concerns about the separate skills needed and about competition might be valid in the case of insurance and capital market supervision, they appear less valid in the case of the supervision of deposit-taking microfinance and cooperative institutions because the required technical skills are similar. Furthermore, given the often vague boundary between traditional banks and deposit-taking MFIs or cooperatives in the eye of the general public, it might be helpful to have one set of regulators for such deposit-taking institutions so as to avoid regulatory arbitrage. It is certainly important that financial cooperatives not be supervised by the general cooperative authority, but by specialized supervisors. There are also political considerations, as well as concerns about the power of bank supervisors and about whether bank supervisors might focus too much attention on stability and not sufficient attention on outreach. A compromise might involve the secondment of staff to a new authority that supervises nonbank deposit-taking institutions.

Another important question revolves around the location of the authority responsible for market development and expansion. While currently often housed in central banks, this raises the issue of a conflict of interest with the prudential task of bank regulators. Yet, the central bank is, in most countries across the region, still the institution with the highest concentration of skills outside financial institutions and often the entity with the best reputation and greatest autonomy.

There has been a recent trend toward a regional regulatory framework. The francophone countries of West and Central Africa are farther ahead in this context, having joint bank regulatory authorities for the two currency unions and one joint insurance regulator and supervisor (the Inter-African Conference on Insurance Markets), though these entities exist more in form than in substance. The authority to license banks is housed with the ministries of finance in these countries, and there is no consolidated supervision, at least not in the UEMOA region. Such regional arrangements can have critical advantages over national supervisors because they are able to address the scale challenge and the governance challenge. By joining forces regionally, bank regulators can create scale economies and build the necessary skills and capacities, while gaining independence from the political sphere and the regulated entities by functioning on the regional level rather than the national level. Attempts to harmonize regulations and supervisory practices, as currently undertaken in other parts of the continent, such as the Southern African Development Community, is an important first step toward the establishment of such regional structures.

From the supply side to the demand side

On a more local level, the risk of overindebtedness among households has been raising concerns since before the microfinance crisis in Andhra Pradesh, India. Initiatives that focus on responsible finance, such as those encouraged by the Consultative Group to Assist the Poor and the International Finance Corporation, commit MFIs to certain minimum standards of individual consumer protection against overindebtedness, including disclosure and transparency standards, but also incentive structures that do not create a bias in favor of lending too much to one client. This refers especially to salary loans, which are considered troublesome especially because of the ease with which creditors can gain access to the salary payments of borrowers.

If voluntary initiatives are not sufficient, more formal structures of consumer protection must be examined. We discuss these in the following.

Focusing on Users: Consumer Protection

Throughout the book, we stress the importance of extending the focus from supply-side constraints to demand-side constraints. This is as important in the area of financial stability as in the areas of expanding access and lengthening contracts. Parallel to financial literacy in the attempt to include a larger part of the population in the financial system, we have to focus on consumer protection to protect current and newly banked segments of the population.

Unlike in the case of capital markets and equity funds, where we advocate a caveat emptor approach to avoid suppressing these nascent segments of the financial system, a *caveat venditor* approach is called for in the case of bottom-of-the-pyramid financial services.[9] Consumer protection has gained increasing importance throughout the world. Across industrialized countries, the aftermath of the global crisis has seen a reemphasis on protecting the unsophisticated consumers of financial services from buying products they do not need or that expose their livelihoods to extreme risk. This focus on consumer protection relates to savings and investment and to credit products, as well as to payment services, such as remittances. It is closely related to the theme of financial literacy discussed elsewhere above, but focuses more on the market-harnessing role of regulation and imposes restrictions on financial service suppliers rather than focusing on (potential) consumers.

Consumer protection can help competition and, thus ultimately, outreach.[10] Better informed customers are able and more likely to shop around, thus incentivizing financial service providers to compete on price and product features. By the same token, marketing tools, including deceptive advertising, can have a major impact on consumer decisions, as a recent study in South Africa shows (Bertrand et al. 2010). Loan offers were mailed to some 50,000 customers. The loans were associated with randomized interest rates and advertising material containing numerous variants on common advertising devices. The researchers found that loan demand was sensitive to the quoted interest rates, but also to several features of the advertising. For example, including a photograph of a woman in the accompanying literature (as opposed to a man) was, in terms of the influence on loan take-up, equivalent to lowering the rate of interest by over 4 percentage points *per month*.

Effective consumer protection in financial services focuses on four key areas: (1) consumer disclosure that is clear, simple, easy to understand, and comparable; (2) prohibitions on business practices that are unfair, abusive, or deceptive; (3) efficient and easy-to-use recourse mechanisms; and (4) financial education that gives consumers the knowledge, skills, and confidence to understand and evaluate the financial information they receive (Rutledge 2010). Consumer protection sets clear rules of engagement between financial firms and retail customers. It helps narrow the knowledge gap between consumers and their financial institutions and increases the ability of consumers to make informed decisions about financial products. Thus, effective financial consumer protection is delivered through regulation (government regulation and self-regulation) and programs of financial education.

No internationally agreed methodology has been developed to assess the quality of a financial consumer protection framework.[11] Nonetheless, the legal, regulatory, and institutional framework is generally stronger in high-income countries than in Africa.

What are the instruments of consumer protection? In line with the motto that transparency is the best disinfectant, disclosure requirements are one of the most basic and important tools. Advising consumers about the returns and the risks of investment products should be the foundation of any sales process in financial services. Providing customers with a clear indication of the monthly costs of credit, including interest, principal, and fee payments, over the complete lifetime of the credit should be a minimum requirement. According to the Making Finance Work for Africa survey (see elsewhere above), most countries require banks, by law, to inform customers about the fees for products before account opening and, subsequently, about any changes to these fees. This is the hallmark of any decent business conduct, and these are rules that can be easily put in place. Consumer protection should also be an integral part of any credit reference bureau, including mechanisms for data disclosure and an appeal process, as in the case of South Africa (box 5.3).[12]

A step up from minimum consumer disclosure rules (which can be enforced by bank supervisors or on a self-regulatory industry-wide basis by the banking association) are government regulations that prohibit financial institutions from selling specific products to all but sophisticated clients (such as corporate clients or high-wealth individuals) and government regulations that impose affordability

Box 5.3   The Consumer Protection Framework in South Africa

A distinct feature of the South African financial system is the presence of the National Credit Act, credit bureaus, the national credit regulator, the Office of the Credit Information Ombud, and the National Consumer Tribunal, which became operational on June 1, 2006.

- *National Credit Act 34 of 2005:* The purpose of the act is to promote and advance the social and economic welfare of South Africans; promote a fair, transparent, competitive, sustainable, responsible, efficient, and accessible credit market and industry; and protect consumers. Specifically, this includes (1) promoting black empowerment and ownership within the consumer credit industry; (2) prohibiting unfair credit and credit-marketing practices; (3) promoting responsible credit granting and use and, for that purpose, to prohibit reckless credit granting; to regulate credit information; to provide for the registration of credit bureaus, credit providers, and debt counseling services; (4) establishing norms and standards relating to consumer credit; and (5) promoting a consistent enforcement framework.
- *National credit regulator:* The national credit regulator is responsible for the regulation of the South African credit industry and has the responsibility to (1) implement education campaigns, (2) conduct research and develop policies, (3) investigate complaints, and (4) ensure compliance with the act. It also has the responsibility to register and regulate credit providers, credit bureaus, and debt counselors.
- *Credit bureaus:* The National Credit Act (1) stipulates that credit bureaus are required to register with the national credit regulator to conduct business legally, (2) sets out the purposes for which consumer credit information may be used and the companies to which the credit bureaus may provide the information, (3) sets out the standards for data accuracy, and (4) ensures that consumers have the right to check their records.
- *Office of the National Credit Ombud:* To resolve disputes between consumers and credit bureau providers, the Office of the Credit Information Ombud was established and is operating.
- *National Consumer Tribunal:* The tribunal hears cases on noncompliance with the act, issues fines, and provides redress to consumers. Consumers and credit providers may appeal any decision of the national credit regulator to the tribunal.

Collectively, the South African consumer protection framework is designed to ensure that, among other protections, (1) the language in credit agreements is simple and understandable;

Box 5.3. The Consumer Protection Framework in South Africa *(continued)*

(2) quotes are given on all credit agreements and are binding for five days; (3) advertising and marketing contains prescribed information on the cost of credit; (4) credit sales at a person's home and workplace are strictly limited; (5) reasons are provided if credit is declined; (6) automatic increases in credit limits are regulated; (7) reckless lending is prohibited; (8) interest and fees are regulated on agreements, including microloans; (9) credit bureaus are regulated, and consumers have the right to free credit bureau records; and (10) overly indebted consumers have access to debt counseling to enable the restructuring of debt.

Although largely applauded for their restrictions on abusive lending practices, the debt restructuring processes embedded in the National Credit Act have attracted criticism from the financial sector. The court-enshrined process has been criticized as too slow. Banks cite the 9,000 cases being submitted to the courts monthly and the resultant backlog as a source of major concern for the industry. Their efforts to establish a national debt mediation association to increase the flow of negotiated interventions for overly indebted consumers is seen as a positive, yet insufficient initiative. It is argued that as few as 5 percent of the estimated 150,000 applications made by consumers since July 2003 have been finalized by the courts.

To create an effective consumer protection framework, the effort must be complemented by an equally effective financial literacy program. The government is determined to raise the level of financial awareness and improve the financial behavior of consumers so that they can make informed financial decisions according to their specific economic and social circumstances. Only a financially literate population will use consumer protection systems. Improving financial literacy strengthens the knowledge, understanding, skills, attitudes, and, especially, behavior that people need to make sound personal finance decisions and that allow people to become more attractive as potential borrowers. The government has to use multiple channels to deliver financial literacy programs, including financial institutions, the education system (financial education in school curricula), the media (newspapers, radio, television, Internet), social marketing (road shows, street theater, targeted entrainment programs), institutional services (debt counseling, mentoring), and other methods.

In South Africa, the Banking Association of South Africa has made representations to the parliamentary portfolio committee on basic education on reforms to the national curriculum on matters of economic management science, including an individual's economic cycle, sustainable growth and development, and managerial, consumer, financial, and entrepreneurial knowledge and skills. Financial literacy programs in the early formative years are accepted as an essential aspect of efforts to improve South Africa's low savings rate of only 15 percent, but also as an essential element of the national empowerment for citizens. The proposed reforms are intended to build on the ongoing Teach Children to Save South Africa Program launched in July 2008, which enables financial sector professionals to share their work-based knowledge and expertise by giving one-hour lessons on savings to grades 4 to 7 learners nationwide. Supported by the Department of Basic Education and integrated in the economic science learning area of the school curriculum, the program has thus far attracted participation from 13 banks and 27 financial sector institutions.

Sources: National Credit Regulator, Johannesburg, http://www.ncr.org.za/; Banking Association of South Africa, Johannesburg, http://www.banking.org.za/.

tests on financial institutions before credit may be extended. However, such regulations impose regulatory compliance costs on financial institutions, might prevent the broadening of the financial system, and require additional institutional capacity among the relevant authorities. South Africa adopted this approach in 2007 through the passage of the National Credit Act and the establishment of the national credit regulator, who is responsible for consumer protection in the area of consumer credits, whether they are extended by banks or by nonbank financial institutions, an experience discussed in box 5.3.

A final set of rules imposes certain minima or maxima on the costs of financial services, including usury interest rates. Such interest rate ceilings (in the case of credit) or floors (in the case of savings products) can, however, easily turn into a restrictive tool that reduces access to services by riskier customers and customers who need smaller transactions and who are thus costlier for financial institutions. According to the Making Finance Work for Africa survey, a third of countries in Africa still have usury ceilings in place, and a fourth impose deposit interest rate floors. This high rate is driven by UEMOA, which caps lending rates at 18 percent for banks and 27 percent for nonbank financial institutions and MFIs, regardless of the purpose or recipient of the loans. Yet, few countries impose limits on fees. This obviously makes interest rate ceilings and floors less effective because fees are a popular escape route for banks facing restrictions on interest rates.

In consumer protection, one size does not fit all. Middle-income countries such as South Africa can afford sophisticated institutional structures. Given the rapid increase in reliance on consumer credit, there is also a stronger need for protection mechanisms in these economies. In the specific case of South Africa, this has also to be seen in the context of the consumer credit boom the country experienced in the early 2000s. Small and low-income countries, in contrast, might not have the necessary resources and capacities to implement such a system and have to rely more on disclosure standards and self-regulatory initiatives. In large and middle-income countries, additional emphasis might have to be put on detecting pyramid schemes in the formal and informal financial services sector.

In terms of institutional structures for simplicity and accountability, it is best to have only one institution to which consumers can submit complaints about financial services (Rutledge 2010). In line with the motto that one size does not fit all, this could be part of an industry association, the regulatory authority, or a separate entity. Dealing effectively with complaints is critical in this context because it is through the complaint process that most consumers will have direct contact with the consumer protection agency, and dealing ineffectively with complaints can lead to cynicism and a general aversion for financial services. However, there might also be a useful link with financial literacy programs, as they can teach (potential) consumers of pitfalls, possible abuse, and remedial opportunities.

Accountability among financial service providers for the products and the information they supply and for the sales processes they rely on is paramount in the protection of consumers. This includes prohibiting unfair and deceptive practices.

Simplicity is key. Disclosure requirements can accomplish much; however, they must be clear and easy to understand and enable users to compare similar products and services. Providing key fact statements, with a summary of the most important terms and conditions written in plain language, and developing standardized contracts can be helpful. It is essential to offer comparable, standardized information about the services provided by financial institutions, for example, the costs of opening, maintaining, and using bank accounts for typical user groups. Financial institutions should also offer contact points where consumers can present complaints.

In terms of consumer protection, all financial institutions should be covered by business conduct regulations, independent of whether they are subject to prudential regulations or not. Obviously, conduct of business regulations and supervision are not as extensive as prudential regulations, so that more emphasis has to be placed on the initial registration process and on following up closely on any complaint. Such a registration process should focus on the integrity and qualifications of the provider. However, there is a trade-off between protecting consumers through a regulatory framework on business conduct and imposing unnecessary regulatory burdens on financial service providers. One has to distinguish among different target groups. Specifically, institutions aiming for the low end of the market certainly deserve closer scrutiny than providers for the high end of sophisticated investors. Put bluntly, caveat venditor should apply to low-end financial institutions, caveat emptor for the high end. Pyramid schemes pop up on a regular basis throughout the developed world and the developing world; continuous monitoring by regulators is therefore required.

Consumer protection is also a critical element in the design of financial infrastructure components such as credit registries. Consumers and businesses need an easy and inexpensive way to verify the positive and negative information that is being collected about them in credit registries, as well as a transparent and swift process to contest information that they think is in error.

Conclusions

The three main messages we discuss in previous chapters also apply to this chapter, though from a somewhat different perspective. In the previous chapters, we advocate for a greater reliance on competition within and across different segments of the financial system so as to reap the benefits of financial innovation. This should not imply that regulators should not follow developments closely and step in when risks to financial stability arise. Allowing competition exerts strain on the regulatory framework and requires more flexibility and more ability in adapting to changing market structures.

While recognizing the potential trade-off between stability and innovation in the financial system, this book advocates a preference for the latter. This also implies, however, that more competition will impose a greater burden on regulators and supervisors. Looking beyond existing institutions and markets to service pro-

224 Financing Africa: Through the Crisis and Beyond

vision is also important in safeguarding finance. Deposit-taking institutions should be subject to prudential regulations and supervision, no matter whether they call themselves banks or not, though the exact nature of the regulatory framework can vary; it must not cause regulatory arbitrage, however. Finally, addressing demand constraints through a greater focus on consumer protection is important in safeguarding finance because this helps expand access and lengthen contracts.

Different countries have different priorities. Countries with more developed financial systems are more likely to have more capacity, but also more need and therefore more motivation to follow closely the regulatory and supervisory upgrades proposed in the G20 reform process and to expand the regulatory perimeter beyond banking. Low-income countries have more immediate needs in regular bank supervision. Consumer protection is important across all countries, though the institutional possibilities and options vary significantly, as we argue. As Africa's financial systems develop, the regulatory and supervisory framework has to adapt to changing circumstances and requirements.

Notes

1. "In a systemic banking crisis," according to Laeven and Valencia (2008, 5), "a country's corporate and financial sectors experience a large number of defaults and financial institutions and corporations face great difficulties repaying contracts on time. As a result, nonperforming loans increase sharply and all or most of the aggregate banking system capital is exhausted. This situation may be accompanied by depressed asset prices (such as equity and real estate prices) on the heels of run-ups before the crisis, sharp increases in real interest rates, and a slowdown or reversal in capital flows. In some cases, the crisis is triggered by depositor runs on banks, though, in most cases, it is a general realization that systemically important financial institutions are in distress." A nonsystemic crisis, meanwhile, affects only (large) financial institutions, without additional negative repercussions on the rest of the financial system.

2. For the following discussion, see Fuchs, Hands, and Jaeggi (2010); Fuchs, Losse-Müller, and Witte (2010).

3. See Making Finance Work for Africa (database), Partnership Secretariat, African Development Bank, Tunis, http://www.mfw4a.org/.

4. In addition to the direct implications of the regulatory reform debate for regulation and supervision in Africa, there are also indirect repercussions. One implication of the Basel reforms described above is that, because smaller banks and banks from developing countries are, on average, less likely to possess sophisticated risk management systems, they will already face a competitive disadvantage in crossborder markets in this respect and will be confronted by higher capital charges as they transition to Basel II and, ultimately, Basel III. Therefore, the Basel capital requirement reforms essentially raise the cost of international bank financing for developing countries and may also reduce their access to external financing.

5. At high cost, Mozambique, Tanzania, and Uganda had to renationalize previously privatized banks because the respective purchasers—various multinational banks—turned out to be too weak (World Bank 2001).

6. Lukonga (2010) documents trends in and the characteristics of large African conglomerate financial institutions and analyzes the stability risks that these pose. As the ex-

ample of Europe shows, a rapid expansion of large, conglomerate financial institutions throughout the continent can raise a number of risks for regional stability that are not adequately mitigated by the current practice in regulatory oversight. These risks mainly arise from (a) the nontransparency of corporate structures, which creates the potential for the unnoticed buildup of group risks and for financial contagion to other banks stemming from problems in separate parts of the corporate group; (b) inadequacies in the risk management of the vulnerabilities inherent in banking and other operations; and (c) potential exogenous shocks from the economic and political environment in which the corporate group operates. The effectiveness of overall supervision is undermined by the inconsistencies in prudential regulation and the lack of supervisory coordination that create opportunities for regulatory arbitrage, by weaknesses in accounting infrastructure, and by the absence of a crisis management framework, an absence that, in the resolution process, could raise the costs of failure.

7. It is important to expand the regulation and supervision of previously unregulated segments of the financial system, such as MFIs and SACCOs, in an incentive-compatible order, that is, first licensing and regulation, before expanding any deposit guarantees to these segments, which could result in large fiscal contingencies and aggressive risk taking.

8. For a discussion relating directly to Africa, see Quintyn and Taylor (2007).

9. In contrast to the caveat emptor approach, the caveat venditor approach (let the seller beware) implies that the seller of the financial product is liable for negative consequences and has to check the financial capacity of buyers.

10. For the following, see the discussion in Rutledge (2010).

11. The World Bank has prepared *Good Practices for Financial Consumer Protection,* which is to be released as a consultative draft for comment by international financial regulators and other stakeholders. See http://go.worldbank.org/CJU6DTRZ20.

12. Detailed diagnostic work has been done on the status of consumer protection in several African countries; see Engels (2011).

Chapter 6

All Financial Sector Policy Is Local

Introduction

The financial sector challenges described in this book are not new. Africa's informal economy, lack of scale, volatility, and governance problems have been discussed extensively. Not new either is a long list of solutions that have been tried in one form or another. Many solutions have been discredited in one decade only to become the preferred flavor of financial reform in the next. Yet, the challenge of limited and costly finance in Africa persists. The importation and application of solutions being implemented on other continents today is not taking place in Africa at a rate sufficient to make a substantial and sustainable impact on the availability of affordable finance.

We argue in this chapter that the problem has not been in the choice of the solutions, but, rather, the direction and quality of the application of these solutions to Africa's local circumstances and the failure to build or scale up homegrown solutions. Or, as one of the leading political economists of our time has put it, "the problem of underdevelopment cannot be solved by economists coming up with better policies for poor countries to adopt. . . . The problem is that they are not adopted" (Robinson 2009, 8). We therefore caution in this chapter that, unless there are changes in the politics of financial reform in Africa, even the recent opportunities of globalization, technology, and regional integration will suffer the same fate as others that once offered promise to resolve Africa's financial constraints.

Modernist Reform Policies: Africa's Achilles Heel

For far too long, the *modernist* policy agenda discussed by Honohan and Beck (2007) has held sway in far too many African financial systems. Governments, regulators, and development partners, encouraged by international financial institutions, have all focused on policies aimed at modernizing the macroeconomic, contractual, and information framework, with the objective of reducing information asymmetries, improving legal certainty, and lengthening the planning horizon of investors. This agenda has included updating the laws governing financial contracts and ensuring their proper and reliable enforcement through judicial reforms to make certain that property rights are clearly defined and enforceable, both in general terms and as they apply to specific modern financial instruments.

The choice of policy instruments has been appropriate. Modernization represents the bedrock of any credible vision for national financial sectors, whether in Africa or elsewhere. The problem has been the application of the modernist agenda according, primarily, to the premise that modernization is equivalent to the best practice of the advanced market economies. Although all stakeholders acknowledge that transplanting best practice that is benchmarked against developed economies is likely to take time, this agenda has been pursued, and the shift in this direction has been accepted as progress. A second problem has centered on the fact that these reforms are necessary, but far from sufficient. They constitute the needed framework in which private providers of financial services can flourish, thus deepening and broadening financial systems. However, they are not sufficient for supplying the required incentives to realize this framework; moreover, they ignore other constraints, including demand-side constraints. As has become clear through our three main messages, financial sector policy has to move beyond the modernist policy agenda, in addition to adjusting it to the African context.

Unless policy makers and the development partners who work with them deliberately redefine progress in financial sector development to suit local African conditions, the modernist agenda will continue to overreach in Africa. We neglect Africa's real local constraints at our own peril. It is not enough that we continue to tweak overambitious structures imported from advanced economies. The evidence of this overreach is clear in the design of African stock markets, in capital regulatory standards for banks, in collateral requirements and the requirements for opening accounts, and in the exclusive nature of payment systems, which are influenced by what is held to be best practice in advanced economies.

Unfortunately, there are numerous examples of real political economy considerations—all well intentioned—that feed the modernist agenda. These include, but are not limited to the following:

- *The global financial architecture:* The well-intentioned work of international standard-setting bodies and international financial sector assessments such as the joint Financial Sector Assessment Program of the International Monetary Fund and World Bank naturally lend themselves to the modernist view. Instead of international standards being judged as benchmarks for certain types of economies and financial institutions, they soon evolve into minimum requirements for *all* economies.

- *International efforts in anti-money laundering and combating terrorist financing:* The work of the Financial Action Task Force in combating money laundering and terrorist financing, which includes the listing of noncompliant countries, has reinforced the desire of all countries, especially developing countries, to comply with a minimum set of standards even if it has been explained that these standards ought to be tailored to national circumstances.

- *National regulatory incentive and cost structures:* National regulators, often the central banks, do not have the incentives or the resources to design and develop regulations that suit national requirements. Regulatory and supervisory skills are in short supply and are often remunerated at less than the rates available in private financial institutions. The cost of adapting regulations to national circumstances can be high; plus there is the additional risk that one may have to explain to ministers of finance and parliaments why the standards fall short of international best practice.

- *The globalization of financial institutions, products, and personnel:* The number of global financial institutions, products, and finance experts has increased tremendously. With the full range of destinations demanding their resources and skills, these experts will first gravitate to countries where standard international best practice is already embedded. National regulators who want to continue attracting international finance and talent are obliged to hesitate before considering any tempering of international standards.

As significant as these pressures are, Africa must overcome them if it is to make meaningful progress in increasing the availability of affordable finance for markets and for growth. *All financial sector policy in Africa is local.* The failure to pay attention to the real national context undermines efforts to build the foundations of an effective financial system for the long run. In the rest of this chapter, we discuss some options for stakeholders involved in financial sector development in Africa. We also discuss the politics of financial sector reform and the various challenges that countries with diverse profiles face in Africa.

The Activist Reform Agenda Revisited: Larger, More Efficient, and Stable Financial Markets

According to Honohan and Beck (2007), the *activist* perspective on finance is concerned with achieving results in areas where the anonymous private financial sector is not conspicuously successful: finance for agriculture and the rural economy, for microenterprises and small enterprises, and for low-income households, as well as long-term finance in general. Inherent difficulties, risks, and costs impede the effectiveness of private financial markets in each of these areas. The activist agenda sees the need for special interventions to help correct market failures. These well-intentioned interventions include enacting protective legislation and efforts at establishing competent and politically independent prudential regulators to guard against the weak, reckless, or corrupt management of financial intermediaries that could cause the collapse of these intermediaries. The activist agenda also sometimes advocates the establishment of a variety of special public, charitable, or otherwise privileged intermediaries who—it is hoped—can help push the financial system toward the frontier in these areas.

Because of the disappointing performance of many publicly owned financial institutions (all too often subverted through politicized management or through corruption), the risk of overreaching in this regard is well known and has caused the activist agenda to be viewed with admirable suspicion (that is, noble in its intentions, disastrous in its unintended consequences). This view is not unwarranted, but it is incomplete. African finance needs a new and positive activist reform agenda, one that expands the reach of financial markets and lengthens financial contracts, yet honors the progress that has been made in making financial systems more stable, one that enables markets rather than replacing them. African finance calls for an activist reform program that is true to the realities of Africa's political economy. While this does not exclude learning from the experience of other regions, such as East Asia (box 6.1), it emphasizes the need to adjust these lessons to the African reality.

The short-term election cycle of African politics is at natural odds with the long-term nature of financial sector development and reform. So is the plethora of po-

Box 6.1 Learning from the East Asian Miracle

The East Asian miracle has often been heralded as proof that unorthodox government interventions can have a positive impact on growth. Specifically, on top of sound macroeconomic policies, many East Asian countries adopted policies that ran counter to the modernist approach, including targeted and subsidized credit, interest rate floors and ceilings, and government-owned banks (World Bank 1993). Most East Asian economies relied on development finance institutions (DFIs) as a catalyst for funding investment projects. What, if any, lessons does the East Asian success story hold for Africa?

There are several important lessons from East Asia for Africa (World Bank 1993). First, macroeconomic stability was key to the success of the East Asian economies. Second, policies to encourage savings in East Asia, accompanied by efficient financial intermediation, were a critical part of the success. Beyond these two important and mostly uncontroversial dimensions, however, East Asian governments intervened heavily in markets. The success of these interventions relied on complementing market-based competitiveness with goverment-induced contests that combined cooperation with competition (World Bank 1993). Rewarding industries and firms that used subsidies successfully, often judged by their ability to export, while withdrawing subsidies from failing enterprises was a critical part of the approach. So, unorthodox instruments were applied, but they were continued only while there was evidence of success, and exports were considered a good indicator and easy to monitor. More importantly, these measures were removed when they did not or no longer worked.

Many of the unorthodox policies successfully implemented in East Asia have not worked in Africa. Financial repression and industrial policies have had little, if no positive impact on financial and economic development in Africa. On the contrary, financial repression has depressed savings and resulted in the misallocation of credit. As discussed above, directed credit and government-owned banking have not only resulted in large losses, but have dis-

Box 6.1   Learning from the East Asian Miracle *(continued)*

torted credit markets and resource allocations, with negative repercussions for economic growth and equity.

Why have government interventions worked in East Asia, but not in Africa? Most activist government interventions have not taken place accompanied by the necessary macroeconomic stability as a fundament; rather, they have undermined stability through large contingent and actual fiscal losses. Decisions on whether to start or continue specific interventions have not been driven by performance criteria, but mostly by political considerations. A more in-depth structural comparison of Africa and East Asia also highlights more deeply underlying factors. First, the lack of scale and limited geographical connectivity reduce the possibility to apply such a contest *cum* cooperation approach in most African countries. Second, limited implementation and monitoring capacity has undermined the success of activist government interventions. Most importantly, however, ethnic fractionalization in most countries of the region explains why the necessary political stability and institutions do not exist that are so critical for the success of government interventions (Easterly and Levine 1997). Ethnic fractionalization can result in uncoordinated rent-seeking activity, exacerbate common pool problems, and lead to the suboptimal provision of public goods. Government interventions are not informed and driven by economic policy objectives, but by private interest; contest *cum* cooperation is not feasible in such an environment. The reliance of many African economies on natural resources increases the incentives for rent-seeking activity and undermines political stability.

East Asia, however, also offers negative lessons for Africa, especially in the wake of the East Asian crisis. Accompanying financial deepening with appropriate regulation and supervision, as well as disclosure and transparency standards, is critical to ensuring sustainable credit growth and growth-conducive financial development and avoiding bubbles ending in financial fragility.

In summary, the East Asian experience underlines the potential for a role for government beyond macroeconomic management and institution building. It also shows the requisite conditions needed to make government intervention work. It shows the potential for the success of activist policies if these are combined with the necessary safeguards, implementation and monitoring capacity, and, most importantly, governance structures. Many activist policies have not worked in the African context. Context-specific and cautious government interventions that try to crowd in rather than replace the market might therefore be more promising in these cases. Recent achievements in macroeconomic stability and bank restructuring in Africa might serve as a basis for more active government participation, with the caveat that any government intervention should not undermine these same achievements.

litically convenient financial sector policies and programs that are incompatible with market-based financial sector development. Ill-designed agricultural subsidies, expensive technological platforms, and poorly governed state-owned financial institutions, to name but a few, continue to act to the detriment of sustainable financial sector policies.

Even if policies have been designed to leverage technical insights, there has been weak implementation. While this weak implementation is partly caused by the shortage of qualified personnel in certain key areas, it is largely caused by inadequate incentives and sanctions and by the pervasive failure to apply appropriate laws and regulations and adhere to established systems and procedures (Ablo, Vantzos, and Sharif 2004).

Regulators routinely acknowledge complete awareness of the technically appropriate policy decisions that are needed to impact the access to and the cost of finance, but are unable to implement them for a host of political economy reasons, the most common of which include the centralized nature of policy making, political patronage, the lack of freedom of expression, and the dominant political elites. These political realities manifest themselves differently across the continent, but, in all cases, they prevent the implementation of optimal solutions.

Instead, the political realities call for the design and development of second-best solutions that go beyond the preoccupation with, for many countries, unachievable optimal policies and that take these governance realities into account more systematically. A study on governance, political economy, and economic development in Zambia (World Bank 2008c) has identified three complementary approaches that can help identify a way forward for financial sector reform in Africa generally, as follows:

- *First, seek out incremental reform options that are feasible given political economy realities.* To contend with political economy realities, a reform agenda must take the interests of stakeholders into account. For instance, stakeholders are generally not interested in achieving some abstract and notionally efficient systemic optimum. Their interests are in achieving better results in relation to concrete goals that matter for them. From this perspective, the challenge is to identify specific reforms that can meet *both* the economic imperatives of improving service provision, reducing poverty, and helping move economic development forward *and* the political imperatives of enjoying the support of influential stakeholders and not generating widespread opposition. Generally, such reforms tend to be incremental. In the financial sector, efforts to establish collateral registries, especially land registries, provide a useful example. This has long been a focus of donor efforts to support reform in the hope that these might unlock credit from the banking sector, with limited success. From a political economy perspective, this failure can be explained in large part by the great number of political and bureaucratic stakeholders that benefit from the existing arrangements for land and by the potentially destabilizing consequences of disrupting a long-standing compromise between customary and statutory arrangements. However, while comprehensive reform may be infeasible, the prospects may be better for an approach that focuses more narrowly on enhancing the transparency of the rules of the game by which individuals gain access to land titles. This would formalize the current system of informal tribute into a set of rules that explicitly support national interests, without challenging directly all the elite interests associated with the current status quo on land.

- *Second, draw on the knowledge of economically optimal policies in the design of reform.* While a necessary step in uncovering politically feasible approaches to reform involves loosening the grip of optimal models as a guide for the design of reform, the point is not to set these models aside entirely. Their normative logic is a useful point of reference, a North Star to help navigate change. Yet, as with ocean-going navigation, the journey is long, and the best route is not necessarily the most direct one. In the financial sector, for example, it is expedient to draw on existing model legislation or policies in the interest of cost-effectiveness and aligning the country to international best practice. Unfortunately, politically, this approach can sabotage internal domestic buy-in into the spirit of the proposed legislation or policies. Expensive as it may be, first strengthening the analytic capacity behind a national policy within and outside government may be more sustainable. Given the dynamics of national decision making, having technically strong policy-making voices inside and outside government that enjoy the respect of national elites could offer a real opportunity to influence public decisions for the better and could help alleviate the ideologically polarized (and not always well-informed) edge that currently characterizes the discourse between development partners and governments.

- *Third, consider the options for strengthening institutions.* The tension between efficient, pro-poor policy on the one hand and governance realities on the other is universal; the quality of a country's governance institutions helps shape the extent to which the result supports or undermines development. Economic development is easier to achieve in countries where political and bureaucratic institutions are strong. So, to support better policy making and implementation, a focus on feasible policies should be complemented by an effort to seek out feasible options for institutional strengthening. In financial sectors where institutions are weak, the key is dependent upon credible mutual commitment among subgroups of the elite to take reciprocal actions. To illustrate, consider the high costs of financial services in many African countries. Part of the problem is consumer acceptance of these high costs of financial services as a given. Yet, currently, the costs are so high that they prohibit greater access to finance. Moreover, despite the high costs of financial services, consumers are unwilling to change banks; not without reason, they view the costs of closing current bank accounts and opening new bank accounts also as too high. A credible commitment to financial literacy and consumer protection is therefore necessary to overcome long-standing public skepticism and the associated resistance to resisting high banking prices. This would require systematic engagement in the reform of the consumer-demand side of the market.

This policy reform agenda requires the deliberate involvement and partnership of key stakeholders on the continent in establishing and executing the reform agenda: politicians, regional bodies, national regulators, international development partners, and beneficiaries of any broadening and deepening of financial services, such as civil society and consumer associations. Before discussing the role of the various stakeholders, however, we turn our attention to the politics of financial sector reform.

The Politics of Financial Sector Reform

Throughout the book, we discuss the policy reforms necessary to expand finance and lengthen contracts, while safeguarding financial systems. However, it is not obvious that policy makers will make the appropriate reform decisions. The view focusing on the public interest has argued that politicians should act to maximize public welfare, but the evidence accumulated by economists, historians, and political scientists has shown a contrary reality.[1] Politicians primarily maximize private interests, whether the interests of their voters or special interest groups. Short-term election cycles undermine the focus on long-term financial development objectives; objectives that maintain the dominant position of elites undermine the incentives of these elites to undertake reforms that can open up financial systems and, thus, dilute the dominant position of the elites.

Path dependence in political structures and the underlying socioeconomic distribution of resources and power make the adoption of growth-enhancing policies, such as financial sector policies, difficult or impossible if the policies threaten to reduce the relative dominance of the incumbent elites.[2] The financial sector is critical for an open, competitive, and contestable economy because it provides the necessary resources for new entrants. Numerous examples in the history of finance have supported the idea that open and thriving financial markets are unhealthy for closed political and economic systems. An incumbent elite that is not willing to be subjected to checks and balances will not be able to agree not to expropriate holders of financial claims against it and will not allow private financial markets to flourish that might provide financing to competing groups.[3]

The three overarching messages of this book are closely related to the discussion on the politics of financial sector reform. An important effect of financial sector deepening and broadening is the increase in competition and contestability throughout the economy (Rajan and Zingales 2003). New players, new markets, and new products undermine the rents of the incumbents not only in the financial sector, but throughout the economy. Having access to transaction and savings services allows larger segments of the population to participate in the modern market economy. Broader access to credit is conducive to a more competitive real economy by fostering new entrants and contestability. The financial infrastructure propagated by the modernist agenda, such as collateral and credit registries, reduces the rents that incumbents gain from their privileges of wealth, a track record, and connections. Thus, creating competition in the financial system fosters competition throughout the economy and ultimately fosters private sector development, which is so crucial for economic growth and poverty reduction; the critical role of competition, however, makes competition more difficult to achieve because incumbent elites are not interested in competition if it will potentially undermine their position.

Pushing a financial system beyond banks toward new providers and products creates the same resistance from incumbent financial institutions, most prominently from banks. Banks typically oppose the introduction of positive information in credit registries because the registries harness the competitive effect of information sharing. Attempts to extend credit registries and payment systems beyond banks will also meet with resistance from banks because these registries and systems will undermine the dominant market position of banks within African financial systems. Similarly, banks might undermine the emergence of powerful capital markets because these markets constitute a threat to the privileged position of banks in bank-based financial systems.

An essential role—we link now to our third message—will be played by the constituency of financial sector reform. The traditional beneficiaries of African finance—blue chip businesses, multinational enterprises, and wealthy individuals—will not push for any financial sector reform that expands financial services, because they also obtain their services from outside the country. Small enterprises and previously unbanked segments of the population constitute the main potential beneficiaries of reform. In the long term, it is crucial to identify and seek the support of the constituency for financial sector reform, which consists of the beneficiaries of a broadening of financial services. Financial literacy can be important in this context, and financial journalists can be major actors in this effort (box 6.2).

The role of technology and globalization

Political economists such as Acemoglu, Johnson, and Robinson (2004) have stressed the importance of path dependence, whereby dominant elites formulate policies that help entrench their socioeconomic and political power. However, they also point to exogenous influences that can shift the equilibrium of influence. Most prominently and related to the themes of our book, globalization and technology can be game changers not only because of the possibilities they represent for deepening and broadening financial systems, but also because they move the playing field. They help create growth coalitions that benefit from financial deepening and broadening. Globalization and regional integration can lead to new opportunities and, thus, new potential winners who will depend on thriving financial institutions and markets to exploit the opportunities. Regional integration and globalization can also help distance the financial sector from the political sphere at the level of financial institutions and at the level of regulators. They are certainly not a panacea, as has been demonstrated by the initial, failed privatization of Uganda Commercial Bank in favor of a foreign investor that was tainted by connected lending and looting. Nonetheless, they offer policy space for financial sector reform. Similarly, technology can create new opportunities and winners rather swiftly, which may give the process of financial broadening critical momentum.

Box 6.2 Financial Journalism

Financial sector issues are rarely treated in the popular media across most of Africa despite the fact that they affect most people's daily lives. At the same time, there is a large knowledge gap on financial sector issues among the population at large. For this reason, the Making Finance Work for Africa Partnership, with support from the Federal Ministry for Economic Cooperation and Development of Germany and in cooperation with DW-Akademie of Deutsche Welle, an international news broadcaster, is now offering training courses on financial reporting for radio and television journalists from across the African continent. The program seeks to support financial literacy and a better understanding of financial sector topics among the African audience. Thus far, 40 television and radio journalists from 24 stations in 11 African countries have been trained in financial reporting for television, radio, and online. During training courses, the journalists have produced over two dozen television and radio reports, as well as online multimedia dossiers on topics ranging from financial capability to microinsurance, the informal financial sector, and access to finance.[a]

The challenge is not so much teaching journalists the technical skills to understand and then report on financial sector issues, but sharing information about everyday problems involving financial sector issues. The ability to describe and communicate real stories is critical so that people can relate financial sector issues such as inflation, high bank fees, or microcredit to their routine experiences. Explaining financial sector issues in simple, easily understandable language helps reach the audience. Journalists can thus play a major role in expanding awareness about relevant financial sector issues beyond specialists and the interested (and often incumbent) elites.

a. See http://mfw4ghana.wordpress.com/ and http://www.mfw4zambia.blogspot.com/ for the dossiers.

Over the short term, activist policies have to take into account the trade-offs we discuss above. In the long term, the objective must be the creation of a constituency for financial sector reform through growth coalitions. While the short-term approach would therefore consist in focusing on homegrown reform agendas that are already supported by political and economic actors, the medium- to long-term approach would include institution building supported by broader growth coalitions.

What is the role of regional integration?

Throughout the book, we point to the benefits of regional integration. Regional integration can help reduce the scale diseconomies stemming from the fixed costs in financial service provision and the fact that most African economies are small. The scale economies of regional integration can be reaped at the level of financial institutions, such as multinational banks, and at the level of financial markets through regional and cross-listing arrangements. However, they can also be reaped at the level of financial infrastructure, including payment systems, credit registries, and even the regulatory and supervisory framework (World Bank 2007a; Irving 2005). Delegating certain politically charged tasks to a supranational platform can also mitigate the political tensions and conflicts of interests that naturally occur in a sensitive sector such as finance. This becomes most obvious in the area of DFIs, in which subregional entities, such as the East African Development Bank, have fared much better than national DFIs. The benefits of regional integration arise across the three aspects of finance on which we focus in this book. Regional financial integration helps expand financial systems by enabling the spread of new products and delivery channels and by enabling larger segments of the population to transfer money across borders, fostering economic integration. Regional financial integration can help lengthen contracts by providing a larger scale. Regional integration is necessary in regulation and supervision in light of the growing role of regional banks.

What are the practical steps to regional integration? One size does not fit all. Some parts of Africa, most prominently the currency unions of Central Africa and West Africa, already have structures in place that can be used to advance integration. In other parts of Africa, most prominently East Africa and southern Africa, there is political impetus for more regional integration. Building on a World Bank study (2007a), we argue that much can still be achieved without waiting for political integration by focusing on the following:

- *Private sector–led efforts:* In many countries, foreign financial institutions have been purchasing local intermediaries. Some now have subsidiaries in several countries within individual regions, and a few have networks that spread across much of Sub-Saharan Africa. These institutions are establishing themselves as regional leaders in integration by the private sector. By addressing intercountry barriers, policy makers should support the efforts of these entities to reduce costs. To reduce costs, institutions need to establish back offices to manage customer relationships, lending, balance sheets, and other business activities on a regional basis.

- *The technical harmonization of regulations:* Policy-level integration is moving slowly on the continent, and more can be achieved. In southern Africa, regulators have started discussing harmonized regulations and a financial reporting framework for banks and insurance companies. Information-sharing agreements are in place; there is crossborder participation in supervision; and there are instances, at least in principle, of single license regimes for financial service firms among groups of countries. This process can be accelerated by encouraging more frequent formal and informal meetings among regulators. Even in the absence of bilateral political agreements, regulators can develop common policies and approaches to supervision on a wider range of issues. Reaching formal and informal standards on ownership, corporate governance, the treatment of nonperforming loans, and other technical issues will make it easier for private sector institutions to cross borders and integrate markets.

- *The physical standardization of financial infrastructure:* While accepting that a regionally integrated payments system may be more efficient and more stable than a purely national one, we recognize that, in many regions, such a system remains an aspiration. The legal framework as a regional solution alone would need to include (1) laws and regulations of broad applicability that address issues such as insolvency and the enforcement of contractual relationships; (2) laws and regulations that have specific applicability to payments systems (such as legislation on electronic signatures, the validation of netting, and settlement finality); and (3) the rules, standards, and procedures to which the participants in a payments or securities system agree. While working toward such a framework, regulators can agree on the standardized physical specifications of the physical payment systems infrastructure. (In southern Africa, many have already done so.) This principle can be applied to other financial sector infrastructure, including credit bureaus. At the regional level, the availability of crossborder credit information would enhance the ability of financial institutions to compete as they do at the national level, but in a larger market; this would encourage competition in both price and innovation and would also benefit borrowers and increase access.

- *Upgrade of information and communication technology* (ICT): To harvest the benefits of technology in the financial sector, it is imperative that efforts be undertaken to upgrade and collaborate in the regional development of ICT networks. ICT is the backbone and future of affordable financial services. A World Bank study of mobile banking services (or m-banking) in southern Africa found countries at different levels of ICT development (see Stone et al. 2009). ICT sectors among the middle-income countries such as South Africa and Namibia were comparatively better developed. In other countries, the telecommunications sector is still mainly characterized by the monopoly of state-owned operators or service providers. Only a few countries in the region have an extensive telecommunications backbone that employs a combination of microwave radio relays and fiber-optic cables; other countries are at an advanced stage in deploying such a backbone. Numerous countries in the region are landlocked (for example, Malawi and Zambia) and do not have the possibility of direct connections to submarine fiber. Such countries will have to rely on expensive satellite links for international traffic and may be unable to afford or access high-bandwidth links. Few countries have an extensive, high-speed backbone and access network to reach out to many users, which creates an artificially low demand for bandwidth. Even where an extensive broadband-capable backbone and access network exist, such as in Namibia and South Africa, the price of high-speed connectivity is substantial and well beyond the means of the majority of the population. Thus, most telecommunications providers in the region aim for low volume and high margins rather than high volume and low margins in the provision of services.

It is a positive that many of these steps are already under way and that there is renewed energy in addressing some of the long-standing barriers to financial integration within four regional economic communities, namely, the Economic and Monetary Community of Central Africa (CEMAC), the Southern Africa Customs Union, the Southern African Development Community, and the West African Economic and Monetary Union (UEMOA) (Wakeman-Linn and Wagh 2008). Between 2000 and 2008, the share of Sub-Saharan African intraregional exports (nonmining) in the total exports of the region increased from 23.3 to 27.7 percent, continuing the trend toward greater intraregional trade since the beginning of the 1990s (Gurcanlar 2010). At the same time, as we discuss in chapter 2, a growing number of private banks headquartered in Sub-Saharan Africa are expanding their networks across the region. For example, Ecobank (Togo) has 600 branches in 29 countries in the region; Bank of Africa (Mali) has 105 branches in 10 countries; and Kenya Commercial Bank has 194 branches in five countries (though most are in Kenya). South-South investment by Nigerian and South African banks is playing a large and expanding role. There is also a growing trend toward the regionalization of stock exchanges, especially an increase in the cross-listing of major companies on several Africa stock exchanges, particularly in Angola, Mauritius, Namibia, Nigeria, South Africa, Tanzania, and Uganda. The issuance of regional bonds by sovereign-linked entities and by large corporations in CEMAC and UEMOA is increasing.

These developments are largely market driven and are occurring in an environment marked by a complex web of overlapping regional trade arrangements. Many countries in Africa belong to several regional trade arrangements with wide variation in country coverage and scope. These range from existing economic and monetary unions such as CEMAC, UEMOA, and the South African Common Monetary Area within the Southern Africa Customs Union to the rapidly emerging common market of the East African Community and the complex trade arrangements of the Economic Community of Western African States, which includes states that are members of UEMOA and states that are not.

The expansion of intraregional trade and the emergence of crossborder banking institutions and capital market operations in this complex environment is remarkable and is testimony to the power of competition among private nonfinancial and financial corporations in increasing private and financial integration across the region, albeit from a low base. However, the small share of intraregional trade in total trade, the limited number of private banks with significant crossborder branch networks, the weak commitment of member states in the case of some regional economic communities as shown by the continued presence of barriers to intraregional payments even within the two CFA franc currency zones in Central Africa and West Africa, the small number of corporations with cross-listings across stock exchanges in the region, and the limited number of countries benefiting from the emergence of regional bond markets are signs of the gaps in private banking and financial integration resulting from the multiplicity of overlapping regional trade arrangements and the wide variation across the legal, regulatory, supervisory, and institutional frameworks facing nonfinancial and financial companies. While the overlapping nature of regional trade arrangements in Africa is an inescapable political reality, the progressive harmonization of the legal, regulatory, supervisory, and institutional framework in existing trade arrangements with best international standards would reduce the variation in business conditions faced by nonfinancial and financial institutions operating across borders in the region and allow these institutions to reap the benefits of scale resulting from deeper integration within and across trade groups (World Bank 2011b).

The Stakeholders

What is the role of the stakeholders in the financial reform process?

Domestic policy makers

As gatekeepers to Africa's financial systems, national regulators have a tremendous responsibility for the sustainable development of financial sectors in the region. They hold the balance between effective modernist and activist financial sector development strategies. However, they operate in a broader political setting of domestic policy makers, including ministries of finance.

The findings of this book suggest that national regulators in many countries deserve credit for their role in strengthening financial systems across the continent. Today, most African banking systems are stable, well capitalized, and liquid. Africa has left behind the traumatic experiences with bank fragility of the 1980s and 1990s, and its resilience during the recent financial crisis is testimony to the effectiveness of the lessons it has learned.

Nonetheless, Africa's challenges are significant. The challenge for regulators is to achieve stability, while pursuing financial deepening and inclusion. This book's findings suggest that regulators should pursue a holistic approach to financial sector reform that begins with a change in perceptions about financial institutions, products, and services in Africa and, subsequently, a change in policies, legislation, regulations, and supervisory practices. In table 6.1, we recap our three main messages and their implications for domestic policy makers across the three themes of the book: expanding access, lengthening contracts, and safeguarding finance.

Table 6.1   Innovation Can Come from Unexpected Quarters

Policy	Expanding access	Lengthening contracts	Safeguarding finance
Fostering competition	1. Innovation can come from an unexpected quarter	4. The need for new providers and products	7. Mitigate the risks of competition
Looking beyond institutions	2. Services matter, but not who provides them	5. Look beyond traditional providers	8. Supervise according to risk, not name
Addressing demand-side constraints	3. Financial literacy	6. Business development, including skill development	9. Consumer protection

Source: Author compilation.

Innovation can come from unexpected quarters: Licensing legislation ought to recognize that financial innovations are no longer the exclusive preserve of banks and financial institutions. Telecommunications companies, grocery stores, bus companies, and other actors that play a significant role in the economic life of Africa have the potential and ought to be encouraged to provide formal and semiformal financial services without having to convert to a formal bank or financial institution as long as the resources put at risk do not represent public savings. The definitions of financial services in current bank-centric legislation need to be revised to accommodate the transformational impact that technology has had on the ability of nonbank actors to provide financial services. Definitions are important and have significant cost implications for service providers. For example, in a number of African countries, licensing requirements still carry physical inspection requirements that are accompanied by costly compliance costs for potential service providers.

Services matter, not who provides them: Connected to the point above, national regulators should focus on the specific financial services offered or proposed, not the nature of the institution providing or aiming to provide the services. This view encourages the unbundling of financial services across banks and nonbank actors. As long as the risk of consumer abuse is adequately catered for, different actors should be encouraged or at least not discouraged from providing narrowly defined services such as the deposit collection services offered by sole proprietors for informal retailers, the payment services and foreign exchange services of domestic and international bus companies, the mobile financial services of telecommunications companies, the credit and crop insurance services of agricultural input supply traders, and the narrow regional or community-based banking services of cooperative associations.

Financial literacy: Broadbased financial literacy programs for children at a young age should be endorsed by national regulators in Africa. Ideally, such programs should be provided by the private sector and agencies other than regulators. The reality of the resource limitations in Africa suggests that national regulators will need to take the first step in developing these programs. Specific roles for regulators include (1) facilitating regular diagnostic reviews of national financial literacy standards to establish regular benchmarks for financial literacy and consumer behavior and (2) working with industry to develop financial consumer awareness campaigns. Specific activities might include the design of graphic tables with comparative information on the full pricing of financial products, community and village road shows to explain major financial concepts, training on the delivery of financial education by retail officers, financial literacy messages in m-banking systems, campaigns on new pension systems, basic brochures on financial services, the inclusion of financial literacy in school curricula, campaigns on the management of debt and the avoidance of overindebtedness, and campaigns on the economics and the benefits of the insurance market. Only with a much higher level of financial awareness and improved financial behavior will consumers be able to make informed financial decisions in the context of their specific economic and social circumstances.

The need for new providers and products: Encouraging new products and services is an art, not a science. It involves regulators' signaling to market participants that the market is open to product innovations without opening the gates to fraudulent products and Ponzi schemes that, after their collapse, leave the public with less confidence in financial services. On the other hand, the government development of specific new institutions and products should (1) be limited to wholesale facilities, (2) enjoy strong private sector buy-in and participation, and (3) be subject to clear sunset clauses and, in the interim, be managed using sound corporate governance structures. State financial institutions, credit guarantee schemes, and mortgage refinancing facilities have a place in the financial system if they meet these three basic criteria.

Look beyond traditional providers: As long as Africa is dominated by banks, finance will remain short term, expensive, and limited in reach. Africa needs to become a laboratory for innovation that provides solutions to the unique problems of the continent in financial sector development, especially with regard to long-term finance. There are many options, including adopting innovative products and solutions in m-banking, enhancing the availability of long-term savings products for recipients of remittances (for example, encouraging investment in housing or insurance products), facilitating the development of housing finance (for instance, providing liquidity facilities such as the one currently being established in Tanzania), significantly deepening the exchange of credit information to encompass supplier credit and thereby enhance the access to formal finance markets, or creating partnerships in such areas as the finance of public-private partnerships (PPPs) and local capital market development. Regulators need to signal to the market their appetite for experimentation and then act upon it.

Business development, including the development of entrepreneurial skills: Firms need to be enabled to identify investment opportunities, assess their own financing needs, and present attractive business proposals to potential financiers. Improving financial capability and the bankability of firms will strengthen the knowledge, understanding, skills, attitudes, and, especially, the behavior requisite to making sound financial decisions and being more attractive as potential borrowers.

Mitigate the risks of competition: Competition is vital to efficiency in the provision of financial services and to expansion in the depth of financial markets. The development and outreach of financial service provision depend on important issues in public policy that regulators must address not only by licensing more banks, but also by more effectively monitoring the behavior of current market participants and making unwarranted anticompetitive behavior public. Allowing more competition also involves risks, however, because national regulators have to adjust constantly to changing market structures, new products, and new providers. The idea is to allow more competition by adopting a more flexible regulatory framework, which allows risk-based supervision, but also more immediate intervention where necessary. This pressure on supervisors can be increased if the competition of international players is allowed.

Supervise according to risk, not name: In pursuit of the modernist agenda, there are many regulatory structures in Africa that are far more unwieldy than the risk they are established to mitigate. Today, for example, nonbank supervision departments supervise microfinance sectors that are miniscule components of the financial sector, and bank inspectors still inspect the physical premises of rural branches to assess the risk of physical theft although commercial insurance can cover most of these physical risks, many of the risks have migrated to technological risks, or the risks should be the primary responsibility of service providers. The increasing complexity of financial institutions and instruments requires greater emphasis on risk-based supervision methods that allocate only limited supervisory resources to assessing the magnitude of risks. National regulators should be encouraged periodically to review their staffing requirements, update their procedures for assessing industry risks, and determine appropriate legislative, regulatory, and supervisory responses.

Consumer protection: As African markets become more sophisticated, national regulators need to strengthen the consumer protection framework in their countries. For many, this should start with a diagnostic review of consumer protection and financial literacy in each country and be followed by the drafting of appropriate regulations and standards to address weaknesses in the current framework that are collectively agreed by the government, regulators, and the financial sector. At a minimum, the regulations are likely to include (1) prohibiting unfair credit and credit-marketing practices and (2) promoting responsible credit granting and use and, for this purpose, prohibiting reckless credit granting. Operationally, two specific elements of an effective consumer protection regime are (1) *the identification of an agency or department* to implement education campaigns, conduct research, develop policies, investigate complaints, and ensure compliance with the law and (2) *the establishment of an effective mechanism for receiving and resolving consumer complaints.* An effective system for handling, analyzing, monitoring, and resolving consumer complaints and disputes will have a strong impact on financial institution behavior. Potential areas of work would include delineating the rules for financial service providers in handling consumer complaints; developing a centralized system to register, track, and analyze data on complaints and complaint resolution; and advising on the creation of an out-of-court mechanism to resolve consumer disputes. In most African countries, there are currently no established procedures for handling consumer complaints within financial institutions and no out-of-court dispute resolution mechanisms.

International development partners

If policy makers are to implement the reforms approach discussed above properly, then development partners must adopt an equally different approach in the way they provide technical assistance for financial sector reforms in Africa.

- *The selectivity of the focus on policy reform:* First, there must be greater selectivity and more careful application of best practice models across heterogeneous African countries. While African financial sector policies share a common thread and common pillars, the interpretation and application may differ according to whether a country is fragile, landlocked, resource rich, governance constrained, or middle income (Addison et al. 2005; Maimbo 2007). Every financial sector strategy should be designed and developed so as to identify the specific limitations within the particular context and seek ways of addressing them that are tuned to local circumstances. At the same time, financial sector policy tools do not need to be reinvented for each country, but need to be adapted and sequenced correctly. The specific needs of African financial sectors require experimentation and innovation to generate African solutions. International best practice has often failed to have an impact in Africa. To this end, development partners need to leverage the diversity of country characteristics to harvest diverse solutions tested in different markets and then scale up in countries with similar characteristics.

- *Policy-based assistance:* Development partners should pursue more policy-based assistance. This change in direction is necessary to achieve the goal of integrated financial sector reform. The need for deeper, comprehensive financial sector policy reform has increased as countries have completed first-generation reform. Many of the challenges African financial systems face today are structural in nature, and this has implications for broad policy reform. In deepening the financial sector reform agenda, many countries have been confronted with a range of issues relating to governance (for example, the cross-ownership of banks and pension funds and the exposure to loss-making state-owned enterprises). They have also been confronted by unfunded (implicit) contingent liabilities, particularly in pensions, as well as unaddressed policy issues relating to transparency in reporting and disclosure and the accountability standards of regulators. Policy-based lending operations are central to embedding financial sector reform within broader structural reform in the economy and ensuring that the reforms are aligned with national development strategy. It is important to highlight that many types of budget-support loans to governments may not be the best vehicle for supporting financial sector reform. Although the focus of this instrument has shifted in recent years toward a growth agenda (as opposed to social sector and public sector reforms), the financial sector remains a modest component of the effort: often only limited attention is paid to the financial sector in these multisectoral operations. Given the long-term and politically contentious nature of financial sector reform and in the absence of complementary support through other vehicles, financial sector reform may not receive the focus, the sustained commitment, and the close supervision needed for success. Policy-based operations are also well aligned with the Paris Declaration principles of (1) reinforcing the ownership of the policy agenda, (2) strengthening harmonization across development partners, (3) customizing programs to suit the circumstances of countries, and (4) selecting only critical actions for government intervention, while encouraging private sector solutions.[4]

- *Investing in capacity development and financial sector deepening:* Policy-based assistance must not supersede traditional technical assistance activities, however. Development partners should continue to invest in the capacity development of country authorities and regulators to enable them to implement policy, safeguard financial sector growth, and create an enabling environment that motivates innovation and ensures stability. Yet, to achieve the ambitions espoused in this book, the technical assistance needs to be broadened to support the entry of new players and expand outreach by requiring the increased use of outreach facilitation instruments, such as partial credit facilities to encourage banks to engage with small and medium enterprises (SMEs) or liquidity facilities to provide banks with longer-term funding to deepen the market for mortgage finance. Promoting innovation will require greater use of instruments that work directly with the private sector to incentivize and support innovation (participation in challenge funds, the funding of product development, and so forth). The targeted scale-up of transaction services will require additional investments in market infrastructure such as regional payment systems, collateral registries, and credit reference infrastructure.

An example of an area in which development partners have the resources and scale to make a significant impact is regional integration. However, given the wide variations in regional economic communities, development partners need to adopt a differentiated approach to regionalization. In existing economic and monetary zones, development partners can focus on strengthening regional institutions, developing crossborder banking, and integrating market infrastructure. In economic communities with a strong political commitment, development partners can support a greater spectrum of activities, including legal and regulatory harmonization, mutual supervisory recognition, infrastructure integration, regional securities markets, regional financing facilities for priority sectors, and regional institutional capacity strengthening for policy formulation and coordination. In communities with weaker political commitment, development partners can initially focus on a narrower range of activities, such as regional payment systems, cross-listing, and cooperation on capital markets, and progressively expand toward a broader financial integration agenda in line with the deepening of political commitment to integration.

Redefine the Role of Government with the Necessary Safeguards

Guided by the generally agreed principle that government intervention should support rather than distort the incentives for the private sector provision of financial services, a formal redefinition of the role of government in the financial sector in each country is proposed. This approach, labeled market-friendly activism, restricts financial service provision by government-owned institutions to a few, selected, and time-bound interventions in areas in which gaps and market failures remain, while policy actions are taken to fill the gaps and remove the market failures, thus opening the market to private initiatives.[5] This approach recognizes that, in some countries, there might be room for well-designed, restricted interventions, in collaboration with the private sector, to foster financial development and broaden access to financial services.

It is important to stress that the space for market-friendly activism varies across countries (Dafe 2011). In general, such policies can be more successful in countries with conditions favorable to minimizing the governance trap. This is typically the case in countries with checks and balances, including beyond the political sphere. A strong private sector can be such a check, as can a thriving media sector that critically analyzes government decisions and programs. More diverse countries have the potential to provide more checks and balances, although they are often also the backdrop for ethnic politics that can easily lead to the abuse of activist policies.

One option often discussed is to move the responsibility for activist policies and market interventions away from the political sphere to (1) donors, (2) supranational regional institutions, or (3) nonprofit organizations. All three options offer advantages in terms of reducing the risk of corruption and graft; all three options, however, also raise concerns among national taxpayers about transparency and accountability.

In summary, in the short to medium term, the conditions in many African countries, especially countries with severe governance challenges, may be such that the responsibility for adopting activist policies and programs will be rather outside the political sphere or, at a minimum, in the political sphere but with strong monitoring and oversight by a third party that does not report to the political sphere. In the long term, however, it is preferable that the necessary country-level checks and balances be developed.

Many governments are turning to the private sector to design, build, finance, and operate infrastructure facilities hitherto provided by the public sector. PPPs offer policy makers an opportunity to improve the delivery of services and the management of facilities. There is no reason why the same principles cannot be applied more intensively to state-owned financial institutions. Indeed, in many countries, this is already taking place, albeit often narrowly centered on the privatization option discussed above.

A holistic review and restructuring of current government institutions and programs could yield substantial economies of scale and reduce the current contamination of private sector–led efforts to increase the access to financial services. Rather than establish a new program each time the government prioritizes a particular sector, region, or activity, the government should focus on using a single agency or institution to prepare and draft the eligibility criteria for the program and then tender the retail implementation of the program to interested institutions. All bank and nonbank financial institutions would be eligible to bid for the tender. By leveling the retail financial sector landscape in this manner, the government would increase pricing and product transparency in the microfinance sector and increase the involvement of the private sector in the delivery of commercially sustainable programs.

There are several well-defined types of PPP and, increasingly, many permutations and combinations. One of the strengths of PPPs is their flexibility in addressing specific situations. Types of PPPs that are relevant for the financial sector include PPPs for service contracts, management contracts, leasing, and joint ventures and partnerships. We discuss several options in box 6.3.

One Size Does Not Fit All

As we emphasize throughout the book, one size does not fit all. While there are commonalities across Africa, as we document in chapter 2, and similar challenges in expanding access, lengthening contracts, and safeguarding finance, there are also significant differences. We cannot design a financial sector strategy for each of the 53 countries of the continent, but we can point to commonalities across groups of countries. The groups are not geographical; rather, we have composed the groups based on the prominence of characteristics of African finance we have identified as challenges. These are size, informality, volatility, and governance, plus any special circumstances. Table 6.2 summarizes the challenges and priorities facing some of these countries.

Low-income countries versus middle-income countries

On average, the financial systems of low-income countries are smaller and less well developed than those of middle-income countries, and the financial reform priorities of the two sets of countries therefore vary. The priorities of countries at low levels of financial development will naturally tend to be included in the *Finance for Markets* agenda rather than the *Finance for Growth* agenda, that is, the priorities will be focused on basic short-term financial services.[6] In addition, low-income countries often also face severe capacity gaps, which may prevent the buildup of regulatory institutions and other elements of financial infrastructure. Middle-income countries, meanwhile, can focus more attention on the Finance for Growth agenda, that is, on long-term financial transactions. Given the higher-income level of middle-income countries, scale diseconomies can be more easily overcome. Many middle-income countries can therefore expand their financial systems more easily beyond the banking sector toward capital markets and contractual savings institutions. Middle-income countries also have more room to address demand-side constraints, including larger financial literacy campaigns and the necessary institutional structures for consumer protection. Low-income countries should focus

Box 6.3   What to Do with State Financial Institutions?

While many African countries have privatized commercial banks, others have recapitalized them. In addition, many countries still maintain DFIs, though, for every active one, there seems to be one that is moribund.

In line with a new role of government, that is, away from a market-replacing activity to a market-enhancing activity, what are the options for state financial institutions? The following are some of the possibilities and the related opportunities and challenges.

Rationalization

First of all, governments need to identify and separate subsidies aimed at solving market failures from the actual financing flowing through financial institutions. Often, subsidies aimed at increasing the use of credit do not address any of the underlying causes of the problems in access. In most countries, governments have provided loans to small producers either through public banks or by using directed credit programs at subsidized rates, while failing to address other business constraints.

Management contracts

Under a management contract, a private firm assumes the overall responsibility for the operation and maintenance of a service delivery system and retains the freedom to make day-to-day management decisions. In many cases, this involves managing the employees of the state financial institution who are employed in the service delivery system. Management contracts generally do not require the implementation of significant institutional changes. Rather, the existing public enterprise generally remains in place, and the personnel of the management contractor assume the line management responsibilities. Whereas the goal of service contracts is to reduce the operating costs of an organization, the goal of management contracts is typically to improve the internal management and operations of an organization. Because this change requires time to implement and take effect, the typical duration of a management contract is three to five years.

In Africa, management contracts have typically been used as precursors to privatization. Yet, there is no reason why they cannot be used as an ongoing renewable arrangement until the institution is able to hire and retain its own qualified management staff. In some countries, preprivatization management contracts have worked so well that the privatization option has been delayed.

In Tanzania, after the performance of the National Microfinance Bank (NMB) began to exceed expectations under management contractors, the privatization of the NMB lost momentum and became more difficult. As the profits of the NMB rose, so did the voices expressing opposition to the privatization. The government was unable to maintain support for the original plan of privatization that called for the sale of 70 percent of NMB shares to a strategic investor. At the height of the heated political debate, the board of directors of the NMB, who had been appointed by the president of Tanzania, publicly expressed their opposition to the privatization. The president responded by replacing the entire board. The result of these political challenges, apart from the delays in the privatization by one and a half years, was an amended privatization strategy, calling for the sale of only 49 percent of NMB shares to a strategic investor. Another 21 percent was to be sold to Tanzanian citizens at a later date.

Box 6.3 What to Do with State Financial Institutions? *(continued)*

As a consequence of the delays in the privatization, the contract for the NMB management contractors was extended several times. The original contract was due to end in April 2001. It was extended to April 2002, April 2003, April 2004, April 2005, and, finally, to December 2005, or until privatization had taken place, whichever came first. Privatization finally took place in September 2005, and the contract was closed.

Privatization

There are various ways to privatize a state financial institution, as follows: (1) sale to a single strategic investor; (2) sale, in part or in whole, to an employee stock ownership plan; and (3) sale of shares to the public through an initial public offering. Each option carries advantages and risks. Strategic investors can inject capital and skills but may be obliged to deal with a public perception that the government has "sold out," especially if the strategic investor is a foreign-owned entity. Employee schemes typically work best as part of an overall privatization scheme, lest the new entity be left with insufficient capital. Public offerings have the additional advantage of supporting the development of local capital markets, but empirical evidence suggests that governments typically underprice the shares in an effort to entice public participation in the market (Caprio et al. 2004).

The lessons of successful privatization efforts suggest the importance of (1) conducting a comprehensive market survey of viable sale options through due diligence of the investor's market reputation (not merely the investor's capital strength), as well as understanding the investor's future intentions in regard to strengthening the capital and management of the bank; (2) involving international bank managers and professional specialists in advising the government on the transaction; (3) dealing swiftly and decisively with nonperforming loans and reversing the weak repayment ethic among borrowers at state banks; and (4) undertaking the privatization process within a strong legal and regulatory framework and supported by an independent central bank.

On the road to privatizing banks, it is necessary to enforce the regulations on all banks, to reveal the weaknesses of the state bank, publish audits, and avoid rapid privatization and excessive delays (Caprio et al. 2004). In the case of Uganda Commercial Bank, the privatization process took too long, and the bank was sold to a buyer without capital, banking reputation, or expertise. The buyer secretly assigned shares to another bank, thereby weakening the sector. This delay impeded competition and efficiency in the credit market and led to a loss of 2 percent of gross domestic product (GDP) during restructuring in 1998. On the political front, the privatization problem of Uganda Commercial Bank was aggravated by the reluctance of politicians to undertake reform because of the fear that they would lose their political influence, as well as their benefits that were associated with directed credit.

Corporatization

Corporatization refers to the transformation of state assets or agencies into state-owned corporations so as to introduce corporate management techniques into the administration of these assets or agencies. The corporatization process involves the sale or attribution of shares to corporate entities by listing the shares of the state-owned corporation as publicly

(Box continues next page)

Box 6.3 What to Do with State Financial Institutions? *(continued)*

traded stocks on stock exchanges. A common model involves corporatizing a state institution so that it is operated as an autonomous joint-stock company, while the state remains majority stockholder and the institution is run by state entities that are separate from the central government administration (Stoyan and Zhang 2002).

A revealing experience is the case of the NMB in Tanzania, which was initially offered for sale to the private sector in 1997 (see above). The government, with the support of the World Bank, sought external managers to lead a restructuring that was intended to make the NMB more attractive to investors. Some NMB products were revamped, which generated an improvement in performance standards, product profitability, and public confidence. There was a concern that the weak credit culture could damage NMB's loan performance, but new loan products were researched, designed, tested, and rolled out. The NMB progressed from a loss-making institution to a profit-making one.

Ownership policy

As the rationalization of existing institutions and programs is taking place, the authorities may wish to examine proposals for state-owned banks in the future within the framework of a formal ownership policy. A case in point is Malawi. The recently proposed Malawi Development Fund, the Financial Inclusion in Malawi Project, and the National Guarantee Scheme, as well as other, future institutions and programs need to be evaluated against an ownership policy that maintains the spirit of divesting government of retail activities. Such a policy should define the government's overall ownership objectives and the government's role in governance and clarify how the objectives and the role should be realized. The ownership policy should be published and should not be subject to frequent change. Specifically, it is important that the government undertake a holistic review of the sector and, for each institution and program, ask the following questions:

- Mandates: Are the policy mandates and objectives clear? These must derive from an adequate assessment of needs. Are perceived market gaps, missing markets, and so on well understood?
- Options: Once the gaps have become well understood, alternative means of meeting the needs should be considered. Is a government institution or program the most cost-efficient means? Can the private sector be leveraged as an alternative means of distribution instead? An assessment of the efficiency of a government institution or program in this regard must explicitly assess the costs inherent in building and maintaining an adequate governance framework in terms of human resources, investment in systems, and maintenance costs.
- Financing: How are the policy objectives (subsidies) to be funded? Subsidies must be made explicit. Allowing funding through cross-subsidies (from the profits on nonpolicy activities) invites mission creep and private financial sector displacement.

Corporate governance

The corporate governance structure for the institution or program must foster complementary private sector support for the institution or program and minimize the risk of political

Box 6.3   What to Do with State Financial Institutions? *(continued)*

interference. A key aspect of this process is ensuring that the management and board of directors are not only competent, but also able to exercise autonomy in the management of the institution or program. This will require key matters to be addressed, as follows:

- What is the composition of the board, and how is the board nominated and selected? Patronage or professionals?

- How is the chief executive officer appointed and compensated? Appointment by shareholders—common among DFIs—affects the quality of the board. The board must be empowered to hire and fire the chief executive officer.

- How well are commercial practices embedded in the governance structure in terms, for example, of internal control, risk management, internal and external audit, and so on? The board must be held accountable for these issues under the legal framework and in practice.

- Do risk management systems simulate the impact of alternative policy programs and the pricing of the same—the level of the subsidies—on the value of the capital so as to enable the provision of quantitative backing to management and the board in making the trade-offs between policy objectives and commercial principles and objectives?

- Is an independent, professional external audit planned? The state auditing agency is no substitute.

- Is there a performance measurement procedure? Financial and commercial performance measures and policy performance measures should be defined in concrete terms. Objective methods for the measurement and evaluation of performance should be established and embedded in the compensation system.

Source: Maimbo and Saranga (2009).

on achieving economies of scale so as to expand payment services and basic credit among the population and capacity building among supervisory authorities.

While the *Finance for All* agenda is important for low- and middle-income countries, the priorities are different in the two sets of countries. In low-income countries, the priority will be on basic transaction services, while it will be on more advanced savings and credit services in middle-income countries. Middle-income countries are also able to pay more attention to specialized areas of finance, such as housing finance and infrastructure finance.

The policy priorities therefore also vary between low- and middle-income countries. Low-income countries focus on basic infrastructure elements, such as payment systems, credit registries, and the regulatory and supervisory framework, while middle-income countries can more easily expand the regulatory realm toward other segments of the financial system and toward consumer protection institutions. Donors also have a different role in low- and middle-income countries: they take a much more prominent role in the former and adopt more of an

Table 6.2 Country Characteristics and the Primary Areas for Financial Sector Policies

Country type	Primary challenge	Focus areas for financial sector policies
Income	low income: provide basic short-term financial services	• payment systems • regulatory framework • supervisory capacity building • financial sector strategies
	middle income: deepen and broaden financial systems	• housing finance • PPPs for infrastructure finance • green finance • innovative solutions • institutional capacity building to support integration with global financial markets • private health insurance, pension reform • capital market development
Size	small: regional integration	• foreign bank entry regimes: licensing • crossborder supervision: home regulatory memorandums of understanding • macroeconomic safeguards to deal with volatility
	large: expand the diversity and penetration of the financial sector	• institutional and product diversification • affirmative regulatory regimes for nonbank financial institutions • capacity building to support coordination among regulators in different sectors
Sparsely populated	expand the reach of the financial sector	• mobile branches, agency arrangements, and technology solutions
Resource rich	turn natural wealth into other forms of wealth	• strengthen the provision of longer-term finance, for example, by using sovereign wealth funds • PPPs for infrastructure finance • build capital markets • promote deepening the provision of finance by banks for SMEs, for example, to support economic diversification • strengthen supervision and financial sector governance • promote innovation and diversity in financial products
Affected by conflict	rebuild basic financial infrastructure	• extend the reach and coverage of microfinance institutions • build payment systems and enable cheaper remittance processes • financial capability • build basic oversight capacity to ensure good governance of the financial sector (including anti–money laundering) • rebuild the banking sector and promote the entry of experienced regional banks • the early decisions on market structure must be accurate

Source: Author compilation.

advisory and analyst role in the latter. Low-income countries often need donor support to implement financial sector strategies and to strengthen retail financial institutions, such as decentralized microfinance institutions, that show potential in the effort to increase outreach and push out the access frontier. Donor support is often provided to middle-income countries in more specialized technical areas.

Basic capacity building is critical for low-income countries, while upgrading skills and ongoing training is more the challenge in middle-income countries.

Small versus large countries

Policy makers in small economies (for example, Seychelles) face different opportunities and challenges relative to policy makers in large economies.[7] In small, low-income countries, the challenges discussed above are exacerbated. The solutions are more costly, and the necessary scale is less likely to be reached. Small financial systems are more concentrated and therefore less competitive. Smaller countries therefore stand to gain more from regional integration in terms of higher-quality and lower-cost financial services. Participating in a regional exchange and a joint regional regulatory framework can help lower costs and extend the access to financial services. These countries may lose some independence in the integration process, but they will gain greater access to a broader range of financial services. Similarly, landlocked countries stand to benefit more from regional integration, including integration beyond financial integration, than countries with direct access to the ports and thus better transportation options.

Smaller countries also stand to gain more from globalization because of the entry of foreign banks. Multinational banks can rely on shared technology and back-office facilities with parent banks and subsidiaries in neighboring countries. Costs thus become lower. However, such gains have often not been exploited fully because of regulatory constraints and differences across countries. Because the market is too small for domestic financial service providers, small countries have to rely more heavily on outside financial service providers, such as foreign insurance companies and international equity funds. Capital account liberalization is more important for small countries needing to attract funding, which puts a higher premium on the macroeconomic safeguards necessary to deal with the ensuing volatility.

On the other hand, larger countries with a critical mass can be more ambitious in creating diverse financial systems beyond banking, especially through contractual savings institutions and capital markets. Larger countries are more likely to have sufficient scale for the private funding of infrastructure and to be able to supply the tools necessary for banks and markets.

Larger countries can offer policy makers more room for activist policies because there are likely to be better checks and balances in these countries. There is also more room for affirmative regulatory actions to push banks toward the frontier without running the risk that the banks will exit the market. Policy makers in large markets can thus be more ambitious, and they have a larger permissible margin of error. As Honohan and Beck (2007) point out, there is likewise more room for an active financial sector dialogue with a larger number of stakeholders and participants and, often, in a more vibrant media landscape.

Sparsely populated countries

Population density is an important predictor of financial development, as we discuss in chapter 2. If a large share of a country's population lives in rural areas or if the population is widely dispersed, this exacerbates the challenges of scale. As Honohan and Beck (2007) indicate, it is important to look beyond population density to the population distribution within a country: is it concentrated in a small area, leaving large parts of the country uninhabited, such as in Algeria or Chad, or is it distributed in smaller population centers across the country, as in Tanzania? One must also look at the income distribution in population centers because less-populated areas may have more resources and, accordingly, the necessary scale to justify financial service provision.

A widely distributed population is especially challenging for the Finance for All agenda because outreach becomes more costly in this case. Innovative solutions are especially important, some of which we discuss in chapter 3. Mobile bank branches, agency agreements, and technological solutions can help overcome the challenges of scale. Viewing beyond the banking system to microfinance institutions and semiformal institutions such as savings and credit cooperatives may be important.

For donors, this is challenging, too. An emphasis on microfinance in rural areas, rather than full-fledged banks, may be useful. Though this may be tempting in such countries, one must not concentrate solely on the capital city area.

The resource rich

The economic structure of many African countries is dominated by commodities, such as aluminum (Mozambique), copper (Zambia), or oil (Algeria and Equatorial Guinea). This dependence on commodity exports might make these countries achieve significantly higher GDP per capita than other countries in the region, but also subjects them to a much larger fluctuation in income levels. Consistent with the Dutch Disease hypothesis, many of these countries also suffer from high real and volatile exchange rates that crowd out noncommodity sectors and industries. Recent cross-country comparisons have shown that economies relying on natural resources benefit as much from financial development in terms of pro-poor growth as other economies and that manufacturing industries more reliant on external funding benefit from financial deepening in resource-based economies more than do corresponding industries in other economies (Beck 2011). This implies that financial sector policies are as important for commodity-exporting countries as they are for other countries. Yet, cross-country comparisons have also shown that commodity exporters have smaller financial systems than predicted by the level of GDP per capita and macroeconomic stability and that banks are more liquid, more well capitalized, and more profitable, but give fewer loans to firms. There is thus a premium on financial sector reform in economies dependent on natural resources; the challenge will be to transform natural wealth into other forms of wealth; the domestic financial system will have a critical role.

Because of the long-term nature of natural resource extraction, a focus on long-term intermediation capacity is important. Sovereign wealth funds can play a major part, though appropriate governance structures are crucial, including the establishment of limits on the contribution of these funds to public deficits so as to ensure long-term sustainability and intergenerational equity. Similarly, other long-term instruments, such as pension funds and insurance companies, can provide key inputs. However, there is a premium on fostering access to credit by SMEs. While some of the commodity exporters have high GDP per capita, income distribution is often highly skewed, and access to financial services is often restricted to a small segment of the population.

Among policy priorities, governance tops the agenda because of the Dutch Disease effect on the governance agenda that has been observed in commodity-exporting countries throughout the world. Large amounts of money invite graft and corruption; the proper handling of these resources for the benefit of the population at large is therefore decisive. Another important priority is macromanagement, that is, carefully managing the capital inflows related to commodity exports and avoiding an overvaluation of the exchange rate. Donors can have a pivotal role in financial sector policy by advising on macropolicy and helping in the design of governance structures, but also by pushing intensely for financial sector reform. Ultimately, commodity-exporting countries could be the drivers of regional financial integration.

Countries affected by conflict

Financial transactions are being undertaken even in the presence of violent conflict and the absence of state authority, which is the case in Somalia. Finance for Markets exists even under the most adverse circumstances; however, it is costly, inefficient, and often excludes large parts of the population. Wherever formal financial systems break down, informal networks expand and take over. Where national currency loses its value completely, foreign exchange takes over. Formal financial service provision is often reduced to urban areas or even limited to the capital city as banks abandon rural areas. Commercial banks often collapse because borrowers are unable to repay and their branches are being looted. A similar fate often hits central banks. The postconflict authorities are presented with destroyed physical and financial infrastructure.

What are the first priorities in the financial sector after a conflict? The priorities of Finance for Markets loom large; among them is the challenge of reestablishing a stable national currency that can be used as a medium of exchange throughout the country, beyond establishing mechanisms of monetary policy that might include the even more basic challenge of reintroducing coins and bills. High on the list is the challenge of building the necessary infrastructure for Finance for Markets, such as the payment system and a basic regulatory and supervisory framework. Simplicity is key in this context given the limited human and financial resources. Often, these challenges consist as much in building physical infrastructure as in building human and organizational infrastructure. However, a chaotic postconflict environment also offers openings for shady businesspeople and shady deals, so that strict rules on anti–money laundering and combating the financing of terrorism might be even more important in the context of postconflict countries than elsewhere.

Rebuilding the formal banking sector is another daunting task. Old bankers might have left for good or are associated with the old regime. The licensing of new banks with appropriate fit and proper standards will be vital. Promoting the entry of reputable and experienced multinational banks from the region or beyond can be useful in rebuilding the financial system; at the same time, it is important to keep the system contestable and open for future domestic or international entrants.

Finance for All challenges also loom large in fragile and postconflict countries. Informal financial arrangements will dominate the financial landscape for many years to come, and the challenge will be to create links between formal and informal financial service providers. Given the destroyed infrastructure, the formal banking system will face a difficult task in seeking to expand beyond urban areas. Promoting the outreach and coverage of microfinance seems a more promising route in this context than focusing on bank outreach. Technology seems a particularly useful instrument in this context of destruction.[8]

Rebuilding the basics of the financial sector is often not on the immediate agenda for postconflict governments and donors, but can play a consequential role in jump-starting the private sector and rebuilding an inclusive market-based economy. Government-to-person payments are often important in the context of rebuilding economies, as are rebuilding contracts given to local contractors, which might require short-term financing. Donors have a decisive role in postconflict economies, but careful hand-holding and supervision are certainly necessary. It is important to focus on basic structures, while developing a comprehensive financial sector strategy with a long-term outlook.[9] Capacity building should top the agenda so as to avoid long-term donor dependence.

Conclusions

Financial sector policies have again moved to the center stage of the development agenda in many African countries. The challenges are similar: expanding access and lengthening contracts, while safeguarding the financial system. However, the circumstances and contexts vary from country to country. The main messages developed in this book are general and have to be translated into specific policy formulations for each country.

Africa's financial systems are on the move. There is a lot to be gained. There is ample evidence that deeper and broader financial systems can help African progress out of poverty. Accepting the opportunities that globalization, regional integration, and technology offer can result in steeper growth trajectories. As we argue in this concluding chapter, these opportunities require a redefinition of the roles of the private sector, the public sector, and donors. They require a look beyond the dichotomy of modernist and activist approaches toward an approach that recognizes that all financial sector policy is local. Reaping the benefits of these opportunities requires a recognition of the politics of financial deepening and the creation of constituencies for financial sector reform. Financing Africa demands that we look beyond the crisis toward the structural challenges and opportunities the continent presents.

Notes

1. For a discussion of these two views in the context of financial sector policy, see Barth, Caprio, and Levine (2006). For a more general survey on the role of politics in financial development, see Haber and Perotti (2007).

2. The general point about path dependence in political and institutional structures is most eloquently and convincingly made by Acemoglu, Johnson, and Robinson (2004).

3. One of the most prominent examples is the greater ease with which the United Kingdom was able to gain access to war finance after the Glorious Revolution of 1688, given that the taxation power was not held by the king, and the checks and balances made a default on government debt less likely.

4. "The Paris Declaration on Aid Effectiveness: Ownership, Harmonisation, Alignment, Results and Mutual Accountability," High-Level Forum, Paris, February 28–March 2, 2005, http://www.adb.org/media/articles/2005/7033_international_community_aid/paris_declaration.pdf.

5. The term market-friendly activism was first used in the Latin America region; see de la Torre, Gozzi, and Schmukler (2007).

6. This does not imply that these countries do not need long-term resources, but rather that the priorities are in the Finance for Markets area.

7. There are large low-income countries, such as Ethiopia and Kenya, but also small middle-income countries, such as Botswana and Mauritius.

8. Donors in Haiti have recently focused on technological solutions for the payouts for government assistance after the recent earthquake.

9. The Iraqi reconstruction offers an interesting example: the objective of introducing the technically most advanced infrastructure for stock exchange trading was repudiated by traders in favor of a simple blackboard solution.

References

Abereijo, Isaac, and Abimbola Fayomi. 2007. "The Attitude of Small and Medium Industrialists to Venture Capital Financing in Nigeria." *Global Journal of Business Research* 1 (1): 127–38.

Ablo, Emmanuel Y., Zoe Vantzos, and Taqi Sharif. 2004. "Republic of Zambia: 1999 CAS Completion Report." In "Country Assistance Strategy for the Republic of Zambia." Report number 27654-ZA (March 9), appendix 8, 91–108, World Bank, Washington, DC.

ACCION. 2011. "EB-ACCION Microfinance." Accion, Boston, http://www.accion.org/Page.aspx?pid=2067.

Acemoglu, Daron, Simon Johnson, and James A. Robinson. 2004. "Institutions as a Fundamental Cause of Long-Run Growth." In *Handbook of Economic Growth*, ed. Philippe Aghion and Steven Durlauf, 385–472. Amsterdam: Elsevier.

Acharya, Viral V., and Matthew Richardson, eds. 2009. *Restoring Financial Stability: How to Repair a Failed System.* Hoboken, NJ: John Wiley & Sons.

Addison, Tony, Alemayehu Geda, Philippe Le Billon, and S. Mansoob Murshed. 2005. "Reconstructing and Reforming the Financial System in Conflict and Post-Conflict Economies." *Journal of Development Studies* 41 (4): 704–18.

Aghion, Philippe, George-Marios Angeletos, Abhijit Banerjee, and Kalina Manova. 2010. "Volatility and Growth: Credit Constraints and the Composition of Growth." *Journal of Monetary Economics* 57 (3): 246–65.

Aghion, Philippe, Philippe Bacchetta, Romain Rancière, and Kenneth Rogoff. 2009. "Exchange Rate Volatility and Productivity Growth: The Role of Financial Development." *Journal of Monetary Economics* 56 (4): 494–513.

Ahmed, Medani M. 2010. "Global Financial Crisis Discussion Series, Paper 19: Sudan Phase 2." February, Overseas Development Institute, London.

Aker, Jenny C., and Isaac M. Mbiti. 2010. "Mobile Phones and Economic Development in Africa." *Journal of Economic Perspectives* 24 (3): 207–32.

Alawode, Abayomi A. 2003. "Analyzing Financial and Private Sector Linkages." Africa Region Working Paper 43 (January), World Bank, Washington, DC.

Albin-Lackey, Christopher, Joseph Bell, Teresa M. Faria, Macartan Humphreys, Peter Rosenblum, and Martin E. Sandbu. 2004. "Proposal for an Oil Revenue Management Law for São Tomé and Príncipe: Explanatory Notes." Center on Globalization and Sustainable Development, Earth Institute, Columbia University, New York. http://www.columbia.edu/~mh2245/papers1/enotes.pdf.

Allen, Franklin, Elena Carletti, Robert Cull, Jun Qian, and Lemma W. Senbet. 2010. "The African Financial Development Gap." Economics Working Paper ECO 2010/24, European University Institute, San Domenico di Fiesole, Italy.

Allen, Franklin, and Douglas Gale. 2004. "Competition and Financial Stability." *Journal of Money, Credit and Banking* 36 (3): 433–80.

Allen, Franklin, and Giorgia Giovannetti. 2011. "The Effects of the Financial Crisis on Sub-Saharan Africa." *Review of Development Finance* 1 (1): 1–27.

Allen, Franklin, Isaac Otchere, and Lemma W. Senbet. 2010. "African Financial Systems: A Review." Wharton Financial Institutions Center Working Paper 10–11, Wharton Financial Institutions Center, Philadelphia.

Al-Sugheyer, Bilal, and Murat Sultanov. 2010. "Leasing in the Middle East and Northern Africa (MENA) Region: A Preliminary Assessment." MENA Financial Sector Flagship Report, October, International Finance Corporation, World Bank, Washington, DC.

Ambrosi, Monica. 2009. "The Development of African Debt Markets: The South African Experience and Key Findings." Paper presented at the International Organization of Securities Commissions' "22nd Africa–Middle East Regional Committee Meeting," Muscat, Oman, March 15–16.

AMIC (Association Marocaine des Investisseurs en Capital) and Grant Thorton. 2010. "Le capital Investissement au Maroc de 1993 à 2008: activité, performance et croissance." AMIC, Casablanca.

ANIMA Investment Network. 2008. "Med Funds Survey: An Overview of Private Equity in the MEDA Region." Notes and Studies 26 (April), ANIMA Investment Network, Marseille.

APSF (Association Professionnelle des Sociétés de Financement). 2010. "Le crédit bail au Maroc." Paper presented at the 2010 Leasing Business Forum, Dakar, Senegal, March.

Arcand, Jean-Louis, Enrico Berkes, and Ugo Panizza. 2011. "Too Much Finance?" Unpublished working paper, Graduate Institute of International and Development Studies, Geneva. http://graduateinstitute.ch/webdav/site/iheid/shared/news/2011_04_27_news/toomuchfinance.pdf.

Aryeetey, Ernest, Hemamala Hettige, Machiko Nissanke, and William F. Steel. 1997. "Financial Market Fragmentation and Reforms in Ghana, Malawi, Nigeria, and Tanzania." *World Bank Economic Review* 11 (2): 195–218.

Asfaha, Samuel G. 2007. "National Revenue Funds: Their Efficacy for Fiscal Stability and Intergenerational Equity." Report, August, International Institute for Sustainable Development, Winnipeg, Canada.

Ashraf, Nava, Nathalie Gons, Dean S. Karlan, and Wesley Yin. 2003. "A Review of Commitment Savings Products in Developing Countries." Draft working paper, Harvard University, Cambridge, MA.

Aterido, Reyes, Thorsten Beck, and Leonardo Iacovone. 2011. "Gender and Finance in Sub-Saharan Africa: Are Women Disadvantaged?" Policy Research Working Paper 5571, World Bank, Washington, DC.

Aterido, Reyes, Mary Hallward-Driemeier, and Carmen Pagés. 2007. "Investment Climate and Employment Growth: The Impact of Access to Finance, Corruption and Regulations across Firms." IZA Discussion Paper 3138, Institute for the Study of Labor, Bonn.

Bankable Frontier Associates. 2008. "Promoting Financial Inclusion through Social Transfer Schemes." Report, December 5, Bankable Frontier Associates, Somerville, MA. http://www.bankablefrontier.com/assets/pdfs/BFA-G2P-DFID-Wkshp Paper-FinalPDF-M-Nov08.pdf.

Banque de France. 2009. "Rapport annuel de la Zone franc, 2009." Banque de France, Paris.

Barth, James R., Gerard Caprio Jr., and Ross E. Levine. 2006. *Rethinking Bank Regulation: Till Angels Govern.* New York: Cambridge University Press.

BCBS (Basel Committee on Banking Supervision). 2006. "Core Principles for Effective Banking Supervision." October, Bank for International Settlements, Basel, Switzerland. http://www.bis.org/publ/bcbs129.pdf.

Beck, Thorsten. 2011. "Finance and Oil: Is There a Resource Curse in Financial Development?" Unpublished working paper, International Monetary Fund, Washington, DC. Previously published as EBC Discussion Paper 2011–004, European Banking Center, Tilburg University, Tilburg, the Netherlands.

Beck, Thorsten, Berrak Büyükkarabacak, Felix Rioja, and Neven Valev. 2009. "Who Gets the Credit? And Does it Matter? Household vs. Firm Lending across Countries." CEPR Discussion Paper 7400, Centre for Economic Policy Research, London.

Beck, Thorsten, Olivier De Jonghe, and Glenn Schepens. 2011. "Bank Competition and Stability: Reconciling Conflicting Empirical Evidence." Unpublished working paper, Tilburg University, Tilburg, the Netherlands.

Beck, Thorsten, and Augusto de la Torre. 2007. "The Basic Analytics of Access to Financial Services." *Financial Markets, Institutions and Instruments* 16 (2): 79–117.

Beck, Thorsten, Asli Demirgüç-Kunt, and Ross E. Levine. 2006. "Bank Concentration, Competition, and Crises: First Results." *Journal of Banking and Finance* 30 (5): 1581–1603.

————. 2007. "Finance, Inequality, and the Poor." *Journal of Economic Growth* 12 (1): 27–49.

————. 2010. "Financial Institutions and Markets across Countries and over Time: The Updated Financial Development and Structure Database." *World Bank Economic Review* 24 (1): 77–92.

Beck, Thorsten, Asli Demirgüç-Kunt, and Vojislav Maksimovic. 2005. "Financial and Legal Constraints to Firm Growth: Does Firm Size Matter?" *Journal of Finance* 60 (1): 137–77.

Beck, Thorsten, Asli Demirgüç-Kunt, and María Soledad Martínez Pería. 2007. "Reaching Out: Access to and Use of Banking Services across Countries." *Journal of Financial Economics* 85 (1): 234–66.

————. 2008. "Banking Services for Everyone? Barriers to Bank Access and Use around the World." *World Bank Economic Review* 22 (3): 397–430.

————. 2011. "Banking Financing for SMEs: Evidence across Countries and Bank Ownership Types." *Journal of Financial Services Research* 39, 35–54.

Beck, Thorsten, Asli Demirgüç-Kunt, and Ouarda Merrouche. 2010. "Islamic vs. Conventional Banking: Business Model, Efficiency, and Stability." Policy Research Working Paper 5446, World Bank, Washington, DC.

Beck, Thorsten, Erik H. B. Feyen, Alain Ize, and Florencia Moizeszowicz. 2008. "Benchmarking Financial Development." Policy Research Working Paper 4638, World Bank, Washington, DC.

Beck, Thorsten and Heiko Hesse. 2009. "Why are Interest Spreads so High in Uganda?", *Journal of Development Economics* 88, 192–204.

Beck, Thorsten, Leora F. Klapper, and Juan Carlos Mendoza. 2010. "The Typology of Partial Credit Guarantee Funds around the World." *Journal of Financial Stability* 6 (1): 10–25.

Beck, Thorsten, and Ross E. Levine. 2002. "Industry Growth and Capital Allocation: Does Having a Market- or Bank-Based System Matter?" *Journal of Financial Economics* 64 (2): 147–80.

Beck, Thorsten, Ross E. Levine, and Alexey Levkov. 2010. "Big Bad Banks? The Winners and Losers from Bank Deregulation in the United States." *Journal of Finance* 65 (5): 1637–67.

Beck, Thorsten, Ross E. Levine, and Norman Loayza. 2000. "Finance and the Sources of Growth." *Journal of Financial Economics* 58 (1–2): 261–300.

Beck, Thorsten, and María Soledad Martínez Pería. 2011. "What Explains the Cost of Remittances? An Examination across 119 Country Corridors." *World Bank Economic Review* 25, 105–131.

Belaicha, Amine, Abdeldjellil Bouzidi, and Daniel Labaronne. 2009. "Un fonds d'investissement d'Etat pour l'Algérie: aproche institutionnelle et confrontation au modèle traditionnels des fonds souverains." Working paper, Faculté des Sciences Economiques, des Sciences de Gestion et des Sciences Commerciales, Univeristé Abderrahmane Mira de Béjaïa, Béjaïa, Algeria. http://www.iefpedia.com/france/wp-content/uploads/2009/12/LABARONNE-Daniel.pdf.

Belke, Ansgar, Rainer Fehn, and Neil Foster. 2003. "Does Venture Capital Investment Spur Employment Growth?" CEPS Working Document 197, Centre for European Policy Studies, Brussels.

Beltratti, Andrea, and René M. Stulz. 2009. "Why Did Some Banks Perform Better during the Credit Crisis? A Cross-Country Study of the Impact of Governance and Regulation." NBER Working Paper 15180, National Bureau of Economic Research, Cambridge, MA.

Benavente, José Miguel, Alexander Galetovic, and Ricardo Sanhueza. 2006. "Fogape: An Economic Analysis." Working Paper SDT 222, Economics Department, University of Chile, Santiago, Chile.

Bennett, Fred, Alan Doran, and Harriett Billington. 2005. "Do Credit Guarantees Lead to Improved Access to Financial Services? Recent Evidence from Chile, Egypt, India, and Poland." Policy Division Working Paper, February, Department for International Development, London.

Berger, Allen N., and Gregory F. Udell. 1996. "Universal Banking and the Future of Small Business Lending." In *Financial System Design: The Case for Universal Banking*, ed. Anthony Saunders and Ingo Walter, 559–627. Homewood, IL: Irwin Publishing.

———. 2006. "A More Complete Conceptual Framework for SME Financing." *Journal of Banking and Finance* 30 (11): 2945–66.

Bernstein, Shai, Josh Lerner, Morten Sørensen, and Per Strömberg. 2009. "Private Equity, Industry Performance and Cyclicality." In *Globalization of Alternative Investments, Working Papers*, vol. 3, ed. World Economic Forum, part 1, 1–23. *The Global Economic Impact of Private Equity Report 2010.* Geneva: World Economic Forum.

Bertrand, Marianne, Dean S. Karlan, Sendhil Mullainathan, Eldar Shafir, and Jonathan Zinman. 2010. "What's Advertising Content Worth? Evidence from a Consumer Credit Market Experiment." *Quarterly Journal of Economics* 125 (2): 263–305.

Bloom, Nicholas, Raffaella Sadun, and John Van Reenen. 2009. "Do Private Equity-Owned Firms Have Better Management Practices?" In *Globalization of Alternative Investments, Working Papers*, vol. 2, ed. World Economic Forum, part 1, 1–23. *The Global Economic Impact of Private Equity Report 2009.* Geneva: World Economic Forum.

Bolzico, Javier, Yira Mascaro, and Paola Granata. 2007. "Practical Guidelines for Effective Bank Resolution." Policy Research Working Paper 4389, World Bank, Washington, DC.

Bourse de Tunis. 2010. "2009 Annual Report." Bourse de Tunis, Tunis.

Bowman Gilfillan. 2009. "Doing Business in South Africa 2009." Bowman Gilfillan Attorneys, Johannesburg.

Boyce, James K., and Léonce Ndikumana, 2001. "Is Africa a Net Creditor? New Estimates of Capital Flight from Severely Indebted Sub-Saharan African Countries, 1970–1996." *Journal of Development Studies* 38 (2): 27–56.

Boyd, John H., and Gianni de Nicoló. 2005. "The Theory of Bank Risk Taking and Competition Revisited." *Journal of Finance* 60 (3): 1329–43.

Boyd, John H., Ross E. Levine, and Bruce D. Smith. 2001. "The Impact of Inflation on Financial Sector Performance." *Journal of Monetary Economics* 47 (2): 221–48.

Boyd, John H., and Bruce D. Smith. 1998. "The Evolution of Debt and Equity Markets in Economic Development." *Economic Theory* 12 (3): 519–60.

Brander, James, Qianqian Du, and Thomas Hellman. 2010. "The Effects of Government-Sponsored Venture Capital: International Evidence." NBER Working Paper 16521.

Brooks, Ray. 2006. "International Experience with Policy Lending." Presentation, International Monetary Fund, Beijing, April 28.

Brown, Michael, Tullio Jappelli, and Marco Pagano. 2009 "Information Sharing and Credit: Firm-Level Evidence from Transition Countries." *Journal of Financial Intermediation* 18 (2): 151–72.

Brunnermeier, Markus. 2009. "Deciphering the Liquidity and Credit Crunch 2007–08." *Journal of Economic Perspectives* 23 (1): 77–100.

Caprio, Gerard, Jr., Jonathan L. Fiechter, Robert E. Litan, and Michael Pomerleano, eds. 2004. *The Future of State-Owned Financial Institutions.* Washington, DC: Brookings Institution Press.

Caprio, Gerard, and Patrick Honohan. 2004. "Can the Unsophisticated Market Provide Discipline." Policy Research Working Paper 3364, World Bank, Washington, DC.

Caprio, Gerard, Luc Laeven, and Ross E. Levine. 2007. "Governance and Bank Valuation." *Journal of Financial Intermediation* 16 (4): 584–617.

CAWTAR (Center of Arab Women for Training and Research) and IFC (International Finance Corporation). 2007. "Women Entrepreneurs in the Middle East and North Africa: Characteristics, Contributions and Challenges." Report, CAWTAR, Tunis.

CGAP (Consultative Group to Assist the Poor) and World Bank. 2010. *Financial Access 2010: The State of Financial Inclusion through the Crisis.* Washington, DC: CGAP and World Bank.

Chander, Anupam. 2001. "Diaspora Bonds." *New York University Law Review* 76, 1005 (October).

Cheung, Yin-Wong, Jacob de Haan, Xingwang Qian, and Shu Yu. 2011. "China's Outward Direct Investment in Africa." HKIMR Working Paper 13/2011 (April), Hong Kong Institute for Monetary Research, Hong Kong, SAR, China.

Christen, Robert Peck, Veena Jayadeva, and Richard Rosenberg. 2004. "Financial Institutions with a Double Bottom Line: Implications for the Future of Microfinance." Occasional Paper 8, Consultative Group to Assist the Poor, Washington, DC.

Christen, Robert Peck, Timothy R. Lyman, and Richard Rosenberg. 2003. "Microfinance Consensus Guidelines: Guiding Principles on Regulation and Supervision of Microfinance." Consultative Group to Assist the Poor, Washington, DC.

Christy, John H. 1998. "Bright Spots on the Dark Continent." *Forbes*, October 5. http://www.forbes.com/global/1998/1005/0113068a.html.

Čihák, Martin, and Richard Podpiera. 2005. "Bank Behavior in Developing Countries: Evidence from East Africa." IMF Working Paper WP/05/129, International Monetary Fund, Washington, DC.

Claessens, Stijn, and Eric Feijen. 2006. "Finance and the MDGs." Unpublished paper, World Bank, Washington, DC.

Claessens, Stijn, and Luc Laeven. 2004. "What Drives Bank Competition? Some International Evidence." *Journal of Money, Credit, and Banking* 36 (3): 563–83.

Claessens, Stijn, Neeltje van Horen, Tugba Gurcanlar, and Joaquin Mercado Sapiain. 2010. "Foreign Bank Presence in Developing Countries 1995–2006: Data and Trends." Unpublished paper, De Nederlandsche Bank, Amsterdam.

Clarke, George, Robert Cull, and Michael Fuchs. 2009. "Bank Privatization in Sub-Saharan Africa: The Case of Ugandan Commercial Bank." *World Development* 37 (9): 1506–21.

Clifford Chance. 2010. "Impact of the 'Volcker Rule' on Non-U.S. Bank Investments in Private Equity and Hedge Funds Outside the United States." Client Memorandum, August 2, Clifford Chance, New York.

Coates, Mike, and Robin Hofmeister. 2010. "Financing Agriculture in Africa: Selected Approaches for the Engagement of Commercial Finance." Unpublished working paper, Deutsche Gesellschaft für Internationale Zusammenarbeit, Eschborn, Germany.

Cole, Shawn, Thomas Sampson, and Bilal Zia. 2010. "Prices or Knowledge? What Drives Demand for Financial Services in Emerging Markets?" Unpublished working paper, Harvard Business School, Harvard University, Cambridge, MA; World Bank, Washington, DC.

Collier, Paul, Anke Hoeffler, and Catherine Pattillo, 2001. "Flight Capital as a Portfolio Choice." *World Bank Economic Review*, 15 (1): 55-80.

Collins, Daryl, Jonathan Morduch, Stuart Rutherford, and Orlanda Ruthven. 2009. *Portfolios of the Poor: How the World's Poor Live on $2 a Day.* Princeton, NJ: Princeton University Press.

Cull, Robert, and María Soledad Martínez Pería. Forthcoming. "Foreign Bank Participation in Developing Countries: What Do We Know about the Drivers and Consequences of this Phenomenon?" In *Encyclopedia of Financial Globalization,* ed. Gerard Caprio. Oxford: Elsevier.

Cull, Robert, and Mircea Trandafir. 2010a. "Banking Sector Consolidation in Nigeria." Unpublished working paper, World Bank, Washington, DC.

———. 2010b. "Credit Market Segmentation in Uganda." Unpublished working paper, World Bank, Washington, DC.

Dafe, Florence. 2011. "The Potential of Pro-Market Activism as a Tool for Making Finance Work for Africa: A Political Economy Perspective." DIE Discussion Paper 2/2011, German Development Institute, Bonn.

Davis, Steven J., John Haltiwanger, Ron Jarmin, Josh Lerner, and Javier Miranda. 2008. "Private Equity and Employment." In *Globalization of Alternative Investments, Working Papers,* vol. 1, ed. World Economic Forum, 43–64. *The Global Economic Impact of Private Equity Report 2008.* Geneva: World Economic Forum.

De Haas, Ralph, and Ilko Naaborg. 2005. "Does Foreign Bank Entry Reduce Small Firms' Access to Credit? Evidence from European Transition Economies." DNB Working Paper 50, De Nederlandsche Bank, Amsterdam.

de la Torre, Augusto, Juan Carlos Gozzi, and Sergio L. Schmukler. 2007. "Capital Market Development: Whither Latin America?" Policy Research Working Paper 4156, World Bank, Washington, DC.

———. 2008. "Innovative Experiences in Access to Finance: Market Friendly Roles for the Visible Hand?" Policy Research Working Paper 3963, World Bank, Washington, DC.

de la Torre, Augusto, and Alain Ize. 2009. "Regulatory Reform: Integrating Paradigms." Policy Research Working Paper 4842, World Bank, Washington, DC.

de la Torre, Augusto, María Soledad Martínez Pería, and Sergio L. Schmukler. 2010. "Bank Involvement with SMEs: Beyond Relationship Lending." *Journal of Banking and Finance* 34 (9): 2280–93.

Deloitte. 2011. "International Tax: Algeria Highlights." Deloitte Global Services Limited. http://www.deloitte.com/assets/Dcom-Global/Local%20Assets/Documents/Tax/Intl%20Tax%20and%20Business%20Guides/2011/dtt_tax_highlight_ 2011_Algeria.pdf.

Demirgüç-Kunt, Asli, Enrica Detragiache, and Thierry Tressel. 2008. "Banking on the Principles: Compliance with Basel Core Principles and Bank Soundness." *Journal of Financial Intermediation* 17 (4): 511–42.

Demirgüç-Kunt, Asli, and Ed Kane. 2002. "Deposit Insurance around the World: Where Does It Work?" *Journal of Economic Perspectives* 16 (2): 175–95.

Demirgüç-Kunt, Asli, Inessa Love, and Vojislav Maksimovic. 2006. "Business Environment and the Incorporation Decision." *Journal of Banking and Finance* 30 (11): 2967–93.

Demirgüç-Kunt, Asli, and Vojislav Maksimovic. 2002. "Funding Growth in Bank-Based and Market-Based Financial Systems: Evidence from Firm Level Data." *Journal of Financial Economics* 65 (3): 337–63.

Detragiache, Enrica, Thierry Tressel, and Poonam Gupta. 2008. "Foreign Banks in Poor Countries: Theory and Evidence." *Journal of Finance* 63 (5): 2123–60.

Djankov, Simeon, Caralee McLiesh, and Andrei Shleifer. 2007. "Private Credit in 129 Countries." *Journal of Financial Economics* 84 (2): 299–329.

Dressen, Robert, Jay Dyer, and Zan Northrip. 2002. "Turning around State-Owned Banks in Underserved Markets." *Small Enterprise Development* 13 (4): 58–65.

Dupas, Pascaline, and Jonathan Robinson. 2009. "Savings Constraints and Microenterprise Development: Experience from a Field Experiment in Kenya." NBER Working Paper 14693, National Bureau of Economic Research, Cambridge, MA.

Easterly, William, and Ross E. Levine. 1997. "Africa's Growth Tragedy: Policies and Ethnic Divisions." *Quarterly Journal of Economics* 112 (2): 103–25.

Ecobank. 2010. "Microfinance and Poverty Alleviation." Ecobank, Lomé, Togo. http://www.ecobank.com/microfinance.aspx.

EMPEA (Emerging Markets Private Equity Association). 2011. "EMPEA Industry Statistics." February 14, EMPEA, Washington, DC. http://www.empea.net/Main-Menu-Category/EMPEA-Research/Industry-Statistics.aspx.

EMPEA (Emerging Markets Private Equity Association) and Coller Capital. 2009. "Emerging Markets Private Equity Survey 2009: Investors' Views of Private Equity in Emerging Markets." EMPEA, Washington, DC; Coller Capital, London.

———. 2010. "Emerging Markets Private Equity Survey 2010: Investors' Views of Private Equity in Emerging Markets." EMPEA, Washington, DC; Coller Capital, London.

Engels, Pim. 2011. "Responsible Finance in Ghana, Kenya, Tanzania, and Uganda." Unpublished synthesis report, Making Finance Work for Africa, World Bank, Washington, DC.

Fall, Muhamet Bamba. 2010. "MIGA and Partial Guarantee Instruments: A Collaborative Framework." Presentation at the Multilateral Investment Guarantee Agency and African Development Bank Workshop, July 21.

Fehn, Rainer, and Thomas Fuchs. 2003. "Capital Market Institutions and Venture Capital: Do They Affect Unemployment and Labour Demand?" CESifo Working Paper 898, CESifo Group, Munich.

Feyen, Erik H. B. 2010. "Finances of Egyptian Listed Firms and the Performance of the Egyptian Stock Exchange." Policy Research Working Paper 5213, World Bank, Washington, DC.

FinAccess. 2009. "Dynamics of Kenya's Changing Financial Landscape: Results of the FinAccess National Survey." June, Central Bank of Kenya and Financial Sector Deepening–Kenya, Nairobi. http://www.fsdkenya.org/finaccess/2009 results.html.

Foster, Vivien, and Cecilia Briceño-Garmendia, eds. 2010. *Africa's Infrastructure: A Time for Transformation.* Washington, DC: World Bank.

Foster, Vivien, William Butterfield, Chuan Chen, and Nataliya Pushak. 2008. *Building Bridges: China's Growing Role as Infrastructure Financier for Sub-Saharan Africa.* Washington, DC: World Bank.

Freund, Caroline L., and Nikola Spatafora. 2008. "Remittances, Transaction Costs, and Informality." *Journal of Development Economics* 86 (2): 356–66.

FSD Kenya (Financial Sector Deepening Kenya). 2008. "SME Risk Capital Funds: Constraints to Kenyan Institutional Investors." July, FSD Kenya, Nairobi.

FSI (Financial Stability Institute). 2004. "Implementation of the New Capital Adequacy Framework in Non-Basel Committee Member Countries: Summary of Responses to the Basel II Implementation Assistance Questionnaire." Occasional Paper 4 (July), FSI, Bank for International Settlements, Basel, Switzerland.

Fuchs, Michael, Richard Hands, and Thomas Jaeggi. 2010. "Recent International Reform Initiatives to Strengthen Post-crisis Banking Supervision and the International Regulatory Architecture: Priorities and Potential Pitfalls for LICs." Unpublished working paper, World Bank, Washington, DC.

Fuchs, Michael, Thomas Losse-Müller, and Makaio Witte. 2010. "The Reform Agenda for Financial Regulation and Supervision in Africa." Unpublished working paper, World Bank, Washington, DC.

Galindo, Arturo, and Margaret Miller. 2001. "Can Credit Registries Reduce Credit Constraints? Empirical Evidence on the Role of Credit Registries in Firm Investment Decisions." Paper presented at the seminar "Towards Competitiveness: The Institutional Path," 42nd Annual Meeting of the Board of Governors of the Inter-American Development Bank and the Inter-American Investment Corporation, Santiago, Chile, March 16.

Galor, Oded, and Omer Moav. 2004. "From Physical to Human Capital Accumulation: Inequality in the Process of Development." *Review of Economic Studies* 71 (4): 1001–26.

Galor, Oded, and Joseph Zeira. 1993. "Income Distribution and Macroeconomics." *Review of Economic Studies* 60 (1): 35–52.

Ghatak, Maitreesh, and Timothy W. Guinnane. 1999. "The Economics of Lending with Joint Liability: Theory and Practice." *Journal of Development Economics* 60 (1): 195–228.

Giné, Xavier, Jessica Goldberg, and Dean Yang. 2010. "Identification Strategy: A Field Experiment on Dynamic Incentives in Rural Credit Markets." Policy Research Working Paper 5438, World Bank, Washington, DC.

Giné, Xavier, and Robert Townsend. 2004. "Evaluation of Financial Liberalization: A General Equilibrium Model with Constrained Occupation Choice." *Journal of Development Economics* 74 (2): 269–307.

Giné, Xavier, and Dean Yang. 2009. "Insurance, Credit and Technology Adoption: Field Experimental Evidence from Malawi." *Journal of Development Economics* 89 (1): 1–11.

GIZ (Deutsche Gesellschaft für Internationale Zusammenarbeit). 2010. "Financing Agricultural Value Chains in Africa: Focus on Cocoa, Cashew, and Pineapple in Ghana." Unpublished working paper, GIZ, Eschborn, Germany.

Goetz, Anne Marie, and Rina Sen Gupta. 1996. "Who Takes the Credit? Gender, Power, and Control over Loan Use in Rural Credit Programs in Bangladesh." *World Development* 24 (1): 45–63.

Goodhart, Charles, and Dirk Schoenmaker. 2009. "Fiscal Burden Sharing in Cross-Border Banking Crises." *International Journal of Central Banking* 5 (1): 141–65.

Gormley, Todd A. 2007. "Costly Information, Foreign Entry, and Credit Access." Unpublished paper, Olin Business School, Washington University, St. Louis.

Gurcanlar, Tugba. 2010. "Global Drivers for Change and Africa Growth, Trade, and Investment." Unpublished working paper, February, World Bank, Washington, DC.

Gylfason, Thorvaldur. 2010. "Natural Resource Endowment: A Mixed Blessing." Unpublished paper, Department of Economics, University of Iceland, Reykjavik. http://www.imf.org/external/np/seminars/eng/2010/afrfin/pdf/Gylfason2.pdf.

Haber, Stephen, and Enrico Perotti. 2007. "The Political Economy of Finance." Paper presented at the Wharton Financial Institutions Center and the Amsterdam Centre for Research in International Finance conference "A Review of Comparative Governance Systems: The Role of Financial Institutions in Corporate Governance," Erice, Italy, April 3–5.

Hallward-Driemeier, Mary, ed. 2011. "Improving the Legal Investment Climate for Women in Africa." Unpublished report, World Bank, Washington, DC.

Hallward-Driemeier, Mary, and Reyes Aterido. 2007. "Impact of Access to Finance, Corruption and Infrastructure on Employment Growth: Putting Africa in a Global Context." Paper presented at the Donor Committee for Enterprise Development's Africa Consultative Conference "Creating Better Business Environments for Enterprise Development: African and Global Lessons for More Effective Donor Practices," Accra, Ghana, November 5–7. http://www.business environment.org/dyn/be/docs/158/Hallward-Driemeier.pdf.

Hassler, Olivier, and Bertrand Renaud. 2009. "State Housing Banks." In *Housing Finance Policy in Emerging Markets*, ed. Loïc Chiquier and Michael Lea, 247–76. Washington, DC: World Bank.

Hernández-Coss, Raúl, Chinyere Egwuagu, Jennifer Isern, and David Porteous. 2005. "AML/CFT Regulation: Implications for Financial Service Providers That Help Low-Income People." CGAP Focus Note 29, Consultative Group to Assist the Poor, Washington, DC.

Heyward, Peter. 2008. "Are Sovereign Wealth Funds a Threat to the U.S. Banking System?" *Banking Law Committee Journal*, March 10, Section of Business Law, American Bar Association, Chicago. http://apps.americanbar.org/buslaw/news letter/0069/materials/pp4.pdf.

Honohan. Patrick. 2008. "Cross-Country Variation in Household Access to Financial Services." *Journal of Banking and Finance* 32 (11): 2493–2500.

———. 2010. "Partial Credit Guarantees: Principles and Practice." *Journal of Financial Stability* 6 (1): 1–9.

Honohan, Patrick, and Thorsten Beck. 2007. *Making Finance Work for Africa*. Washington, DC: World Bank.

Honohan, Patrick, and Michael King. 2009. "Cause and Effect of Financial Access: Cross-Country Evidence from the Finscope Surveys." Paper presented at the World Bank Conference "Measurement, Promotion, and Impact of Access to Financial Services," Washington, DC, March 12–13. http://www.tcd.ie/Economics/staff/phonohan/Honohan%20King%20Mar%209.pdf.

Houston, Joel, Chen Lin, Ping Lin, and Yue Ma. 2010. "Creditor Rights, Information Sharing and Bank Risk Taking." *Journal of Financial Economics* 96 (3): 485–512.

IFC (International Finance Corporation). 2007. "A Survey of the Leasing Market in Rwanda." Leasing Development Program, Competitiveness and Enterprise Development Project, IFC Rwanda, Kigali, Rwanda.

———. 2009. "Leasing in Development: Guidelines for Emerging Economies." 2nd ed., IFC, Washington, DC.

ILO (International Labour Organization). 2010. *Governance of Social Security Systems: A Guide for Board Members in Africa*. Turin, Italy: International Training Centre of the ILO.

IMF (International Monetary Fund). 2011. "Global Recovery Advances but Remains Uneven." World Economic Outlook Update, January 25, IMF, Washington, DC.

———. Various. Global Financial Stability Report Series. IMF, Washington, DC. http://www.imf.org/external/np/mcm/financialstability/index.htm.

Ioannidou, Vasso P., and María Fabiana Penas. 2010. "Deposit Insurance and Bank Risk-Taking: Evidence from Internal Loan Ratings." *Journal of Financial Intermediation* 19 (1): 95–115.

IODSA (Institute of Directors in Southern Africa). 2009. *King Report on Governance for South Africa 2009*. Johannesburg: IODSA.

Irving, Jacqueline. 2005. "Regional Integration of Stock Exchanges in Eastern and Southern Africa: Progress and Prospects." IMF Working Paper 05/122, International Monetary Fund, Washington, DC.

ISSA (International Social Security Association). 2004. "Guidelines for the Investment of Social Security Funds." Technical Report 13, Study Group on the Investment of Social Security Funds, ISSA, Geneva.

Jappelli, Tullio, and Marco Pagano. 2002. "Information Sharing, Lending and Defaults: Cross-Country Evidence." *Journal of Banking and Finance* 26 (10): 2017–45.

Jerome, Afeikhena Theo. 2008. "Private Sector Participation in Infrastructure in Africa." Unpublished working paper, African Peer Review Mechanism Secretariat, Johannesburg.

Kapchanga, Mark. 2010. "Kenya's Leasing Sector Set for Drastic Changes." *East African*, September 13. http://www.theeastafrican.co.ke/news/-/2558/1008918/-/opavqhz/-/index.html.

Kasekende, L. A. 2001. "Capital Account Liberalisation: The Ugandan Experience." *Development Policy Review* 19 (1): 101–20.

Kaufman, Daniel, Aart Kraay, and Massimo Mastruzzi. 2009. "Governance Matters VIII: Aggregate and Individual Governance Indicators, 1996–2008." Policy Research Working Paper 4978, World Bank, Washington, DC.

Keeley, Michael C. 1990. "Deposit Insurance, Risk and Market Power in Banking." *American Economic Review* 80 (5): 1183–1200.

Ketkar, Suhas L., and Dilip Ratha. 2010. "Diaspora Bonds: Tapping the Diaspora during Difficult Times." *Journal of International Commerce, Economics and Policy* 1 (2): 251–63.

Klapper, Leora. 2006. "The Role of Reverse Factoring in Supplier Financing of Small and Medium Sized Enterprises." *Journal of Banking and Finance* 30 (11): 3111–30.

Kortum, Samuel, and Josh Lerner. 2000. "Assessing the Contribution of Venture Capital to Innovation." *Rand Journal of Economics* 31 (4): 674–92.

Kose, M. Ayhan, Eswar Prasad, Kenneth Rogoff, and Shang Jin-Wei. 2009. "Financial Globalization: A Reappraisal." *IMF Staff Papers* 56 (1): 8–62.

KPMG and SAVCA (Southern African Venture Capital and Private Equity Association). 2010. "Venture Capital and Private Equity Industry Performance Survey of South Africa Covering the 2009 Calendar Year." May, KPMG Services, Johannesburg. http://www.kpmg.com/Global/en/IssuesAndInsights/Articles Publications/Emerging-markets-Africa/Documents/private-equity-survey-july-2010.pdf.

Kumar, Kabir, Claudia McKay, and Sarah Rotman. 2010. "Microfinance and Mobile Banking: The Story So Far." Focus Note 62 (July), Consultative Group to Assist the Poor, Washington, DC.

Laeven, Luc, and Fabian Valencia. 2008. "Systemic Banking Crises: A New Database." IMF Working Paper 08/224, Washington, DC, International Monetary Fund.

La Porta, Rafael, Florencio Lopez-de-Silanes, and Andrei Shleifer. 2002. "Government Ownership of Commercial Banks." *Journal of Finance* 57 (1): 265–301.

————. 2006. "What Works in Securities Law?" *Journal of Finance* 61 (1): 1–32.

La Porta, Rafael, Florencio Lopez-de-Silanes, Andrei Shleifer, and Robert W. Vishny. 1997. "Legal Determinants of External Finance." *Journal of Finance* 52 (3): 1131–50.

Larraín, C., and J. Quiroz. 2006. "Estudio para el fondo de garantía de pequeños empresarios." Unpublished working paper, March, Banco del Estado, Santiago, Chile.

Lelarge, Claire, David Sraer, and David Thesmar. 2010. "Entrepreneurship and Credit Constraints: Evidence from a French Loan Guarantee Program." In *International Differences in Entrepreneurship*, ed. Joshua Lerner and Antoinette Schoar, 243–73. Cambridge, MA: National Bureau of Economic Research; Chicago: University of Chicago Press.

Lerner, Josh, Morten Sørensen, and Per Strömberg. 2008. "Private Equity and Long-Run Investment: The Case of Innovation, In *Globalization of Alternative Investments, Working Papers*, vol. 1, ed. World Economic Forum, 27–42. *The Global Economic Impact of Private Equity Report 2008*. Geneva: World Economic Forum.

Levine, Ross E. 2002. "Bank-Based or Market-Based Financial Systems: Which is Better?" *Journal of Financial Intermediation* 11 (4): 398–428.

————. 2005. "Finance and Growth: Theory and Evidence." In *Handbook of Economic Growth*, vol. IA, ed. Philippe Aghion and Steven A. Durlauf, 865–934. Amsterdam: North-Holland.

————. 2010. "An Autopsy of the U.S. Financial System: Accident, Suicide or Negligent Homicide?" *Journal of Financial Economic Policy* 2 (3): 196–213.

Levine, Ross, Norman Loayza, and Thorsten Beck. 2000. "Financial Intermediation and Growth: Causality and Causes." *Journal of Monetary Economics* 16 (1): 31–77.

Levine, Ross E., and Sergio L. Schmukler. 2006. "Internationalization and Stock Market Liquidity." *Review of Finance* 10 (1): 153–87.

Levine, Ross E., and Sarah Zervos. 1998. "Stock Markets, Banks, and Economic Growth." *American Economic Review* 88 (3): 537–58.

Littlefield, Elizabeth, Jonathan Morduch, and Syed Hashemi. 2003. "Is Microfinance an Effective Strategy to Reach the Millennium Development Goals." CGAP Focus Note 24 (January), Consultative Group to Assist the Poor, Washington, DC.

Losse-Müller, Thomas. 2010. "African Financial Sector in Times of Global Crisis: What Lessons Have We Learned?" Unpublished working paper, Making Finance Work for Africa, World Bank, Washington, DC.

Love, Inessa, 2003. "Financial Development and Financing Constraints: International Evidence from the Structural Investment Model." *Review of Financial Studies* 16 (3): 765–91.

Lukonga, Inutu. 2010. "The Cross Border Expansion of African LCFIs: Implications for Regional Financial Stability and Regulatory Reform." With Kay Chung, Research Paper, September, International Monetary Fund, Washington, DC.

MAC SA. 2010. "Le secteur du leasing en Tunisie: Un secteur qui gagne du terrain sur le paysage financier tunisien." Unpublished working paper, Département Recherches, MAC SA, Tunis.

Maimbo, Samuel Munzele. 2001. "The Regulation and Supervision of Commercial Banks in Zambia: A Study of the Design, Development and Implementation of Prudential Regulations by the Bank of Zambia between 1980 and 2000." PhD thesis, University of Manchester, Manchester, United Kingdom.

———. 2007. "Remittances and Financial Sector Development in Conflict-Affected Countries." *AfricaGrowth Agenda*, January–March: 26–29.

Maimbo, Samuel Munzele, and Dilip Ratha, (eds). 2005. Remittances: Development Impact and Prospects. Washington, DC: World Bank.

Maimbo, Samuel Munzele, and Tania Saranga. 2009. "State-Owned Financial Institutions and Programs in Malawi, Mozambique, and Zambia." Unpublished working paper, World Bank, Washington, DC.

Maimbo, Samuel Munzele, S. Strychacz, and T. Saranga. 2010. "Faciliating Cross-Border Mobile Banking in Southern Africa." *Africa Trade Policy Notes*. World Bank: Washington, DC.

Marcus, Alan J. 1984. "Deregulation and Bank Financial Policy." *Journal of Banking and Finance* 8 (4): 557–65.

Mas, Ignacio, and Daniel Radcliffe. 2010. "Scaling Mobile Money." Bill & Melinda Gates Foundation, Seattle, WA. http://www.mobilemoneyexchange.org/Files/5ac0df5c.

Mazhar, Farida. 2005. "Privatization Guarantees for Regulatory Systems for Power Distribution in Uganda and Romania." Paper presented at World Bank Energy Week, Washington, DC, March 14–16.

Mazzucato, Valentina, Bart van den Boom, and N.N.N. Nsowah-Nuamah. 2004. "The Impact of International Remittances on Local Living Standards: Evidence for Households in Ghana." Paper presented at the conference "Migration and Development," Accra, Ghana, July 18–20. http://ghanatransnet.org/output/documents/MDCONF-Mazzucato.pdf.

McKenzie, David, and Michaela Weber. 2009. "The Results of a Pilot Financial Literacy and Business Planning Training Program for Women in Uganda." Finance and PSD Impact Note 8, World Bank, Washington, DC.

Miller, Margaret. 2011. "Financial Literacy across Africa." Background paper for Thorsten Beck, Samuel Munzele Maimbo, Issa Faye, and Thouraya Triki, *Financing Africa: Through the Crisis and Beyond*. Washington, DC: World Bank.

MIX (Microfinance Information Exchange) and CGAP (Consultative Group to Assist the Poor). 2010. "Sub-Saharan Africa 2009: Microfinance Analysis and Benchmarking Report." MIX and CGAP, Washington, DC.

Moss, Todd, Vijaya Ramachandran, and Scott Standley. 2007. "Why Doesn't Africa Get More Equity Investment? Frontier Stock Markets, Firm Size and Asset Allocations of Global Emerging Market Funds." Working Paper 112, Center for Global Development, Washington, DC.

Naouar, Riadh. 2009. "Bank Leasing in Africa: Case Study, Ghana." Unpublished report, Africa Leasing Facility, International Finance Corporation, Johannesburg.

Napier, Mark. 2011. "Including Africa: Beyond Microfinance." Report, Centre for the Study of Financial Innovation, London.

Nasr, Sahar. 2008. *Access to Finance and Economic Growth in Egypt.* Washington, DC: World Bank.

Ndikumana, Léonce, and James K. Boyce. 2008. "New Estimates of Capital Flight from Sub-Saharan African Countries: Linkages with External Borrowing and Policy Options." PERI Working Paper 166, Political Economy Research Institute, University of Massachusetts, Amherst, MA.

Ndulu, Benno J. 2006. "Infrastructure, Regional Integration and Growth in Sub-Saharan Africa: Dealing with Disadvantages of Geography and Sovereign Fragmentation." *Journal of African Economics* 15 (2): 212–44.

Nyirinkinda, Emmanuel. 2005. "The Uganda Distribution Concession." Paper presented at World Bank Energy Week, Washington, DC, March 14–16.

Pagano, Marco, Otto Randl, Alisa A. Röell, and Josef Zechner. 2001. "What Makes Stock Exchanges Succeed? Evidence form Cross-Listing Decisions?" *European Economic Review* 45 (4–6): 770–82.

Peachey, Stephen, and Alan Roe. 2006. "Access to Finance: Measuring the Contribution of Savings Banks." Working paper (October), World Savings Banks Institute, Brussels; Oxford Policy Management, Oxford.

Pearson, Roland V., Jr., and Craig Kilfoil. 2007. "Dowa Emergency Cash Transfer (DECT) Wider Opportunities Evaluation and Recommendations: Solid Lessons and a Promising Vision." DECT Wider Opportunities Report, June, Concern Worldwide, Dublin; U.K. Department for International Development–Malawi, Lilongwe.

PEI (Private Equity International). 2010. "The Walls Go Up." PEO Friday Letter, August 6. Private Equity Online. http://www.privateequityonline.com/Pages .aspx?pageID=1223.

Pickens, Mark, David Porteous, and Sarah Rotman. 2009. "Banking the Poor Via G2P Payments." Focus Note 58 (December), Consultative Group to Assist the Poor, Washington, DC. http://www.cgap.org/gm/document-1.9.41174/FN58.pdf.

Porteous, David. 2010. "Mobile Financial Services in Africa: The Next Generation." Unpublished working paper, World Bank, Washington, DC.

Quintyn, Marc G., and Michael William Taylor. 2007. "Building Supervisory Structures in Sub-Saharan Africa: An Analytical Framework." IMF Working Paper 07/18, International Monetary Fund, Washington, DC.

Rajan, Raghuram G. 2010. *Fault Lines: How Hidden Frictions Still Threaten the World Economy*. Princeton, NJ: Princeton University Press.

Rajan, Raghuram G., and Luigi Zingales. 1998. "Financial Dependence and Growth." *American Economic Review* 88 (3): 559–86.

———. 2003. *Saving Capitalism from the Capitalists*. New York: Crown Business.

Ratha, Dilip, Sanket Mohapatra, and Sonia Plaza. 2008. "Beyond Aid: New Sources and Innovative Mechanisms for Financing Development in Sub-Saharan Africa." Policy Research Working Paper 4609, World Bank, Washington, DC.

Robinson, James A. 2009. "Industrial Policy and Development: A Political Economy Perspective." Paper presented at the World Bank's "ABCDE Conference," Seoul, June 22–24.

Rodrik, Dani. 1998. "Who Needs Capital-Account Convertibility?" Essays in International Economics 207 (May): 55–65, International Economics Section, Princeton University, Princeton, NJ.

Rudolph, Heinz. 2009. "State Financial Institutions: Mandates, Governance, and Beyond." Policy Research Working Paper 5141, World Bank, Washington, DC.

Rutledge, Susan. 2010. "Consumer Protection and Financial Literacy: Lessons from Nine Country Studies." Policy Research Working Paper 5326, World Bank, Washington, DC.

SAVCA (Southern African Venture Capital and Private Equity Association) and DBSA (Development Bank of Southern Africa). 2009. "The Economic Impact of Venture Capital and Private Equity in South Africa." Report, SAVCA and DBSA, Johannesburg.

Schaeck, Klaus, Martin Čihák, Andrea Michaela Maechler, and Stéphanie Stolz. Forthcoming. "Who Disciplines Bank Managers?" *Review of Finance*.

Schaeck, Klaus, Martin Čihák, and Simon Wolfe. 2009. "Are Competitive Banking Systems More Stable?" *Journal of Money, Credit and Banking* 41 (4): 711–34.

Schneider, Friedrich, Andreas Buehn, and Claudio E. Montenegro. 2010. "Shadow Economies All Over the World: New Estimates for 162 Countries from 1999 to 2007." Unpublished working paper, World Bank, Washington, DC.

Senbet, Lemma W., and Isaac Otchere. 2006. "Financial Sector Reforms in Africa: Perspectives on Issues and Policies." In *Annual World Bank Conference on Development Economics 2006: Growth and Integration*, ed. François Bourguignon and Boris Pleskovic, 81–120. Washington, DC: World Bank.

Sengupta, Rajdeep. 2007. "Foreign Entry and Bank Competition." *Journal of Financial Economics* 84 (2): 502–28.

Shendy, Riham, Zachary Kaplan, and Peter Mousley. 2011. *Toward Better Infrastructure: Conditions, Constraints, and Opportunities in Financing Public-Private Partnerships.* World Bank Studies. Washington, DC: World Bank.

Sheppard, Robert, Stephan von Klaudy, and Geeta Kumar. 2006. "Financing Infrastructure in Africa: How the Region Can Attract More Project Finance." Gridlines Note 13 (September), Public-Private Infrastructure Advisory Facility, World Bank, Washington, DC.

Sole, Juan. 2007. "Introducing Islamic Banks into Conventional Banking Systems." IMF Working Paper WP/07/175, International Monetary Fund, Washington, DC.

Stewart, Fiona, and Juan Yermo. 2009. "Pensions in Africa." OECD Working Papers on Insurance and Private Pensions 30, Organisation for Economic Co-operation and Development, Paris.

Stiglitz, Joseph E. 2010. "Lessons from the Global Financial Crisis of 2008." *Seoul Journal of Economics* 23 (3): 321–39.

Stiglitz, Joseph E., and A. Weiss. 1981. "Credit Rationing in Markets with Imperfect Information." *American Economic Review* 71 (3): 393–410.

Stone, Robert, Jerry Grossman, Philippe Breul, Abigail Carpio, and Mateo Cabello. 2009. "Trade in Financial Services: Mobile Banking in Southern Africa." Policy Research Working Paper 50975, World Bank, Washington, DC.

Stoyan, Tenev, and Chunlin Zhang. 2002. *Corporate Governance and Enterprise Reform in China: Building the Institutions of Modern Markets.* With Loup Brefort. Washington, DC: World Bank and International Finance Corporation.

Swiss Re. 2010. "World Insurance in 2009: Premiums Dipped, but Industry Capital Improved." Sigma 2/2010, Swiss Re Insurance Co., Zurich.

TheCityUK. 2010. "Sovereign Wealth Funds 2010." Brief, March, Research Centre, TheCityUK, London.

Thorne, Janine, and Charlotte du Toit. 2009. "A Macro-framework for Successful Development Banks." *Development Southern Africa* 26 (5): 677–94.

Wakeman-Linn, John, and Smita Wagh. 2008. "Regional Financial Integration: Its Potential Contribution to Financial Sector Growth and Development in Sub-Saharan Africa." Paper presented at the International Monetary Fund seminar "African Finance for the 21st Century," Tunis, March 4–5.

Walley, Simon. 2010. "Financing Africa: Housing Finance." Unpublished paper, World Bank, Washington, DC.

White, Ed. 2009. "White Clarke Global Leasing Report 2010: Global Leasing Business Contracts by 15% as Industry Hunkers Down to Ride a Bigger Storm." White Clarke Group, Milton Keynes, United Kingdom.

World Bank. 1993. *The East Asian Miracle: Economic Growth and Public Policy.* World Bank Policy Research Reports. Washington, DC: World Bank; New York: Oxford University Press.

————. 2001. *Finance for Growth: Policy Choices in a Volatile World.* Policy Research Report, April. Washington, DC: World Bank; New York: Oxford University Press.

————. 2003. *Kenya: A Policy Agenda to Restore Growth.* Report 25840-KE (August 18), World Bank, Washington, DC.

————. 2005. "Meeting Development Challenges: Renewed Approaches to Rural Finance." Consultant report, Agriculture and Rural Development Department, World Bank, Washington, DC.

————. 2007a. "Financial Sector Integration in Two Regions of Sub-Saharan Africa: How Creating Scale in Financial Markets Can Support Growth and Development." Making Finance Work for Africa Working Paper 1, World Bank, Washington, DC.

————. 2007b. *Nigeria: Competitiveness and Growth; Country Economic Memorandum.* Report 36483-NG. 3 vols. Washington, DC: World Bank.

————. 2008a. *Finance for All: Policies and Pitfalls in Expanding Access.* Policy Research Report. Washington, DC: World Bank.

————. 2008b. *Payment Systems Worldwide, a Snapshot: Outcomes of the Global Payment Systems Survey 2008.* Financial Infrastructure Policy and Research Series. Washington, DC: World Bank. http://siteresources.worldbank.org/INTPAYMENTREMMITTANCE/Resources/Global_Survey_Book.pdf.

————. 2008c. "Zambia: Governance, Political Economy, and Development Strategy." Policy Note, March 28, World Bank, Washington, DC.

————. 2009a. *Banking the Poor: Measuring Banking Access in 54 Economies.* Washington, DC: World Bank.

————. 2009b. "Making Finance Work for Uganda." Report, December, Financial and Private Sector Development, Africa Region, World Bank, Washington, DC.

————. 2010a. *World Development Indicators 2010.* Washington, DC: World Bank.

————. 2010b. "What Can Be Done about Nigeria's 'Credit Squeeze'?" Unpublished working paper, World Bank, Washington, DC.

————. 2011a. *Migration and Remittances Factbook 2011.* 2nd ed. Washington, DC: World Bank.

————. 2011b. "Africa Financial Sector Development Strategy." Policy Note, Africa Financial and Private Sector Development, World Bank, Washington, DC.

World Bank and IFC (International Finance Corporation). 2008. "Financing Homes: Comparing Regulation in 42 Countries." World Bank, Washington, DC.

————. Various. *Doing Business Report Series.* Washington, DC: World Bank.

Wurgler, Jeffrey. 2000. "Financial Markets and the Allocation of Capital." *Journal of Financial Economics* 58 (1–2): 187–214.

Index

Boxes, figures, notes, and tables are indicated with *b*, *f*, *n*, and *t* following the page number.